The Chaos of Cults

Books by J. K. van Baalen

THE CHAOS OF CULTS

THE GIST OF THE CULTS

OUR CHRISTIAN HERITAGE

COMFORT TO SPARE

IF THOU SHALT CONFESS

THE COMPENDIUM WITH OUTLINES

THE CHAOS OF

CULTS

A STUDY IN PRESENT-DAY ISMS

BY

JAN KAREL VAN BAALEN

Second Revised and Enlarged Edition

1956

WM. B. EERDMANS PUBLISHING COMPANY
GRAND RAPIDS, MICHIGAN

THE CHAOS OF CULTS
by J. K. VAN BAALEN, TH.M.

Copyright 1938, 1951, 1956 by
Wm. B. Eerdmans Publishing Co.

LIBRARY OF CONGRESS NUMBER LC 39-11391

Set up and printed, 1938
Sixteenth printing, July 1956
(First revised and enlarged edition, July 1951)
(Second revised and enlarged edition, July 1956)

PRINTED IN THE UNITED STATES OF AMERICA

PREFACE
to the
SECOND REVISED AND ENLARGED EDITION

Nothing is more characteristic of our times than their kaleidoscopic aspect. In politics as in economics, in international relations and in religious novelties, there is a ceaseless change that might well have staggered the imagination, not of the ancients alone, but of men and women of a fairly modern era.

Since the writer of this volume first took up the study of cults, new isms have appeared on the horizon of thought and of action, and some already have had their little day.

To keep up with all the religious oddities and monstrosities would take more spare time than the author has available for this hobby; and also, a mere reference to most of them would enlarge the present work far beyond all reason. Besides, such movements as *The Landone Foundation*, Winter Park, Florida, appear to center so largely around the founder (Brown Landone) and his successor (Clark Maxwell); while others, such as *Men of Goodwill* (11 West 42nd St., New York) show such clear resemblances to movements dealt with in the book (Theosophy), that it seems superfluous to devote separate chapters to them.

Moreover, the books and pamphlets dealing with psuedo-Christian cults are growing in number, and it is not necessary to repeat what many have said elsewhere.

That this book continues to appear in new editions is largely due to the zeal of the publishers and the courtesy of the readers; and since there is a demand, the author has deemed it his task to bring, as much as possible, existing chapters up to date.

For this he has had unexpected opportunity because during the first year of a temporary sojourn among our northern neighbors, he has, among the intelligent Canadians, for the first time met with a group that asked him to teach the textbook of which so many others had made use before him. As this has afforded an occasion, at long last, to see from an objective standpoint, the existing gaps in previous editions, it is hoped with some little confidence that those who have so kindly used the book before, will find that it has gained in usefulness.

Were it for brevity's sake alone, I would not here repeat the little incidents mentioned in one or two previous editions of the book concerning a few personal contacts I have had with propagandists of the cults here described. The reader may well be informed that *The Chaos of Cults* is not a book written by a reporter who has placed himself under the spell of personalities, but (though on a very modest scale) the result of an objective study of the tenets of men and women, regardless of their personal charm or lack of charm. That in a few cases individual idiosyncrasies have affected a cultist's views and system (polygamous Joseph Smith, self-assertive "Pastor" Russell), cannot and need not be denied or ignored.

As to Seventh-Day Adventism I only wish to repeat briefly that although it maintains many fundamental Christian doctrines, it belongs with the cults as long as its defenders condemn the entire Christian church as "rejecting the Christ with the pierced hands," call themselves "the church of the remnant," and fight every attempt of evangelical churches for Sabbath recognition. A movement which, as much as Eddyism and Mormonism, boasts an inspired prophetess, is bound to remain outside the pale of recognized churches from the standpoint of evangelical Christianity.

Interest in the cults is on the increase. It is no longer as it was in 1914 when the present writer, coming to Princeton for postgraduate theological studies, discovered that here, as well as in Europe, the cults were ignored while philosophers such as Hegel and Fichte received a measure of attention. The vigorous propaganda of cultists who reach their thousands where scholars approach only scores of men and women, may largely be responsible for this; for all that, it is all to the good that the cults receive attention.

Also, there are indications that it is being understood more and more that only indoctrination as to the main tenets of the holy catholic Christian church can offset the vicious and ceaseless propaganda of errorists.

It is hoped that the questions appearing at the end of each chapter may facilitate teaching and studying the book.

The author's thanks are expressed to the Baker Book House, Grand Rapids, Michigan, for permission to reprint the chapter "Approaching Adherents of the Cults" from the book *Reformed Evangelism*, 1948.

Should this second revised and enlarged edition help a little in the direction of understanding truth as distinct from religious error, the author would be grateful to the good Lord Himself and to a patient public.

J. K. VAN BAALEN

Lynden, Washington
June, 1956

CONTENTS

The Chaos of Cults

1

THE ISSUE DEFINED

In a recent study of "Bavinck as a Dogmatician" the noted Dutch scholar Dr. G. C. Berkouwer remarks that Bavinck's great work on Dogmatics (1918) is by no means antiquated, and that not only because the truth according to Scripture remains unaltered, but even more so because Bavinck's *magnum opus* contains much that is of an apologetic and polemic nature. And, says Berkouwer, in reading Bavinck one is again and again impressed with the fact that many of the problems that engaged the mind of the great Dutch theologian have returned in our own day with but slight variations. Thus the demythologizing of which Bultmann now speaks in Germany differs but very little from the antipathy of the older "higher critics" to miracles in the Bible.

This also holds for the cults. There is little that is new under the sun. Or, how could there be when Spiritists boldly claim their religion to be the oldest and most fundamental of human cults, when Theosophists call their system now Esoteric Buddhism and at another time Esoteric Christianity?

Here lies one reason why the present book could be published and re-published since 1929.

There is, however, at once an amount of progress and of historic development. And that calls for new and revised editions. The founders of the more popular cults are by no means all finished scholars; too often they are bunglers who stumble upon an idea, and afterward bolster it with pickings from many fields.

In the case of some religious systems later changes are mostly a slightly different emphasis. Such is the case with

13

Modernism, which now lays more stress upon sin, but loathes the Scriptural doctrine of justification by faith as much as ever. Here, therefore, a few citations from more modern works should suffice to show that "liberal theology" has altered but little in its opposition to the Biblical doctrine of an alien and forensic righteousness imputed to man. What is new in a chapter like that will therefore be found in the second part, which gives quotations from various authors.

Quite to the contrary the change from the old Buchmanism to the new MRA has been so great that the chapter had to be largely re-written, although for historic reasons much of the older material has been incorporated.

I have deemed it necessary to add but one more cult — where is the end? — namely, Swedenborgianism, perhaps because in Edmonton, Alberta, where I lived from 1950 to 1955, much house-to-house canvassing was done during my stay.

More and more I have come to the conclusion that we can learn from cultists, not only noting what not to believe, but also bearing in mind that "the cults are the unpaid bills of the church."

In general it may be stated that the cults are gradually dropping some of the old belligerency: even Jehovah's Witnesses are more sparing of vehement invectives. Having obtained a hearing and a following, they no longer go about carrying a chip on their shoulder. George Channing, CSB, writes, "The Christian Scientist does not feel superior to the adherents of any denomination. Every man is free to demonstrate the efficacy of his own faith; each is entitled to encouragement in his pursuit of spiritual objectives. Mrs. Eddy said: 'A genuine Christian Scientist loves Protestant and Catholic, D. D. and M. D. . . . loves God, good; and he loves his enemies.' "[1]

---

1. "What Is a Christian Scientist?" in *Guide to the Religions of America.*

The newer spirit of ecumenicity, world-wide unity, finds an eloquent expression in such books as *Radhakrishnan. Comparative Studies in Philosophy*, Presented in Honour of His Sixtieth Birthday (Harper and Brothers, 1950). Here a group of twenty scholars from Asia, England, and America openly suggest a philosophical synthesis of East and West which will, in its own way, contribute to the growth of a world community. To these men religion is not a creed or a code, but "an insight into reality." If only the West will give up its age-old prejudice against re-incarnation, it would be discovered that East and West are not so far apart.

And Professor Toynbee states that the Western world must produce a new religion, a universal cult, and it must be made up of Christianity, Buddhism, Hinduism and Islam. A contributor to the Letterbox of the *Edmonton Journal* (Jan. 25, 1955) wrote: "Christianity expresses belief in one God, in life everlasting for each individual soul, and in the status of women as 'persons.' By contrast, Hinduism expresses belief in many gods; Buddhism in the eventual absorption of one's soul into Nirvana; and Islam holds for the predominance of the male sex, among other things. Yet with terrifying calm the Professor announces that there must be a synthesis of these religions which have divergent fundamental beliefs. Truly, his universal religion would belong to a composite order of architecture, a nightmare edifice looking like a combination of the Mosque of St. Sophia, Bombay Temple and Rheims Cathedral, with probably a gigantic image of Buddha dominating the interior."

This is of a piece with the words of the late Dean Inge, who wrote of Buddhism and Christianity: "There is a cardinal affinity between the two religions in their attitude toward their divinized founders. There are differences due to the historical circumstances in which the two religions have grown up, and of the different demands of the peoples they were intended to lead; but the religious foundation of both is the same."

But in the words of John A. Mackay, President of Princeton Theological Seminary: "In the interest of world-loyalty
mutuality should be promoted between East and West, each
sharing with the other its ideals. But how utterly unreal
is such a proposal at a moment in history when the traditional ideals of both East and West are passing away, and
when a tremendous force, that of Marxist Communism,
proclaims around the world that what matters is not the
mutuality of ideals but the common recognition of realities."[2]

The Bible-believing Christian may easily detect that to
which all this is bound to lead. The true Christians will be
hated of all men for their aloofness, their refusal to recognize others as equally good; they will be accused of holding
back unity and progress, world-peace, and similar desirable goods. Probably it will all end in renewed persecution.
Already the unbalanced genius of Hitler has accused Christianity of standing in the way of the *Pax Germana* that was
to bless the world through the race with the *Weltgeist*.

Paganism or Christianity?

There is a sufficient number of books on the market
today that cater to this conciliatory spirit. Among these
Braden's *These Also Believe* and Bach's *They Have Found
a Faith* and *Faith and My Friends* occupy a prominent
place. According to such books faith is of value because of
its psychological effect rather than through its object.
Writes Chester E. Tulga: "A world-religion is on the way,
but it will be religious rather than Christian: it will be
human rather than divine, it will be natural rather than
supernatural. Its God will be its servant not its sovereign,
its Christ will be its leader not its king, its political econ-
omy will be a democracy not a theocracy: its saints will be
its socialists not its seers, its goal will be a human utopia
not the Kingdom of the coming King. The coming world-

2. *God's Order*. The Ephesian Letter and this Present Time. (New
York: Macmillan, 1953), page 46. One of the truly great books of
the decade.

religion is envisioned by liberals as the harbinger of the 'Kingdom' but by the biblical writers as the forerunner of the anti-Christ (II Thess. 2:3-12)" (*The Case Against Modernism*, 1950, p. 58). With this agree, from the opposite camp, such items as one reads from time to time, for example, a January 5, 1951, AP report, quoting Abdel Rahman Azzam Pasha, secretary-general of the Arab League, saying that "a spiritual alliance of the Moslem and Christian world would group more than one half of the men of the earth together against a common enemy." "The two religions," said the Arab leader in Rome, "are founded upon an exquisite high spirituality and are menaced by the same enemy, atheistic materialism."

Besides these we have the books that, like Frank S. Mead's *Handbook of Denominations in the United States*, 1951, write "with malice toward none, but in justice to all," yet do not only describe all cults as "churches," but dedicate their writings to "Those in the Church who see that the great truths we hold on common ground are of more importance to God and man than the little fences and barriers which divide us."

Among these must now also be numbered President Eisenhower's favorite Elton Trueblood, whose final chapter, "The Ground of Hope" in *Declaration of Freedom*, 1955, ends with these words, "This faith is so strengthening that it ought to be uniting. The chasm between a merely secular conception of the world and any conception in which the Personal Basis of the moral order is recognized is so great and so crucial that those who believe in the latter are foolish to let their particular differences divide them. Moslems and Christians and Jews and many more need to know that they have the greatest things in common. The question of the particular banner is secondary."

Over against all such lowering of the Christian standard the present volume maintains with H. Bavinck and B. B. Warfield that there are but two religions in the world. The one is autosoterism, that salvation is from man. The other ascribes the entire work of salvation from the world's ills to God. Christianity is the name of the latter. It matters not under what flag the former sails: it stands in opposition to the Christian, that is, the true religion.

Even the most cursory examination of the ethnic religions should convince one of this truth. The ancient Egyptians taught, "Prepare for the judgments of Osiris by observing the rules of right conduct." The Norsemen dictated, "Fight a good fight." Confucious prescribed, "Walk in the trodden paths; be a good citizen of the celestial empire." While in India the Buddha advised, "Walk the Noble Eightfold Path." Islam enjoins, "Stand by the Five Pillars of Conduct." All these religions instruct men to work out their own salvation.

Nor is this all. The ethnic religions not only teach men to save themselves; they also promise a salvation which is quite naturalistic in its concept. It is the life of this earth lived again, minus its disappointing features. To the Mohammedan, it means "places of innumerable sensuous joys — shadowy groves, fountains, fruits hanging low so as to be easily gathered, and wives *ad libidum*." To the old Norse king, heaven means, "Quickly, quickly, seated in the splendid habitation of the gods I shall be drinking beer out of a curved horn." Buddha not only said with dying lips, "Henceforth be ye to yourselves your own light, your own refuge, seek no other refuge. Look not to any one but yourselves as a refuge," but the salvation thus to be obtained by human effort is that "night of hopelessness," "to break through the prison walls, not of life only, but of being."

Even Zoroastrianism, the highest of the non-Christian religions except Judaism in its unadulterated form (and that was rare), taught that there is no saviour. Man must suffer the penalty of whatsoever evil he has done. The only saviour, so it asserted, is a virtuous life.

Aim of this Book

1. A study of cults will convince evangelical Christians of the necessity of studying more carefully *the faith which*

was once for all delivered unto the saints. Mormons, Jehovah's Witnesses and Seventh-Day Adventists have their "prooftexts" at their fingers' tips, often carrying Bibles with passages marked in red and blue. Adherents of the sound doctrine, on the contrary, quite frequently are unable to match these texts with convincing and final arguments from Scripture.

2. In proportion as we study false creeds, we shall learn to appreciate the doctrine that is unto godliness.

3. As we mark the fundamental difference between autosoterism and the "Just as I am, without one plea" note of all true Christianity, we shall learn to think less severely of the many subordinate, and racial and national tenets that too often keep Christ's disciples apart. There still is too much of the spirit of "We forbade him because he followeth not with us" (Luke 9:49).

4. At the same time, a study of the cults may well humble us because most of them are the result of an insufficient emphasis by Christians upon some valuable point of Biblical teaching: the boast that we preach "the full counsel of God" is all too often vain, untrue, and the fruit of a narrowed view which is due to a refusal to look beyond one's own small group. The true Biblical doctrine would envisage not only doctrine but also ethics, economics and sociology as much as a personal code of conduct, art in music, sobriety in public prayer, and beauty in church architecture. Few, if any, are capable of such all-embracing views.

Questions

1. Why is the study of cults useful?

2. What is the cardinal difference between Christianity and non-Christian religions?

3. Is certainty in religion obtainable? Where and how may it be found?

2

SPIRITISM

The word "Spiritism" deserves preference over the more popular "Spiritualism," first, because it emphasizes the admitted fact that this system claims to deal with spirits, and also because it is rather difficult to see where its alleged spirituality enters.

Historical

The beginnings of Spiritism are lost in antiquity. We are probably dealing with the oldest religious delusion in existence. It results, first, from the desire to obtain information concerning the life beyond. Will the next life be as full of sorrow as the present is? Shall we be happy? Are we to have bodies? Next, Spiritism is the fruit of the wish to be still in touch with departed loved ones.

This will explain why this cult is the first one to be taken up. One could hardly look for Christian Science or modern Theosophy among the ancients, although these cults may have absorbed and assimilated ideas which also prevailed among the ancients. But we do find traces of Spiritism among ancient Chinese, Hindus, Babylonians, and Egyptians; Spiritism can be traced through the Roman Empire and the Europe of medieval times. Of the present-day religious delusions it is therefore the only one which existed in Biblical times, and the Scriptures are anything but silent on it.

There have, of course, been periodic revivals of Spiritism. The last three revivals are those caused by the Fox sisters and by the bereavements resulting from the two world wars.

In its modern form, Spiritism goes back to two American girls. Mr. John D. Fox, his wife and six children in December, 1847, entered a house in the village of Hydeville, N. Y. The two youngest children, Margaret and Kate, respectively twelve and nine years old, soon afterward heard knockings in different parts of the house, which at first were accounted for as coming from rats and mice. However, when bedclothes were pulled off the bed by invisible hands, chairs and tables removed from their places, and a cold hand was felt on the youngest daughter's face, and when no effort to explain these phenomena in a natural manner succeeded, Kate hit upon the idea of getting in touch with "Old Splitfoot." Snapping her fingers, she said, "Here, old splitfoot, do as I do." Instantly the knocking responded. As this was repeated several times, it was concluded that something supernatural was at work. The two girls devised a means of intelligent communication with the author of the noises, who would reply to questions by a number of raps. He revealed himself as Charles Rosma, a married man and a peddler, who, at the age of thirty-one had been murdered by one John Bell, a blacksmith and former tenant of the Fox home. The body was said to lie ten feet under ground in the cellar; the murderer had remained unpunished. Portions of a human skeleton were actually found in the cellar.

From this widely advertised event spiritistic séances spread all over the United States. In England, "table-turning" was already popular among the social elite. Hence the American mediums found a fertile soil there also, when in 1852 the "spirits" announced to American devotees that they were going to invade England, and would be "very religious and very scientific" over there. Other European lands also were successfully visited by American Spiritists.

From 1850 to 1872, according to an official report, local organizations sprang up throughout the U. S., but no attempt was made to organize a national association until 1863. In 1863 the *National Spiritualist Association of the*

U. S. of A., was organized as now constituted. Its members were officially reported as 126,000, its churches 682, and its ministers as 600 for the year 1923. The 1945 Yearbook of American Churches gives a total of 228,000 "spiritualists" in the U. S. scattered over four organizations. The *British Spiritualists Union's* 18,000 members meet in 500 "churches" — usually hired rooms, garages, or private drawing rooms, but sometimes in rooms equipped with pews, harmonium and lectern.[1]

The Claims of Spiritists

Spiritists teach the following *doctrines*:

They emphasize right living here on earth, believing that their condition in the spirit world depends entirely upon what they do while in mortal form. "They believe in Infinite Intelligence, and that the phenomena of nature, physical and spiritual, are the expressions of Infinite Intelligence; that the existence and personal identity of the individual continue after the change called 'death,' and that communication with the so-called 'dead' is a fact scientifically proven by the phenomena of Spiritualism." They believe in the "Golden Rule" and that man makes his own happiness or unhappiness as he obeys or disobeys "Nature's psychic laws." The doorway to reformation is never closed against any human soul, here or hereafter.

The spirit world is said to be the counterpart of the visible world, only more beautiful and perfect. Those who enter it must be free from the impress of evil wrought while in the body. There is final restoration to happiness for all souls. But they who have lived on earth contrary to the laws of Intelligence will suffer in the hereafter the punishment of desiring to continue their evil course without the ability to do so. This will lead to remorse, and remorse to purification. Some Spiritists hold that life in the hereafter will be spent in seven different circles or spheres, which

---

1. *Newsweek*, Apr. 12, 1948.

surround the earth, each succeeding circle being around the former one, as the skin of a fruit surrounds the fruit, or the bark covers the trunk of a tree. Some hold that the lowest spirits are in a low, "earthbound" sphere, where they are taught by spirits in a higher sphere. The spirits of those who have died recently are quite near the earth; they can hear us, and they know of us. As the spirit becomes more perfect it passes into a higher sphere, and gradually loses its interest in the life we live in the flesh. Spirits are believed to have a body, although one that differs from the one we now have on earth.

Spiritists are opposed to war, to capital punishment, and to every form of tyranny. They do not believe in forgiveness of sin, but each person has to work out his own destiny through moral or spiritual evolution.

Spiritistic phenomena (the events whence such information reaches our Spiritists) are numerous. All men, so it is said, have *psychic force* (*psychic*, from the Greek *psyche*, soul, hence soul-force). While physical force resides in the muscles, psychic force rests in the minds of men. They who possess this force in greater measure than others are likely to become mediums. A *medium* is a go-between, the instrument through which spirits transmit supernatural knowledge to the *sitters* at a *séance*, the usual term for a spiritistic *session* or meeting.

Since psychic force is supposed to be enhanced when several people concentrate on it, and when they strengthen one another by physical contact, the simplest spiritistic phenomenon is perhaps that of *table tilting*, or *rapping*. The sitters spread their hands on the surface of a table around which they are seated. There is to be an unbroken circle, each sitter's two thumbs are to touch each other, while his little fingers touch those of the sitters next to him. The table begins to lift two or more legs off the floor, and bounds back. The sitters agree with the "spirit" that one thud will mean the letter "A," two thuds "B," and so on; and the message is conveyed through the number of thumps. Or, the sitters suggest a name, or a noun, and the "spirit" voices its assent when the right word is spoken.

A more advanced phenomenon occurs when the medium goes into *trance*. This is an unconscious or insensible condition, a state in which bodily consciousness and sensation are suspended for a time. The medium reports what he, more often she, hears and sees in this condition. At times the medium answers questions which the sitters ask the spirit.

Again the spirit, called the *control* of the medium, makes the latter *write*. When the medium comes out of the trance, she seldom remembers what she has said or done, but is much fatigued.

There are numerous other phenomena, some of which do not impart any information concerning the beloved dead or the hereafter but seem to aim only at impressing the sitters with the supernatural power of the spirit. Examples are the *floating* of objects through a room, the apparition of visible spirits, hands and arms. This is called *materialization*. In a typical materialization séance ectoplasm is said to emanate from the mouth and body of the medium, which foggy, smokelike substance is then shaped into forms by the chemist in the spirit world. (Ectoplasm is defined as exteriorized protoplasm, which latter is described by Webster as "the physical basis of life," "ordinarily a thick viscous semi-fluid of almost jelly-like, colorless, translucent material containing a large percentage of water, and holding fine granules in suspension.")

Great Britain and the United States alike in World War II witnessed a revival of interest in Spiritism, and even before that, "Books for the Occult, Psychic and Mystical Library" advertised on the jacket of Stewart Edward White's *The Betty Book* numbered more than fifty. The chief difference between the later and the earlier spiritistic literature lies in the fact that the later books are written in a more gentle tone. Instead of deriding or vehemently accusing the doctrines of the universal Church, they conveniently ignore them. The main thesis, however, remains unaltered: Death itself need not be feared, for it is only a gentle passing into a life very similar to the one just left behind.

Many soldiers who died on the battlefield awoke as out of sleep and inquired in a somewhat bewildered way what had happened to them and where they were: those who had gone before were "kept busy" assuring them that all was well and they were still in the same world from which they had arrived.

Of Stewart Edward White's *The Betty Book* (1937), *Across the Unknown* (1939), and *The Unobstructed Universe* (1940), the second volume is introduced as "A Formula for Living," and of the third the publishers state, "In answer to the desperate need of a stricken world, this book offers a new pattern for individual and social living—based on recapture of faith, not in the *thereness* of immortality, but in its *hereness.*"

In these more than 900 pages God is not mentioned; only in the concluding pages some references occur to the Bible as "full of stepladders" to spiritistic truth.

Yet of *The Betty Book* John Haynes Holmes, minister of the Community Church at New York, could only state that he found "an honest report of firsthand and unquestionably genuine experience, had by sincere and intelligent persons, moved by sober scientific interest, embodying a system of spiritual truth as sane as it is sublime. The important thing is to recognize the reality of what is here set down."

Thus Modernism, which itself has discarded the authority of Scripture in matters of faith, welcome books which indeed contain sane advice concerning control of temper, worry and other faults, but which lead one far afield from all that Christendom has ever held dear, whether in its Eastern or Western branch.

When the devil comes in velvet slippers, is he less dangerous than he once was when he decreed through Spirittists, "We abrogate the idea of a personal God"? Are the thousands who have read the sixteen printings of *The Unobstructed Universe* which came off the presses between September, 1940, and October, 1941, on the right track? Did Mr. White himself, when he passed into the beyond on September 1, 1946, find what he expected to find? Or did he, together with the thousands who followed his guidance, meet with disastrous disillusion, having bypassed God's own revelation?

These questions will not down; too much depends upon their answer.

Mr. White (1873-1946) is known as the talented author of many books of adventure and travel. During the last twenty years of his life he added to his travels through Africa and Alaska an itinerary far into another land, a territory more unknown, yet close around us.

It began in 1919, when Mrs. White—the "Betty" in the three books—was summoned by "Invisibles" (spirits in the beyond) to take psychic matters seriously and to develop her natural gift for communication with the dead.

For many years Mr. White and others took down a vast mass of what was revealed to "Betty," and when in 1939 the wife died, the husband continued his wife's explorations, got in touch with her, and at the age of 67 completed the message for the guidance of seekers after truth and comfort.

Fundamental in the White trilogy is the thought that "there is only one universe." Both "heaven" and "hell" are right here, hell being only suffering from frustrated urge, "since in the hereafter all are bound to desire the progress of evolution."

Betty states, "I am right here. There is only one universe. There is no other 'heaven.' It is only that you cannot see me. Your eyes are not attuned to the color, your ears to the sound. I am in the unobstructed phase of the one and only universe. That is all. It is only that my I-Am is separated from the obstruction that was my body. My world is your world *plus*."

Man is "a bit of individualized consciousness," and "the only rock" is "recognition of the creator as greater than the thing created," "acceptance of the Oneness of Consciousness as a whole."

Thoroughly pantheistic is the new Spiritism as was also the old.

When asked how she could formerly pray the Lord's Prayer while yet "always beyond the anthropomorphic idea," Betty replied from the beyond that she was wont to address her prayer "to consciousness." "Did you think of consciousness with personality, warmth, such warmth as comes with personality, I mean?" "As though I were drowning in a great sea, and there was a shipful of people, any or all of whom could help me."

While in his earth-life, man has two bodies, the Alpha and the Beta body. The Beta is "the actual invisible substance which you have for long termed soul or spirit." It has weight and if a man had scales he might weigh the medium before the cold goes into the room and after: the difference would be the weight of the cold which is the Beta going out in response to a magnetic call of another consciousness to his own. When this going out is done under proper conditions and in the right mood, great good may result, for one can get in touch with "the oversoul" only through the subconscious, which is in the Beta, while the conscious mind is in the Alpha body.

Spiritism, then, is the very opposite of Russellism with its rationalistic praise of "the intellect." White belittles the intellect, "the brain." It is "a marvelous mechanism," but effective only "in combination with the inner self." It is "a machine which must be worked by the other, wiser guiding consciousness."

Thus the man—the "person" is said to be in the Beta—is left a prey to all sorts of suggestions from the "spiritual world."

Mr. White did not receive vulgar, obscene, irreverent, silly information, as have countless other Spiritists before him. And there are beautiful literary touches, fine illustrations in the White books. The mysteries of spiritistic phenomena become quite plausible events when he speaks on "Orthos and the Essences": Time, Space, Motion, Frequency, Conductivity.

Take a few samples.

Time has three aspects. The first is *sidereal time* (from Latin *sidera*, the stars). The term stands for our ordinary time, determined by the stars and ticked off by the clock. Already here, however, we know that there is a different aspect of time, which may be called *psychological time.* An hour is not always the same: five minutes may seem like sixty when we wait for a pot to boil. Fifteen minutes may seem endless when we nervously wait for a train to arrive; let the same fifteen minutes be spent in intent survey of beautiful surroundings, and the train arrives before we realize we have waited any time at all. Thus time is elastic, not fixed at all.

There is also a third time, *orthic time* (*orthos* being the Greek word for right, correct, as most people know from the word orthodox [right in opinion]). This orthic time, in which those live who have graduated from our life, is also "malleable"; it expands and contracts; it is a timeless present, of which we have a slight experience when we pace about oblivious to past and future moments. The "dead," therefore, are far from dead: they are like the Old Testament Jehovah who said "I Am," not I was or will be, but just *am.* Just plain being is the time condition of the hereafter.

There are also three aspects of *space.*

The first is determined by the *geometrical distance* between two points. *Psychologically*, however, that distance varies: long if we walk it, footsore and weary; short if we ride over a concrete road in a modern car geared to do 70, 80, 100 miles an hour. When we sleep in a Pullman compartment we may awake at a distance of many miles, but

all that space has vanished. What obstructs us is not the
number of miles but "our inexpertness in telescoping
them, or, if you will, telescoping through them."

In the third, or *orthic space,* those who have gone on before live in the same universe in which we dwell, but are
minus the obstructions of the dense Alpha body, and they
know that space itself is not solid. They pass right through
it at will.

There is also an *orthic motion.* In the universe in which
we live, the obstructed universe, motion is real: the train
may move faster and faster, though only up to a certain
point. It may also stand still and yet be in motion, because
it moves through space with the earth on which it stands.
But in Betty's universe motion is obstructed neither by
time nor space: "In orthos, motion is instant."

No wonder the wise Spiritist does not fear death. He
gladly anticipates it. It will be a permanent laying aside
of all obstructions, something he has done quite frequently
for a while, if, namely, he has developed the psychic
aptitude of leaving the Alpha body and stepping out in the
Beta. It is "a pleasurable releasing, quite different from
the death-agony idea."

Nor can those "stepladders" to which Mr. White referred fail to lead some poorly instructed souls astray. For
many other Spiritists freely and with gusto point to the
facts that Abraham, Moses, Saul, Samuel, Isaiah, Daniel,
and Paul all were psychics and had definitely spiritistic
experiences, while Jesus was the greatest medium of all.
He was clairvoyant, Matthew 21:2; clairvoyant and clair-
audient, Matthew 3:17; telepathic, John 4:17-19; and He
was a materializing medium, Luke 9:28-30.[2]

Besides, all the information from the other side points
to the happy existence of the Invisibles. As the older
Spiritists spoke of seven spheres all around the earth as
the layers of an onion around its core, so White speaks of
different "levels" of existence hereafter. Those on the first

2. See Marcus Bach, *They Have Found a Faith,* Ch. 4.

level are guided on toward the next and more felicitous by those already inhabiting them.[3]

To the Christian, however, this fast-and-loose play with the Bible is self-condemnatory. For if all the information by so-called visiting spirits from the beyond says that "there is nothing in death to fear," that "life goes on exactly as it did here," then Jesus must have been a poor medium. For Moses and Elijah discussed with Him His *exodus* at Jerusalem, that is, His death, resurrection, and ascension; yet the same gospel from which the Spiritists endeavor to prove Jesus a materializing medium, continues to describe His anguish in Gethsemane at the approach of death. Do we have "the greatest medium" so out of harmony with the unanimous testimony of the spirits; or shall we scrap the comparatively large sections of the four Gospels describing His death-agony?

Yes, it is all very attractive and quite scientific. It is as Darby concludes in *The Unobstructed Universe*: ". . . so inclusive a philosophical structure, so closely knit, so airtight logically: one that proceeds through so wide a range of subjects and interlocks them all so perfectly that not a seam shows; and, with all that, expresses it so simply and so clearly." And there is a gradual development from the first book through the second and the third, beginning with the demonstration that psychic phenomena are possible; continuing to show how it should be tried and what pitfalls to avoid; and working up toward a climax which leaves little to be asked.

Explanation of Phenomena

There is so much counterfeit Spiritism that the appraisal of the phenomena becomes a complicated task. We have:

(1) *Fraudulent Spiritism*

Under the cover of darkness (spirits are said to be sensitive to light) and with the aid of electricity, phonographs

---

3. For a somewhat detailed description of existence in the "seven spheres," cf. Charles S. Braden, *These Also Believe*, pp. 344-346.

and numerous other modern inventions, there is not a
genuine spiritistic phenomenon that cannot be reproduced
a hundred-fold for commercial reasons. There is a host of
well-organized crooks who gather information concerning
prospective dupes in the most systematic manner, who
carefully file such information for future reference, or sell
it to other mediums. With the information obtained be-
forehand, the sitter is duly impressed with the knowledge
of the medium, the voice of the "spirit" is produced seem-
ingly from the "ether," and the dupe is gradually enslaved
by the medium, until he is advised where to invest his
capital. When the victim at last awakes to the fact that he
has been misled, the medium goes scot-free; she has only
plied her "religion." Thus a gang of crooks discovered
that a sitter was a musician whose favorite master was
Brahms. A supposed medium, an able pianist, herself actually memorized the chief works of Brahms. The sitter was
then asked to summon his favorite musician through the
medium, who sat at the piano in a supposed trance, and
was guided by the "spirit of Brahms" to play the master's
works called for by the sitter. Struck with awe, our mu-
sical dupe surrendered to the medium, lost his fortune,
and committed suicide. The extent of this fraudulent Spiritism is so large that it is difficult to know where it begins
and where it ends.[4]

But our difficulties increase when we consider the fact
that even genuine psychics have been caught in fraud time
and again. This is supposedly due to the fact that psychic
force does not always work when the medium wants it.
Consequently, when the scene has been set for a séance
and the sitter expects results, the medium often resorts to
trickery. Thus the Fox girls admitted that their early raps

4. This side of the matter is well described by E. H. Smith in an
article "Crooks of Ghostland" in *Saturday Evening* Post, April 24,
1920; *Behind the Scenes with the Medium* by D. P. Abbott; *Houdini's
Spirit Exposés and Dunninger's Psychical Investigations*, New York,
1928. "I've Unmasked a Thousand Frauds" by Mackenberg and
Fishman in *Saturday Evening Post*, March 3, 1951; Miss Mackenberg
asserts that she has never found a genuine medium.

were achieved by the snapping of the joints of their toes. Eusapia Paladino, most famous medium in her day, was caught deceiving at least twice. In short, the original P(sychical) R(esearch) S(ociety), which consists of eminent scholars and has investigated spiritistic phenom-ena since 1882, has found only two or three mediums above suspicion during a period of forty years. To this one may add that such prominent advocates of Spiritism as Sir Wm. Crookes in 1874, *Light* in 1909, and Sir Conan Doyle in 1919 have admitted that there is no test known where-by we may determine whether information which does come from departed spirits, comes to us bona-fide or from a "naughty spirit" or *Poltergeist* bent upon deceiving.

Besides all this, good spirits may attempt to convey a message through a medium's *control,* the spirit who com-municates with her in her trance condition. But the con-trol itself at times seems to take a wicked pleasure in twisting the information of the good spirit. Thus we have a confused mass of information by so-called Shakespeares and Carlyles who cannot spell their own names; and upon such dubious sources we depend for our information con-cerning the hereafter.

However, let us give our Spiritist friends the benefit of the doubt. Let us rule out of court the fact that undoubtedly the bulk of spiritistic phenomena is deceptive, and likewise the consideration that it is very difficult for the average man to know whether he deals with a fake or with a gen-uine medium, and she in turn with a true or a fraudulent source of information. In other words, let us consider

(2) *Bona-Fide Spiritism*

Here we have the following opinions:

1. Spiritists themselves assert that such *information* as they believe has reached them through honest channels *has come from the spirits of departed human beings* who live in the spheres close to our own world. Since this is known to be contrary to the teachings of Christianity, prominent Spiritists do not hesitate to denounce Christian

leaders as incompetent judges. Sir Oliver Lodge may be
thought to speak the mind of modern Spiritism when he
informs us that "the clergy can hardly form a good court
of enquiry" since they "look at the matter from the Christian standpoint." He wants us to lay aside all "prejudice" and to "proceed hypothetically." At the same time,
however, Sir Oliver admits that his own conviction remains a hypothesis, although he states, "It is not an unreasonable hypothesis. It is the hypothesis to which I have
been impelled after thirty years of study." In itself this
would not be so bad, since the doctrines of Christianity
are as much a "hypothesis" from the standpoint of the
exact sciences as the doctrines of Spiritism or any other
metaphysical opinions and convictions. After all, we all
walk by faith. We maintain, however, that the Christian
faith is based upon such well-established historic facts
that we should not discard them for something so un-
proven and so diametrically at variance with the doctrines
of Christianity itself. It is not concerning the *facts* of
genuine Spiritism that we contend; it is the interpretation,
the *alleged source* of these facts, which we dispute. That
information reaches the medium, we have no doubt. But
why must Sir Oliver Lodge inform us with passion that
the hypothesis that such information comes from our departed dear ones is superior to any other hypothesis? This
hypothesis leads Sir Oliver himself to discard all the "ter-
ribly depressing doctrines, about repose in graves and
fleshly resurrection at some long distant day," and similar
"mediaeval absurdity." If it remains a matter of one hypothesis versus another, we Christians have a full right, it
would seem, to refuse to surrender the heritage which the
Church has so painstakingly and universally derived from
the Bible. And when we add that, in general, the findings
of Spiritism are in direct opposition to all that Bible and
Church teach, can we be rightly blamed for refusing the
"hypothesis" of Spiritism?

2. A second *account* is that *all communications come
from medium and audience.* In Spiritism we are dealing

with physical phenomena (moving of heavy bodies without contact, alteration in weight, the appearance of hands and other limbs), and with psychical phenomena (knowledge in the medium in trance condition which cannot be traced to any known source). It is alleged that all men have *physical, electric, and psychic* force; that the physical phenomena of Spiritism are due to exceptional physical force, or, to unusual power of mind over matter; that the psychic features are the result of phenomenal psychic force. Under this head come *telepathy* (thought-transference from sitters, or others, to the medium) ; *mind-reading* (in some cases the subconscious mind of the medium is even asserted to read the subconscious mind of the sitter, (and to read long-forgotten data from his memory) *clairvoyance* and *clairaudience* (ability to see and to hear below or beyond the ordinary amount of ether thrillings seen and heard by human beings) ; and similar attributes of the soul that are only partially known quantities. The book of Dr. A. T. Schofield, an English physician and psychologist, contains much of interest in this connection. It remains noteworthy that so little of even that which is *known* of these forces is really *understood,* that prominent Spiritists themselves have admitted that many so-called spirit-manifestations may be due to these mysterious qualities of the soul.

The writer heard Dr. C. Eaton state that he had demonstrated the truth of this theory time and again by the following challenge. He would open a book in the presence of a medium in trance, read the number of the page, turn the book upside down, and ask the medium to mention the number of the page. This she could invariably do, since she read the number from his mind. He would then close the book and re-open it while it was upside down. In this way "no one on earth knew the number of the page at which the book had been opened, and the same medium would invariably guess the page wrongly."

This is indeed a remarkable test. Moreover, in the light of the fact that mental telepathy and mind reading occur

in almost every human life some time or other, we do not
wonder that psychics are said to have this mysterious
power in a great measure, especially when in trance, that
is to say, when their conscious mind has surrendered to
the play of their unconscious mind. The well-known novel
Jane Eyre presents, a case of mental telepathy which
might be duplicated today. One of the present writer's
professors told him that two days after he had spent a
night celebrating with fellow students, a letter arrived
from his mother in a distant city inquiring why he had
not been in bed that night, as it had worried her until the
early morning hours.

We are not surprised, therefore, to discover that men
who, like the Sadducees, say that there is no resurrection,
neither angel, nor spirit, attribute all spiritistic phenomena to these natural forces. This means, of course, genuine
phenomena, since throughout we should bear in mind that
there is much deception. Thus table-tilting is produced by
means of a hook and chain connecting the table with the
medium's clothing, or through a hollow table-leg which is
being moved by an accomplice in a room below the sitters,
and so forth. For those who deny the spiritual world, the
above is the logical interpretation of all Spiritism that is
genuine.

3. There remain, however, two difficulties in the way of
accepting this theory as explanatory of all spiritistic phenomena.

a. Spiritists who have gone into the matter deeply have
occasionally confessed to obsession by vile and evil spirits.
E. F. Hanson's excellent book contains several pages filled
with quotations from such spiritistic authorities as the
magazine *Mind and Matter* in which it is admitted that
mediums are at times subject to the control of evil spirits.
He mentions a medium who was in such poor physical condition that a "spirit doctor" commanded an evil spirit to
leave the body of the medium-victim, after which he in-
vited, equally successfully, a gentler spirit to take control
of the mediumistic patient.

In support of this is the testimony of mediumistic or
psychic people who, after a few experiments, discarded
Spiritism entirely because the information they received
was so unspeakably vile, obscene, and blasphemous that
they were fairly shocked out of Spiritism. It will not do
to blame all of this on the medium's or sitter's subliminal
self, as honest Spiritists have admitted, for, as Mr. Wal-
lace the Spiritist states, "then that second self is almost
always a deceiving and a lying self, no matter how moral
and truthful the first self may be." This, he calls a "stu-
pendous difficulty."

To this we may add that the physical effects upon the
medium are often of such painful or violent character "as
have been (to quote a Spiritist) in all ages imputed to
possession by evil spirits." They are, in point of fact, the
same as they were in Jesus' day, the symptoms of the
demon-possessed, to wit, prostration, foaming, and similar
phenomena.

b. This leads us inevitably to the second obstacle in the
way of attributing all spiritistic phenomena to psychic
force. The Bible, in both the Old and the New Testaments,
apparently warns severely against Spiritism as demonology. In this connection we take issue with the assertion
of Canon Barnes and Jane T. Stoddart, "that the worst
way of attacking spiritualism is to admit its fundamental
claim that communication with 'spirits' can be set up, and
then to assert that the 'spirits' with whom intercourse is
established are evil."

Contrary to this, we maintain that there is a marked
difference between the "fundamental claim" that contact
can be established with departed mortals, and the Christian view that it cannot be done. We also assert that those
seeking after such contact fall an unknowing prey to evil
spirits, that is, to demons, whose very existence they deny.
We can see no yielding of ground to Spiritism in this view.

In defending this latter position as explanatory of at
least part of the spiritistic phenomena, we present the
following cumulative argument.

1. Spiritism has always existed, and its history may be traced through the centuries. It has ever revealed the same characteristics, according to the spiritist Colville as well as the ex-Spiritist Hanson. Accordingly the *International Psychic Gazette* for Setember, 1916, contained the interesting information that an English medium, Mr. W. W. Love, held a spiritist seance in a Chinese temple in the presence of Chinese priests who considered him "a brother spiritist" and who expressed their surprise that he, a European, should know so much about spirit manifestation.

2. But to these priests in their Chinese temple their Spiritism was undoubtedly religion. Is it, then, so far amiss to remind ourselves of the fact that Scripture warns against heathen idolatry as against the worship of demons?

3. Certainly Scripture teaches that demons can influence human beings. Read Genesis 3:1; Revelation 12:9; I Kings 22:19-23; Ezekiel 28:11-19 (observe that here the king of Tyre is addressed in language partly fitting him, and partly only his satanic master, the inference being that they must have worked much together); John 8:44; Ephesians 6:11, 12.

4. In perfect harmony with this, Scripture teaches that men may worship demons under semblance of worshiping "god," Deuteronomy 32:17; I Corinthians 10:20.

5. To this it may be added that demon-possession was of frequent occurrence in Bible times, especially when the devil ("God's ape" according to Luther) imitated the incarnation of the Son of God by taking possession of the bodies of human victims. It is preposterous to assert that evil spirits cannot do in "these last days" what they did in the first century of our era.

We may state in this connection that, in our own opinion, a combination of views two and three is the most satisfactory. We hold that many spiritistic phenomena are the natural result of little-studied soul force, but that in some, perhaps in fewer, cases demons are at work. Nor do we consider it at all strange that a medium who has surrended his mind to the dictation of outside influences, should at times become the willing instrument of a strong human will and mind, and at other times the unsuspecting tool of superhuman spirits who have equal access to him in his trance condition.[5] And this view, it would appear, accounts fully for the notorious fruit of Spiritism, namely, The Three Black I's: *Infidelity, Insanity, Immorality.* However, in making this statement we must bear in mind that, like other "liberal" cults and currents of thought, modern Spiritism has absorbed something of the spirit of the times, that is to say, the newer writers and practitioners of Spiritism, instead of decrying Christianity as absurd, false, and the like, maintain that it is essentially in agreement with its own teachings.

There remains the task of examining briefly, first, Scripture's attitude toward Spiritism; and secondly, Spiritism's attitude toward Scripture and Scriptural truth. As to the first,

The Bible on Spiritism

The Scriptures contain many references. For an intelligent understanding of these the following definitions from the International Standard Bible Encyclopaedia may serve.

Consulter with a familiar spirit: One who was possessed of a python or soothsaying demon. (I Sam. 28; Acts 16: 16-18).

Divination: the art of obtaining secret knowledge, especially that which related to the future, by means almost exclusively within the reach of special classes of men.

---

5. This is, of course, widely different from attributing insanity to direct influence of evil spirits. Dr. Mulder shows conclusively that many symptoms formerly ascribed to demonic influence have only a disturbed physical background, such as hysteria. Dr. Mulder seems to incline toward the view that at Endor the presence of an evil spirit may be suspected. Cf. *Essays on Mental Disturbance and Demon Possession* by Jacob D. Mulder, M.D., Grand Rapids, Michigan. The present writer, in view of the *energeia tou satana* predicted of "the lawless one" in II Thess. 2:9, would not wonder if toward the end of time demon-possession, as manifest in Jesus' days, occurred on a limited scale.

Familiar spirits: spirits which were supposed to come at the call of one who had power over them. They were probably called "familiar" because it was a servant (*famulus*), belonging to the family (*familiaris*) who might be summoned to do the commands of the owner. The Hebrew word means *hollow*, because the voice of the spirit might have been supposed to come from the one possessed, as from a bottle, or because of the hollow sound which characterized the utterance, as out of the ground (Isa. 29:4).

Necromancy: consultation with the dead. The attempt was condemned though the end could not be attained.

Sorcerer: one who muttered incantations or spoke in ventriloquial whispers, as if under the influence of the spirits of the dead.

Witch: "one who knows." The Hebrew word means "a woman that hath a familiar spirit."

Wizard: "a knowing one." The word in the Old Testament always denotes a man who can interpret the ravings of the medium.

Among the Scriptural passages are Leviticus 19:26, 31; Deuteronomy 18:9-14; I Samuel 28; II Kings 21:2, 6; I Chronicles 10:13, 14; Isaiah 8:19-22; 19:3; Acts 16:16-18. There are likely to be many more, though some of the divinations mentioned were of a different character. These are certain, and they teach:

1. That all seeking of the dead was forbidden (Ex. 22:18; Lev. 20:6).

2. That Spiritism caused the destruction of seven nations; and, together with other sins, the death of Saul (1 Chron. 10:13).

3. That Israel was as much in danger of resorting to this sin as are "Christians" today.

4. That Egypt, in punishment for its sins, was abandoned by God to Spiritism (Isa. 19:3).

5. That its sinful character consists of finding out things hidden, apart from the divine revelation. (Deut. 18:11, 14, 15, 20; Isa. 8:19, 20).

6. That Spiritism is the rejection of Christ. (Deut. 18: 14, 15).

7. In the light of the foregoing texts the modern revival of Spiritism seems to be clearly predicted in I Timothy 4:1, and perhaps in Revelation 16:13, 14 (as frogs live in water or on the earth, so demons live in the air or in human beings).

The Seance at Endor

That Spiritists cannot appeal to I Samuel 28 to support the view that the Old Testament sanctions communication with the dead, forbidding only iniquitous practices attending Spiritism in its decadent form, is evident from I Chronicles 10:13, 14. Even if Samuel did appear, this passage would only mean that God upset the séance and intervened.

That this is what happened is held by Keil, Haldeman, Pink, Gray, Panton, Schofield, and many others. Their arguments are:

1. The medium was terrified when the *unexpected* happened.

2. Scripture speaks five times of *Samuel*.

3. The prophecy was fulfilled: Saul died the next day and his army was routed.

Yet the only apparent indication of Samuel's return is vs. 15, "And Samuel said to Saul." If, however, other considerations prove that Samuel did not appear, these words must be explained:

a. As a rendering of what the woman said to Saul.

b. Or, as calling Samuel what looked like Samuel, just as angels appearing like men are called men (Gen. 18:1, 2; Dan. 9:21) ; and men called *gods* because they resemble or represent God in certain aspects or positions (Ps. 82: 6).

That Samuel did not appear is held by Hanson, Bavinck, Orr (*Intern'l Stand. Bible Enc.*) and Honig.[6] Their argu-

---

6. *Handboek v. d. Geref. Dogmatiek*, Kampen, 1938, p. 796, quoting extensively from the 18th century Dutch theologian P. van Mastricht.

ments seem clinching, although they differ as to what did happen. We advance:

1. Neither the woman nor her familiar spirit ("control") had power over Samuel. God had. But He refused to answer Saul (v. 6) ; surely, He would not answer him now that Saul took refuge to forbidden means, least of all by doing a thing He has never been known to duplicate.[7]

2. After Samuel informed Saul that God had rejected him, the prophet had no more dealings with the king.

3. The true Samuel would not have lied, by saying that Saul had disturbed his rest, if not Saul but God had ordered him; nor by saying that Saul would be with him the next day, cf. Luke 16:26.

4. After rejecting Saul for the sin of disobedience and subsequently ignoring him for years, God would not at the last moment

a. have catered to Saul's desire to receive another revelation;

b. have acted contrary to the conviction He has always impressed upon His people, namely, that there is no contact between the living and the dead (Job 7:10; Eccl. 9:6; Isa. 63:16; Luke 16:31;

c. have created the impression that seeking information from the dead is not so bad, since elsewhere He has commanded this sin to be punished with death (all Spiritists appeal to this passage) ;

---

7. Houdini, lifelong antagonist of spiritism, promised his wife that, if at all possible, he would visit her after his death. For years Mrs. Houdini waited in accordance with her late husband's instructions. At last she extinguished the light she had left burning to guide the spirit in his search for her.

Clarence Darrow, the agnostic, promised Claude Noble, Detroit businessman and musician, "that if he found an after life he would manifest it on the anniversary of his death." On March 13, 1942, Mr. Noble made his fourth annual attempt in Jackson Park, Chicago, to contact Darrow. It was in vain as in previous years. Even recital of the Lord's Prayer could not aid in producing the promised "violent vibration of Noble's arm." And no wonder: the Lord's Prayer cannot avail in an attempt to run afoul of the Lord's written Word.

d. have stated that Saul had to die because of this thing
in which God yielded to his request (I Chron. 10:13).

5. Saul told the medium whom to call up. In accordance
with our explanation of psychic phenomena the *sensitive*
(medium) would thereupon read from Saul's mind what
Samuel looked like, and describe him *as Saul had been wont
to see him* (not as he was after death).

6. The woman was afraid:

a. Because in her trance she recognized Saul (v. 12),
    who was known as a mighty enemy of the medium
    (mind reading) ; see verse 3; or

b. Because she saw *elohim, spirits,* hover above the ap-
    parition, who, with "lying wonders" (II Thess. 2:9),
    impersonated Samuel.

7. Saul never saw Samuel; he *perceived* from the woman's description what *she* saw in her trance.

8. As to the prophecy, here are several possibilities:

a. The woman read Saul's dread that his end was com-
    ing. This she predicted.

b. The woman read the prophecy by Samuel (I Sam.
    15:16, 18) which had haunted Saul (I Sam. 16:2;
    20:31, etc.) in his frightened mind, and told him
    what he expected to hear.

c. If a demon, impersonating Samuel, spoke through the
    medium, it would remember Samuel's prophecy and
    make use of it.

Spiritism on the Bible

Lest we repeat ourselves in Chapters 2-12, we shall merely present statements by prominent cultists on various important and generally accepted Christian points of doctrine.
In Chapter 17 we shall briefly recall that these doctrines
are indeed contained in Scripture and believed by "the holy
catholic church" of the ages. It will be observed, we trust,
that the various antichristian "Isms" reveal their true character when they denounce the revealed truth of the Word of
God.

As to Spiritism, it teaches — which means sundry Spiritists teach, there being no official creed of Spiritism — as
follows:

God

"We abrogate the idea of a personal God."[8]

"It should be understood that there are as many Gods as
there are minds needing Gods to worship; not only one, two,
or three, but many . . . The noble forest trees, sun, moon,
and stars, all things are Gods to you, for they minister unto
the needs of your soul. It is vain to suppose you can all bow
down to, and truly serve one God."[9]

Q.   (by Mrs. Connant, medium). "Do you know of any
such spirit as a person we call Devil?"

A.   (through the controlling spirit at séance) : "We certainly do, and yet this same Devil is our God, our Father."[10]

Jesus Christ

"What's the meaning of the word Christ? Is it not, as is
generally supposed, the Son of the Creator of all things?
Any just and perfect being is Christ."[11]

"It seems nevertheless that all the testimony received
from advanced spirits only shows that Christ was a medium and a reformer in Judea; that he now is an advanced
spirit in the sixth sphere." — DR. WEISSE.[12]

"High above all these is the greatest spirit of whom they
(the spirits) have cognizance — not God, since God is so
infinite that He is not within their ken — but one who is
nearer God and to that extent represents God. This is the
Christ Spirit. His special care is the earth. He came down
upon it at a time of great earthly depravity — a time when

8. Wilkins, *The Physical Phenomena in Spiritualism Revealed*,
quoting "one of the presidents at a national camp of Spiritualism."
9. *The Banner of Light*, Feb. 3, 1866.
10. *Ibid.*, Nov. 4, 1865.
11. *Spiritual Telegraph*, No. 37.
12. Dr. Weisse, as quoted by Hanson, *Demonology or Spiritualism*,
p. 147.

the world was almost as wicked as it is now, in order to give the people the lesson of an ideal life. Then he returned to his own high station, having left an example which is still occasionally followed. That is the story of Christ as spirits have described it.[13]

"Christ was a good man, but He could not have been divine except in the sense perhaps that we are all divine." —MESSAGE BY A "SPIRIT."[14]

"I do not find that Christ claimed for Himself more than he held out as possible for others. When He identifies Himself with the Father, it was in the oneness of mediumship. He was the great Medium or Mediator." — GERALD MASSEY.[15]

"As God is Spirit, that is the Infinite Spirit's presence acting by the law of mediation, the Apostle with a singular clearness of perception pronounced the Nazarene a Mediator — i. e. a Medium — between God and man." — DR. J. M. PEEBLES.[16]

"In the Spiritualist hymn-book the name of Jesus is deleted — for example, 'angels of Jesus' reads 'angels of wisdom.' At their services His name is carefully omitted in the prayers." — REV. F. FIELDING-OULD.[17]

"The miraculous conception of Christ is merely a fabulous tale.[18]

"Christ arose in spirit. It was the spirit that appeared to the disciples so constantly after the crucifixion. It was a spirit that ascended into heaven, and it is a glorious spirit

13. A. Conan Doyle, *The New Revelation*, p. 57.
14. Quoted by Raupert, *Spiritistic Phenomena and their Interpretation*, p. 47.
15. Quoted by Pollock, *Modern Spiritualism Briefly Tested by Scripture*, p. 13.
16. *Ibid.*, p. 14.
17. In *Light*, July 12, 1919.
18. *Spiritual Telegraph*, No. 37.

that appears and has appeared during the long centuries to thousands of wearied Christians on earth." — COLVILLE.[19]

"I, Jesus, appeared in spirit in 1861, and do say and declare unto the world that the new era or dispensation has commenced, called the coming of Christ. It commenced about the year 1847, and as represented and spoken of by the prophet Daniel and others, by my coming as a cloud in the heavens, with tens of thousands of angels, to overshadow the earth with my glory."[20]

"This is the second coming — a coming in power and glory — a coming of ministering angels and spirits — a coming to morally and spiritually enlighten all conscious intelligences. It is the overshadowing return of the living Christ. There will be no such personal return as theologians have taught. This will be, and is, the spiritual return to his people, by the voice of his messengers speaking to those whose ears are open; even as he said. . ." — STAINTON MOSES (Imperator).[21]

The Atonement

"Your atonement is the very climax of a deranged imagination, and one that is of the most unrighteous and immoral tendency." — A. J. DAVIS.[22]

"The orthodox doctrine of Atonement was a survival of the greatest abuses of earliest time, and it was immoral to the core. . . The reason for this doctrine is that you are born into this world a lost, ruined, hell-deserving sinner. But

---

19. *Universal Spiritualism*, p. 234. It deserves attention that these are the words of a modernist preacher (F. Phillips) which the spiritist Mr. Colville quotes "without addition of our own to make their salutary influence felt upon every attentive reader's mind." That also other Modernists are in perfect agreement with the spiritist idea of Christ's appearance as materializations, see *Princeton Theol. Review*, July, 1922, p. 487.

20. Opening words of the book *New Dispensations*, quoted by Hanson, *op. cit.*, p. 212.

21. Colville, *op. cit.*, pp. 322, 323.

22. *Nat. Div. Rev.*, p. 576.

what an outrageous lie! . . . Does not your blood boil with indignation at such a doctrine?"[23]

"One can see no justice in a vicarious sacrifice, nor in the God who could be placated by such means." — A. CONAN DOYLE.[24]

Man

"Never was there any evidence of a fall." — A. CONAN DOYLE.[25]

"We must reject the conception of fallen creatures. By the Fall we understand the descent of spirit into matter."— G. G. ANDRE.[26]

Bible

"We must have no desire to hide the plain fact that there is much in some parts of the Bible which does not amalgamate with our teaching."[27]

"To assert that it is a Holy and Divine Book, that God inspired the writers to make known His Divine will, is a gross outrage on and misleading to the public."[28]

Hell

"Hell, I may say, drops out altogether, as it has long dropped out of the thoughts of every reasonable man. This odious conception, so blasphemous in its view of the Creator, arose from the exaggeration of Oriental phrases, and may perhaps have been of service in a coarse age when men were frightened by fires, as wild beasts are scared by the travelers. Hell as a permanent place does not exist. But the idea of punishment, of purifying chastisement, in fact of Purgatory, is justified by the reports from the other side." — A. CONAN DOYLE.[29]

23. R. B. Jones, *Spiritism in Bible Light*, p. 172, quoting the spiritist paper *Medium and Daybreak*.
24. *Op. cit.*, p. 55.
25. *Loc. cit.*
26. *The True Light*, p. 162.
27. *Spirit Teachings*, p. 74.
28. *Outlines of Spiritualism*, p. 13.
29. *Op. cit.*, p. 68.

"It [the ancient Egyptian view of transmigration] is immeasurably superior to any view of endless, useless torment such as many benighted Christian theologians have proclaimed . . . a conception for which there is neither rational explanation nor apology." —COLVILLE.[30]

"There is nothing that can properly be called Hell in the mediaeval sense of eternal hopelessness; but yet Hell in very truth in so far as they suffer the pangs of remorse when their rebellious spirit is broken, and when in their felt poverty of soul they begin to long to return to the Father." — SIR OLIVER LODGE.[31]

"Hell is a great remedial agency. The punishment of sin is remedial. No great gulf is fixed between Heaven and Hell." — "JULIA," a supposed spirit speaking thru W. T. STEAD.[32]

Spirits

"All spirits in the other world are nothing else but the souls of those who have lived here."—LANSLOTS.[33]

"If for convenience we designate the high ranks (of the departed) Angels, and the lower as Evil Spirits, let us be careful not to lose sight of the fact that they differ only as elder and younger."—G. G. ANDRE.[34]

The Church

"Step by step the Christian Church advanced, and as it did so, step by step the torch of Spiritualism receded, until hardly a flickering ray from it could be perceived amid the deep darkness. . . . For more than 1800 years has the so-called Christian Church stood between mortals and spirits, barring all chance for progress and growth. It stands today

30. *Op. cit.*, p. 82.
31. *Raymond; or Life and Death with Examples of the Evidence for the Survival of Memory and Affection After Death.*
32. Quoted by A. T. Schofield, *Modern Spiritism, Its Science and Religion*, p. 65.
33. *Spiritism Unveiled*, p. 36.
34. *Op. cit.*, p. 76.

as complete a barrier to human progress, as it did 1800 years ago."[35]

"It (Spiritualism) is vastly more firmly fixed than the rock on which it has been falsely said, Jesus Christ founded his church. . . . It is for that reason that we have felt it our duty, as a sincere friend of Spiritualism, to show what Christianity is. . . . If the latter lives, Spiritualism must die; and if Spiritualism is to live, Christianity must die. They are the antithesis of each other. . . . Modern Spiritualism has come to give it its *coup de grace;* and those who would hold back that flow are the enemies of spiritual truth."[36]

"Resolved: (1) That Sunday Schools should be discontinued; (2) That all Christian ordinances and worship should be abandoned; (3) That sexual tyranny should be denounced; (4) That abstinance from animal food should be affirmed." — Spiritist Conference held in Providence, Rhode Island (1920?) [37]

"I will exercise that dearest of all rights. . . the right of maternity — in the way which to me seemeth right; and no man, nor set of men, no church, no State, shall withhold me from the realization of that purest of all inspirations inherent in every true woman, the right to re-beget myself when, and by whom, and under such circumstances as to me seem fit and best." — J. M. SPEAR, a medium.[38]

Conclusions

That Spiritism has again called attention to the existence of a spiritual world, to life hereafter, to future retribution in a time of gross materialism, we can appreciate. But when we see that this spiritual conception is accompanied by such hatred of Biblical truth, and leads to such disastrous physical and mental results, we can only condemn it from the Christian standpoint. Christianity and Spiritism can-

35. *Mind and Matter*, May 8, 1880.
36. *Ibid.*, June, 1880.
37. Cited by Vine and Pollock.
38. Waggoner, *Modern Spiritualism*, p. 147.

not go together. We think Rudyard Kipling was warranted
in saying,

> *Oh, the road to En-dor is the oldest road,*
>   *And the craziest road of all.*
> *Straight it runs to the witch's abode,*
>   *As it did in the days of Saul.*
> *And nothing has changed of the sorrow in store*
> *For such as go down on the road to En-dor.*

For You to Answer

1. Why is Spiritism the first cult we consider?

2. What tends to revive interest in Spiritism?

3. Would you call Spiritism a cult that stresses clearly
defined doctrines? In this respect is it similar to, say, Mormonism, Russellism?

4. What do Spiritists mean by the terms: séance, trance,
a psychic, materialization, Invisibles?

5. Has the new Spiritism a different attitude toward
the Church than had the older type? Is this spirit characteristic of our time?

6. What is a fundamental thought in White's exposition
of Spiritism?

7. Do Spiritists believe in a personal God? Do they believe
man is soul and body?

8. What does Mr. White understand by the terms orthic
time, orthic space, orthic motion; and why does he consider
our universe to be obstructed?

9. If the modern philosophy of Spiritists is logically airtight, why can it still be wrong?

10. Is there much fraudulent Spiritism? Why are there
no proven methods whereby genuine Spiritism may be dif-
ferentiated from spurious Spiritism?

11. How many differing interpretations are there of
spiritistic phenomena? Why can we not accept the explanation of Spiritists themselves? What do you think of the
second one? Can you give any reasons for thinking that at
least some phenomena are caused by evil spirits?

12. Do the Old and New Testament indeed refer to Spiritism? Does the Bible express itself as to the source of spiritistic phenomena? Why does it forbid all Spiritism?

13. Do you think Samuel appeared to Saul at Endor?

14. Mention some cardinal doctrines that are taught in Scripture and denied by Spiritism. Why does Spiritism deny these?

15. A student asked, "Would it be wrong for me to attend a séance in a 'Spiritualist Church' merely to see what goes on?" What would you reply? Give your reasons.

3

THEOSOPHY

Theosophy, or Divine Wisdom, is the apostate child of Spiritism mixed with Buddhism. It is far more complicated and more intricate than Spiritism; at the same time its world-and-life view is more complete and fascinating.

History

Helena Petrovna, a Russian girl, at the age of seventeen, married N. B. Blavatsky in 1848. She deserted him after two months, and led a wandering life for twenty-five years. She flitted between Paris, London, Russia, Greece, the United States, Mexico, and India. She became a spiritistic medium early in life, and for ten years was under the "control" of a spirit calling himself John King. In 1857 "Madame" Blavatsky tried to found at Cairo a spiritistic society, but failed. Coming to New York in 1873, she sought co-operation with mediums; but just then so much fraud was exposed that she wearied of the Spiritism of the day.

In 1875 she founded the Theosophical Society in New York, aided by Colonel Olcott, a colonel in the Civil War. She said of it, "It is the same Spiritualism, but under another name." In 1882 Blavatsky and Olcott visited India together, and rounded out their system by adding Hindu and Buddhist elements. Blavatsky died in 1891, aged sixty years.[1]

Her greatest successor was Mrs. Annie Besant (1847-1933), daughter of an English minister, later wife of one. She left her husband in 1873, and, after challenging the

---

1. Braden shows conclusively, not only that "H. P. B." was personally interested in Spiritism, but also that she wrote in defense of it repeatedly, *op. cit.*, 225.

doctrine of the Church of England, she identified herself with Free Thought and radical political movements. Then suddenly Mrs. Besant was converted to Theosophy. She became a scholar, public speaker, and voluminous writer. She died September 20, 1933, in her eighty-sixth year. Her outstanding claim was that her adopted son, Krishnamurti (also called Krishnaji) was the new Messiah, or the re-incarnation of the World Teacher (see below). This she discovered on December 28, 1925. In 1926, Baron Philip Van Pallandt gave his large estate at Ommen, Netherlands, to be the headquarters of the new Messiah. Here annual conferences were held with, at first, as many as two thousand attendant disciples, while in 1928 there were seventeen hundred fifty women and eight hundred men. Some of these ladies slept with the picture of Krishnamurti under their pillows. At Krotona, California, the American headquarters of Theosophy, Krishnaji announced on November 20, 1931, that he had become convinced that he was not the Messiah, and refused to receive further adoration. "I am not an actor; I refuse to wear the robes of a Messiah; so I am again free of all possessions. I have nothing except my creed." Since then he has lived in retirement, giving lectures occasionally. Mrs. Besant died in 1933, and was succeeded by George S. Arundale, who upon his departure was followed by C. Jinarajadasa, the president of the Society since 1945. He is a prolific writer; among his works is *The Golden Book of the Theosophical Society*, published upon the fiftieth anniversary of the Society at Adyar, 1925.

Teachings

Theosophy, called by L. W. Rogers "a religion, a philosophy, a science and yet, accurately speaking, none of these, for it is truly all of them, and yet something beyond them," can here be described only in briefest outline. Since the doctrine of God is always determinative for an entire system, we shall first inquire into Theosophy's very complex ideas concerning God.

God

Theosophy, like its prototype, Buddhism — which was originally a reaction against the polytheism of India — is on the whole remarkably silent or evasive in its statements concerning God. It is pantheistic and teaches an impersonal God. "God is all, and all is God." Over and over again theosophic writers speak of *the unity of all life.* From this principle considered fundamental, follow many doctrines. If "everything that is, is God," and this God is thought of as "Universal Life, the Limitless Consciousness, the Eternal Love, the very source and heart of all that is," it follows that every form of activity is conceived of as "wave after wave of this Life pushing its way up through matter."

Given this, we do not marvel that all religions are esteemed fundamentally one. There may be a different emphasis, but "the Brotherhood of Religions" is the first plank in the platform of the Theosophical Society. "Every religion has a note of its own, a color of its own, that it gives for the helping of the world . . . blended together they give the whiteness of truth, blended together they give a mighty chord of perfection" (Besant).

To be sure, this impersonal God, from which all religions emanate, when occasionally described, is spoken of as a Trinity. But this is a Trinity in name only, for it is "a threefold manifestation of Power or Will, Wisdom, and Activity," to quote Mrs. Besant. Elsewhere she expresses this thought as follows, "Trinity of Divine Beings [sic], one as God, three as manifested Powers." Worse than this, we are told there is "a fourth Person or in some religions, a second Trinity, feminine, the Mother. This is That which makes manifestation possible, That which eternally [!] in the One is the root of limitation and division, and which, when manifested, is called Matter. This is the divine Not-Self, the divine Matter, the manifested Nature. Regarded as One [later on "She" is regarded as triple] She is the Fourth, making possible [!] the activity of the Three, the

Field of Their operations by virtue of her infinite divisibility, at once the 'handmaid of the Lord' (S. Luke 1, 38) and also His Mother, yielding of her substance to form His Body, the Universe, when overshadowed by His power."

Let us give one more taste of this. The Second Person is revealed by interaction between "Her"—divine Matter— and the Third Person of the Trinity, and thus becomes the mediator; hence "the Second Person of the Trinity of Spirit is ever dual; He is the One who clothes Himself in Matter, in Whom the twin-halves [!] of Deity appear in union, not as One."

We shall not vex the reader with more of a similar nature; the above may suffice to show that the theosophic conception of the Godhead is widely different from that held in "the holy Catholic Christian Church." *It* is impersonal; *It* lies at the root of all existence; *It* manifests itself as Power, as Wisdom and as Activity when considered as a spiritual entity. Besides, *It* also manifests itself as Divine Matter which is the necessary condition for *Its* manifestation. The second Person, Wisdom, is dual in nature, spiritual as Reason, material as Love.

Cosmogony

Theosophy, considering matter eternal, reckons the cycles of the universe by the millions. We are at present in the fifth subrace of the third human rootrace, and even a subrace goes on for millennia without any visible changes preparing for a new subrace. The present subrace, called the *Teutonic*, is a subrace of the Aryan rootrace; the latter has been preceded by the Atlantean, and this in turn by the Lemurian race; this was the first that can be truly called human, as it was preceded by semi-animal races. The proper history of man, according to Blavatsky, began no less than 18,000,000 years ago. As a result of "clairvoyant investigation" (getting in contact with *devas* and *mahatmas*, see below), Theosophists publish maps of the world as it was 800,000 years ago, and again as it appeared 11,500 years ago. We are told of the Atlantean race, living on the At-

antean Continent 800,000 years ago. This continent formed
a belt around the earth, stretching almost uninterruptedly
from Mexico, right across the (present) Atlantic Ocean, on
to Egypt and Asia. An older continent, the Lemurian, once
stretched from the Indian Ocean to Australia. From the
same "occult" source of information Theosophists know that
during the Atlantean period very early immigrations resulted in the grand civilization of Egypt, which was in
progress long before the time assumed by modern historians. Of this early civilization little is left beyond the
pyramids, because of the great convulsion which is said
to have taken place 11,500 years ago. At the time, of the
Atlantean Continent only an island was left, about as large
as all modern Europe minus Russia. Owing to a cataclysm
this island subsided with terrific suddenness, "and the sea,
which then covered what is now the desert of Sahara, was
driven eastward so as to completely deluge Egypt." In support of this clairvoyant assertion a Mexican document is
proudly pointed to, which was translated in 1893. It "is
in itself an ancient manuscript of immense antiquity, and it
says that the catastrophe took place '8060 years before the
writing of this book.' Ten countries, it says, were torn a-
sunder in the convulsion, and sank with their 64,000,000
inhabitants."

"Man, Whence? What? Whither?"

This conception of the world makes room for the countless reincarnations of millions of human souls as taught by
Theosophy. Man is said to be a "Divine Fragment, the
Divinity becoming patent"; and his ultimate destiny is to
return to God (the impersonal *It*). He attains to this goal,
the Buddhist nirvana, only through a process of evolution,
calling for many incarnations. The idea of reincarnation,
itself of ancient Hindu origin, has been civilized in so far
as Theosophists do not teach that a man may be reborn as
an animal, as was the teaching of the East. Nevertheless,
it was not introduced by the authors of Theosophy (Madame H. P. Blavatsky and Colonel H. S. Olcott) until after

their journey to India. At first they considered reincarnation exceptional. Since 1882, however, this purged Hindu
idea has become the "pearl doctrine" of theosophy. "The
actual number of incarnations for each monad is not far
short of eight hundred," says A. P. Sinnett, an Englishman
to whom Madame Blavatsky wrote many letters, and an
author of theosophical literature.

In speaking of man's *bodies*, Theosophy becomes be-
wildering. "Man has a 'natural body,' which is made up of
four different and separable portions, and is subject to
death." "Man has further a 'spiritual body.' This is made
up of three separable portions, each portion belonging to
one of, and separating off, the three Persons in the Trinity
of the human Spirit." Let us consider the "natural body."

The natural body of theosophic speculation consists of *a
physical body* with its *etheric double, and* an *astral body,* and
a mental body. These bodies occupy the same space, just as
"the space in a bowl can be occupied by a sponge and by
water that fills it, because the latter grade of matter inter-
penetrates the former." The physical is the body of activity;
the astral the body of emotions, the "desire-body"; the mental body is the body of thought.

In sleep and in trance-condition man leaves his physical
body and, in his astral and mental bodies, dwells in the astral
world. Here Theosophy reveals its kinship to Spiritism. We
have seen that, according to Spiritists, a medium's subconscious mind gets into contact with the spirit-world through
telepathy and clairvoyance. According to theosophists it is
the man himself who *leaves* the physical body, and visits the
astral plane. The latter is thought of as "an envelope, sur-
rounding the earth," at the same time penetrating it, "just
as water penetrates the pores of a wet sponge. It is infused
in all matter as a salt dissolved in water exists in association with all of its molecules."

The astral world, thickly populated with all sorts of
people formerly in the flesh, is described much after the
manner of Spiritism's lower spheres beyond the veil. While

man in his astral body visits the astral world, the etheric
double (of the dual physical body) may be abused" by "a
disembodied entity living in the astral world, to reestablish
his connection with the physical." This is mediumship,
which is dangerous. Thus Theosophy, a true apostate, at
once acknowledges and discourages the phenomena of
modern Spiritism.[2] What does it propose instead? That
man should learn both to remember his "dreams," and to
dwell on the astral plane even in his waking condition, that
he may learn from the astral beings. He should reach a
point where he can dwell with equal ease in the physical or
in the astral world.

Man's third body is the mental body. It requires a still
higher stage of evolution to withdraw from both the physical and the astral bodies, and in the mental body to dwell
in the corresponding mental world, or the world of thought.
Here again Theosophy reveals its spiritistic origin. The
mental world, also called *Devachan,* is the abode of *devas,*
or angels. They are the spirits of those who have graduated
from the astral world. Few people "at this stage of human
evolution" are able to withdraw into the mental world.
Those who, through the practice of yoga, have learned to do
so (advanced Theosophists), receive "inspirational thought
forms" from the devas.

---

2. The kinship between Spiritism and Theosophy reveals itself in
various other ways; for instance, in the fact that the *Catalog of
Theosophical Publications and Importations* advertises books by Sir
A. Conan Doyle, the Spiritist; and that Colville, the Spiritist, in
describing *The Spirit World,* inserts a chapter by C. W. Leadbeater,
prominent theosophist, afterward bishop for Australia of the *Liberal
Catholic Church,* which is an offshoot of the Theosophical Society.

It seems, moreover, that Spiritism is moving more in the direction
of Theosophy. Consider the following from White's *The Betty Book,*
p. 108: "Apparently some part of Betty, call it whatever you like,
has left the body lying on the couch and has visited and reported
back from other states of being. That some part of her has left the
body has been sufficiently proved to us by her reports of distant
actual physical things of this world. I say, some part of her; and
you can call it her clairvoyant sense; or her acute consciousness; or
herself; or whatever you please."

"The Path"

To man, who does not reach his final goal in a few incarnations, "each life on earth is like a day in school." "The normal interval between one life and another varies from a few score years in the case of an undeveloped soul to twenty centuries or even more in the case of a far advanced type." Meanwhile he first pays the price of every uncontrolled passion and appetite of the ignoble sort in the astral world. He does so by literally starving those passions to death, which means keen suffering. In this respect theosophic teachings run parallel with those of Spiritism. Afterward man dwells in Devachan (heaven). Sooner or later he returns to earth, being born anew in an infant body, to work out his *Karma*.

This Karma — a Buddhist idea — is described as "the law of Action and Re-action," or "the Law of Causation"; or in the Scriptural phrase, "As a man soweth so shall he also reap" (Besant). It means "actions pursuing the soul through successive births and compelling it to reveal by its conditions and reflect by its experiences in each birth the experiences of the previous birth." Karma might also be called the divine law of retribution. "When a man has created a vice by evil desire, evil thought, and evil act, he, its creator, can also be its destroyer by good desire, good thought and good act." "We can build our character as surely as a mason can build a wall, working with and through the law. As by law we suffer, so by law we triumph." This then, must be largely done in future lives.

Thus Theosophy reveals its kinship to Buddhism in the autosoterism it proposes. Buddhism teaches salvation through *The Noble Eightfold Path*. Besant and Krishnamurti speak of a *Fourfold Pathway* which man must tread in order to become an *Initiate*.

For advanced Theosophists, however, the system has a shortcut to perfection in the practice of *yoga*, that is meditation, holding the breath, and similar exercises.

The Mahatmas

Even the merest outline of Theosophy should not fail to
refer to the Mahatmas, beings of the greatest importance
to the system. They parade also under the names of Masters, Adepts, Initiates, the Great White Lodge, the Occult
Hierarchy, Brotherhood of Teachers. Mrs. Besant is credited with the saying, "If there are no Masters, then the
Theosophic Society is an absurdity." They are "the finished
products of human evolution," "divine men made perfect."
Sinnett says they are as far above ordinary mankind as
man is above the insects of the fields. Their habitat is Tibet.
They are ready to reach Nirvana, but they remain in order
to supervise human evolution. According to Annie Besant,
"They have many ways of working in the world; through
their own subtle, spiritual bodies they work, sending out
floods of blessing over the whole world." They become incarnate in the body of a Theosophist who has reached that
stage of inspiration "at which the mind and emotions of
the man no longer sway his body, but the body is wholly
taken possession of and used by One greater than himself."
To their information and inspiration Theosophy owes its
complete knowledge of occult matters. Most of their inspiring work is done on the astral and the mental planes. When
a human being has traveled the path of evolution to the
end, he becomes an Initiate; he is welcomed by the Great
Brotherhood of Teachers.

Above all these teachers there is *One Supreme Teacher.*
When *he* becomes incarnated we have a Christ among us.
Yet — for such is Theosophy's faith in the divinity of man
— Mrs. Besant states, "Every man is a potential Christ."

What Is Coming?

There have been three human races thus far: the Lemurian, the Atlantean, and the Aryan. Each one of these
has developed several subraces. The present, or Aryan,
"rootrace," has now its fifth subrace, the Teutonic. It is
soon to be followed by a sixth subrace. Each subrace makes

a distinct contribution to the race. The present subrace is that of the *intellectual* man. This, at first sight, looks rather flattering. But hear the end of the tale! The sixth subrace will be that of the — *spiritual* man. The present brotherhood-feeling and unity-efforts are a direct preparing for the sixth Aryan subrace. Now at the beginning of each subrace the "Supreme Teacher of the World" becomes incarnate to contribute to the evolution of that race. He does so by entering into the body of a disciple who is ready for initiation; in this body he dwells among men. He has been among us five times in the Aryan race: first as Buddha (rather, in the Buddha's body) in India (first subrace); next as Hermes (Egypt, second subrace); then as Zoroaster (Persia, third subrace); again as Orpheus (Greece, fourth subrace); finally as Christ, when the disciple Jesus surrendered his body to the World Teacher upon the occasion of his baptism. He is shortly to appear again, since the sixth subrace is in the making.

Each time the Supreme Teacher becomes incarnate, he contributes to the human race, not the totality of his divine knowledge (which would be "crushing") but as much as the race can bear at that state of its evolution. It follows at once that Theosophists can speak dearly of Christ Jesus as the greatest revelation of God the world has witnessed thus far; and, that the next Christ will be a greater one than the Christ in Jesus' body, because the *spiritual man* will be superior to the *intellectual man*. The particular task of the coming Messiah will be "again to strike the keynote of a new civilization, gathering all the religions of the world under that supreme teaching of His own."

Theosophy in its modern form, claiming to be "nothing less than the bedrock upon which all phases of the world's thought and activity are founded" (Cooper), lays itself open to criticism as a philosophy and as a religion.

Philosophy

1. Theosophy has endeavored to swallow too large a lump. It tries to be philosophy and theology at once. And

this creates a dualism which affects its views of God and of
man. Trying to prove to the mind that which can only be
known by faith, it has called for proof and it loudly denounces those who doubt its evidence. Such assertions as
the insistence upon a revelation from the masters of Karma are simply to be accepted upon the word of Theosophists, and although this, in the abstract, may not be a
larger *tour de force* than any other religious axiom or dogma, it certainly is not a sufficiently clear intellectual prem-
ise to serve as a foundation for a philosophy of life.

2. Theosophy suffers from a mixture between monism
and dualism. While avowedly pantheistic in its concept of
God, and while considering God a spiritual being, Theosophy at the same time speaks of the material side of God
and this material is thought of as ethereal, *geistleiblich*, a
sort of dream-entity, the existence of which again must be
accepted merely upon theosophical authority.

3. It is difficult to understand whence arrives the human will, the intellect, and the personality of man since
man is a spark of divinity encased in matter. Since the
creation, or rather the evolution, of man is the result of divine interaction between the Self and the Not-self in the
impersonal God, and since it is the purpose of man to be
again absorbed into the impersonal Godhead, whence comes
the personality of man, his distinct knowledge and will?
Pantheism and the polytheism of the Hindus are mixed in
Theosophy.

4. Again, we object to the reincarnation theory from a
philosophic standpoint. It is beyond comprehension that
the human soul, after having escaped through evolution,
first into the astral world, and hence into the higher spiritual world of *Devachan* or heaven, should long for the
lower life in the grossly material body. Why should man,
who is on the way to escape from earthly sorrowful experience, "thirst for more experience . . . such as may only
be gained on earth"? It is, say Theosophists, because the
man in the higher worlds, not quite perfected, is not fully
attuned to the prevailing vibrations there, hence cannot

be fully conscious. He must therefore return to taking on the coarser bodies in which he can feel fully at home. But the constant boast of evolution upon which the entire system rests would rather suggest that the man, having dwelt in the mental world, should return to the astral, than all the way back to the physical; while the inability to receive all the impact of the higher worlds, the semi-consciousness that is due to incomplete perfection, appears to contradict the claim of man's great felicity in "Devachan."

5.   The Karma doctrine we hold to be untenable. Experience teaches that it is not correct to ascribe all suffering to evil done in a former period of existence. We suffer much as a result of the misdeeds of others.

6.   There can be no merit in suffering for sins done in a former existence since the sufferer has no knowledge of his former life, cannot trace cause and effect. The assertion that the soul remembers, although it cannot communicate through the brain, is a mere subterfuge.

7.   The Karma doctrine is unjust. Why should one after death suffer the penalty of evil doers in the astral world, and later on another penalty for evil deeds in lives to come? Here the Spiritism of Blavatsky's first period and the Buddhism of her second period have been joined together in a fruitless effort to arrive at unity.

Religion

1.   As a religion, Theosophy is *gnosticism*. Knowledge is enthroned, and the ignorant are to be pitied.

a.   It is a religion for the initiate, not for the masses. Consider the following announcement of an expensive publication: *Theosophic Glossary. Gives information on the principal Sanskrit, Pahlavi, Tibetan Pali, Chaldean, Persian, Scandinavian, Hebrew, Greek, Latin, Kabalistic and Gnostic words and Occult Terms Generally Used in Theosophic Literature. Shows Elaborate and Extraordinary Scholarship.* Does the "Path" to God require that much "scholarship"?

b. Its gnosticism fosters pride. Sinnett derisively calls those who deny the existence of astral faculties *deafmutes, O. P.'s* (ordinary persons).

c. The gnostic character of Theosophy makes the system look suspicious, to say the least. Besant, calling one of her books *The Lesser Mysteries,* states, "The Greater will never be published through the printing-press; they can only be given by Teacher to pupil, 'from mouth to ear'." Blavatsky wrote, "Being obliged to start an esoteric section, to teach those things which it was impossible to impart to the students except under the bond of an oath between the teacher and pupil, I carefully prepared those whom I could trust, so that they would not drift back into the worldly methods. I sought in this way to impart magnetic and sexual truths which could be imparted only from ear to ear."

2. Theosophy on the one hand declares the seat of evil to be in matter, and on the other hand speaks of matter as emanating from God. Thus it actually blames God for evil, something Manicheism dared not do: it declared matter, the seat of evil, to be eternally existent beside God. Here lies also another inconsistency. Why speak of matter as an emanation of the divine Logos, while at the same time speaking of man's "physical bondage"? Annie Besant said, "Each successive body is a fresh limitation, or an increased dimming of our vision."

3. Theosophists parade as mystics who live in continual fellowship with God. So do all pantheists. At the same time, however, one finds very scanty reference to God in theosophical writings. God, to them, is a great unknown quantity. But what good is a fellowship with a God who either is unknown and not understood, or who is one with us because we are sparks of God? It is at best a mystic feeling of unity with an impersonal something which pervades us as well as other things.

Theosophy, then, notwithstanding its high-sounding phrases, does not rank more highly as a religion than it does as a philosophy.

Theosophy and Christianity

1.   Occultism, as exemplified by Theosophy, not only fosters unbelief in regard to other religions; it is likely to lead to superstition and spirit-worship, since the spirits with whom we are supposed to come into contact are conceived of as more or less omniscient. It is exactly in this attitude of mind that we are in danger of being influenced by supernatural spirits from below. M. E. Sloan informs us that "in explanation of Blavatsky's constant inconsistencies, Olcott advanced the theory that she was subject to the influence of 'incarnating entities,' resulting in 'double personality,' and producing the 'second self' in place of the 'Normal self.' " "He was correct," adds Mr. Sloan, "but failed to recognize the real import of the situation." In this we are inclined to follow this able critic of Theosophy. Very insufficient attention is paid today to the Biblical warning against "doctrines of demons."

2.   The Karma doctrine is the sworn enemy of forgiveness. The proud Theosophist needs no forgiveness. He is willing to work out his own destiny.

3.   Notwithstanding Krishnamurti's "path of *Desirelessness*," Theosophy is selfish to the core. Its aim is self-improvement, evolution as an end in itself. It lacks the Bible's "unto Him are all things."

4.   Like Mormonism, Theosophy is anti-scriptural in teaching the pre-existence of the human soul. Scripture teaches that God first formed the body of man, then gave him the breath of life, making him a living soul.

The Liberal Catholic Church

Numerically, the Liberal Catholic Church is so small that we might ignore it. Yet the tendency that "all faiths and no faith can dwell together in harmony" appears so clearly here that it merits attention.[3]

---

3. Under date March 1, 1951, Miss Marion M. Matthews, Provincial Secretary-Registrar, wrote as follows from the Provincial Head-

The Liberal Catholic Church (hereafter L.C.C.) pretends to be a Christian Church, and one catering to the needs of those cultured and mystical souls who feel the need of concerted worship in a beautifully appointed building, and with a great deal of ritual and "atmosphere." Among such there is, quite naturally, a group that refuses to be held down by any creedal commitments. They want to "feel" Christianity rather than think it through.

Here the L.C.C. offers an ideal scheme. Its "Statement of Principles" begins as follows: "The L.C.C. exists to forward the work of her Master — Christ — in the world, and to feed His flock. It is an independent and autonomous body, in no way dependent upon the See of Rome, or upon any other see or authority outside its own administration. It is neither Roman Catholic nor Protestant — but Catholic."

Here then we have a sort of original World Council, the "twin-half" to the goddess "Ecumenicity."

"The apostolic succession of the L.C.C. is derived from the ancient Church of Holland, sometimes called 'Jansenist.' With characteristic hospitality the Dutch people had given sanctuary to many unfortunate Jansenist refugees who had fled from France and Belgium to escape Jesuit persecution." There was some subsequent friction between the Jansenists and the holy see at Rome, which culminated in the organization of the Old Catholic Church when the former refused to bow to the 1870 dogma of the infallibility of the pope. The Dutch bishops consecrated some English bishops, one of whom, James I. Wedgwood, in turn con-

---

quarters of the Liberal Catholic Church, 2041 North Argyle Avenue, Los Angeles 28, California:

There are now twenty-three Centers of the Liberal Catholic Church now functioning.

Both Bishop Leadbeater and Bishop Cooper have passed on. There are two Liberal Catholic groups in this country. One is headed by Bishop Newton Dahl in Minneapolis. The other by Bishop Matthews who is the Regionary Bishop for the Liberal Catholic Church in the Province of the United States and the Province of Canada. As you will note above, his office is located here, above address, the Provincial Headquarters for the United States.

secrated Charles W. Leadbeater, Mrs. Besant's co-discoverer of Krishnamurti, as bishop for Australia of the L.C.C. Bishop Wedgwood one year later (1917) consecrated as bishop for the U. S. A. Irving Steiger Cooper.

Aided by Wedgwood, Leadbeater set to work on the liturgy of the L.C.C., and wrote the volume *The Science of the Sacraments.* Thus the new liturgy, to borrow Mr. Ferguson's spicy speech, "was modeled after that of Rome and has since been filled with the ghosts of Theosophy, so that not so much as an article remains without a spooky and cryptic reference of one sort or another."[4]

If this should sound irreverent, consider a few samples.

The L.C.C. has all the features of a regular Church. It has a summary of doctrine — but no dogma ("The L.C.C. permits to its members entire freedom in the interpretation of Creeds, Scriptures and Tradition, and of its Liturgy and Summary of Doctrine"). It uses the Holy Scriptures, creeds, and other traditions of the Church as the vehicle in which the teaching of Christ has been handed down to His followers. "It deduces from them certain principles of belief and conduct . . ." Thus baptism "is a sacrament by which the recipient is solemnly admitted to membership of Christ's holy Church and 'grafted into his mystical body' " — the mystical body interpreted theosophical fashion. For: "The Sacrament of Baptism takes on a new significance when we realize *that man is essentially an unfolding spiritual intelligence* who expresses himself through a physical body. Thus in an infant the body only is new; the soul standing behind and animating it is old — with a long past behind him."

"The Holy Eucharist is the central act of Christian worship." But how does it work? "Each time it is celebrated, there passes forth into the world a wave of peace and strength, the effect of which can hardly be overrated. . . This flood of spiritual force affects the spiritual body of the recipient . . . to unfold his latent powers . . ."

---

4. Charles W. Ferguson, *The Confusion of Tongues*, p. 282.

There are healing services, and sermons; and the vesper service "ends with prayers, asking God's help and protection"; but when the beautiful benediction of the Church of England is used the Trinitarian formula is understood in the sense of the Summary of Doctrine: "The manifestation of God in the universe under a triplicity — Father, Son and Holy Ghost."

And the return of Christ is expected after the theosophical manner: "We look for the Lord Christ, the Great Teacher of Angels and of men, to walk once more as a Man among men in the not far distant future, so that He may give this new, yet old teaching, which will place religion on a basis of science as well as revelation."

To these samples I add only that Leadbeater's book on the sacraments is said to be "scientific, because it is the testimony of a great physicist of the spiritual worlds to the things which he has observed, and with which in all reverence he has experimented."

For all this, the writer is convinced that many mystically inclined folk might walk into one of these "churches" and follow its worship without sensing the serious deviation from the age-old tenets of the Christian Church. Is it not time, then, for us to teach the youth of our churches not only *what to confess*, but also *how to understand their confession?*

The Bible and Theosophy

Such Scriptural passages as plainly teach the fundamentals of the Christian faith may be used, of course, with equal force against any system denying those doctrines. It remains remarkable, however, that certain passages seem to have a distinct bearing upon theosophical errors. We submit the following:

1. Against the claim, *ex oriente lux,* Isaiah 2:6, "For Thou hast forsaken thy people, the house of Jacob, because they are filled from the east."

2. Against the universal brotherhood of men, Matt. 12:50, John 1:12, 13.

68 THE CHAOS OF CULTS

3. Against brotherhood of all religions, Gal. 1:8, II John 10, 11.

4. Against the gnostic distinction between the disciple Jesus and the Christ making use of his body, I John 2:22.

5. Against new revelation beyond that in Christ Jesus, John 1:14; 14:9; II Cor. 4:3, 4; Col. 1:19, 20, 25, 26: Heb. 1 and 2; I John 5:20; II John 10, 11; Jude 3; Rev. 22:18, 19.

6. Against disembodied state in an astral world: II Cor. 5:1-4; Phil. 3:21.

7. Against reincarnation (a) of Jesus, Heb. 9:26; (b) of the rest of us, Heb. 9:27.

8. Against Mahatmas and Christs in the caves of Tibet, Matt. 24:24-26.

9. Against Karma, Isaiah 1:18; I John 1:9.

Theosophy and the Bible
Angels

"We regard those mighty archangels and angels as the product of the evolution of older worlds than this, as those who have won beyond the point towards which we now are climbing . . . their younger brothers who are treading the Path that they have trod so long ago in the days of their struggle, ere their victory was won."—A. BESANT.[5]

Blood Atonement

"For what is the doctrine of Atonement as seen from the Theosophical standpoint? It is the declaration that the Atonement wrought by Christ lies not in the substitution of one individual for another, but in the identity of nature between the divine man and men who are becoming divine."—A. BESANT.[6]

"Karma takes no account of custom; and the Karma of cruelty is the most terrible of all . . . Superstition is another mighty evil, and has caused much terrible cruelty. . . . Think of the awful slaughter produced by the superstition that

5. *Is Theosophy Anti-Christian?* p. 11.
6. *Ibid.,* p. 15.

animals should be sacrificed, and by the still more cruel superstition that man needs flesh for food. Many crimes have men committed in the name of the God of love, moved by this nightmare of superstition."—KRISHNAMURTI.[7]

Brotherhood of Believers

"Objects of the Theosophical Society:

"1.   To form a nucleus of the Universal Brotherhood of Humanity, without distinction of race, creed, sex, caste, or color."[8]

"The stately figure of the Ancient Wisdom named The-osophy,' after the Greek 'divine Wisdom,' enters the field as a unifier and peacemaker in religion. 'Sirs, ye are brethren, why do ye wrong one another?' is the expostulation that falls from her lips."[9]

Christ

"This word, 'the Christ,' means to us more than the name of one, however lofty, or however holy, and to us the Christ is less an external Savior than a living Presence in the human Spirit, a Presence by which the human Spirit un-folds its innate divinity, so that in time all men become Christ."—A. BESANT.[10]

Man

"When your body wishes something, stop and think whether *you* really wish it. For *you* are God, and you will only what God wills; but you must dig deep down into your-self to find the God within you, and listen to His voice which is *your voice*."—KRISHNAMURTI.[11]

"Man is a Spiritual Intelligence, a fragment of Divinity clothed in matter."—A. BESANT.[12]

---

7. *At the Feet of the Master*, pp. 64, 67.
8. I. C. Cooper, *Theosophy Simplified*, p. 1.
9. *The Brotherhood of Religions*, p. 8.
10. *Op. cit.*, p. 16.
11. *Op. cit.*, p. 10.
12. *Man's Life in Three Worlds*, p. 3.

"Lastly we come to the true man, the soul, of whom it is said in an ancient scripture: 'He is not born, nor does he die, nor having been ceaseth he any more to be.' Unborn, perpetual, eternal and ancient, he is not slain when the body is slaughtered."—I. S. COOPER.[13]

"The popular conception is that God created the world and mankind as a mechanic creates a complicated machine — a thing apart from himself. . . . On this great central problem of life Theosophy is, as on all other matters, in perfect agreement with science, showing that creation is the act of God, but that his process of creation is an evolutionary one; that the life of the supreme Being, permeating every atom of the universe . . . is slowly evolving into higher and higher powers of consciousness through gradually increasing complexities of form."—L. W. ROGERS.[14]

Inspiration of the Bible

"I confined myself to the Hindu scriptures, and in all cases I stated that I regarded these scriptures and the Hindu religion as the origin of all the scriptures and all the religions."—MRS. BESANT.[15]

"The doctrines of the Gospels, and even of the Old Testament, have been taken bodily from the book of Enoch.

"In its hidden meaning, from Genesis to the last word of Deuteronomy, the Pentateuch is the symbolical narrative of the sexes, and is an apotheosis of Phallicism, under astronomical and physiological personifications."—BLAVATSY.[16]

Forgiveness of Sins

"The word Karma simply means action . . . Hence Karma may be called Causation, or the Law of causation. Its scientific statement is: 'Action and Reaction are equal and opposite' . . . This sane and true teaching bids man . . . surrender

13. *Theosophy Simplified*, p. 30.
14. *What Theosophy Is*, p. 8.
15. *The Daily Chronicle*, April 9, 1894.
16. *The Secret Doctrine*, III, 87, 172.

all the fallacious ideas of 'forgiveness,' 'vicarious atonement,' 'divine mercy,' and the rest of the opiates which
superstition offers to the sinner."—BESANT.[17]

Hell

"If this (Luke 13:23, 24) be applied in the ordinary protestant way to salvation from everlasting hell-fire, the statement becomes incredible, shocking. No Savior of the world
can be supposed to assert that many will seek to avoid hell
and enter heaven, but will not be able to do so. But as applied to the narrow gateway of Initiation and to salvation
from rebirth, it is perfectly true and natural."—BESANT.[18]

Mediator

"It is the event of the Baptism which marks the coming
of the Christ . . . and it is *then,* from the occult point of view,
that the *Jesus* became the *Christ* . . . Jesus the Hebrew, the
individual, the spiritual man, stepped out of the body that
he had been dwelling in through all those years and preparing for the coming of his Lord, giving it over as a holy temple for the incoming of the supreme Teacher, so that the
body became the habitation of the supreme Teacher, for
the three years of his ministry." — A. BESANT.[19]

Prayer

"Whether the person pray to Buddha, to Vishnu, to
Christ, to the Father, it matters not at all."—A. BESANT.[20]

"The action of prayer—which is concentrated thought."
—A. BESANT.[21]

"Then he learns that Divinity lies hidden within himself,
and that nothing that is fleeting can satisfy that God within; that only union with the One, the Perfect, can still his
cravings. Then there arises within him the will to set him-

---

17. Leaflet *Karma.*
18. *Esoteric Christianity*, p. 42.
19. *The Changing World*, p. 306.
20. *The Seven Principles of Man*, p. 58.
21. *The Changing World*, p. 68.

self at one with the Divine; . . . he has risen above all prayer, save that which is meditation and worship; he has nothing to ask for, in this world or in any other." —A. BESANT.[22]

Providence

"Man, an immortal soul, is the moulder and master of his own destiny, because he has started and will start all the forces which mould the circumstances in which he lives . . . No one is to blame except ourselves for our birth conditions, our character, our opportunities, our abilities, for all these things are due to the working out of forces we have set going either in this life or in former lives . . . From the seed of good and bad actions spring the harvests of pleasant and unpleasant physical circumstances; . . . from the seeds of good and evil thoughts and desires spring the harvests of good and bad character."—I. S. COOPER.[23]

For Discussion

1. What is the difference between the Christian and the theosophical conception of the divine Trinity?

2. Point out the affinity between Spiritism and Theosophy as to clairvoyance. What does Theosophy substitute for contacting disembodied spirits?

3. Describe the "astral world," and the human "astral body."

4. What is the resemblance and what the difference between the spiritistic and the theosophical conception of "hell," or rather, "purgatory"?

5. What is meant by "Karma"; what by "Mahatmas"?

6. Describe the difference between the theosophical and the Christian idea of incarnation.

7. State your objections to Theosophy as a philosophy; also as a religious system of thought.

8. Do certain passages of Scripture indeed apply directly to certain theosophical ideas?

---

22. *Esoteric Christianity*, p. 257.
23. *Op. cit.*, p. 55.

9. Trace evidences of pantheism in quotations from spiritistic and theosophical writers; see pp. 43-48 and 67-70.

10. Point out similarities and differences between the Christian and the theosophical understanding of Jesus Christ as Mediator.

11. Can you agree with the late Dr. Francis L. Patton of Princeton: "The strongest argument against theosophy is that there is no argument in its favor"? (Machen, *What is Christianity?*, p. 70).

4

ROSICRUCIANISM

Rosicrucianism is powerful in California, headquarters of so many false cults. From Oceanside the widow of Max Heindel, late apostle of modern Rosicrucianism, sends forth the copyrighted reprints of her husband's profound and voluminous tomes (*The Rosi-crucian Cosmo-Conception or Mystic Christianity*, 606 pp., 5x51/2 in. page), *The Rosi-crucian Philosophy in Questions and Answers* (426pp.), *The Rosicrucian Christianity Lectures* (347 pp.), and numerous pamphlets and correspondence courses.

There may be some small comfort in the knowledge that the Rosicrucians, too, are divided against one another. The lady who sold me the books informed me that the "AMORC" (see Bibliography at the end of this volume) have lost their title to the name Rosicrucians because "they commercialize religion, whereas *we* only charge for the books."[1]

She also informed me that she had been "a member of the Mother Church for twenty-five years prior to joining the Rosicrucian Fellowship, but made the change because here truth is taught so much more clearly." This at once suggests that Rosicrucianism and Christian Science are related; and they are, as all forms of pantheism are related.

Approaching Rosicrucianism more closely, however, we soon discover that it far more intimately resembles Theosophy. In fact Rosicrucianism admits being "the Western

---

1. On the third floor of the Arcade Building in Seattle the average Christian worker may receive an eye opener. Rosicrucians, Baha'is, the Unity School of Religion, Astrologists, Spiritists, all have their studios; and each studio has not only a rack or a bookcase with literature, but there are chairs which are arranged in class-room fashion: the cultists are evidently of the opinion that religion can be taught. Had the evangelical churches done more doctrinal teaching, there would today be fewer victims of all these strange cults.

teaching given to the Western people at this time for their
advancement." "If we take Theosophy as meaning *Theo
Sophia* (Divine Wisdom), then, of course, the Rosicrucian
Philosophy is only part of that Divine Wisdom, like all other
religious systems. But if we take theosophy to mean the
philosophy promulgated by the Theosophical Society, or
Societies, for there are several brands, then we may say
that the Rosicrucian teaching is much more comprehensive
and complete." Besides, Rosicrucianism is opposed to the
arrogant attitude of Theosophy in regard to other systems
that also have the idea of universal brotherhood at heart.
"It is not necessary to be a theosophist in order to follow
that object, but it is necessary to be an occultist in order to
follow the third object of the Theosophical Society, namely,
the study of the unexplained laws of nature and the powers
latent in man." "The Theosophical Society is simply an
exoteric organization [I wonder how the Theosophists like
that "exoteric"!] for the dissemination of a certain philosophy, mostly derived from the Eastern religions, while the
Rosicrucian Fellowship aims to promulgate the teachings
of the Western Mystery School, the Order of Rosicrucians,
which is secret and not accessible to anyone except upon
direct invitation."[2]

I believe, if I were to choose between the two, I'd choose
Rosicrucianism. From a purely philosophical viewpoint
it seems to me the more acceptable of the two. It does not
believe in Karma, but holds that, though every Ego is re-
incarnated many times, each individual birth brings one
into the world innocent because the evil has been purged
away; yet one is born with certain tendencies which may
develop into vices, therefore we must be tried to see whether
we will develop virtue.

And I would prefer Rosicrucianism to Christian Science
from a medico-religious viewpoint because, all according to
the nature of the malady and the bias of the patient, I
should be allowed to choose between employing a Christian

---

2. *The Roisicrucian Philosophy*, pp. 358-360.

Science practitioner, a Faith Healer of some other brand
"materia medica used in conjunction with astrology," or
even be permitted to "attempt to cure the ills from which
we suffer in any other way possible that appeals to us."

However, as a Christian I need not choose between Theosophy and Rosicrucianism, but may have the clear and
sufficient teachings of the Scriptures which leave enough
unexplained as to the manner of Christ's return and the
hereafter for *faith* to be satisfied for the time being without
sight; and so there is no need of the ill-founded vagaries of
the occult.

And here, perhaps, we touch upon the fundamental fruit
of the "Rosicrucian Philosophy." There is literally nothing these people cannot and do not explain. One marvels at
the patient digging and the interminable babbling that produces a never ending stream of facts and subjects, all fitting neatly within the confines of this all-absorbing system. And, of course, there is no argument against information that obtains from an "occult" source. If you do
not believe it, you simply are on the outside.

The Rose Cross

The name of the cult itself is an apt illustration of this
uncanny ability to interpret all things and make them fit. It
happens that in the thirteenth century a man named Christian Rosenkreuz began to bring out into the open teachings
which hitherto had been promulgated only in secret. Christian Rosenkreuz, what a name to conjure with! He founded
the mysterious order of Rosicrucians with the object of
throwing occult light upon the misunderstood Christian
Religion and to explain the mystery of Life and Being from
the scientific standpoint in harmony with Religion.

All of which, it will be seen, might have been written by
a theosophical Rogers or Sinnett; all except for the "symbolical name Christian Rosenkreuz."

The Rosicrucians have taken the offense out of the Cross
(and they call that esoteric Christianity!). The Cross
should not be interpreted as an emblem of suffering and

shame, so reads the amazing account of this "mystic Christianity."

What then did and does it stand for? Ask Plato, who was an initiate, and wrote, "The world-soul is crucified." With these words, we are informed, the Greek philosopher gave out occult truth. And what is that truth? That "the Cross is symbolical of the life currents vitalizing the bodies of plants, animal and man"; it is "symbolical of man's past evolution, present constitution, and future development."

"The mineral kingdom ensouls all chemical substance of whatever kind, so that the Cross, of whatever material it is made, is first symbol of that kingdom.

"The upright lower limb of the Cross is a symbol of the plant kingdom because the currents of the group spirits which give life to the plants come from the center of the earth where these group spirits are located and reach out toward the periphery of our plant and into space.

"The upper limb of the Cross is the symbol of man, because the life currents of the human kingdom pass downward from the sun through the vertical spine. Thus man is the inverted plant, for as the plant takes its food through the root, passing it *upward,* so does the man take his nourishment by way of the head, passing it *downward.* The plant is chaste, pure and passionless, and stretches its creative organ, the flower, chastely and unshamed *toward the sun,* a thing of beauty and delight. Man turns his passion-filled generative organ *toward the earth.* Man inhales the life-giving oxygen and exhales the poisonous carbon dioxide. The plant takes the poison exhaled by man, building its body therefrom, and returning to us the elixir of life, the cleansed oxygen.

"Between the plant and the human kingdom stands the animal with the horizontal spine, and in the horizontal spine the life currents of the animal group spirit play as they circle around the globe. Therefore the horizontal limb of the Cross is the symbol of the animal kingdom."[3]

---

3. *Ibid.*, p. 202.

"The animal, which is symbolized by the horizontal limb of the Cross, is between plant and man. Its spine is in horizontal position and through it play the currents of animal group-spirit which encircle the Earth. . . .

"To keep him steadfast and true through adversity, the Rose Cross holds aloft, as an inspiration, the glorious consummation in store for him that overcometh, and points to Christ as the Star of Hope, the 'first fruits,' who wrought that choicest of all gems, the Philosopher's Stone while inhabiting the body of Jesus."[4]

This, then, interprets the Rosicrucian emblem: the Cross as well as the Star against which it stands; while the garland of roses around the center of the Cross points to yet another symbolism. "In the form where it is represented with a single rose in the center it symbolizes the spirit radiating from itself the four vehicles: the dense, vital and desire bodies plus the mind; where the spirit has drawn into its instruments and become the *indwelling* human spirit." But there was a time when that condition did not obtain, a time when the threefold spirit hovered above its vehicles and was unable to enter. Then the Cross stood alone without the rose, symbolizing the condition which prevailed in the early third of Atlantis. There was even a time when the upper limb of the Cross was lacking and man's constitution was represented by the Tau (T). That was in the Lemurian Epoch when he had only the dense, vital and desire bodies, but lacked the mind. Then the animal nature was paramount. Man followed desire without reserve. At a still earlier time, in the Hyperborian Epoch, he was also minus the desire body and possessed only the dense and vital bodies. Then man-in-the-making was like the plants: chaste and devoid of desire. At that time his constitution could not have been represented by a Cross. It was symbolized by a straight shaft, a pillar (I).

Thought and voice, we are told further, are both creative but the selfish, dominating creative faculty (symbolized

4. *Cosmo-conception,* pp. 86, 519.

by the larynx, at the crossing of head and body) must give way to a less selfish creative force. It is here that the roses enter; for "the rose, like any other flower, is the generative organ of the plant. Its green stem carries the colorless, passionless plant blood. The blood-red rose shows the passion-filled blood of the human race, but in the rose the vital fluid is not sensuous; it is chaste and pure. Thus it is an excellent symbol of the generative organ in the pure and holy state to which man will attain when he has cleansed and purified his blood of desire, when he has become chaste, pure and Christ-like."

Thus we get the Cross, the long limb representing the body, the two horizontals the two arms, and the short upper limb the head, with the circle of roses around the center instead of the larynx. "Therefore the Rosicrucians look ardently forward to the day when the roses shall bloom upon the cross of humanity, therefore the Elder Brothers greet the aspiring soul with the words of the Rosicrucian Greeting: 'May the Roses bloom upon your Cross,' and therefore the greeting is given in the meetings of the Fellowship Centers by the leader to the assembled students, probationers and disciples who respond to the greeting by saying, 'And on yours, also.' "[5]

It is all very profound, quite esoteric, and eminently fitting the name of Christian Rosenkreuz of the thirteenth century. Perhaps, though, the name was not quite as accidental as an outsider might surmise: we are told that this Mr. Rosenkreuz, or rather the Ego dwelling in him, was already then "a high spiritual teacher." His birth as Christian Rosenkreuz merely marked the beginning of a new epoch in spiritual life in the Western world. And he has since that day "taken a new body when his successive vehicles have outlived their usefulness, or circumstances rendered it expedient that he change the scene of his activities. He inspired Bacon's works (altho through an

5. *Ibid.*, pp. 534ff.

intermediary), and he enlightened the mystic Jacob
Boehme. He is also embodied today, an Initiate of high
degree, an active and potent factor in all affairs of the
West—although unknown to the World" (1909, but still
printed in the 1944 edition of the *Cosmo-conception*).

In accordance with such symbolism Christian emblems
of long standing are made to fit in. "In esotericism the
Cross was never looked upon as an instrument of torture,
and it was not until the sixth century that the crucified
Christ was shown in pictures. Previous to that time the
symbol of the Christ was a Cross and a lamb resting on
its foot, to convey the idea that at the time when Christ
was born the sun at the vernal equinox crossed the equator
in the sign of Aries the Lamb . . . Some claimed that the
vernal equinox at His birth was really in the sign of Pisces,
the Fishes, and that the symbol of our Savior should have
been a fish. It is in memory of that dispute that the Bishop's
mitre still takes the form of the head of a fish."[6]

The apostle John evidently lacked this occult information,
and in his ignorance interpreted the Lamb in Old Testament style as a sacrifice that takes away the sin of the
world. And the early Christians, who for fear of being be-
trayed to the enemy, drew a fish in the sand to see if there
were an understanding response, interpreted the symbol of
the fish as follows: ICHTHUS (Greek for "fish"): *I
(esous) CH(ristos) TH(eou) U(ios) S(oter)*, *i. e.* Jesus
Christ, God's Son, Saviour.

The Worlds

The explanation of the Cross, however, contains sufficient
hints at other Rosicrucian doctrines to launch us upon a
more complete, though ever so brief, exposition of this complicated system of thought. For we have heard of the various bodies of man, of many spirits, of evolution through
reincarnation, and of many races.

---

6. *Rosicrucian Philosophy*, p. 203.

There are seven Worlds which together form the Universe. Each one is amenable to laws which are practically inoperative in the other. For instance, the laws of gravitation, and of contraction and expansion to which matter is subject in the Physical (the lowest) World, do not exist in the next higher or the Desire World. Neither is there heat or cold there.

Each World is subdivided into seven Regions or subdivisions of matter. In the Physical World we have denser forms, namely, solids, liquids and gases; and also four ethers of varying densities. But ether still remains a physical matter. The four etherics together form the Etheric Region. Above all this is the Universal Spirit, expressing itself in the visible world as four great streams of Life, at varying stages of development. This fourfold spiritual impulse molds the chemical matter of the Earth into variegated forms of the four kingdoms—mineral, plant, animal and man.

The Etheric Region of the Physical World is as tangible to the clairvoyant as are the solids, liquids and gases of the Chemical Region to ordinary people. The clairvoyant sees four ethers: Chemical Ether, Life Ether, Light Ether, Reflecting Ether. Rather than invent instruments to learn the secrets of nature (as does the scientist), the occulist would develop the investigator himself.

Thus we may find that our senses or faculties may become the "open sesame" in searching for truth. The trained senses of the clairvoyant see clearly the interaction between the physical and the etheric body of man.

For example, the Chemical Ether expels from the physical body of man the materials in food which are unfit for use (negative pole) and also assimilates that which can be incorporated into the body (positive pole).

The Life Ether, also working through a positive and a negative pole, takes care of the forces of propagation, the positive working in the female during the period of gestation, and the negative pole of life enabling the male to produce semen.

Light Ether negatively operates through the senses, manifesting the passive functions of sight, hearing, feeling, tasting, smelling; it also builds and nourishes the eye; positively, it is the avenue of the forces that circulate the blood. In plants and animals Light Ether is responsible for color.

Reflecting Ether has in it the reflections of the memory of nature (as the giant ferns of the childhood of the Earth have left their pictures in the coalbeds). But no clairvoyant likes to read in this book of memory, as the pictures are blurred. Spiritist mediums and psychometers may be forced to do that sort of thing: the Rosicrucian clairvoyant rises to greater heights, knowing that in higher Worlds nature has better memories.

The Desire World, like the Physical World, and like every other realm of nature, has the seven subdivisions called Regions, but it does not have the four great etheric divisions. "Desire stuff" in the Desire World persists through its seven subdivisions or regions as material for the embodiment of desire.

The desires, wishes, passions and feelings of man express themselves through these seven regions of "desire matter," which is only one degree less dense than the matter of the Physical World. It is not a *finer* physical matter: rather it is in unceasing *motion*, whereas the matter of the Physical World is *inert*. The Desire World is ever-changing light and color, in which forces of animal and man intermingle with the forces of innumerable Hierarchies of spiritual beings which mold our desires. Our desires in turn create *interest*. Interest, once it is thoroughly aroused, starts the forces of *attraction* and *repulsion*.

Observe now the following verbatim citation, to point out the close resemblance of the "western" occultism to the "oriental" "esoteric" Christianity."

"The Physical and the Desire Worlds are not separated from each other by space. They are 'closer than hands and feet.' It is not necessary to move to get from one to the other, nor from one Region to the next. Just as solids, liquids, and gases are all together in our bodies, interpenetrating one another, so are the different Regions of the Desire World within us also."

The World of Thought also consists of seven Regions of varying qualities and densities, and, like the Physical World, the World of Thought is divided into two main divisions: the Region of Concrete Thought, composing the four densest Regions, and the Region of Abstract Thought, comprising the three Regions of finest substance. All of this is also thought of as consisting, if not of material, at least of "mind-stuff." The *thought-forms* are acting "as regulators and balance wheels upon the impulses engendered in the Desire World by impacts from the phenomenal World."

The Evolution of Man

As to the evolution of man and the growth of the soul, we find a more sensible account here of the character of dreams than we met in Theosophy. When during sleep the desire body does not fully withdraw from the vital body, but remains connected with it, the vehicle for sense perception and memory has its "axis askew," and the memory becomes confused. For sleep is just that: a withdrawal of the higher vehicles from the dense body which then gets a rest and a chance to rebuild itself.

Death is something else again. Here the higher vehicles leave the dense body more completely, though for a while remaining connected by "the silver cord." One end of the silver cord is fastened to the heart by means of the *seed-atom,* and it is the rupture of the seed-atom which causes the heart to stop. The cord itself is not snapped until the panorama of the past life, contained in the vital body, has been reviewed. At death the dense body at once loses weight because *not the soul* but the vital body has left.

In his vital body the man still has all his desires, but he lacks the organ to satisfy them. This causes the sufferings of *purgatory*; for example, a miser may hover over his bonds and stocks in his invisible desire body, trying to hang on to them, but his relatives go right through him and take them away. He may even hear them mock "the old tightwad." A drunkard may penetrate the dense body of a drinker in a tavern, but he lacks a stomach and the organs of taste, therefore can but very slightly satisfy his craving for drink.

Thus, through suffering, the departed person finally learns to despise and relinquish the vices of his former days on earth, and he becomes ready to go to heaven.

However, there are three heavens, just as there were three regions of the Desire World (purgatory). In the *first heaven,* located in the three highest regions of the Desire World, the results of the soul's sufferings are "incorporated in the seed-atom of the desire body, thus imparting to it the quality of right feelings, which acts as an impulse to good and a deterrent from evil in the future."

"At last the man, the Ego, the threefold spirit enters *the second heaven.* He is clad in the sheath of Mind, which contains the three seed-atoms, the quintessence of the three discarded vehicles." Upon arrival in the second heaven follows "the great Silence," and after this period of wonder the awakening. The spirit is now in its home-World. Here it hears "the music of the spheres," and learns to do many-sided work. It prepares for the next life. Before reincarnation, however, the spirit must first dwell in the third heaven, the higher Region of the World of Thought.

But why should the human spirit experience another "dip into matter" at all? Because the purpose of life is not pleasure but experience, which is knowledge of the effects which follow acts. If I did not feel pain when I put my hand on a hot stove, my hand might burn off without my knowing it; but now my experience teaches me to be more careful next time.

It would take us too long to speak of the "preparations for re-birth." Suffice it to say that each re-birth (about every one thousand years) begins with a birth of the *dense* body; that the *vital* body is formed within this in the seventh year; that the *desire* body is formed at the time of puberty; and the mind is not completed until the twenty-first year.

As the Etheric Region extends beyond the atmosphere of our dense Earth, the Desire World extends out into space further than the Etheric Region, and the World of Thought further into interplanetary space than either of the others, so also the seven Worlds and Cosmic Planes are not one above another in space, but the seven Cosmic Planes interpenetrate each other and all the seven Worlds. They are states of spirit-matter, permeating one another, so that God and the other Great Beings are not far away in space. They pervade every part of their own realms and realms of greater density than their own. (Here the apostle Paul is quoted, "In Him we live, and move, and have our being.")[7]

The Great Being called God "proceeds from the Root of Existence." He is the Absolute, but "positively not Christ." This threefold Supreme Being exists as *Power*, the *Word* and *Motion*; and from this threefold Supreme Being proceed the seven Great Logoi. In the Highest World of the seventh Cosmic Plane dwell the God of our Solar System and the Gods of all other Solar Systems in the Universe. These great beings are also threefold in manifestation. Their three aspects are *Will*, *Wisdom* and *Activity*.

With the aid of diagrams (pictures of things seen in clairvoyant state), we are told of the evolution of the earth and its inhabitants, and with all of this agrees an "Occult analysis of Genesis."

In every Period of evolution there are those who "fall behind," the *stragglers*. Thus "the lower monkeys, instead of being the progenitors of the higher species, are stragglers occupying the most degenerate specimens of what was once the human form." Instead of man having ascended from the anthropoids the reverse is true: these have degenerated from man. The mosses likewise are the lowest degeneration of the plant kingdom. "Material science, deal-

---

7. Ask your teacher to explain to you the difference between the doctrines of pantheistic immanence, deistic transcendence of God, and theistic teaching of the Trinity which includes both these elements. Or, see my volume *Our Christian Heritage*, on the subject.

ing only with the Form, has thus misled itself and drawn erroneous conclusions in this matter."

Apart from these stragglers, then, there is a continuous upward movement. Thus we also have *newcomers*, which we might call converted stragglers. And here a remarkable feature enters. Most human beings are not in need of salvation. For "progression with our present wave of evolution is what is meant when 'salvation' is spoken of in the Christian religion, and it is something to be earnestly sought, for though the 'eternal damnation' of those who are not 'saved' does not mean destruction nor endless torture, it is nevertheless a very serious matter to be held in a state of inertia for inconceivable milliards of years, before a new evolution shall have progressed to such a stage that those who fail here can have an opportunity to proceed. The spirit is not conscious of the lapse of time, but it is none the less a serious loss, and there must be also a feeling of unhomelikeness when at last such spirits find themselves in a new evolution."[8] The atonement was wrought by Christ for such as these. For Christ, who is the highest initiate of the Sun Period, became the Regent of Earth at Golgotha, his mission being the salvation of those who had bogged down in matter. These "lost ones" he saved "by raising them to the necessary point of spirituality, causing a change in their desire bodies which will make the influence of the life spirit in the heart more potent."[9]

This theory of "vicarious atonement" is not to be objected to on the ground that each must be willing to take the consequences of his own act; for it is perfectly just: it is like a man placing a rope above the cataract at Niagara: this he does that others, in danger of falling down, may have something to hold to even though he knows that in doing so he must go down himself: should or would that prevent any one else in danger from taking hold of the rope?

---

8. *Cosmo-conception*, p. 230.
9. *Ibid.*, p. 403

Universal Evolution

The axiom for the understanding of all this ceaseless activity of evolution is the Hermetic axiom, "As above, so below," and vice versa. There is a constant flaming out and dying down of activity in every department of nature.

In the beginning of a *Day of Manifestation* a certain *Great Being* (called a *God* only in the Western World) limits himself to a certain portion of space, in which he elects to create a Solar System for the evolution of added sense consciousness. It all begins with the *Cosmic Root Substance* which is an expression of the negative pole of the Universal Spirit, while the great Creative Being we call God (of whom we, as spirits, are part) is an expression of the positive energy of the same Universal Absolute Spirit. From the work of one upon the other, all that we see about us has resulted.

Now there are seven Worlds, not separated by space or distance (as is the earth from the other planets) but by their rate of vibration. The highest Worlds are the first to be created, the densest World last. But every World, as well as man, passes through seven Periods of Rebirths. The names of the seven Periods are as follows:

1. The Saturn Period
2. The Sun Period
3. The Moon Period
4. The Earth Period
5. The Jupiter Period
6. The Venus Period
7. The Vulcan Period

These names have nothing to do with our planets, but they are the Rosicrucian names for the successive rebirths of our Earth.

We know nothing of the six Cosmic Planes above our own except that God, "the Architect of our Solar System, is found in the highest division of the seventh Cosmic Plane, which is his World." But we do know that our own Plane during its Saturn Period (the first or lowest Period of its existence) traveled in its evolutionary impulse seven times around seven Globes, and when that laborious process ended, there followed the first Cosmic Night after the First Day of Creation, after which the Sun Period dawned. Here the same process of the life-wave circling seven times around the seven Globes was repeated, and the Moon Period was entered. From here on, we are told, the evolution of the Universe cannot be understood except by students of Arithmetic and the "Fourth Dimension."

It is interesting to learn, however, that even during the Saturn Period "great creative Hierarchies," far more perfectly evolved spirits, helped man in his evolution. These Hierarchies called "Thrones" in the Bible, worked on man of their own free will.

Among these the *Lords of Flame,* emitting a strong light, "by repeated efforts during the first Revolution, succeeded in implanting in the evolving life the germ which has developed our present dense body."

During this Saturn Period the Lords of Flame also labored on other spirits, namely, the *Lords of Wisdom,* spirits not as highly evolved as themselves. But during the second, or Sun Period, the Lords of Wisdom aided man "by radiating from their own bodies the germ of the vital body, making it capable of interpenetrating the dense body and giving to the germ the capability of furthering growth and propagation and of exciting the sense centers of the dense body and causing it to move. This work occupied the second, third, fourth, and fifth Revolution of the Sun Period."

And so it continues and will continue. Spiral evolution for the ordinary people, with spirals within spirals, and the "straight and narrow path" of access to divinity for the initiate. The *Conscious soul* of man will be absorbed by the divine spirit in the seventh Revolution of the Jupiter Period; the *Intellectual soul* will be absorbed by the life spirit in the sixth Revolution of the Venus Period; the *Emotional soul* will be absorbed by the human spirit in the fifth Revolution of the Vulcan Period.

Since the mind is the most important instrument possessed by the spirit, and its special instrument in the work of creation, at this stage of human development "the spiritualized and perfected larynx will speak the creative Word, but the perfected mind will decide as to the particular form and the volume of vibration, and will thus be the determining factor. Imagination will be the spiritualized faculty directing the work of creation."

In the Jupiter Period the human mind will imagine forms which will *live* and grow, like plants. In the Venus Period of that distant stage he can create living, growing, and *feeling* things. And when at the end of the Vulcan Period man reaches perfection, he will be able to "imagine" into existence creatures that will live, grow, feel, and *think*.

He will, in other words, do for plants and animals, and even for minerals, what the *Lords of Mind*, those ancient Hierarchies, did for him in the ages of long ago; he will help them acquire dense bodies, desire bodies, mind bodies, and other equipment.

Finally the divine Spirit, God, will absorb man. His spirit will be merged into God from Whom it came, to re-emerge at the dawn of another Great Day, as One of His glorious helpers. "During its past evolution its latent possibilities have been transmuted to dynamic powers. It has acquired *Soul power* and a *Creative Mind* as the fruitage of its pilgrimage through matter. It has advanced from *impotence to Omnipotence, from nescience to Omniscience."*

The question remains how man in his present average stage of evolution may acquire first-hand knowledge of the truth of all the foregoing.

The answer is that as a mechanic is a better worker in proportion to the precision of his tools, so man must develop his various bodies. The dense body must be trained by means of the proper food (pages and lists of minerals and vitamins in the right combinations are given). The diet must, of course, be vegetarian. The sex impulse must be trained to produce spiritual rather than material creative force.

Moreover, man must learn to use the pituitary body and the pineal gland, two small organs in the brain. He must thus become a clairvoyant, which is far more difficult than becoming a medium. The latter is merely a revival of the mirror-like function possessed by man in the far past, by which the outside world was involuntarily reflected in him.

The clairvoyant cannot live to eat and drink and gratify the sex-passion in an unrestrained manner. Because he lives a life that causes less confusion in the dense body, he need not spend his entire period of sleep in repairing the damage done in the day time by means of the desire and vital bodies, leaving no time for outside work of any kind. Thus it becomes possible to leave the dense body for long periods during sleeping hours, and function in the inner worlds in the higher vehicles. (*Tout comme chez nous*, the Theosophist might well say.)

Next it is necessary to reach a state in which the spirit is within the bodies and in full control of the faculties, as it is in the waking state, and yet able to work inwardly and properly sensitize the spirit's vehicles.

Concentration in such a state (not *yoga*, because the vehicles of the Caucasian are so very differently constituted than those of the Hindu that the methods of *yoga* — union with the Higher Self—would not benefit us), *Meditation, Observation, Discrimination, Contemplation, Adoration*, these are the words used in the description of how to become an initiate; but it would lead us too far afield for our purpose to inquire into the how of all these things.

Evaluation

1. Max Heindel's textbook *The Rosicrucian Cosmo-conception or Mystic Christianity* begins as follows:

"The founder of the Christian Religion stated an occult maxim when He said: 'Whosoever shall not receive the kingdom of God as a little child shall not enter therein' (Mark 10:15). All occultists recognize the far-reaching importance of this teaching of Christ and endeavor to 'live' it day by day."

Thus a system that denies and perverts everything taught by Christ and concerning Christ appeals to the authority of His name in order to make us see the necessity of coming to the Rosicrucian occultism with minds that are completely blank, divested of all opinion, and shorn of any and all "preference" and "prejudice." In all occult schools the pupil is first taught to forget all else when a new teaching is being given, allow neither preference nor prejudice to govern but to keep the mind in a state of calm, dignified waiting."

This is impossible for any one who knows that he is twice-born as a result of the regenerating power of the Holy Spirit. Once a Christian by the saving and renewing grace of Christ, a man cannot possibly start with a blank mind, but is inwardly and outwardly bound to compare a new teaching with what he has found to be the universally and age-old accepted teachings of the Scriptures.

2. We readily grant that the Rosicrucian philosophy has many fine points, such as its inexorable logic. It gives a more plausible reason for rebirth than does Theosophy. It appears to present a better cause for a clean and lofty life than do the "ear-to-ear and mouth-to-mouth" secrets of a Blavatsky. But all this logic and all this loftiness cannot annul the fact that the entire structure is built upon a false foundation, namely, another than the Christ of the Scriptures.

3. Many points of criticism that have been advanced against the kindred systems of Spiritism and Theosophy hold true also against Rosicrucianism: when the mind and heart are left blank to be played upon by outward forces, it may, according to Scripture, be expected that "doctrines of demons" will be infused from without. It is no wonder that astrology and spiritism and necromancy are so consistently forbidden in the Old Testament. Attention should be given, therefore, to the great similarity among these various cults.

4. The crowning test of a religious or philosophical system of thought from the viewpoint of the present volume

must always be: How do its statements compare with what
has been held to be in harmony with Scripture by the entire
Christian Church? When we do this, we reach the conclusion that the apostle Paul would say of the followers
of the Rose Cross that they are "enemies of the cross of
Christ."

Rosicrucians and Biblical Doctrine
Christ

(a) *His Person*

"In the Christian creed occurs this sentence: 'Jesus
Christ, the only begotten Son of God.' This is generally
understood to mean that a certain person Who appeared in
Palestine about 2000 years ago, Who is spoken of as Jesus
Christ—one separate individual—was the only begotten
Son of God. This is a great mistake. There are three distinct and widely different Beings characterized in this
sentence. It is of the greatest importance that the student
should clearly understand the exact nature of these Three
Great and Exalted Beings—differing vastly in glory, yet
each entitled to our deepest and most devout adoration.

"The student is requested to turn to diagram 6 and note
that 'The only begotten' ('The Word' of Whom John speaks)
is the second aspect of the Supreme Being.

"This 'Word,' and It alone, is 'begotten of His Father [the
first aspect] before all Worlds.' . . . Therefore the 'only
begotten' is the exalted Being which ranks above all else
in the Universe save only the Power-aspect which created
It."—M. HEINDEL[10]

(b) *His Sacrifice*

"We are now approaching the winter solstice, the darkest
days of the year, the time when the light of the sun has
almost faded, when our Northern Hemisphere is cold and
drear. But on the longest and darkest night the sun turns
on its upward path, the Christ light is born on the earth

---

10. *Ibid.,* p. 374.

again, and all the world rejoices. By the terms of our
analogy, however, when the Christ is born on earth He dies
to heaven. As the free spirit is at the time of birth finally
and firmly encased in the veil of flesh which fetters it all
through life, so also the Christ Spirit is fettered and ham-
pered each time He is born into the earth. This great Annual Sacrifice begins when our Christmas bells are ring-
ing, when our joyful sounds of praise and thanksgiving
are ascending to heaven. Christ is imprisoned in the most
literal sense of the word from Christmas to Easter."—M.
HEINDEL[11]

(c) *Second Coming*

" 'The law and the prophets were until Christ,' it is said,
but we know that even today law is, and is necessary.
Therefore, it is evident that law was not abolished at the
physical coming of Christ. It is the coming of Christ into
'the within,' the inner nature of man, that is to abolish law.
Paul speaks of this advent as the 'Christ being formed in
ye,' and until Christ has been formed in us we are not ready
for the Second Coming . . . The Second Coming of Christ
depends upon how soon a sufficient number of people have
become Christ-like and attuned to the Christ principle, so
that, as tuning forks of the same pitch sing together when
one is struck, they will be able to respond to the Christ vibrations that will be set up at the return of the Savior. Every
time we endeavor to imitate Christ and fulfil His teachings,
we are hastening His Coming; so let us thus strive."—M.
HEINDEL[12]

Jesus

"*I understand you to say that the Christ has been incarnated only once in Jesus; was he not previously incarnated
in Gautama Buddha and still earlier in Krishna?*

"*Answer*: No. Jesus Himself was a spirit belonging to
our human evolution, and so was Gautama Buddha. The

11. *The Mystical Interpretation of Christmas*, p. 21.
12. *The Rosicrucian Philosophy*, p. 206.

writer has no information concerning Krishna, but is inclined to believe that he was also a spirit belonging to the human race, because the Indian stories concerning him tell of how he entered heaven and what took place there. The Christ spirit which entered the body of Jesus when Jesus himself vacated it, was a ray from the cosmic Christ. We may follow Jesus back in his previous incarnations, and we can trace his growth to the present day. The Christ spirit, on the contrary, is not to be found among our human spirits at all."—M. HEINDEL[13]

God

(a) *Trinity*

" 'The Father' is the highest Initiate among the humanity of the Saturn Period. The ordinary humanity of that Period are now the Lords of Minds.

" 'The Son' (Christ) is the highest Initiate of the Sun Period. The ordinary humanity of that Period are now the Archangels.

" 'The Holy Spirit' (Jehovah) is the highest Initiate of the Moon Period. The ordinary humanity of that Period are now the Angels."—M. HEINDEL[14]

(b) *The Holy Spirit* (Rev. 1:4)

"It is necessary for all beings high or low in the scale of existence, to possess vehicles for expression in any particular world in which they may wish to manifest. Even the Seven Spirits before The Throne must possess these necessary vehicles, which of course are differently conditioned for each of Them. Collectively, They are God, and make up the Triune Godhead, and He manifests in a different way through each of Them."—HEINDEL[15]

13. *Ibid.*, p. 181.
14. *Cosmo-conception*, p. 376.
15. *Ibid.*, p. 252.

Man

(a)   *Races of man*

"The Bible does not state anywhere that the negroes are
the descendants of Ham; besides it is well known that the
Biblical ethnology as commonly understood among orthodox people is an utter impossibility in view of the facts of
geology and ethnological research. . . The Biblical ethnology
also has the exact year of the flood and similar events fixed,
but from the occult point of view, which is derived from a
direct reading in the picture gallery of the past, which we
call *the memory of nature,* the case is very different. . . We
find there that there have been various epochs or great
stages of unfoldment in the earth's history, and that the
negro was the humanity of the third of these epochs, the
Lemurian.   The whole human race of that time was black
skinned.   Then came a time, called the Atlantean Epoch,
when humanity was red, yellow, except one race which was
white.   These people were original Semites, the fifth of the
Atlantean Races.   These Atlanteans are called Niebelungen,
or *children of the mist,* in the old folk stories, for at that
time the atmosphere of the earth was a very dense fog.   In
the latter half of the Atlantean Epoch this atmosphere con-
densed, floods resulted and gradually the sea covered the
larger part of the globe.   Then the atmosphere became clear
above the earth.   This point in evolution is described in the
Bible where Noah, the leader of the Semites, came out
from the drowning Atlantis and first saw the rainbow, a
phenomenon impossible in the foggy atmosphere of early
Atlantis.   We also hear of that emigration in the story of
Moses and the Israelites coming out from Egypt while the
Egyptian king and his men drown in the waters of the Red
Sea.   These people had been chosen to become the progenitors of our present Aryan races, but not all of them
were true to the command of their leader.   There were some
of them who 'went after strange flesh,' and that is the
greatest crime possible at such a time, for when a leader
is aiming to instill new faculties into a new race, the ad-
mixture of strange blood has a tendency to frustrate his

plans. Therefore, some of these chosen people were lost,
that is to say, they were abandoned by their leaders and
did not become the forebearers of the new humanity. *Those
who were thus lost or left behind are, strange to say, the
present day Jews,* who at one time married into the families of their Atlantean brethren, contrary to the commands
of their divine leader, and yet today think themselves the
'chosen people' of God."—M. HEINDEL[16]

(b) *Divinity of man*

"There is endless progress, for we are divine as our
Father in heaven, and limitations are impossible."—M.
HEINDEL

Pantheism

"We would ask, what do you mean by nature? Bacon
says that nature and God differ only as the print and the
seal. Nature is the visible symbol of God, and we are too
apt to think of nature nowadays in a materialistic sense.
Back of every manifestation in nature are forces, *not blind
forces, but intelligences* . . . What we speak of as electricity,
as magneticism, as expansion in steam, etc. are intelligences
which work unseen to us when certain conditions are
brought about. Nature spirits build the plants, form the
crystals of the rock, and with numerous other hierarchies
are working around and about us unseen, but nevertheless
busy in making that which we call nature."—M. HEINDEL[17]

Parenthood

"Unless there is an Ego seeking embodiment through a
married couple, their efforts will be fruitless. . . . We know
that if we mix hydrogen and oxygen in proper proportions
we always get water; we know that water will always flow
downhill; and thus all the laws of nature are invariable,
so that unless there were another factor than the chemical
mixture of semen and ova there would always be issue.

16. *Rosicrucian Philosophy,* p. 54.
17. *Ibid.,* p. 85.

And this unknown and unseen factor is the reincarnating
Ego which goes where it pleases and without which there
can be no issue. If the inquirer will pray earnestly to the
angel Gabriel, who is the ambassador of the Regent of the
Moon to the Earth, and therefore a prime factor in the
generation of bodies (vide the Bible), it may possibly avail
to bring the desired result. The best time is Monday at sun-
rise, and from the new Moon to the full."[18]

Prayer

"*Hallowed be Thy Name*: prayer of the Human spirit
to the Holy Spirit for the desire body.
Thy kingdom come: prayer of the Life Spirit to the Son
for the vital body."—M. HEINDEL[19]

Hints

1. In what particulars does this system resemble Spiritism; Theosophy?

2. In which points do these cults differ?

3. What is the meaning of the Cross, and what that of
the Roses in Rosicrucianism?

4. What is the place of God in this philosophy?

5. How many Worlds are there said to be, and through
how many periods of evolution is each World said to pass?

6. Is Christ a Person or an impersonal spirit according
to this ism?

7. Do you find any elements of superstition in this boast-
fully superior system of thought?

---

18. *Ibid.*, p 64.
19. *Cosmo-conception*, Diagram 16.

5

CHRISTIAN SCIENCE

We live in a fast moving world. A storm of protest went up in 1930 when Edward F. Dakin published his highly entertaining book, *Mrs. Eddy, the Biography of a Virginal Mind.* The publishers were deluged with abusive attempts at boycotting, and found it necessary, backed by leading authors and magazines in America and England, to insert in the two-dollar edition of their five-dollar book a pamphlet, "The Blight that Failed." "The American bookbuyer and bookseller," announced the pamphlet, "have prevented the smothering of an outstanding biography, and circumvented the blight that would have fallen upon our constitutional liberties of free speech, free thought, and a free press."

Having failed in the attempt to prevent the selling and reading of Dakin's book, the devotees of Mother Eddy came in the same year, 1930, with a new biography by Lyman P. Powell, of which "self-portrait of Mrs. Eddy" W. E. Garrison wrote, "Already a gospel of the infancy is springing up. Pre-natal influences are stressed. Her mother 'was filled with the Holy Ghost . . . and felt the quickening of the babe.' " And he added, "Half of this statement lacks evidence, and the other half scarcely needs it."

But now the hatchet has been buried, and Mrs. Eddy's Church is stressing the teachings and healing practice rather than the life of Mrs. Eddy, just as Jehovah's Witnesses no longer bother about "Pastor" Russell's court cases which have long since been forgotten.

One may spend many charming hours with this fascinating literature. To wade through the trumped-up tradition which Eddyists have established and the unvarnished facts concerning Mary Baker Glover Patterson Eddy, is a delightful task.   But the problem as to how much Mrs. Eddy was indebted to "Doctor" Quimby — a clockmaker by trade, and a doctor only by courtesy — for her system, and as to whether he only spoke of *Mental Healing* or also of *Christian Science;* as to whether the term "malicious animal magnetism" is Mrs. Eddy's own contribution or not — these and similar interesting points of discussion have little to do with the *system* erroneously called "Christian Science."

Historical

There can be no doubt as to the following few and sober facts.   Mary Baker was born on a farm at Bow, near Concord, New Hampshire, on July 16, 1821.   She was the child of a headstrong and religious New Englander; and she herself was abnormally nervous in childhood and early married life.   She was subject to what the neighbors called "fits." When she was physically full grown, her father constructed a specially built cradle in which she could be rocked to sleep.   In 1843 she married George Washington Glover, a bricklayer, who died one year later.   In 1853 she was married, "cradle and all," to Dr. Daniel Patterson, an itinerant and none too affluent dentist who left her because of her tantrums.

In 1862 Mrs. Patterson visited P. P. Quimby, who suggested to his patients that "they were not cured by medicine but by the state of their minds."   She stayed three weeks, read his manuscripts, and was healed of her nervous troubles.   She revisited him in 1864, staying three or four months.   It is strange, perhaps, that she soon afterward began to go into trances and represented her brother Albert as a spiritistic medium.

Mrs. Patterson praised Quimby abundantly, wrote poetry about him, gave him credit for her ideas ("P. P. Quimby rolls away the stone from the sepulchre and health is the resurrection").   Later she repudiated Quimby, stating that her "Divine Science" had come to her directly from God.

This "revelation" she dated in various books as having occurred in 1844, 1853, 1864, 1866.[1]

She was desperately poor for many years, and did not become successful until she forgot Quimby and began to practice Healing in her own name. Then, also, she published *Science and Health With Key to the Scriptures* in 1875. In 1877 she married Asa Gilbert Eddy, who made the book a financial success. She established her "Metaphysical College" at Boston, where she charged three hundred dollars for a course of twelve lessons, and two hundred dollars for a course of six lessons. She sold 400,000 copies of her book, on which she realized a million dollars. She left an estate of three million dollars. She died, "a very old and toothless woman," on December 3, 1910, in spite of her denial of sickness and death.

One hardly knows what to marvel at mostly in Mrs. Eddy. Perhaps it is her indomitable will power, her dogged adherence to one idea notwithstanding the fact that her own life disproved that idea time and again. She did not become successful in any phenomenal sense until she had been forsaken by one husband and had buried two others. She called a doctor when her beloved Eddy was too far gone to be healed, and afterward "explained" his death as the result of "arsenic mentally administered." She conquered a world, built a church, received the worship of thousands, and amassed a fortune, after she was sixty-one years old and a widow once more. And she lived long enough to spend her last years in utter loneliness and in mortal fear of the "malicious animal magnetism" which her enemies were said to direct against her to kill her mentally. She died at eighty-nine, worn out and silent, yet leaving behind a host of followers ready to defend the legend of her supernaturalness.

---

1. Mrs. Eddy's indubitable dependence upon Quimby, and her treacherous subsequent denial of it; and her dependence upon the Rev. J. H. Wiggin (her literary editor and ghost writer: "I often feel as if the Lord spoke to me through you") have been recently "demonstrated" from unimpeachable sources by W. Martin and N. Klann, *The Christian Science Myth.*

She reasoned with the utmost self-confidence about problems which were far and wide beyond her mental grasp and her meager education. And she probably never spoke a truer and more witty word than when she acknowledged that Bronson Alcott, on reading *Science and Health,* said that no one but a woman or a fool could have written it.

Yet there are other humorous touches. There is the fact that she maintained that her book had been dictated by God so that it would have been very unseemly for her to speak of it in a modest manner. When, afterward, it was observed that she had hired a clergyman to correct her poor English, and when the alleged inspiration was disputed, she asserted that the mistakes were not at all contrary to the divine inspiration. She had been so filled, she affirmed, with Science that "grammar was eclipsed."

What, then, is the charm and power of this system? Mrs. Eddy's followers were reported to have reached 268,915 in 1947. They implicitly obey Mother's orders that religious services must be without preaching. A Christian Science service always consists of one reading from Scripture and one from *Science and Health,* the singing of a few hymns, the repetition of the Lord's Prayer as amended by Mrs. Eddy, and no more nor less than these. An air of mystery is left over it all.

Thus, "the cult of American ladies" (seventy-five per cent are said to be women) hides its nakedness under a cloak of profundity. The old gentleman who was asked why Mrs. Eddy had not removed error from her hymnal answered with a dazed look, "Oh, Christian Science is a life-long study." It had never dawned upon him that the system is so simple as not to merit the name of a philosophy, it being merely an "elaborate idea."

For all that it would be an interesting study to discover how many elements have entered into the making of Christian Science. Thomas Cuming Hall charges it all off to the emotional hunger after the Civil War which, in the case of many, found Moody's revivalism too noisy, and yet craved the "exceedingly self-centered and individualistic gospel" that Eddyism is. This undoubtedly goes too far, although it contains an element of truth. On the other hand, the Pundita Ramabai exaggerated in another direction when she remarked, upon coming to this country in 1898, that the "new" philosophy of America, called Christian Science, was nothing new to her. It had been taught, she added, in her country these four thousand years; and it had wrecked thousands of lives in India through its lack of sympathy. It could not show sympathy since it considered both suffering and sufferers unreal.

On June 8, 1943, Mrs. Daisette D. S. McKenzie of Cambridge, for 56 years a Christian Scientist and a member of the first class taught by Mary Baker Eddy, was elected president of the Mother Church, the First Church of Christ, Scientist. She succeeded Mrs. Elizabeth F. Norwood of Brooklyn.

John Randall Dunn, C. S. B., of Boston, was at the same time appointed editor of three Christian Science publications.

The System

Mrs. Eddy taught that "God is divine *Principle*, supreme incorporeal Being, Mind, Spirit, Soul, Life, Truth, Love." The "fundamental propositions are summarized in the four following, to me *self-evident*, propositions. 1. God is All-in-all. 2. God is Good. God is mind. 3. God, Spirit, being all, nothing is matter. 4. Life, God, omnipotent good, deny death, evil, sin, disease. — Disease, sin, evil, death, deny good, omnipotent God, Life."

Should you ask whence sickness, hunger, and numerous other things which we associate with the material world, arise, the answer is that all these lack reality. They do not actually exist. They are mistaken notions of *Mortal Mind*, And the grand ideal of Christian Science is to *demonstrate* the non-existence of all these things.

In other words, all people, including Christian Scientists, in the present stage of development, are under the "tyranny of mortal mind." As long as this tyranny cannot be broken, it is better to substitute a more refined "error" for a grosser error. Hence, although there is no body to get hungry (since all is Mind, God), if mortal mind makes me feel hungry, it is better to eat and to suffer mentally from the delusion that I have a well-fed body than to suffer from the delusion that I have a painfully hungry body. Marriage is allowed, as long as we think, or feel we have bodies; but the ideal is that there shall be no marriage.

It is difficult to give a somewhat full epitome of the teachings of this system; for it has been correctly stated that it does not attain to the height of a system of thought, but is actually only "an elaborate idea." And that idea is that since God is All-in-All, everything else lacks reality or substance. If God is All, naturally all things are divine, or else non-existent, and God is conceived of after the manner of an extreme pantheism. Christ becomes a divine idea, and the Holy Spirit is interpreted as Divine Science. Adam becomes Error; Death is but a "Belief," "a dream from which mortals must waken"; the church is defined as "the structure of Truth and Love; whatever rests upon and proceeds from divine Principle"; the thing, and virtually the only thing that counts is that Man can destroy all evil with his thought. We must "demonstrate against" all error, be that mental or physical. We shall no doubt continue to exist somehow after the delusion of death; but how and where is not nearly as important as to demonstrate in the present life that the here and the now can become free from anxiety and suffering.

Can you blame critics of "Divine Science" when they point out the suspicious truth that Mrs. Eddy asserted that in the present stage of our understanding Science, we can only demonstrate against sickness, and not against hunger and money?

The term "animal magnetism" is prevalent in the literature of Christian Science. It is understood that thought influences mind. "Practitioners" are advised to be alone with a patient whose sickness they argue out of existence, for when others who think the sickness to be real are pres-

ent, their influence upon the "mortal mind" of the patient
may be stronger, and may neutralize the influence of the
practitioner and the patient. This is a clever excuse whereby the death of a person is ascribed not to the failure of
"Science," but to the influence of evil mortal mind which
reaches us from every side.

Mrs. Eddy herself attributed the death of her husband
Asa Eddy to "arsenic mentally administered," and also to
"mesmeric" (*i. e.,* mental, hypnotic) "poison." Of this
Martin and Klann write: "Here is an emotionally confused
and frustrated woman who frantically attempts to establish what is a medical absurdity, namely, that Asa Eddy's heart was destroyed by 'mesmeric poison' directed at
him by a metaphysical enemy."[2]

Christian Science As a Philosophy

1.   Mrs. Eddy has been charged with spoiling Quimby's
philosophy because she failed to grasp it. Whatever there
may be to this, she certainly produced a system which is
pantheism gone to seed. It has been called "precisely acos-
mic pantheism, that, all that, and nothing but that." Pantheists before Mrs. Eddy identified God with the creation,
conceived of the material world as of some part of God:
God the soul, matter the body of the universe. Mrs. Eddy,
on the contrary, denied the existence of matter. This is
highly unscientific, since every form of experience teaches
that matter does indeed exist.

2.   Many have thought that Eddyism is inconsistent because it denies the existence of evil and sickness, and, in the
next breath, refers to the positive cure of pneumonia and
other diseases. Christian Scientists, with their mysterious
air of wisdom, will reply, "Yes, that is the way it looks to
non-Scientists, but it is perfectly logical." They are right.
The truth is that as long as mortal mind tyrannizes, it is
consistent to speak of sickness as existing. This is merely
condescending to our present condition. *Science and Health,*
as Dr. Swain has taught us, can be "read like a primer"

2. *Op. cit.,* p. 76.

once we realize that it contains "the trick of two languages": the one, affirming evil things, is the language of Mortal Mind! the other, denying them, is the language of Divine Science.[3]   This double use of language, however, does not make for Sincerity and Truth (to borrow Mother Eddy's Love for Capitals).

3. Christian Science, for all that, is glaringly inconsistent. If there is nothing but God, Mind, Truth, Love, whence cometh this Mortal Mind? If "Life, God, omnipotent good deny death, evil, sin, disease," how can there be a Mortal Mind in God? Who is there to suffer even from a fictitious sense of pain and hunger? This pivotal question, Dr. Swain discovered, Scientists are not ready to discuss.

4.   "Has the Christian Scientist ever paused to answer the following problem: If I cannot trust my senses when they report death and pain, how can I trust them when I read the works of Mary Baker Eddy? The latter data are far less compelling than the former."[4]

5.   Closely related to this inconsistency — in fact, included in it — is the fact that Mrs. Eddy did not understand her own terminology. "Christian Science," wrote Dr. Atkins, "is not monism; it is rather a dualism; it confronts not one but two ranges of reality and it is compelled to admit the existence of the reality it denies."   And this is probably due to Mrs. Eddy's failure to realize that *experience is real* just as much as matter is real, that not all reality has to be tangible reality.

As a System of Healing

Christian Science has outwitted numerous other systems of faith-healing and mind-healing. In fairness to Mrs. Eddy we should state that she wants her Science to be called Mind-healing, with a capital M.

1. It is natural that a system which heals people of physical diseases gets a hearing. Strictly speaking, Christian

---

3. R. L. Swain, *The Real Key to Christian Science.*
4. E. J. Carnell, *A Philosophy of the Christian Religion,* p. 292.

Science does not heal, for there is no one to be healed and nothing to be healed. Christian Science demonstrates that there is no sickness to begin with. However, let us make use of our privilege by using the language of Mortal Mind.

We see at least three reasons why Christian Science has been successful, even beyond the faith healers of its earlier days.

a. Many diseases are mental, imaginary, as all physicians and psychiatrists know today.

b. Even where physical disturbance exists, the power of mind over matter, of soul over body is known to be great. We gratefully acknowledge that Eddyism has again emphasized this truth. It is superfluous, however, to say the least, to do this by means of denying God and Christ.

c. Faith healers direct the mind to a Power outside the sick person. If that Power does not respond quickly, the patient is likely to lose his faith in the existence of this Power. Eddyism, however, not only directs the mind to itself (which the mind could not well refuse), but prescribes several treatments for the training of the mind. And this undoubtedly leaves a greater chance for kind Doctor Nature to cooperate with the patient's desire to get well.

2. Eddyism, therefore, has little to boast of beyond patent medicine, Roman Catholic shrines, and other aids to the power of the human mind. The "I believe in Christian Science because it has healed me" is an erroneous conclusion, a ladies' leaping at conclusions.

Moreover, it has been *demonstrated* that Christian Science patients often die of the very troubles of which they had been "healed."

3. Over against the alleged cures, which in many cases are undoubtedly genuine, we have a long list of deaths caused by neglect and failure to call in medical help. This cruelty has been punished by our Courts.[5]

---

5. A partial account of such cases may be found in Stephen Paget, *The Faith and Works of Christian Science*, 151-180; W. A. Purrington, *Christian Science, an Exposition of Mrs. Eddy's Wonderful Discovery, including the Legal Aspects, a Plea for Children and other*

As a Religion

1. Christian Science is the least of all the systems. True, it is popular as a system which combines religion with the healing-bait ever will be, but what is, after all, a religion which is not even autosoteric? If our objection to the ethnic religions and the common run of cults is that they teach man that he can and must save himself from sin and its aftermath, what must be our opinion of a "religion" which teaches that there is nothing to be saved from, and no one to be saved from, and no one to be saved? Christian Science does not even recognize the evil of which Theosophy speaks. God is All. Salvation is superfluous.

2. Christian Science is not only immoral with its teaching that marriage can only be tolerated while Mortal Mind reigns, and that in any event it should be childless (children are so many more delusions of Error, Mortal Mind); it is most dangerous in that it teaches that the flesh is an illusion, our life on earth a dream-life, sin non-existent. "The moving pictures of the sensuous life together with the lusts of carnal nature will do the rest," says Dr. Marsten, "and it will be nothing strange if the dream of the Nicolaitans of the first century is dreamed over again in this twentieth century." Yes, and with wars and rumors of wars and crime waves pressing upon us, we need not teach the rising generation that sin has no reality. Nor need we teach men that from the standpoint of "Divine Science" Jesus Christ came to lay down His life for *nothing*.

3. The method of the *Key to the Scriptures* is what Scripture calls handling the word of God deceitfully (II

Helpless Sick. See also Marsten, *The Mask of Christian Science*, pp. 167-170 and Swain, *op. cit.*, 82-95. Since several of the older works are now difficult to obtain, we can only rejoice that many of such cases have been dug up from original sources in the excellent work by Martin and Klann (*The Christian Science Myth.* 1954, chap. VIII). It appears in general that only such cases yield to suggestion as have been caused by suggestion, while those that are of an organic nature not only refuse to respond to this so-called healing system, but "Scientists" from Mrs. Eddy down have repeatedly gone to physicians and dentists to have their troubles treated, novacaine included.

Cor. 4:2). When Mrs. Eddy paraphrases as follows, "As in Adam (error) all die, even so in Christ (Truth) shall all be made alive," she commits a travesty upon language, upon the plain meaning of Scripture, which is rank dishonesty.

4. Like Theosophy, Christian Science must be condemned as sheer gnosticism. Gnosticism taught that salvation could come only through knowledge; hence it was selfish, and had no message for the ignorant. Christian Science teaches that sickness, sin, and disease disappear in proportion as we understand that God is all. It is this knowledge that sets us free. Gnosticism, moreover, taught that God is opposed to matter; that Christ emanated from God and liberated the spirit from matter; that, since matter is evil, Christ could not have a human body; consequently that His sufferings were not real, but only an appearance. Who does not recognize here the language of Mrs. Eddy? B. B. Warfield was right, then, when he concluded, "You can have a little Christian Science in your Christianity just as little as you can have a little water in your fire; and a little Christianity in your Christian Science just as little as you can have a little fire in your water. The things are mutually exclusive."[6]

And Dr. R. L. Swain, himself a liberal, not only stated, "I have practiced healing on myself, and upon patients formerly treated both by Christian Science and the Immanuel Church. It would be foolish, however, to suppose that I have powers which these Churches do not possess. My success is quite in keeping with theirs, and subject to the same limitations. Healing without medicine is a good thing in its place, but a curse the moment it transcends its proper bounds." But he also added this terse critique: "Now, in spite of the absurd notion that human beings do not exist, that the things for which they daily strive are 'nothing' . . . that there is nothing to improve, since God's

---

6. *Counterfeit Miracles*, p. 220.

ideas, the only realities, are perfect. . . . They give the lie to their philosophy. . . . Though they deny the existence of all mortals, yet they are ever striving to instruct these 'non-existent beings' with the fine faith that they will succeed. Though their theoretical inconsistencies undo them, yet their practical inconsistency in repudiating their theories in daily life saves them in part."

Truly, such candid and uncompromising condemnations of a system that is neither Christian nor scientific in any sense of the word, are greatly to be preferred to the present-day "objective" descriptions with a laudatory remark about the good Eddyism accomplishes by healing the sick.[7]

The Bible and Christian Science

Not referring now to individual doctrines of Christian Science, the system *in toto* and its methods of approach have been well characterized by the inspired apostle Paul in such lines as these,

". . . according to the working of Satan with all power and signs and lying wonders, and with all deceit of unrighteousness of them that perish; because they received not the love of the truth that they might be saved" (II Thess. 2:9, 10).

"But refuse profane and old wives' fables" (I Tim. 4:7).

"For of these are they that creep into houses, and take captive silly women laden with sins, led away by divers lusts, ever learning, and never able to come to the knowledge of truth" (II Tim. 3:6, 7).

"Men who overthrow whole houses, teaching things which they ought not, for filthy lucre's sake."

Christian Science, like other antichristian isms reveals its true character in the manner in which it denies true Scriptural doctrine.

---

7. W. W. Sweet in his admirable study *The Story of Religion in America* goes so far as to suggest, "And perhaps the growing interest in psychiatry as a new technique is not unrelated to Christian Science." p. 377, third ed.

Christian Science and Biblical Truth

Angels

"Angels are pure thoughts from God, winged with Truth and Love, no matter what their individualism may be . . . My angels are exalted thoughts."—MRS. EDDY.[8]

Atonement

"One sacrifice, however great, is insufficient to pay for the debt of sin. The atonement requires constant self-immolation on the sinner's part. That God's wrath should be vented upon His beloved Son, is divinely unnatural. Such a theory is man-made. The atonement is a hard problem in theology, but its scientific explanation is, that suffering is an error of sinful sense which Truth destroys."

"The efficacy of Jesus' spiritual offering is infinitely greater than can be expressed by our sense of human blood. The material blood of Jesus was no more efficacious to cleanse from sin when it was shed upon 'the accursed tree,' than when it was flowing in his veins as he went daily about his Father's business. His true flesh and blood were his Life; and they truly eat his flesh and drink his blood who partake of that divine Life."—MRS. EDDY.[9]

Death

"What appears to the sense to be death is but a mortal illusion, for to the real man and the real universe there is no death-process."

"Death.—An illusion, the lie of life in matter; the unreal and untrue."

"His disciples believed Jesus to be dead while he was hidden in the sepulchre, whereas he was alive, demonstrating within the narrow tomb the power of Spirit to overrule mortal material sense."—MRS. EDDY.[10]

---

8. *Science and Health*, ed. 1910, p. 298.
9. *Ibid.*, pp. 23, 25.
10. *Ibid.*, pp. 289, 584, 44.

Devil

"Christian Science teaches us that 'the evil one,' or one evil, is but another name for the first lie and all liars."

"DEVIL, evil, a lie, error, neither corporeality nor mind."—MRS. EDDY.[11]

Evil

"If God, or good, is real, then evil, the unlikeness of God, is unreal."

"All sin is insanity in different degrees."

"Man is incapable of sin, sickness, and death."—MRS. EDDY.[12]

Fall of Man

"If man was once perfect but has now lost his perfection, then mortals have never beheld in man the reflex image of God. The *lost* image is no image. The true likeness cannot be lost in divine reflection [that is, man]. Understanding this, Jesus said: 'Be ye therefore perfect even as your Father which is in heaven is perfect,'"— MRS. EDDY.[13]

God

"God is All-in-All."

"God is incorporeal, divine, supreme, infinite Mind, Spirit, Soul, Principle, Life, Truth, Love."

"Life, Truth, and Love constitute the triune Person called God, that is, the triply divine Principle, Love . . . the same in essence, though multiform in office; God the Father-Mother; Christ the spiritual idea of sonship; divine Science or the Holy Comforter."

"The theory of three persons in one God (that is, a personal Trinity or Tri-unity) suggests polytheism, rather than the one ever-present I Am."—MRS. EDDY.[14]

Inspiration of Scripture

"The Bible has been my only authority. I have had no other guide in 'the straight and narrow way' of Truth.

11. *Ibid.*, pp. 331, 256.
12. *Ibid.*, pp. 470, 407, 475.
13. *Ibid.*, p. 259.
14. *Ibid.*, pp. 113, 465, 331, 256.

"Genesis 2:7. Is this addition to His creation real or unreal? Is it the truth, or is it a lie concerning man and God? It must be a lie, for God presently curses the ground." —MRS. EDDY.[15]

Jesus Christ

"God is indivisible. A portion of God could not enter man; neither could God's fulness be reflected by a single man, else God would be manifestly finite, lose the deific character, and become less than God."

"Jesus is the human man, and Christ is the divine idea; hence the duality of Jesus the Christ."

"The Christ dwelt forever an idea in the bosom of God, the divine Principle of the man Jesus, and woman perceived this spiritual idea, though at first faintly developed."

"Christ, Truth, was demonstrated through Jesus to prove the power of Spirit over the flesh. . . . Jesus represented Christ, the true idea of God."

"The Virgin-mother conceived this idea of God, and gave to her ideal the name of Jesus."

"Jesus was the offspring of Mary's self-conscious communion with God."

"Mary's conception of him was spiritual, for only purity could reflect Truth and Love."

"Jesus bore our sins in his body. He knew the mortal errors which constitute the material body, and could destroy those errors; but at the time when Jesus felt our infirmities, he had not conquered all the beliefs of the flesh or his sense of material life, nor had he risen to final demonstration of spiritual power."

"Our Master fully and finally demonstrated divine Science in his victory over death and the grave. . . . The persecutors had failed to hide immortal Truth and Love in a sepulchre."—MRS. EDDY.[16]

15. *Ibid.*, pp. 126, 524.
16. *Ibid.*, pp. 336, 473, 29, 316, 29, 332, 53, 45.

Justification by Faith

"Final deliverance from error, whereby we rejoice in immortality, boundless freedom, and sinless sense, is not reached through paths of flowers nor by pinning one's faith without works to another's vicarious effort."—MRS. EDDY.[17]

Marriage

"Until time matures, human growth, marriages, and progeny will continue unprohibited in Christian science." —MRS. EDDY.[18]

"Until the spiritual creation is discerned and the union of male and female apprehended in its soul sense, this rite should continue."[19]—MRS. EDDY.

"Until it is learned that generation rests on no sexual basis, let marriage continue."[20]—MR. EDDY.

"Until it is learned that God is the Father of all, marriage will continue."[21] —MRS. EDDY.

Prayer

"Desire is prayer. Such a desire has little need of audible expression. It is best expressed in thought and life."

"Shall we ask the divine Principle of all goodness to do His own work? His work is done.

"God is not influenced by man."

"The mere habit of pleading with the divine mind, as one pleads with a human being, perpetuates the belief in God as humanly circumscribed—an error which impedes spiritual growth."

"Here let me give what I understand to be the spiritual sense of the Lord's Prayer:

Our Father which art in heaven,
Our Father-Mother God, all-harmonious,
Hallowed be Thy name.

---

17. *Ibid.*, p. 22.
18. *Miscellaneous Writings*, p. 289.
19. *Science and Health*, ed. 1881, p. 152.
20. *Ibid.*, ed. 1889, p. 274.
21. *Ibid.*, ed. 1910, p. 64.

> *Adorable One.*
> Thy kingdom come.
> *Thy kingdom is come; Thou art ever-present.*
> Thy will be done in earth, as it is in heaven.
> *Enable us to know — as in heaven, so on earth, —*
> *God is omnipotent, supreme.*
> Give us this day our daily bread;
> *Give us grace for today; feed the famished affec-*
> *fections;*
> And forgive us our debts, as we forgive our debtors.
> *And Love is reflected in love;*
> And lead us not into temptation, but deliver us from
> evil;
> *And God leadeth us not into temptation, but deliv-*
> *ereth us from sin, disease, and death.*
> For thine is the kingdom, and the power, and the
> glory, forever.
> *For God is infinite, all-power, all Life, Truth, Love,*
> *over all, and All."*—MRS. EDDY.[22]

Sacraments

"Our baptism is a purification from all error." "*Baptism*: Purification by Spirit; submergence in Spirit." [Note: Baptism is not a sign and seal; baptism itself is spiritualized away.—V. B.]

"The true sense is spiritually lost, if the sacrament is confined to the use of bread and wine. . . . Jesus prayed; he withdrew from the material senses to refresh his heart with brighter, with spiritual views . . . and this supper closed forever Jesus' ritualism or concessions to matter. His followers partook of the heavenly manna, which of old had fed in the wilderness the persecuted followers of Truth. Their bread indeed came down from heaven. It was the great truth of spiritual being, healing the sick and casting out error . . . they had borne this bread from house to house, *breaking* (explaining to others), and now it comforted themselves.

"For this truth of spiritual being, their Master was about to suffer violence and drain to the dregs his cup of sorrow

---

22. *Ibid.*, pp. 1, 11, 3, 7, 2, 27.

... Christians, are you drinking his cup? Have you shared the blood of the New Covenant, the persecutions which attend a new and higher understanding of God? If not, can you then say that you have commemorated Jesus in his cup? Are all who eat bread and drink wine in memory of Jesus willing truly to drink his cup, take his cross, and leave all for the Christ-principle? Then why ascribe this inspiration to a dead rite ... ?

"What a contrast between our Lord's last supper and his last spiritual breakfast with his disciples in the bright morning hours at the joyful meeting on the shore of the Galilean Sea! ...

"This spiritual meeting with our Lord in the dawn of a new light is the morning meal which Christian Scientists commemorate. They bow before Christ, Truth, to receive more of his reappearing and silently to commune with the divine Principle, Love. They celebrate their Lord's victory over death, ... and his spiritual ascension above matter, or the flesh, when he rose out of material sight."—MRS. EDDY[23]

Consider

1. Is "Christian Science" among the more profound substitutes for Christianity, or is it one of the most superficial?

2. Is it possible to be an intelligent "Christian Scientist" and an intelligent Christian at the same time?

3. What is the great inconsistency in Eddyism?

4. How do you account for Mrs. Eddy's popularity?

5. Mention some cardinal Christian doctrines and show how "Christian Science" denies and perverts them.

6. Is "Christian Science" only unchristian, or is it also unscientific? Would you prefer a "practitioner" to a physician?

7. What is "the grain of truth in the bushel of Christian Science"?

---

23. *Ibid.*, pp. 32-35, 581.

6

THE UNITY SCHOOL OF CHRISTIANITY

Charles W. Ferguson has, in his inimitable style, defined Unity as "an enormous mail order concern dispensing health and happiness on the large scale of modern business enterprise. It is mass production in religion and its work is carried on shrewdly and systematically . . . It has transformed the United States Mail into a missionary machine. . . . It is the work of a retired realtor and his inspired wife, and with its tedious array of tabular facts and its insufferable efficiency, it suggests pretty well what Americans want in the realm of the spirit."[1]

Side by side with this we submit Dr. Atkin's opinion on New Thought: "It is the apotheosis of what James called, 'The Religion of Healthy Mindedness'; it all fits easily into the dominant temper of our times and seems to reconcile that serving of two masters, God and Getting On, which a lonely teacher long ago thought quite impossible."

These two opinions of two writers on two religious cults coincide thus remarkably because the two cults are almost one, being as two branches on the same tree. There is a third branch, and we have come to know it as Christian Science.

Origin

To understand the interrelationship of these three cults we should go back to Franz Anton Mesmer, the great German physician who, from 1774 to 1814, wrestled with the problem of psychotherapy, as we call it today. Mesmer, however, incidentally discovered the power of one man over another; but his discovery was too great for his genius. He

---

1. *The Confusion of Tongues, passim.*

did not understand his own remarkable find, so unorthodox in his day, and attributed the powers of the subconscious mind to magnetism, later on to a fluid supposed to emanate from the healer and to affect the patient. Mesmer, though by turns worshipped and despised, adored and hated, never commercialized his find, never lost faith in his discovery, and never used his great power to take advantage of others.

But what Mesmer would not have thought of doing, his disciples, the one hundred percent and the forty percent disciples and the ten percent followers of this remarkable man, have not hesitated to do. Just as the bona-fide evangelism of America's earlier days has degenerated into a loudly screaming, money-making scheme which has destroyed its own usefulness, so the hypnotists and the mesmerists and the spiritists and theosophists, together with the host of faith healers and mind curers, have misused the newly discovered fact of the power of mind over matter for the sake of filthy lucre. They have amassed large fortunes. And they have helped suffering humanity to forget its nervous troubles and its organic diseases just as many have found relief and "healing" from the use of the Owens Electric Belt, the Oxypathor and the Oxygenor, the Electro-Chemical Ring, the Rice Rupture Cure, and Swoboda's Conscious Evolution which "has made possible for everyone the possession of super-health, super-vitality, super-courage, super-aggressiveness, super-mental power, and super every power." And as these officially condemned and exposed quacks could nevertheless produce testimonies of physicians as well as of those who had benefited by being fleeced by them, so Unity and New Thought and Christian Science can boast of swarms of people who would lay down their lives in gratitude for the obtained salvation. For in one respect the Mardens and Eddys and Fillmores have outwitted the ordinary quacks: they have turned their healing recipes into the conundrums of a deeply mystic religion, thereby adding a fervor and a flavor which the common garden variety of healer has missed.

To Count Maxime de Puységur belongs the honor of having discovered in 1784 that Mesmer's alleged magnetic fluid is indeed a power of the human mind, and he opened up the large field of hypnotism and somnambulism. Charles Poyen, a French hypnotist, introduced the revived mesmerism to the gullible American public of the New England states in 1836. Phineas Park Quimby heard Poyen lecture at Belfast, Maine. Poyen told "Park" that he had vast psychic power. Quimby, the clockmaker, began to experiment with sick folk, used his rare hypnotic power upon suffering New England, and in his own right discovered the power of mind over matter.

Quimby became the pioneer mental healer of his day and country. It was not medicine but faith in medicine which healed people, according to Quimby. He wrote his philosophy in ten volumes of longhand. These manuscripts he generously lent to his disciples and patients, being of the old style which did not think of healing in terms of self-aggrandizement. He disclaimed divine inspiration when his admirers tried to force it onto him, and he was glad to have others spread his knowledge.

Among those who benefited by Quimby's manuscripts and methods of healing were Mrs. Eddy, who, as Mrs. Patterson, came to him in 1862 (when he was 60 and she 41), and Julius Dresser. Mrs. Eddy plagiarized the Quimby manuscripts after Quimby's death and denounced the man to whom she had earlier written poetry, "To P. P. Quimby, Who Heals the Sick as Jesus Did." Meanwhile, Dresser became one of the early propagandists of "New Thought."

Observe then the following dates: *Science and Health* was first printed in 1857; the name *New Thought* first appeared as the title of a small magazine devoted to mental healing in 1894; Mrs. Fillmore and her husband decided in 1889 to devote themselves to propagating their "discovery" of health and harmony through "practical Christianity" which is the very name that was in use for New Thought in the West. No wonder there is a great family likeness among these three.

Charles Fillmore was a cripple from infancy. He suffered from a hip disease. Besides, he had curvature of the spine, and was deaf in his right ear. When his wife contracted tuberculosis, they lived for six years in Texas and Arizona, hoping to find health in the arid climate. During a boom Mr. Fillmore amassed a fortune of $150,000 in real estate, but he lost it all during a depression. Penniless and sick, they saw little ahead that was hope-inspiring. It was then that Myrtle Fillmore, so the Unity literature has it, heard a lecture "by a now all-but-forgotten metaphysical lecturer that marked the turning of the tide in Mrs. Fillmore's life, and through her, in that of others. From that lecture one idea stood out in her mind, 'I am a child of God, and therefore I do not inherit sickness.' " "This idea," so the pamphlet continues, "was far reaching." And indeed it was. The good lady's tuberculosis vanished, "and she began healing her children and neighbors." "Gradually the influence of Mrs. Fillmore began to take on the aspects of a religious movement." The husband also became interested in the work of his wife. He, too, regained his health. By 1889 they decided not to take any more risks in real estate, but to make others share in their religio-medico find.

A letter from "The Society of Silent Unity" ("Unity School of Christianity") dated March 17, 1942, states: "Myrtle Fillmore passed on in October of 1931. The present Mrs. Fillmore was formerly Cora Dedrick, Charles Fillmore's secretary, and she is of invaluable help to him in his work."

That the aged gentleman continued long to "prove" his theories appears from the following citation from his article on "The Atomic Prayer" in *Unity*, November, 1945.

"Our modern scientists say that a single drop of water contains enough latent energy to blow up a ten-story building. This energy, existence of which has been discovered by modern scientists, is the same kind of spiritual energy that was known to Elijah, Elisha, and Jesus, and used by them to perform miracles.

"By the power of his thought Elijah penetrated the atoms of hydrogen and oxygen and precipitated an abundance of rain. By the same law he increased the widow's oil and meal. This was not a miracle — that is, it was not a divine intervention supplanting natural law — but the exploitation of a law not ordinarily understood. Jesus used the same dynamic power of thought to break the bonds of the atoms composing the few loaves and fishes of a little lad's lunch— and five thousand people were fed."

The article continues as follows:

"The foregoing extract is from our *Health and Prosperity Column* in *Unity* for May, 1927, some eighteen years ago. Comparison with our class words for this month shows that those comments are peculiarly applicable to the present and also to a subject that has been agitating the public mind for some time, the atomic bomb.

"Of all the comments on or discussion of the indescribable power of the invisible forces released by the atomic bomb none that we have seen mentioned its spiritual or mental character. All commentators have written about it as a force external to man to be controlled by mechanical means, with no hint that it is the primal life that animates and interrelates man's mind and body.

"The next great achievement of science will be the understanding of the mental and spiritual abilities latent in man through which to develop and release these tremendous electrons, protons, and neutrons secreted in the trillions of cells in the physical organism. Here is involved the secret, as Paul says, 'hid for the ages and generations . . . which is Christ [superman] in you, the hope of glory.' It is through release of these hidden life forces in his organism that man is to achieve immortal life, and in no other way. When we finally understand the facts of life and rid our mind of the delusion that we shall find immortal life after we die, then we shall seek more diligently to awaken the spiritual man within us and strengthen and build up the spiritual domain of our being until, like Jesus, we shall be able to control the atomic energy in our body and perform so-called miracles."

However, on July 5, 1948 Charles Fillmore, too, "passed on" and joined the ranks of the immortals.

Today the Unity School of Christianity, with headquarters at Kansas City, Missouri, has its own broadcasting station, an efficient and large office force, the "best vegetarian café in the world," its own oil wells; and it sends by telegram or telephone, prayers and healing thoughts to those in need of them. The Unity Training School Prospectus each year offers a summer schedule with an elaborate course in Healing, Prayer, Bible Interpretation, with a regular Teaching Staff and Great Teachers, with large and well-equipped class rooms and dormitories, various Conferences for Leaders and for Youth, an attractive picture of what "Unity City" will look like in the future, and the general encouraging information, "Rooms are nearly always used to capacity."

The literature of this amazing religious fungus, apart from textbooks and pamphlets carried by "national lecturers," comprises six magazines, *Unity, Unity Daily Word, Weekly Unity, Progress, Wee Wisdom,* and *Good Business.*

System

Unity is so much like Christian Science and like New Thought that a few comparisons must be drawn. These three systems—although New Thought was from the start almost too evasive, too unorganized to merit the name of system — all believe in healing through the mind. Mrs. Eddy, to be sure, repudiated the term mental healing. She preferred to say that Mind, with a capital *M*, demonstrates that there is no such thing as sickness. But the effect is the same. Patterson, New Thoughter, said "Christian Science and the New Thought agree that all life is one; that all intelligence is one; that God is all in all. And they disagree on the following points: Christian Science says that the visible world is mortal mind [that is, an illusion]; the New Thought declares the visible world to be an expression of God's handiwork. Christian Science asserts that sin, sickness, and death have no existence. The New Thought affirms that they have an existence; but that their existence is only limited and their destruction comes through right thinking and hence right living."

And the Unity literature warns that "many of those not acquainted with the distinctions of metaphysical thought class Unity with Christian Science because of a common emphasis on healing; nevertheless Unity, in nearly all its expositions of Truth, is quite distinct from Christian Science. To class them together, except in the fundamental conception of the being of God, common to all religions, is a mistake. It has also been said that Mr. and Mrs. Fillmore were at one time associated with the Christian Science church. This is also a mistake. While the Fillmores were not students of Mary Baker Eddy, nor connected with the Christian Science church in any way, a friendly feeling is always expressed by Unity and its workers toward Christian Science and all other religions. 'God is no respecter of persons' or of sects."

We shall have to be quite careful, then, lest we fall into Error and Delusion in identifying these various "religions." We maintain, however, that they are as much alike as triplets. In Unity we find the same vagueness we meet with in the New Thought literature; also the same key-words, such as *harmony, prosperity, affirmation, health, poise, affluence.* Unity recommends that its disciples shall go into silence, there to repeat "Unity Class Words," "Unity Daily Words," and to meditate upon its "Suggestions for Daily Meditation." The truth of the matter is that at first, owing to the founders' own physical troubles, the emphasis in the Unity movement was mostly upon physical healing, while later on a greater stress was laid upon prosperity and happiness. We offer the following samples, taken at random from its magazines.

"God in the midst of me is mighty to quicken and to illumine. Through the power of God in Christ Jesus I am saved from sin, sickness, and death. Through the power of

God in Christ I am saved from the thought of lack, and I am made rich in all my affairs."

"No longer looking to any external place or to any future time for heaven, I find the kingdom of God — the kingdom of peace, joy, health, and plenty — within me."

"I have faith in God to supply all men's needs everywhere."

"I always think of substance as being abundant and sufficient for all needs. Therefore my material needs are always bountifully supplied."

"Prosperity follows prosperous thinking. For this reason I am thinking prosperous thoughts, wasting no time worrying about what I am to lack."

Marden's chapters on "Power of the Mind, The Law of Opulence," "Imagination and Health," "Why Grow Old?" "How Mind Rules the Body," "Thinking Brings Success," simply abound with almost identical statements, as every student of New Thought knows.

As to Mrs. Eddy, one only needs to glance at the chapter on "Physiology" in *Science and Health* to find the parallel words, "Science can heal the sick, who are absent from their healers, as well as those present, since space is no obstacle to Mind."

Of death Mrs. Eddy wrote, "Sin, disease and death have no foundation in Truth." And again, "DEATH — An illusion." Charles Fillmore has this to say of death, "God is not dead; he does not recognize or countenance death; neither does man when freed from its delusion. . . . The first step in demonstrating over death is to get the belief entirely out of the mind that it is God ordained, or that it is of force or effect anywhere in the realm of Pure Being. The next step is to live so harmoniously that the whole consciousness shall be not only resurrected from its belief in death, but also so vivified and energized with the idea of undying life that it cannot dissolve or separate."

From such quotations it is easily seen that the common pantheistic paternity of these systems has bequeathed to them many fundamental points of similarity. Could pantheism express itself more alike than in Mrs. Eddy's "What is God? God is incorporeal, divine, supreme, infinite Mind, Spirit, Soul, Principle"; and Mr. Fillmore's, "The truth is, then: That God is Principle, Law, Being, Mind, Spirit, All-Good"? Furthermore, he continues as a good brother to Mrs. Eddy: "That God is individually formed in consciousness in each of us, and is known to us as 'Father,' when we recognize him within us as our Creator, as our mind, as our life, as our very being."

On the other hand, Unity has some ideas that are found neither in Christian Science nor in New Thought. Among these the doctrines of reincarnation and of the "regeneration of the body" are noteworthy. Death is but a temporary laying down of the body. Man is a complex being. At death "the spiritual ego reverts to its original essence in the bosom of the Father; soul falls asleep until the next incarnation. Body and sense consciousness are earthbound and in due season they disintegrate." It is not necessary to die. If one believes faithfully in the Christ life he will never die, but continue to live in one's last and final body. "Here," wrote Dr. Braden, "is a daring doctrine." Indeed, it is. But not only is it contrary to Scripture, but with it goes what Paul undoubtedly would have called a doctrine "forbidding to marry." "Through the sins of the sex-life the body is robbed of its essential fluids and disintegrates. The result is called death, which is the last great enemy to be overcome by man. Immortality in the body is possible to man only when he has overcome the weakness of sensation and conserves his life substance. . . . So long as your eyes see sex and the indulgence thereof on any of its planes, you are not pure. You must become mentally so translucent that you see men and women as sexless beings — which they are in the spiritual consciousness."[2]

---

2. Charles Fillmore in *Twelve Powers of Man*, as quoted by Charles S. Braden, *These Also Believe*.

Our Estimate of Unity

1. It may be well for us to remind ourselves once more that it would be neither wise nor in the interest of truth to deny whatever good elements an Ism may contain. Truth is never helped by untruth. Hence we admit that Unity, for all its antichristian elements, emphasizes certain elements of truth which would be well for Christians to bear in mind more generally. Thus the Sermon on the Mount certainly forbids worry as a sin of the Gentiles. The child of God should not be anxious for the morrow, but should know himself to be safe in the Father's loving care. Thousands of orthodox Christians, however, will admit, at times even boast, that they are "the worrying kind." New Thought and Unity deserve a vote of thanks for reminding such Christians that fear is our worst enemy and that no good whatever can result from worry.

For all that, is it not possible to insist upon Jesus' teaching against worry, so deeply religious in Matthew 6, without turning this antiworry principle into the grossest parody upon the choicest parts of Scripture? Or, what else is it but blasphemous parody when the Twenty-Third Psalm is paraphrased as follows — and here it is remarkable how the pantheistic ignoring of a personal God leads to the most brutal materialism:

"The Lord is my banker; my credit is good.
He maketh me to lie down in the consciousness of omnipotent abundance; He giveth me the key to His strong-box.
He restoreth my faith in His riches,
He guideth me in the paths of prosperity for His name's sake.
Yea though I walk through the very shadow of debt I shall fear no evil, for Thou art with me; Thy silver and gold, they secure me.
Thou preparest a way for me in the presence of the collector;
Thou fillest my wallet with plenty; my measure runneth over.

Surely, goodness and plenty will follow me all the days
of my life;
And I shall do business in the name of the Lord forever."[3]

It is also true that the reading of such literature as these
cults produce may be an aid to the discouraged by directing
their attention to the recuperative powers laid by God within the human mind and body. However, here, too, though a
Christian may find sentiments which he may well utilize
against his own believing background, such sentiments and
elements of truth cannot atone for the violently antichristian teaching which underlies the entire cult of the Unity
School. Nor should it be forgotten that when Dr. Braden
visited the Kansas City institution in 1945 he was frankly
informed that in order to be healed the Unity way, it was
neither required to have a physician's diagnosis of one's
trouble nor even desirable that the healing should be at-
tested to by medical authority. "The whole operation is
based," said a leader of the cult, "on faith — not upon
proof, and the intromission of an intent to prove might
even be counter-productive and lessen men's faith rather
than increase it."[4]

2. It is not necessary for Unity to spiritualize story after
story from the Bible, until there is nothing left of the story,
as is done continually in its Sunday School lessons. Thus
the parable of Dives and Lazarus is reconstructed as being
a parable which speaks of one man, and not of two. The
rich man is said to be the outer personality. Dives is self-
indulgent. Lazarus, on the other hand, is the undeveloped
psychic or spiritual body, which Dives neglects and allows
to suffer and starve. The two characters represent each
one of us. Each person is double. The fight of the dual
man results either in Dives becoming Lazarus, as Saul
became Paul, or in Dives gaining the upper hand as Mr.
Hyde defeated Dr. Jekyll.

In a similar manner we are informed in the discussion of

---

3. Fillmore, *Prosperity*, p. 60.
4. *Op. cit.*, p. 150.

the International Lessons: "King Herod represents the ego in the outer or sense consciousness. The Herod man is temporal because he does not understand his origin or the law of his being. He is narrow, jealous, and destructive. His destructive thoughts react upon his body, making it full of pain and misery. Such a man does not fulfill the divine idea of a man, and another ego must supplant him. Jesus represents God's idea of man in expression: Christ is that idea in the absolute [again: compare Mrs. Eddy on Jesus Christ] . . . The Wise-men from the east are the inner planes of consciousness, which, like books of life, have kept the records of past lives and held them in reserve against the great day in which the soul should receive the supreme ego, Jesus.

"When the Jesus ego first appears in the subconsciousness, it is a mere speck of light, a 'star in the east.' The East is the mystical and occult realm where great wisdom and rich presents await the one who is born 'King of the Jews.'"

And so it goes *ad infinitum*. In the same lesson-notes from which the above is taken (*Unity*, Vol. 72, No. 1) we find such gross teaching as, "Galilee represents the life activity or soul energy of man acting in conjunction with substance. Nazareth, a city of Galilee, means a *sprout*, a small thing held of slight significance, hence a term of reproach. It typifies the commonplace mind of man; but it is in the commonplace mind actuated by the soul energy of true substance that the Christ idea takes root and grows up in consciousness."

Or, take this example of pantheistic spiritualizing of truth: " 'And there shall come forth a shoot out of the stock of Jesse, and a branch out of his roots shall bear fruit.' The meaning is 'Jah, Jehovah, or I AM,' representing eternal existence. The shoot or *sprout* out of Jesse therefore, would typify the dawning realization by men of the eternal existence of I AM . . .''

And this is Sunday School instruction! And thousands

are said to swallow this teaching as though it were Christian doctrine. Poor America! How we agree with the conclusion of Dr. Atkins, "There is need of a vast deal more of sheer teaching in all the churches. The necessity for congregations and the traditions of preaching conspire to make the message of the Church far less vital than it ought to be. Preaching is too much declamation and far too much a following of narrow and deeply worn paths."

3. Like Christian Science and New Thought, Unity overemphasizes the importance of intellectual considerations. It will meet with no objections on our part if anyone teaches the primacy of the intellect. But these cults stress the intellect at the expense of the totality of human experience. Thus it is good to be an optimist, but to deny the very possibility of evil is as dangerous as pessimism itself.

4. In the light of Unity's travesty upon the cardinal doctrines of Scripture we wonder why this school should call itself a School of Christianity, why its prospectus should present a well-known portrait of Jesus.

Here are a few excerpts from the literature of Unity:

God

"The author of Genesis was evidently a great metaphysician. He described Being as God, Lord God and Adam. We would express the same truth in the terms Mind, Idea, and Manifestation . . . But Mind, Idea and Manifestation are one. Manifestation rests upon, and is sustained by the Idea, and the Idea is encompassed by the Mind that conceives it; therefore the Real of Adam is the Lord God, and the Omnipresent Fount of the Lord God is the One God.

"Man is by nature an organizer. It is his function in the God-head to formulate the potentialities of the Principles."[5]

"God is not loving . . . God does not love anybody or anything. God is the love *in* everybody and everything. God is

---

5. Charles Fillmore, *Christian Healing*, pp. 133, 217.

love ... God exercises none of His attributes except through the inner consciousness of the universe and man."[6]

"Never be formal with God. He cares no more for forms and ceremonies than do the principles of mathematics for fine figures or elaborate blackboards. . . . You cannot use God too often. He loves to be used, and the more you use Him, the more easily you use Him and the more pleasant His help becomes . . . He will do you a favor just as quickly if you ask in a jolly, laughing way as He would if you made your request in a long, melancholy prayer. God is natural and He loves the freedom of the little child."[7]

Trinity

"The Father is Principle, the Son is that Principle revealed in a creative plan. The Holy Spirit is the executive power of both Father and Son carrying out the creative plan."[8]

Jesus Christ

"The Bible says that God so loved the world that he gave his only begotten Son, but the Bible does not here refer to Jesus of Nazareth, the outer man; it refers to the Christ, the spiritual identity of Jesus, whom he acknowledged in all his ways, and brought forth into his outer, until even the flesh of his body was lifted up, purified, spiritualized, and redeemed. Thus he became Jesus Christ, the Word made flesh. And we are to follow him into this perfect state and become like him for in each of us is the Christ, the only begotten Son. We can, through Jesus Christ, our Redeemer and Example, bring forth the Christ within us, the true self of all men, and be made perfect even as our Father in heaven is perfect, as Jesus Christ commanded his followers to be. Paul wrote to the Galatians, 'It was the good pleasure of God . . . to reveal his Son in me.' We do most certainly

---

6. *Jesus Christ Heals*, Unity School of Christianity, Kansas City, Missouri, 1944, pp. 31-32.
7. *Ibid.*, p. 15.
8. *Metaphysical Bible Dictionary*, Unity School, p. 692.

Man

accept the divinity of Christ and of Jesus Christ, and we believe most thoroughly in the work which he did for mankind."[9]

"In his true estate man is the Christ, the head of the body . . . The *I am*, or Christ, goes through the body to each center, quickening, cleansing, purifying the consciousness with the Word of Truth."[10]

"Statements for the Realization of the Son of God:

"I am the Son of God, and the Spirit of the Most High dwells in me."

"I am the only begotten Son, dwelling in the bosom of the Father."

"I am the Lord of my mentality and the ruler of all its Thought-People."

"I am the Christ of God."

"Through Christ I have dominion over every thought and word."

"I am the Beloved Son in whom the Father is well pleased."

"Of a truth I am the Son of God."

"All that the Father hath is mine."

"He who hath seen me hath seen the Father."   "I and my Father are one."[11]

"As the oak is in the acorn, so God is in man."[12]

Sin

"There is no sin, sickness or death."[13]

"As we explore the mental realm . . . we find it filled with a whole legion of narrow beliefs, foolish, ignorant beliefs, selfish beliefs, and discordant beliefs. These we have lumped together and denominated 'mortal mind' or 'carnal

---

9. *Unity*, Vol. 57, No. 5, p. 464; also *Unity*, Vol. 72, No. 2, p. 8.
10. *Unity*, Vol. 48, No. 2, p. 128.
11. Fillmore, *Christian Healing*, p. 26.
12. *What Practical Christianity Stands For*, Unity School, p. 3.
13. *Unity*, Vol. 47, No. 5, p. 403.

mind.' It is here we first do our 'raising of the dead.' Each of these beliefs of mortality is a sin."[14]

Atonement

"The atonement is the union of man with God the Father, in Christ. Stating it in terms of mind, we should say that the atonement is the at-one-ment or agreement or reconciliation of man's mind with Divine Mind through the superconsciousness of Christ mind. The very foundation of the Christian religion is the atonement of Jesus Christ; but the results of the past teachings show that there has been a misconception of the nature and scope and object of this atonement, else the race would not now still be suffering from the results of the fall. Jesus came to redeem men from sin, and salvation through Him is complete . . . So long as the belief is held that man must worry along somehow with all the afflictions of sin and be taken to a heaven somewhere after death, just so long will the blessings of the atonement be delayed. A living faith in the atoning grace of Jesus Christ will prepare the way to an understanding of His mission and will open the consciousness to the saving Christ power, which alone can, here and now, make the transformation of the soul and body that is called redemption."[15]

Heaven

"It is often assumed that Jesus went away into the skies to prepare a material heaven with golden streets, but the Spirit of truth reveals that the place that Jesus went to prepare is here. 'Lo, I am with you always.' That place is in the mind. 'The kingdom of God is within you.' By his redeeming work Jesus Christ is forming and establishing a new consciousness, into which all may enter. He went first into the interior spiritual realm of consciousness,

---

14. Fillmore, *Christian Healing*, p. 164.
15. *What Practical Christianity Stands For*, p. 5.

and thus opened and prepared the way for all to follow Him and enter with Him into the realization of a perfect union with the Father-Mind."[16]

Resurrection (rejected for *Reincarnation*)

"We believe that the dissolution of spirit, soul and body, caused by death, is annulled by rebirth of the same spirit and soul in another body here on earth. We believe the repeated incarnations of man to be a merciful provision of our loving Father to the end that all may have opportunity to attain immortality through regeneration, as did Jesus. 'This corruptible must put on incorruption.' "[17]

Prayer

"We believe that creative Mind, God, is masculine and feminine, and that these attributes of Being are fundamental in both natural and spiritual man. . . . Almighty Father-Mother, we thank Thee for this vision of Thine omnipotence, omniscience, and omnipresence, in us and in all that we think and do, in the name of Jesus Christ. Amen."[18]

"*Society of Silent Unity*: It is with joy and gratitude that I report to you that I am entirely healed of the trouble about which I wrote to you — varicose veins and an ulcer on my ankle. When I first wrote to you asking for your prayers I was in bed in a rather serious condition. My recovery has been slow and at times I seemed to lose ground. But the months have been a season of renewing, of rebuilding." —Mrs. B. G. T., Chattanooga, Tenn.[19]

"*Society of Silent Unity*: About a month ago I wrote to you asking for prayers for my skin. I had boils on my face. I had tried creams, salves, and many other things without obtaining relief. Your wonderful prayers did the work of healing." —Mrs. C. H. C., Los Angeles, Calif.[20]

16. *Ibid.*, p. 11.
17. *Unity's Statement of Faith*, Art. 22.
18. *Ibid.*, Arts. 16, 32.
19. *Unity*, Vol. 72, No. 3, p. 72.
20. *Unity*, Vol. 72, No. 1, p. 71.

To Aid Digestion (metaphysically conceived)

1. What is the common source of New Thought, Christian Science and Unity?

2. How were "miracles" performed by Elijah, Jesus, and others, according to Unity?

3. Explain the use of atomic energy according to Unity leaders.

4. What is the difference in understanding of "sin" in the three above-named systems?

5. Is death a reality to Unity minds?

6. Give some samples of spiritualizing truth as found in Unity literature.

7. What is wrong with the Unity concepts of God, Jesus Christ, Atonement, Heaven, Resurrection, Prayer?

7

BAHA'ISM

"There is a snag," wrote Dr. E. Stanley Jones, "in the statement of the Theosophists and the Baha'is that all religions are basically one and the same, and are equally good, therefore join the Theosophical Society or the Baha'is on that basis. If they are all the same, why another?" It would indeed seem superfluous. Yet Baha'is report "a much stronger response from the public during recent years than ever before." Perhaps Ferguson was right when he stated that "no cult bears a gospel better suited to the temper of our times than the Bahai."[1]

A movement which claims something over one million aherents "in nearly every country of the world" is worth studying. Dr. Atkins was right in observing that there is among all the cults "nothing more curious than that the old controversy as to the true successor of Mohammed the prophet should at last have issued in a universal religion with a temple of unity on the shores of Lake Michigan."

History

Baha'ism is of Persian Mohammedan origin, tracing its beginning to the Mohammedan belief "that the last true successor of Mohammed who disappeared in the tenth century never died, but is still living in a mysterious city, surrounded by a band of faithful disciples and 'that at the end of time he will isue forth and fill the earth with justice after it has been filled with iniquity.'" This hidden successor is said to have revealed himself from time to time through those to whom he has made known his will, and

---

1. *The Confusion of Tongues*, p. 231.

who are known as *Babs* or *gates,* "the gate, that is, whereby communication was reopened between the hidden one
and his faithful followers."

The last one of these Babs was a young Persian merchant,
named Mirza 'Ali Muhammed who took the title of Bab in
1844 and who "had much the same relation to Baha'u'llah
as John the Baptist had to Christ." The Bab's career was
short-lived; he died a martyr's death at the hand of Persian
Mohammedans at the age of thirty years, A.D. 1850. He had
constantly pointed to a divine prophet who was shortly to
succeed him. Before his death he sent his signet rings and
writings to one of his friends and foremost supporters, one
Mirza Husayn 'Ali, his senior by two years. The two had
never met, and were not related. 'Ali at first continued the
teachings of the Bab; but soon afterwards announced himself as the divine manifestation predicted by him. He is
known as *Baha'-u'llah,* that is, *Glory of God.* The followers
of the cult then changed their name from Babs to Bahais
and proceeded to ascribe to Baha'u'llah divine honor and
worship. Like the Bab, Baha'u'llah and his disciples suffered
much from persecution and exile, which, of course, only
proved once more that "the blood of the martyrs is the seed
of the church."[2]

Baha'u'llah passed away in May, 1892, at the age of seventy-five, after forty years of hardship, imprisonment, and
exile, in his villa of Behje near Akka (Palestine, "the Holy
Land"). He was succeeded by his son Abbas Effendi, born
in Teheran, Persia, May 23, 1844, "on the very day upon
which the Bab made his declaration to the disciples in
Shiraz." Abbas, who had shared his father's hardships as
well as his greater ease in his declining years, is known

---

2. The matter is so stated in J. E. Esslemont, *Baha'u'llah and His
Message;* also in S. G. Wilson, *Baha'ism and Its Claims,* p. 22. W. E.
Miller, however, identifies Baha'u'llah with Baha, half-brother to
Mirza Yahya, which latter reigned undisputed from 1852-1863, when
Baha gained the ascendency. In his earlier work Miller states that
"the more the Baha'i doctrine spreads . . . the more the true history
and nature of the original Babi Movement is obscured and distorted."
Baha'ism: Its Origin, History and Teachings, p. 90.

among Bahais as *'Abdu'l-Baha,* that is, *The Servant of God.*
He became "the authoritative interpreter" of the teachings
of "The Master," Baha'u'llah. He, too, has known adversi-
ties and persecutions, although not as severe or numerous
as those of his predecessors in the Cause. In 1912 he visited
the United States, where the first disciples were won in
Chicago and where the Cause has since grown more rapidly
than in any other country except Persia. 'Abdu'l-Baha died
on November 28, 1921, aged seventy-seven years. The leadership of the movement, after some wranglings, fell to his
eldest grandson, Shoghi Effendi, the head of a Committee
of Nineteen, and known by the title of *Guardian of the
Cause.*

Teaching

Baha'ism is the unifying cult *par excellence.* "It has," in
the words of Mrs. Chandler, "accepted all the religions of
the world, found them fundamentally and essentially alike,
and reveres equally as divine all nine of the prophets. So
it may appeal equally to Hindus, Moslems, Christians, and
Jews; it admits the divinity of the prophet or Messiah of
each. It does not even claim any greater divinity for its
own particular prophet, Baha'u'llah. It merely claims that
the Great Beauty of Blessed Perfection, coming later, has
brought the latest message from the Divine Source to the
peoples of the world, and that the message doesn't differ
fundamentally, or in essence, from the message of his prede-
cessor, but is, one might say, brought up to date in dealing
with certain specific matters that didn't concern the people
whom Christ or Mohammed addressed."

In the words of another Baha'i writer, "Jesus could not
speak of international problems; his people did not know
of the existence of Japan." A new revelation for our modern day must therefore complete that brought by Jesus.
When Jesus warned to "watch and pray" for the coming
of the Lord He meant, "Receive Baha'u'llah." This prophet,
therefore, referred to Jesus as "the Son of God," or "a

Manifestation of God," but claimed to be, himself, "a later Manifestation."

In accordance with these fundamental ideas, and to attain to their unifying ideal, Baha'is present the following "principles" for which they strive:

"The Oneness of God and Oneness of Religion;

The Oneness of Mankind;

Independent Search After Truth;

All Prejudices must be Abandoned (to wit, religious, color, national, class, sexual, and personal prejudices) ;

International Peace;

International Auxiliary Language;

Education for All;

Equality for the Sexes;

Abolition of Industrial Slavery (Abolition of Wealth and Poverty) ;

Personal Holiness (Work in the Spirit of Service is Worship)."

Baha'ism claims that unity and brotherhood are the only important things and not doctrine. "Love" is the ever-recurring word in its literature. But its conception of love is neither correct, nor consistently carried out. In the first place Baha'ism itself proves that "love" without certain definite teachings is untenable. When in New York in 1912, 'Abdu'l-Baha was approached by two Baha'is who, arguing a point of Baha'i teaching, asked him to decide who was right. The answer of 'Abdu'l-Baha was: "Neither is right. To be a Baha'i there must never be any discord; all must agree. Unity is the aim." And yet this same system now insists "that nothing whatever should be given to the public by any individual among the friends, unless fully considered and approved by the Spiritual Assembly in his locality."[3] The implication is that it is not safe to let individuals air their views on Baha'i teaching except after official approval of their views. The *Star of the West* is the official organ of the movement in America. And, in the

---

3. Shoghi Effendi in a letter addressed from Haifa, March 12, 1922, to "Dear Fellow-Workers in the Cause of Baha'u'llah."

next place, if a member of the Baha'is leaves the movement
because of changed views, he — or, generally *she*, for this
is a ladies' cult like Christian Science — has good reason
to hide as far as possible out of reach of the leaders of this
loving cult.   The last statement can, in the nature of the
case, not be backed up by references; but the author vouches
for its truth.   There is no salvation for apostate Baha'is
according to the system.

The Wilmette Temple

One would think that the frightfully outlandish names
in use among Baha'is tend to make the movement unpopu-
lar.   The Baha'is, however, do not shrink from pointing to
their great temple as *Mashriqu'l-Adhkar*.[4] And with this
temple they conjure.   It has cost more money and time to
complete this temple than seems to have been originally expected, and the dream of building similar structures in
every State of the Union has, for the time being at least,
been abandoned.

The temple at Wilmette, near Chicago, embodies in visible form many of the ideals of the cult, and is its chief
means of propaganda.   In an illustrated pamphlet on "The
Baha'i House of Worship, An Institution of the World Order of Baha'u'llah," Genevieve L. Coy informs us that, as
musicians, artists, poets receive their inspiration from another realm, so the late Louis Bourgeois, architect of the
Temple, "through all his years of labor was ever conscious
that Baha'u'llah was the creator of this building to be erected to his glory. . . . When the man-made creeds are stripped
away from all the religions we find nothing left but harmony.   Today, however, religion is so entangled in the su-
perstitions and hypotheses of men that it must needs be
stated in a new form to be once again pure and undefiled.
Likewise in architecture those fundamental structural lines
which originated in the faith of all religions are the same,

---

4. Also spelled Mashrak - ul - Azkar, and meaning "The Dawning-
place of Praises."

but so covered over are they with the decorations picturing creed upon creed and superstition upon superstition that we must needs lay them aside and create a new form or ornamentation. Into this new design, then, of the Temple, is woven, in symbolic form, the great Baha'i teaching of unity — the unity of all religions and of mankind. There are combinations of mathematical lines, symbolizing those of the universe, and in their intricate merging of circle into circle, of circle within circle, we visualize the merging of all the religions into one."

We shall not weary the reader with a detailed account of the cost ($895,000 has been spent, and the end is not yet). "When the *Mashriqu'l-Adhkar* at Wilmette is completed it will include a hospital and dispensary, a school for orphan children, a hospice, and a college for higher scientific education. In these institutions the principle of the oneness of mankind will be put into concrete practice. Their services will be dispensed irrespective of color, race, or nationality." The scientific college, we are told, is included because "religion and science are the two wings upon which man's intelligence can soar into the heights, with which the human soul can progress."

There are nine entrances into the "nonagon Temple," each one representing one of Nine Great Religions, and all together leading into the inner sanctuary of Truth. From the headquarters of the "National Spiritual Assembly of Baha'is of the U.S. and Canada" we are also informed that "when the interior decoration is completed, the central hall of the Wilmette Temple will be open for daily prayer and meditation and for meetings consisting only of reading from the words of Baha'u'llah and 'Abdu'l-Baha."

The work on the great temple appears to proceed but slowly. In a letter dated February 21, 1942, Mr. Horace Halley, secretary of the National Spiritual Assembly of the Baha'is, of Wilmette, Illinois, informs me thus: "Since the pamphlet by Genevieve L. Coy was published, the work of external decoration has been carried forward to a point very near completion. The enclosed photograph, taken

December 18, shows the progress on the main story, which is now nearly completed, except for two of the nine sides. We hope that this work can be done before the fall of 1942 and at the same time construct the circular steps which are to surround the building.

"When this construction work is finished, the exterior of the building will be complete, but the work of the interior is still to be done. We do not plan any immediate work on the interior, but assume that after a few years a definite scheme of interior decoration and arrangement will be undertaken."

Compare with this slow financial sacrifice for the movement's chief enterprise the remark of W. M. Miller: "It is startling to read in the census statistics as given by the Bahais of America that whereas the property of the Bahai Temple in Chicago is worth more than a million dollars, the amount given in 1936 by the members of the Cause to charity was only $281. Even if this figure is incorrect, we wish that the Bahais would show their 'love' more in deed than in word, if they would win our confidence. How much more convincing a great medical mission in India or Tibet than a million-dollar Temple in Chicago, beautiful as the Mashriq-ul-Azkar may be!"

To this may be added that *The Baha'i Centenary*, 1844-1944, published in 1944 by the Baha'i Publishing Co., Wilmette, Illinois, states that the superstructure was finished in 1931 and the exterior ornamentation was completed between 1932-1943. From the same source we learn that four Baha'i schools have been established in the United States, some of which, judging from the photographs, are quite elaborate. Of the Temple this source states: "Records of daily visitors kept since July 1, 1932 show that the total number who went through the building with Baha'i guides up to October 1, 1943, was 164,360. To deal with this throng of inquirers a body of Temple guides has been rendering service, its members prepared by a special course of instructions based upon long experience with the types of question asked and the information desired."

The year 1953 marked a Holy Year for Baha'is, it being the one hundredth anniversary of the call of the founder Baha'u'llah, to his mission. Pioneers went as far north as Yellowknife, Alberta, Whitehorse, Baker Lake and Arctic Bay. This was the opening of a ten-year crusade by Ruhiyyih Khanum, the former Mary Maxwell of Montreal, and the wife of Shoghi Effendi, the present guardian and international head of the faith. Baha'is consider it encouraging that during these one hundred years Baha'ism from its native land, Iran, has spread to 124 countries. "Its followers are of diversified cultures, races and nations. Its teachings are based upon the principles of the oneness of mankind, the unity of religions, and justice without principles."

Appraisal

It is evident that a movement which so strongly stresses the unity of all religious forces in the world should be somewhat vague and general. There are not many points of Christian doctrine upon which the cult teaches. It rather ignores them one and all. Perhaps it is exactly here that we should start.

1. It should be clear that Baha'ism has some very fine points which, from the Christian standpoint, make it all the more dangerous *as a religion*. The last three words are underscored with a purpose. Who would not praise it in the Baha'is when they advocate world peace? Who has not grasped by this time the terribleness of a universal war fought with modern means of wholesale destruction, and in the interest of international investments of large capital? Who does not realize that modern warfare comes as close to hell as anything on earth can well come? Or, who does not realize that it is more than a noble gesture for a white man from the South (conceivably) to lay a sick negro child in the bed next to his own in the same ward, and tend to both with equal tenderness? For all that, there are great gifts of what Calvin called God's common grace. But all such nobility of character does not atone for sin. It

is not religion.   Least of all is it a religion superior to
Christianity.

2. With its plainly implied pantheism Baha'ism is one
more example of what Dr. Abraham Kuyper called many
years ago "the irresistible tendency of our age to change
along every line the God-man into the Man-god."   As pantheism, Baha'ism stands condemned from the standpoint
of Christianity.   Not man's reaching up to ever higher
manifestations of the divine, but the transcendent God de-
scending to man in divine revelation, is the way out of
human ills.

3. Baha'ism has much in common with Theosophy.   Both
emphasize the idea that one more divine spokesman must
add to Jesus' words.   But, whereas Theosophists are looking for this man to appear since Krishnamurti stepped down
from "the throne that was Christ's" Baha'is assert that this
man has appeared in Baha'u'llah.

With Theosophists the Baha'is also agree that all religions are one.   We remember Annie Besant's words, "Blended together they give the whiteness of truth, blended together they give a mighty chord of perfection."   This is due, of
course, to their common pantheism.

4. Baha'ism has much in common with Spiritism and
Free Masonry.

Of Spiritism Sir Arthur Conan Doyle wrote, "To me it *is*
religion — the very essence of it."   He called it "the great
unifying force, the one probable thing connected with every
religion, Christian or non-Christian, forming the common
solid basis upon which each raises if it must needs raise,
that separate system which appeals to the varied types of
mind."   How greatly like Baha'ism that sounds!

The discussion of Free Masonry in a separate chapter
has been omitted from this volume.   It had been inserted in
Our Birthright and the Mess of Meat.[5]   The writer realizes

---

5. The first edition of the present work.   An up-to-date appraisal
of Lodgism may be found in *A Handbook of Organizations* by Theodore Graebner (St. Louis: Concordia Publishing House, 1948).

that Free Masonry is not a cult like the other isms here
discussed. To a great many Free Masons the lodge is the
badge of sociability, mutual helpfulness. They laugh at
the idea that the Masonic lodge or the Independent Order
of Odd Fellows should be considered a competitor, let alone
a substitute, for the Christian religion.

Nevertheless, many leaders of the Masonic movement, the
officially recommended literature of the movement, its signs
and emblems which are all borrowed from oriental pagan
religions, all these and other things show Free Masonry
to be such that Dr. Torrey was right in saying, "A man
can be a Christian and a Free Mason, but he cannot be an
intelligent Christian and an intelligent Mason at the same
time."

Without wanting to give offense, therefore, to Christian
Masons we would ask of them to study such works as *An
Encyclopedia of Freemasonry and its Kindred Sciences*,
1914; *Lexicon of Freemasonry; Masonic Ritualist;* all by
Albert G. Mackey, M.D. 33. *Freemasonry and the Ancient
Gods* by J. S. M. Ward, 1926; *New Odd-Fellows' Manual,*
by Rev. A. B. Grosh, 1882. We would ask Freemasons to
consider why there is a *Co-masonic Order* in the Theosophical Society. We would ask why the assertion that all religions are one, should be tolerated in Free Masonry, but
condemned in Theosophy and Baha'ism. Said Baha'u'llah
in his "Last Will and Testament":

"O ye people of the world! The religion of God is for the
sake of love and union; make it not the cause of enmity and
conflict . . . The hope is cherished that the people of Baha
shall ever turn to the Blessed Word: LO: ALL ARE OF
GOD:—"

Said the Supreme Council of the 33d Degree, F.A.A.M.,
Southern Jurisdiction of the U.S. in 1874, "Freemasonry
is a worship, but one in which all civilized men can unite;
for it does not undertake to explain or dogmatically to settle

those great mysteries that are above the feeble comprehension of our human intellect."⁶

And Mackey wrote, "If Free Masonry were simply a
Christian institution, the Jew and the Moslem, the Brah-
man and the Buddhist, could not conscientiously partake of
its illumination. But its universality is its boast. In its
language citizens of every nation may converse; at its altar
men of all religions may kneel; to its creed disciples of every
faith may subscribe."⁷

5. Whereas Baha'is claim for their religion a later emphasis upon the same truth taught also, among others, by
Christianity, we maintain that it is, at least in its manifestation in Christian lands, a sad imitation of the Christian
religion. Baha'u'llah as final manifestation of God in the
flesh we believe to be an imitation of the incarnation as seen
in Jesus Christ; Baha'i "inspired tablets" we consider fake
scriptures. Their "spiritual baptism," "Holy Land," "Be-
atitudes," "Unity Feast" (for the Lord's Supper), their
imitation Pentecost (a surprising peace is said to fill the
souls of those who repeat ninety-five times daily the words
Alla hu Abha)— these would-be Christian touches, apparently calculated to catch Christians, do not increase our
respect for Baha'ism.

Editorially, the *Christian Century* of September 25, 1946,
informs us that the Baha'is have decided to begin to advertise their cause in a twofold manner: for the rank and
file, through *Newsweek* and similar periodicals, while others
will be reached through trade journals of the publishing
and broadcasting industries. This is interesting, first, because we are now prepared to look for a more open method
of propaganda by this cult that teaches the unity of any
and all religions. Secondly, however, we get an interesting

---

6. *Morals and Dogmas of the Ancient and Accepted Scottish Rite of
Freemasons.* Prepared for the Supreme Council of the 33rd Degree
for the Southern Jurisdiction of the U. S. and published by its
authority, New York, 1874, p. 526.

7. *An Encyclopedia of Freemasonry and Its Kindred Sciences.*
Subtitle: *Christianization of Freemasonry.* Two volumes. (New York
and London: the Masonic History Co., 1914).

glimpse of the mentality of Modernism, when we see the
editor of Chicago's modernist journal of religion go so far
in his vehement antagonism against "denominationalism"
as to write: "The plan is all right. *The Baha'is have something to sell* . . . It is interesting, and may be helpfully sug-
gestive to other religious bodies, to see how *this worthy
group,* which had its origins among the Mohammendans of
Persia about a century ago, makes use of the most modern
techniques for making friends and influencing people."
(Italics mine).

Baha'ism and Scripture

God

"'Further than this [Baha'u'llah] man has no other
point for concentration. He is God."[8]

Sin

"The only difference between members of the human
family is that of degree. Some are like children who are
ignorant and must be educated until they arrive at matu-
rity. Some are like the sick and must be treated with
tenderness and care. None are bad or evil. We must not
feel repelled by these poor children. We must treat them
with great kindness, teaching the ignorant and tenderly
nursing the sick."

"Evil is imperfection. Sin is the state of man in the
world of the baser nature, for in nature exist defects such
as injustice, tyranny, hatred, hostility, strife: these are
characteristics of the lower plane of nature. These are the
sins of the world, the fruits of the tree from which Adam
did eat. Through education we must free ourselves from
these imperfections."—'ABDU'L-BAHA.[9]

Jesus the Only Name

"Christ was the Prophet of the Christians, Moses of the
Jews — why should not the followers of each prophet rec-

---

8. *The Star of the West* (official organ of the movement in America), Feb. 7, 1914.
9. *The Wisdom of 'Abdu'l-Baha,* pp. 128, 155.

ognize and honor the other prophets also? If men could only learn the lesson of mutual tolerance, understanding, and brotherly love, the Unity of the world would soon be an established fact."—'ABDU'L-BAHA.[10]

"The revelation of Jesus was for His own dispensation —that of 'the Son.' Now it is no longer the point of guidance to the world. We are in total darkness if we are refusing the revelation of the present dispensation. Bahais must be severed from all and everything that is past — things both good and bad — everything. Now all is changed. All the teachings of the past are past. 'Abdu'l-Baha is now supplying all the world."—C. M. REMEY.[11]

Faith Versus Reason

"There are two kinds of light. There is the visible light of the sun by whose aid we can discern the beauties of the world around us—without this we could see nothing.

"Nevertheless, though it is the function of this light to make things visible to us, it cannot give us the *power* to see them or to understand what their various charms may be, for this light has no intelligence, no consciousness. It is the light of the *intellect* which gives us knowledge and understanding, and without this light the physical eyes would be useless.

"This light of the intellect is the highest light that exists, for it is born of the *Light Divine.*

"The light of the intellect enables us to understand and realize all that exists, but it is only the Divine Light that can give us sight for the invisible things, and which enables us to see Truths that will only be visible to the world thousands of years hence."—'ABDU'L-BAHA.[12]

"We must not accept traditional dogmas that are contrary to reason, nor pretend to believe doctrines which we

10. *Ibid.*, p. 43.
11. *Star of the West*, Dec. 31, 1913.
12. *Op. cit.*, p. 62.

cannot understand. To do so is superstition and not true religion."—J. E. ESSLEMONT.[13]

Sufferings of Christ

"Why did Christ Jesus suffer the fearful death on the Cross? Why did Mohammed bear persecutions? Why did the Bab make the supreme sacrifice and why did Baha'u'llah pass the years of his life in prison?

"Why should all this suffering have been, if not to prove the everlasting life of the Spirit?

"Christ suffered, He accepted all His trials because of the immortality of His spirit. If a man reflects he will understand the spiritual significance of the law of progress; how all moves from the inferior to the superior degree."— 'ABDU'L-BAHA.[14]

We hold that Baha'ism stands condemned by the following statements of Scripture:

Matthew 24:24, 26: "For there shall arise false Christs, and false prophets, and shall show great signs and wonders; so as to lead astray, if possible, even the elect . . . If therefore they shall say unto you, Behold, he is in the wilderness; go not forth: Behold, he is in the inner chambers; believe it not."

Colossians 1:19: "For it was the good pleasure of the Father that in him should all the fulness dwell; and through him to reconcile all things unto himself, having made peace through the blood of his cross; through him, I say, whether things upon the earth, or things in the heavens."[15]

---

13. *Baha'u'llah and His Message*, p. 11.
14. *Op. cit.*, p. 85.
15. We have purposely presented Baha'ism as it reveals itself in its Western cloak. It will be noted that even this is, more or less openly, antichristian. And this is an adaptation of Persian Baha'ism for consumption in the West. A close student and adherent spoke of "Persian Baha'ism and not that American fantasy which bears its name." The original Baha'ism is far more hateful toward its opponents; it advocates bigamy rather than equality of sexes; its literature is replete with historical and religious falsehoods. For that matter, the statement that the Bab pointed to an early successor of his, is itself untrue, although now believed by Baha'ists both in the East and the West. In Persia the movement is now boosted with the legend that half America is Bahai. Cf. the well documented works by S. G. Wilson and W. Miller, previously cited.

Pointers

1. Why is Baha'ism suited to our times?

2. What is the relation between Bab, Baha'u'llah, 'Abdu'l-Baha, Shoghi Effendi?

3. Can you mention some cardinal teachings of this system?

4. Is Baha'ism as tolerant as it pretends to be?

5. Why have Baha'is made but little financial sacrifice for their views?

6. What do you think of the stand of the Christian Reformed and other churches who maintain that lodge membership and church membership are inconsistent and incompatible?

8

MORMONISM

We are taking quite a leap. We are leaving the isms which have been more or less directly influenced from the East. We are bidding farewell to the out-and-out pantheistic cults (although there are many more). And we are turning to isms of a simon-pure American make. Among these Mormonism, Seventh-Day Adventism, and Russellism are perhaps the most persistent propagandists; hence we intend to devote considerable attention to these three.

Mormonism is a marvelously composite faith. It has developed over a period of time, and as it went along it took over some of the most divergent elements from other sects and groups. They brewed, to speak with Mr. Ferguson, a synthetic religion in Utah.

A Charming People

There is an imposing story of Mormonism's accomplishments that makes not only good reading, but cannot fail to arouse admiration. It is the story of how, all before their first centennial, the Mormons have not only encircled the globe, with their missionaries donating a year or two of their youthful lives, but also of how the later Mormons have succeeded in blotting out the dark record of early Morman antisocial doings in Illinois and Missouri. "These amazing Mormons" have indeed come near to approaching the ideal state. Their co-operatives in matters socio-religious have yielded astonishing fruit. In war or depression, no Mormon becomes a burden upon the state and no help from the national capital is accepted. By means of a strictly enforced sense of stewardship, which does not only involve money but also physical and mental faculties, an unemployed man may hold his head as high as the captain of industry; for does not his donated labor fill the warehouses and the granaries of "Zion" from which in time of distress all will receive the just rewards of their former labors? Enormous business enterprises such as the U and I (Utah and Idaho) sugar industry with its sugarbeet fields and refineries throughout western states are all under the control of the Church's hierarchy. For the Church, like the business organization that it really is, is headed by a "President" with a staff of numerous lesser officials with high-sounding titles, who not only watch over the moral but also over the business conduct of the citizen-members.

A high level of family life is maintained which is, compared with the rest of the nation, remarkably free of juvenile and adult delinquency. Not only religious exercises in the strict sense of the word, beginning with the celebrated first "testimony" of small youngsters in Sunday Schools, but also dances and other recreational enterprises are sanctioned with a bishop's prayer and made to redound to the increase of the Church of Latter-Day Saints. Mormons have indeed the right to ask proudly, "Can you point me to a better group of citizens, one that has resulted in greater willingness to lend support to education and removal of poverty and disgrace?" And Fundamentalists whose "uneasy conscience" may have occasion to rebuke them for letting Satan have his way with the world, and Calvinists who withdraw from all cooperation with other Christians because "we must be separate," may well stop to see the bold attack that is launched under their noses by such groups as Mormons and Jehovah's Witnesses, who go into all corners of the world to propagate without ever a fear that they might "lose their distinctiveness."

Only a vigilant and agressive Christianity, such as Abraham Kuyper endeavored half a century ago to make victorious in "brave little Holland," one that has the promise of the life that now is and of the life that is to come, can successfully oppose the mushroom growth of these movements. And such a Christianity is all the more necessary today since Unitarianism-Modernism has so misplaced the emphasis as to make the average man think that the best Christianity is that society which, regardless of religious doctrine, improves the lot of man upon the earth and maintains a high standard of economic and personal ethics.

Since, however, Christianity is supposed to be a *salt* retarding corruption, a *leaven* that permeates, and a *light* that shines in darkness, and since only the Christ according to the Scriptures is the Light of the World, Mormonism must stand condemned. It is not only guilty of many crimes in its earlier history, but, for all its sociological improvements, it is guilty of the two cardinal sins of our time: first, it identifies the kingdom of God with a here-and-now social utopia; and secondly, it fosters the essentially pagan idea that salvation is by works rather than of grace.

History

The Mormon "prophet" Joseph Smith, Jr., was born on December 23, 1805, in Sharon, Vermont. He was reared in ignorance, poverty and superstition. Moreover, he was indolent in his youth. However, quite in keeping with the superstitious atmosphere in which he breathed he claimed to have visions and divine revelations as early as 1820 and 1823. In the latter year the angel Moroni revealed to him the spot where golden plates lay buried containing the history of ancient America in "reformed-Egyptian *caractors.*" Smith undoubtedly meant *characters,* but, unlike Mother Eddy, he had never known enough grammar for it to be "eclipsed" by a divine revelation; hence he made occasional grammatical errors.

In 1830 "Joe," as he was known, organized the "Church of Jesus Christ of Latter-Day Saints" at Fayette, New York. This he accomplished after having convinced a few friends that his "translation" of the Golden Plates — afterward duly returned into the hands of the angel Moroni — had been done, not as was maliciously slandered, with the aid of "a peepstone in a hat," but with the assistance of the proper "Urim and Thummim" which the obliging angel had provided. The plates are stated to have been hidden in the earth from the year 420 of our era until September 22, 1823, when "Joe Smith" discovered them in the "Hill Cumorah"; and yet the Book of Mormon, being a faithful rendering of the said plates, gives extensive quotations from the Bible in —: the King James Version! (1611) It contains modern phrases and ideas that could not have been known to its supposed author in 420 A. D. It puts the words of Jesus (though often twisted) into the mouths of men alleged to have lived centuries before Christ. It was not only written in a poor imitation of Biblical style; it also undermines the Bible by declaring it *insufficient,* by *adding to and changing many Biblical passages,* "by divine revelation." For such reasons as these it could hardly have been revealed by an angel. Its story of the ancient inhabitants of America, the supposed ancestors of the "Latter-Day Saints," contains twelve historical errors.

The Book of Mormon is officially recognized by both branches of Mormonism as of equal authority with the Bible, and practically receives honor far beyond the Bible. But there is an abundance of incontestable evidence that the origin of the Book of Mormon must be sought in Solomon Spaulding's unpublished and stolen novel, *The Manuscript Found.* The Mormons try to obliterate this evidence by referring to another manuscript, *The Manuscript Story,* by the same Spaulding; they prove that the Book of Mormon is not a copy of the latter manuscript. The unknowing are thus convinced that Joseph Smith did not copy from "*the* Spaulding manuscript"; but the real argument, that the "Golden Bible" is the work of copying and embellishing by Rigdon and Smith, remains unanswered.

In June, 1831, a "revelation" commanded the Saints to settle in Missouri, the "land of Zion." Kirtland, Ohio, and Zion, Missouri, now became headquarters of the movement. But for some pagan reason or other the "Gentile" neighbors did not trust the Mormons, and accused them of various crimes. The Saints did not hesitate to denounce the Gentiles as "enemies of the Lord." When the "Safety Bank" at Kirtland, a Mormon enterprise, failed in 1838, Smith and his friend, Sidney Rigdon, fled to Missouri. From Missouri they were driven away by order of Governor Boggs in 1839.

Finding a welcome in Illinois, they erected the city "Nauvoo." Here our prophet made his biggest display, announcing himself, among other feats, candidate for the presidency of the United States. Accused of gross immorality, counterfeiting, sheltering criminals in the act of fleeing from justice, and other misdeeds, Smith was arrested, but a mob stormed the jail and shot to death both prophet Joseph and his brother Hyrum.

This was rather unfortunate for the anti-Mormon cause, since the prophet now became a martyr. When his indictment was in sight and the movement might have died a natural death, hotheaded men with a just grievance killed their cause by immortalizing their opponent and giving his followers a supposed occasion for seeking revenge upon the wicked inhabitants of Gentile America and their descendants.

Brigham Young came from England, where he had been proselytizing, and by the force of his personality put several rivals out of commission. He become the recognized leader of the large majority of Mormons. Young was a strong man. With only eleven days of formal schooling he went far in this world and became a statesman and leader of no mean proportions. With the simple faith of an uneducated mind Young believed in Joseph Smith, and remained true to the "prophet" all his life.

Brigham Young led the thousands of disciples amid untold sufferings until, in July 1847, they reached Utah, which was then unoccupied Mexican territory. Young did not know himself whither the long trek was. Now and then he would say, "I will know the place when I see it." When the outposts of the travelers reached Salt Lake, he announced his one and only "revelation," to wit, the Lord had revealed

to him that here would be the place where the Saints would
be free from Gentile American persecution.

The Mormons under Young's leadership became excellent
pioneers.   For many years they had things entirely their
own way.   The incident of the sea gulls that ate the grasshoppers which had settled upon their first crop, convinced
them that the Lord was with them and approved their new
venture.   Hard pioneering conditions, frugal habits, tithing
in the interest of their Church, made the early Mormons
and their Church rich.   Soon missionaries were sent to England and other European countries to fetch converts, especially women.   Young, who had twenty-five wives, ruled
with an iron hand in the colony.   As to his rule in the Bee-
hive and Lion's House, the opinions of his runaway wife,
Ann Eliza, and his daughter, Susan, differ somewhat.

When in 1849, at the close of the Mexican War, Utah be-
became American territory, the Mormons refused to be
ruled from Washington.   Had they not fled from the U.S.
because of "persecution"?   There followed a long history of
diplomatic and other blunders on both sides, until finally
Young, the first governor of the State of Utah, had to admit another governor.   Young, however, remained the First
President of the Church.   He was assisted by twelve apostles.

Notorious is the incident of the Mountain Meadow Massacre.   In 1857 an entire group of immigrants on their way
from Arkansas to California (during the gold rush) was
murdered in Utah.   For this the Mormon John D. Lee was
executed by the U. S. government in 1877.[1]

Brigham Young lived to the age of 76 and died in 1877.
After the United States obtained greater influence, the Mormons became known as good pioneers, although also as
political intriguers.   They continued to erect costly temples.
Among these is the great ninth, or Mesa temple in Arizona,

---

1. *The Mountain Meadows Massacre* by Juanita Brooks (Palo
Alto: Stanford University Press, 1950). The writer is a Mormon, who
admits that the murder of the unarmed men by the armed Mormons
who were supposed to protect them against the Indians, was a Mormon crime which she attributes to mob hysteria.

built in 1927. Here visitors from every State are shown
mural paintings portraying the history of Mormonism as
twisted by the Mormons. In 1937 two more temples, at Los
Angeles and Idaho Falls, were on the program of the
Church at a total cost of $2,600,000. On the hill Cumorah
in New York, a tall monument now convinces large numbers of people of the truth of the Moroni Urim and Thummim legend.

In 1956 Utah announced the opening of "one of the biggest tourist attractions in California," to wit, their tenth
temple, the Los Angeles Temple of the Church of Jesus
Christ of Latter-Day Saints, erected at a cost of six million dollars, covering twenty-five acres, at a height of 257
feet, topped by a golden statue of the Angel Moroni. Besides an assembly room (capacity 2,600), a marriage "sealing" room, a room for the instruction of brides, a huge bap-
tismal font, the second floor of the Temple contains "the
Five Rooms" — "a series of class rooms explaining the purpose of life, where we come from, what we are doing, where
we are going." These rooms are called successively the
Creation Room — oval-shaped, with murals of the sun and
moon. No. 2 is the Garden of Eden," "where," reads a sign,
"Adam and Eve made their great decision." Next is the
World Room, with murals inspired by Death Valley, which
"represents the lone and dreary world, the testing ground."
No. 4 is the Terrestrial Room, "fourth stage on the path to
celestial glory, the step before entering the Celestial Kingdom." One of its walls opens onto the fifth room decorated
as a luxurious sitting room, with well-upholstered chairs
and settees, delicate murals and elaborate chandeliers. This
represents the Celestial Kingdom itself, "where exalted
man may dwell in the presence of God."

The other nine temples of the Utah Mormons are in Lo-
gan, Utah; Cardston, Alberta; St. George, Utah; Manti,
Utah; Mesa, Arizona; Honolulu; Salt Lake City; Idaho
Falls; Bern, Switzerland. In addition to the temples, the
most extensive building program in Mormon history is go-

ing on of "stakes," centers of Mormon activity in many college towns, on or nearby the campuses.[2]

At the death of George Albert Smith, distant relative of Joseph and eighth "prophet, seer and revelator," in April, 1951, the Council of Twelve Apostles chose as his successor David O. McKay, who thus began his administration at the age of 77. He has paid less attention to business than did some of his predecessors, and has emphasized making converts to the Mormon faith.

In 1948 the writer was treated to a lecture given at the end of a conducted tour through the Utah temple grounds. In this lecture the tremendous organization of the Mormon Church in the direction of social security was duly stressed. The lady who spoke said, "Not only do I and many others freely donate our time to conduct these tours; I have at the present two sons who are on a one-year missionary tour. For all Mormon young men are required to donate from one to two years of their time going forth preaching the gospel at no other pay than their room and board. These are supported as much as possible by parents and other relatives. In addition to that we live on two meals one Sunday a month, have a meatless day once a month, and the amount so saved is given to the church for distribution among the poor." This custom was begun during the great depression in the nineteen-thirties. The unemployed donated their time, working in charity houses where surplus grain and other staples are taken care of. For the work done these received their "keep"; and thus the central clearing house in Salt Lake City has provided, all by means of mutual aid and self-help, for all members of the Church, so as to cast no one at any time on public relief.

These and other laudable works of the Mormons are described in a booklet published by the Deseret Book Company in Salt Lake City, *These Amazing Mormons* by Joseph H. Weston.

---

2. *Life* magazine, Jan. 16, 1956.

Perhaps these means toward social security, together with the enormous zeal of six thousand Mormon "missionaries" touring the continent, are largely responsible for the growth of the Utah Mormons from 215,796 in 1906 to 870,346 in 1946. For almost any system that stresses, as does Mormonism, "temporal salvation" as well as "spiritual salvation," is bound to receive a hearing in these days when people ask for material results rather than for doctrinal foundation.[3]

The Two Factions

At the death of Joseph Smith, Jr., the Prophet, the Mormons broke up into numerous groups. Brigham Young succeeded in combining most of these under his leadership, with the exception of a small minority which, as "The Reorganized Church of Latter-Day Saints," or Josephites, settled in Missouri. They chose the leadership of a son of Joseph Smith. The re-organized group felt the restraint put upon them by their Christian environment in the East to the extent of their repudiating polygamy altogether. They have since put forth brave efforts to fasten the guilt of po-

---

3. Canada has 25,000 Mormons, 15,000 in small towns of southern Alberta, the rest scattered throughout Canada. A $1,000,000 temple is in Cardston (that and the one in Laie, Hawaii, being the only two outside continental U.S.A.), headquarters for the Alberta Stake (diocese) with 6,100 members. There are two other Canadian stakes, Taylor with 3,800 and Lethbridge with 5,000 members. Cardston was founded by Charles Ora Card, who had three wives and trekked into Canada in 1886, four years before plural marriage was abandoned, because U. S. marshals were after him. —*MacLean's Magazine*, Jan. 15, 1951.

The Mormon Church claims 12,000 members in New Zealand, as of Dec., 1951. It has launched a $2.8 million building program. "Plans envision a coeducational agricultural boarding school in the north island, completion of a large church and administration center in Auckland, and extension of schools and church halls in other areas. To secure materials for their projects, the Mormons have bought a timber mill and erected a plant which is turning out 3,000 concrete blocks a day. Most of the converts to Mormonism in the commonwealth are Maoris." —*The Christian Century*, Jan. 9, 1952.

The Utah Branch in April, 1953, reported at their 123rd annual conference, held in Salt Lake City, a membership of 1,189,053, at their 125th annual conference (Jan. 1, 1955), 1,302,240 members — an increase of 55,878 in one year, with 10,814 missionaries.

lygamy onto the sister-body which, under Young, went
to Utah. At that time Utah was unoccupied Mexican territory, and the system could be practiced to the heart's content. But the facts are overwhelmingly against their contention. Not only did Smith undoubtedly write the *Revelation on Celestial Marriage,* but, of Joseph's followers,
twenty thousand went with polygamous Young over against
one thousand who went with the Josephites. In fact, polygamy was taught and practiced by all the original twelve
Mormon apostles and by at least six factions of the Church
as it became disrupted at Smith's death. Moreover, prominent leaders of the early Josephites have admitted the Josephite origin of the doctrine, whereas the denials by later
Josephites prove to be flimsy upon closer scrutiny. They
also "are often rather vague and uncertain in fixing the
responsibility for polygamy and the time when it was introduced into the church." Fawn M. Brodie lists forty-
eight wives of Joseph Smith himself.[4]

There are, then, certain differences between the teachings
of the Brighamites and those of the Josephites. These center chiefly around prophetic succession and polygamy.

1. The Josephites claim that the President of the
Church must be "of the seed of Joseph Smith." Charles A.
Shook has wittily remarked, "It appears to me that if they
would split the difference they would have about the truth,
and that, as it now stands, the Josephites have the president and the Brighamites the church."[5] Another convert
from the Re-organized Church, however, repudiates on
good grounds the alleged hint of Joseph Smith that his son
should succeed him, while the Josephites admittedly were
without the President from 1852, the year of their organization, until 1860, when Joseph's son joined their ranks.
Where, then, was the "Church" from 1844-1860 if the Josephites are right?

2. Again, the Josephites reject polygamy. But this is
just as illogical on their part as is the Utah rejection of the

---

4. *No Man Knows My History. The Life of Joseph Smith.*
5. *The True Origin of Mormon Polygamy.*

"Inspired Translation" of the Bible which the Josephites accept.

3.   The Josephites reject *in toto* the Adam-god doctrine of the Brighamites. But they do believe in many gods, and gods with flesh and bones, as does the Utah group.

What Constitutes Mormonism

Thus the differences are few, and with the exception of the Josephite rejection of polygamy, insignificant. Both groups hold before the public misleading documents supposed to state their beliefs, but in reality concealing them. "But the real beliefs," to quote a lifelong student of Mormonism, "are essentially in common, as follows: Smith a prophet; continuous revelation through him and others; the *Book of Mormon* and *Doctrine and Covenant* as such revelations; the *Pearl of Great Price* as translated by Smith, parts of which are parts of the 'Inspired Translation' by him; more revelations yet to come — at least equal to the Bible; Melchizedec and Aaronic priesthoods; gathering; tithing; flesh-and-bones God; many gods logically involved in this (but not often advocated by Josephites); Christ and the Spirit (but not Bible conceptions); sin a necessity for man; hell a saving agency; salvation through works instead of by faith in Christ; baptism (immersion) essential to salvation; pre-existence of all men; apostasy of the Christian church; authority; organization of the church, on their style; punishment after death temporary and measured by sins; premillennialism; the Bible defective and practically superseded by their revelations; their President alone the mouthpiece of God, etc."

Quite a list of rarities, yet one that does not lay claim to completeness. As to that, the Rev. Van Dellen reminds us that their system contains elements borrowed from such widely divergent sources as Christianity, Judaism, Mohammedanism, Fetishism, Communism, Manicheism, Campbellism, and other isms. To discuss and trace all these errors one by one, he adds, one ought to write a voluminous book on the doctrine of Mormonism alone, and in it discuss well-nigh all religious sects of earlier and later times. It is, indeed, next to impossible to give a concise view of its many heterogeneous elements. Its earlier advocates were anything but theologians.

The Re-organized Church launched a $500,000 campaign in November, 1951, toward the completion of their temple, construction of which was begun in 1926. The copper-sheathed dome was finished during the summer of 1951. The main "auditorium" is to seat 6,700, and a basement section to give room for 3,000 temporary seats.

The Doctrine of Polygamy and Its Development

It is well known that many pagan religions have arrived at what Paul describes in Romans 1 as the logical outcome of heathenism, the deification of the sexual life. Thus many ancients deified the steer as an emblem of fertility. The refined Greeks had their temples for pederasty. Popular Hinduism of today has traveling temple cars with grossly sensual carvings, while dancing-girls, the professional prostitutes of India, are supposed to be married to the gods in whose temples they serve.

1. With Mormonism, polygamy was not an afterthought; it was one of the first thoughts that entered into the lustful brain of Joseph Smith when he perceived that certain people could be made to believe in him as a prophet. But the "doctrine" was at first communicated to a few select of the inner circle only; the surroundings in New York, Ohio, Missouri and Illinois were too antagonistic to it. And to the very end of Joseph's career (April 1830 to June 1844) it was understood that this "strong meat" was not to be fed to "the Gentiles," who were to receive only the "first principles." The first public announcement of polygamy was in Utah, in 1852; and here it also became a popular hobby. Nor was the practice officially abandoned till after a long legal battle. Even after President Wilford Woodruff published his manifesto against polygamy because of strong

government opposition (1889), it was practiced in secret. At the present time it may not be widely practiced; it may be true that "the average young Mormon has no use for it." It is also true that Mormon missionaries, when pressed for an answer, will say, "We believe in it, but we do not practice it." And since the Mormon belief is that a polygamous priesthood is to rule the earth, it is justifiable to believe that the old Danish Mormon was correct when he stated that loud denunciations of polygamy from the Salt Lake City tabernacle are "yust to fool the Yentiles." Young Mormons still give an entire year, in their early twenties, to go forth as "missionaries" among "Gentiles," being supported entirely by their families; and these do propagate the old Mormon teachings. Yet their Conferences now deal more with purely ethical problems. Thus, for instance, an AP report from Salt Lake City, Oct. 7, 1946, states: "From comment on labor-capital relations to discussions on world peace, the 117th semiannual conference of the Latter Day Saints (Mormon Church) cut a wide swath through temporal affairs." We are reminded of Dr. James H. Snowden's comment in 1926: "It seems to me if they would give up their prophet and their Bible, they might be taken into the other churches."[6] This, of course, they will not do; but the emphasis seems to be more on general humanistic principles, as is the case in the modernist churches.

Early in 1944, however, a scandal filled our daily papers for several days. Moving simultaneously in Utah, Idaho, and Arizona, Federal and state law-enforcement officers arrested forty-six members of the Fundamentalist sect. The charges against them — both by state and Federal governments — were severe: Mann Act and Lindbergh kidnap law violations; mailing obscene literature; conspiracy; unlawful cohabitation. Nine young women "cheerfully" faced charges of advocating polygamy and had their group picture published in *Newsweek* for March 20, 1944. Several indictments followed the court trials. It was found that the

6. *The Truth About Mormonism*, p. 46.

magazine *Truth,* of which the seventy-one-year-old sect leader was editor, was devoted chiefly to propagandizing polygamy. Mormons of the "orthodox Church" commended officials for making the arrests, but "doubted that the new drive would stamp it out entirely." "Of course we believe in what we are doing," said Mrs. Rhea A. Kunz in an interview with the Salt Lake *Telegram.* "This thing is far bigger than the individual, for it inevitably will encompass much more than the man-made laws by which the world lives and will become a fundamental component in the lives of all right-living people."[7]

Why is the practice hard to stamp out? A Baptist minister to whom the writer gave a copy of his booklet *The Gist of the Cults* at the time, said, "I was naturally interested in your treatment of Mormonism, for I have been a minister for many years in Salt Lake City, and have had frequent contacts with Mormons. Your view is entirely correct: Mormonism is a fleshly religion, and the Fundamentalists of whom we read so much of late, learned the theory from the official Mormons. When the matter became public, they threw them out to save their own face."

---

7. On Nov. 18, 1946, the Supreme Court of the U. S. upheld the Salt Lake City convictions of the following six "Fundamentalists" who had practiced polygamy: Heber Kimball Cleveland, David Brigham Derger, Theral Ray Dockstader, L. R. Stubbs, Follis Gardner Petty and Vergel Y. Jessop. The majority of the Court, as represented by Justice Douglas, held that polygamy is not excluded from the Mann Act. The minority of the Court (Justices Hugo L. Black, Robert H. Jackson and Frank Murphy) dissented. Said Justice Murphy: "Marriage, even when it occurs in a form of which we disapprove, is not to be compared with prostitution or debauchery or other immoralities of that character." He said that the Court's majority decision was but another consequence of its long-continued failure to recognize that the white slave traffic act is aimed solely at the diabolical interstate and international trade in white slaves. The argument of the defense that the six cult members were motivated by a religious belief, "claims too much," in the words of Justice Douglas. "If upheld, it would place beyond the law any act done under the claims of religious sanction."

After the U. S. Supreme Court had refused to reconsider this verdict the Utah Supreme Court on Dec. 16 confirmed the conviction of twenty Fundamentalist cult members on charges of conspiring to violate state laws prohibiting plural marriages.

2. The Mormon theory of polygamy may have followed in the wake of its practice, but it has become an integral part of the doctrine. Elder William Clayton, who was the confidential clerk of the Prophet, told in his affidavit what he learned of Joseph Smith concerning it in these words, "Of him I learned that the doctrine of plural and celestial marriage is the most holy and important doctrine ever revealed to man on the earth, and that without obedience to that principle no person can ever attain to the fulness of exaltation in celestial glory." This does not mean that "Joe" Smith desired or allowed people to live in promiscuity without due regard to the wishes of the Prophet. In his Diary he wrote (Oct. 5, 1843) :

"Gave instructions to try those persons who were preaching, teaching, or practicing the doctrine of plurality of wives; for, according to the law, I hold the keys of this power in the last days, for there is never but one on earth at a time on whom the power and its keys are conferred; and I have constantly said no man shall have but one wife at a time unless the Lord directs otherwise."

This statement is in full harmony with the guarded language in which the Book of Mormon, as early as 1830, hinted at polygamy. After the statement (introduced by the usual "Behold" for which the book is noted) that "David and Solomon truly had many wives and concubines, which thing was abominable before me, saith the Lord," the people are admonished not to "do like unto them," but to "keep my commandments." But this passage is followed by words that leave a loophole: "For if I will, saith the Lord of Hosts, raise up seed unto me, I will command my people; otherwise they shall hearken unto these things." The Josephite exegesis that the word "otherwise" here means "in other words" is plainly born of embarrassment; the evident import of the clause is in full accord with the passage in Smith's Diary.

3. The *Doctrine and Covenants* which was written at a later date by Smith, when opposition to the doctrine had sufficiently waned among the Saints, contains a "Revela-

tion on the Eternity of the Marriage Covenant, including Plurality of Wives, Given through Joseph, the Seer, in Nauvoo, Hancock County, Illinois, July 12th, 1843." Here the plural wives of David and Solomon are stated to have been given by the Lord. Here also occurs this noted passage: "And again as pertaining to the law of the Priesthood: If any man espouse a virgin, and desire to espouse another, and the first give her consent; and if he espouse the second, and they are virgins, and have vowed to no other man, then he is justified; he cannot commit adultery, for they are given unto him; for he cannot commit adultery with that that belongeth unto him and to no one else. And if he have ten virgins given unto him by this law, he cannot commit adultery for they belong to him, and they are given unto him, therefore is he justified."

These references, although the last one has been removed from the *Doctrine and Covenants* by the Josephites, prove that the real Mormon doctrine on this point is taught in Utah; and they corroborate the evidence that the *Revelation on Celestial Marriage* came from Joseph.

The Theory Underlying Polygamy

That so much attention is paid to this feature of Mormonism is not because we consider it a bit of spicy gossip. Rather, we are convinced that polygamy is part and parcel of the system, and that true Mormons must long for the time when the practice of polygamy shall be restored. Young's daughter informs us, "The principle of plural marriage was adopted by my father as it was taught him by the Prophet Joseph Smith, after great inner struggle and earnest prayer. His strict puritanical training ill-fitted him to accept such a doctrine. He foresaw — as who would not? — the storm of abuse and opposition which such action would arouse. And it was as death to him ... But the fact remains that the men and women who entered into that relationship in early days, did so from purely religious motives. It was a high and sacred undertaking with them, involving much suffering and sacrifice on the part of both men and women."[8]

Perhaps the picture of the ideal home life in Young's family as presented by Mrs. Gates, with all the fifty-six children and the "aunties" living in perfect mutual love and understanding, is somewhat colored by the love for propaganda. Perhaps, also, Young was not quite the indifferent husband Ann Eliza makes him out to be. Whatever may be the truth of this, we gladly accept Mrs. Gates' statement on the principle that led to polygamy. We have no desire to speak of Mormon polygamy in the light vein of Mark Twain's *Roughing It*.

The fact that someone does something because of principle does not, however, make that principle right. The question remains why self-willed, headstrong Brigham Young yielded to the unwelcome doctrine. And why is this principle considered so highly important that it clings with tenacity even after its practice has been officially suspended?

1. Mormons proceed from the thought that a marriage that has been solemnized for this life amounts to but little. Husband and wife must be united for eternity. "Be fruitful and multiply" is the great commandment. Upon its keeping depends the future glory of the married. Woman cannot be saved apart from man; at any rate, she cannot attain to the highest glory possible for woman. It is therefore the man's duty to take pity upon woman, and to marry her. Better to be a plural wife than no wife at all. When, hereafter, the saved Mormon reigns, a king in a new world, his wives will be enthroned as queens at his side.

2. The doctrine as contained in Smith's *Revelation on Celestial Marriage* contains two elements. The first is termed *plurality of wives;* the second, *spiritual wifery.* Marriages are not valid for eternity except there be spiritual affinity, and such marriages can be solemnized only

---

8. Susan Young Gates, *The Life Story of Brigham Young*, p. 321.

in the Mormon secret temples which continue to appear. The element of secrecy and the high-sounding titles of almost every Mormon, be it said by the way, remind us that all the original Mormons were at one time Freemasons. What wonder then, if a man discovers, after some years of married life, that there exists spiritual affinity between himself and some other woman, that he betakes himself to the Temple in order to be "sealed for eternity," if not "for time *and* eternity," to his newly discovered attraction? Or, what wonder that women who have been taught since infancy that man is to be woman's saviour, defend the doctrine, and would rather share eternity as polygamous wives in the highest glory than occupy the role of servants in the hereafter?

3. The gods of Mormonism are "big men, like Brigham Young," graduates, one might say, of the school of human life, and post-graduate students in the sacred science of procreation. One of the earliest conspirators with Rigdon and Smith was Parley P. Pratt, who was converted to Mormonism and became a missionary in August 1830. This "Saint" wrote the following on our subject: "O candidates for celestial glory! Would your joys be full in the countless years of eternity without forming the connections, the relationship, the kindred ties which concentrate in the domestic circle, and branch forth, and bud and blossom, and bear fruits of eternal increase? Would that eternal emotion of charity and benevolence which swells your bosoms be satisfied to enjoy in 'single blessedness,' without an increase in posterity, those exhaustless stores of never ending riches and enjoyment? Or, would you, like your heavenly Father, prompted by eternal benevolence and charity, wish to fill countless millions of worlds with your begotten sons and daughters and to bring them all through all the gradations of progressive being, to inherit immortal bodies and eternal mansions in your several dominions?" And a little further, "The eternal union of the sexes, in and after the

resurrection, is mainly for the purpose of renewing and continuing the work of procreation."[9]

Endless, aimless procreation. If that is not the religion of phallicism, what is it? Meanwhile, the manner in which the saintly lords in Utah exercised "eternal benevolence and charity" from their "swelling bosoms," in anticipation of greater bliss to come, may be learned from the sober, but eloquent and heart-rending tale in Ann Eliza Young's *Wife No. 19*.[10]

Polygamy Influencing the Entire System

The hankering after sexual indulgence that characterized Smith, Young, Pratt, and other founders of the Mormon system, resulted in the doctrine of polygamy. This, in turn, became so basic to the theory that polygamous marriage was transfered from life on earth to that in heaven hereafter. And that influenced the entire view of heaven and God, whose dwelling-place is heaven. And since one's view of God naturally determines his conception of sin against God, of salvation, and of Christ the Saviour, it becomes evident that the phallicism of Mormonism is responsible for the strange mixture of doctrines that seem to be borrowed on every hand.

Since the highest conception of bliss is that of begetting sons and daughters, God Himself becomes a polygamist.

Men who attain to that blissful state hereafter have reached the pinnacle, and are gods themselves. Thus a gross polytheism is taught.

It follows that every god was a man on earth at one time. These gods and their wives beget children as spirits; these spirit-children are waiting for an opportunity to come to earth to receive bodies.

---

9. Under date May 15, 1947, "Elder" H. Harris writes to me from Llano, New Mexico, concerning this telling quotation: "I think it is quite beautiful, easy to believe, and lots more logical than the theology of modern-day, so-called 'Christianity' (like playing harps forever!)"
10. This interesting book is difficult to obtain. I have been told that Mormon missionaries buy up copies and send them to Utah for confiscation.

Hence it is the duty of every woman to be married, and of every man to beget as many bodies as possible. The doctrines of the pre-existence of the human soul and of the duty of polygamy are thus seen to be closely interwoven. Is it a strange thing that Mormon missionaries will state that "we hope for a better day when polygamy will again be practiced"?

The gods being conceived as such, Christ becomes the ordinary child of Adam-god and one of his wives. He cannot be a Saviour in any sense.

Nor is sin against a once earthly and still human god anything so very dreadful. Man becomes his own saviour. And, since salvation is only obtained in the Mormon pathway — it is a peculiarity of all the non-Christian sects that they condemn every doctrine but their own most severely — Mormons have an authoritative priesthood with a baptism that is absolutely necessary unto salvation.

And this, in turn, results in the doctrine of *baptism for the dead*. Mormons are kept busy looking up their genealogies, and some have been baptized "by proxy" fifty and more times for the benefit of their "Gentile" ancestors. This is always done in the secret temples, and by immersion.[11]

---

11. It is considered highly important to have lived and died a Mormon; and Mormon missionaries, even today when outsiders almost welcome this sect as one more Christian denomination, display charts teaching the following with graphs: At death all who have not accepted the doctrines of Joseph Smith go to a "Spirit Prison." Here they receive a chance to accept "the Truth" (as per the much abused passage in I Peter 4:19, 20, Mormon version). All good Mormons go to the *celestial* degree of glory, where God the Father and the Son dwell. Non-Mormons who have led a fairly good life are assigned to the *terrestial* degree of felicity, visited occasionally by Christ. The wicked go to the *telestial* abode, there to be ministered to by good spirits from the celestial sphere.

Another diagram shows the "revelation" that the steps leading to heaven are: Faith, Repentance, Baptism, Confirmation, and that there are degrees of glory in heaven parallel to one's services rendered the Church on earth as Deacon, Teacher, Priest, Elder, Bishop, Seventies, Apostles, President.

Other Groups

I have come into contact with a third group, perhaps the most subtle of all. It calls itself "The Church of Christ, Headquarters on the Temple Lot, Independence, Missouri." It Publishes *Zion's Advocate,* a monthly journal, of which W. A. Sheldon, 11427 E. 16th St., Independence, Missouri, is Editor-in-Chief.

The subtlety of this group lies in the fact that they disclaim the name Mormons as well as that of Latter-Day Saints, and even refuse to admit that they are followers of Joseph Smith. "We are no more Mormons because we believe the Book of Mormon to be inspired than you would call yourself a Catholic because you believe the Bible to be inspired," one of their "elders" informed me. "We are just the Church of Christ; we only recognize the Bible and the Book of Mormon as authoritative. We only follow Joseph Smith in so far as he received a divine revelation in addition to the Bible."

All authentic books written by prominent Mormons are brushed aside with the words, "That was published in Utah, and we do not recognize it." Even "The Holy Scriptures Translated and Corrected by the Spirit of Revelation by Joseph Smith, Jr., the Seer," is ruled out of court with, "That was put out in Iowa by the Reorganized Church of Jesus Christ of Latter Day Saints: we are not Latter Day Saints, we are just the Church of Christ."

Meanwhile this group has all the earmarks of Reorganized Mormonism: their missionaries labor among church members, whom they endeavor to wrest away from evangelical churches; they teach them the doctrine of a flesh-and-bones God, at any rate a God who has a body as well as a spirit; the message of God's Word has been obscured until Smith found the Book of Mormon; salvation is by the blood of Christ, "which cannot be taken literally, but *typifies* his life and the power that sustained him, and supports and sustains *every* man who is saved to the uttermost. God is the Supreme Saving Power — He sent his Son to make the terms of Salvation known to man — The Son appointed the Holy Ghost as his successor to guide and to teach, and to help the obedient on to perfection. When the body of Christ, his Church, has the living blood, the real life of the body, in it as a spiritual force to develop and cleanse, then there is joy and hope of victory."[12] This means salvation by character, a truly Mormon teaching. They re-baptize their converts, and impart to them "the Holy Spirit" by the laying on of hands. They are ruled by twelve apostles, and have a bishop who receives "all tithes, offerings, consecrations and donations to the Temple Fund and Storehouse" (all Mormons and Seventh-Day Adventists are supposed to tithe their income for their Church).

This movement appears to be growing; the monthly paper contains news items from many quarters. Their faith in the fulfillment of predictions made in the Book of Mormon remains unshaken, and accounts for the missionary zeal toward the Navahos and other American Indians. Thus we are told that the literal seed of Abraham, Isaac and Jacob are the American Indians, whose seed, the Lamanites, are to be visited by a return of Jesus Christ. These American Indians therefore always refer to themselves as "the People," and the Hopi Indians of the Southwest have a legend of a "white brother" who is to come in the future and decipher the predictions found on a sacred prayer stone. This "white brother," according to these Mormons (with reference to I Nephi 3:192-237) is one of the white or Nephite Indians whose people have been preserved "somewhere deep in that jungle country of Central America or Mexico." Then the Father shall commence his work; then the Indians will build the Temple of the Lord upon the temple-lot in Independence, Missouri, where Joseph Smith laid the corner stone, and they will do so with the aid of the Gentiles converted in the meantime (III Nephi

---

12. *Zion's Advocate*, Jan., 1942, p. 15.

10:1-5), "and they shall build up a holy city unto the Lord like unto the Jerusalem of old."[13]

Meanwhile Clarence and Angela Wheaton report in a "Letter to the Church," that they have actually located these White Indian people "and that they live in a walled city secluded deep in the jungle country of southern Mexico." These White Indians have golden plates, bracelets and legends predicting the time of their going north (to Missouri).[14]

Since the missionaries and "elders" of this group will admit faith in the Book of Mormon as divinely inspired, we here append a few remarks which, taken by themselves, ought to be sufficient to convince any one that the Book of Mormon is a rank fake. We acknowledge our indebtedness to the thorough work of the Rev. M. T. Lamb, in which much more of a similar nature may be found.[15] However, we have carefully checked all references, and are quoting from the Seventh Independence Edition, printed at the Zion's Printing and Publishing Company, Independence, Missouri.

1. The book is written in a would-be imitation Bible style, a) pompous, verbose, and b) full of incorrect grammar and nonsense.

a) Take this: *Book of Alma,* Ch. 5, p. 249:

> 49. And now I say unto you, that this is the order after which I am called; yea, to preach unto my beloved brethren; yea, and every one that dwelleth in the land; yea, to preach unto all, both old and young, both bond and free; yea, I say unto you the aged, and also the middle aged, and the rising generation; yea, to cry unto them that they must repent and be born again;

---

13. "The Relationship of the American Indians to the Restoration," a sermon by Apostle Clarence L. Wheaton in *Zion's Advocate,* Dec., 1950.

14. *Zion's Advocate,* Jan., 1951. Frank S. Mead, *Handbook of Denominations in the United States,* also numbers these under Mormons; and besides this "Church of Christ (Temple Lot)" he gives three more small Mormon bodies: Bickertonites, Cutlerites, and Strangites, all under the official name "Church of Jesus Christ."

15. *The Mormons and Their Bible.*

50. Yea, thus saith the Spirit, Repent, all ye ends of
the earth, for the kingdom of heaven is soon at hand;
yea, the Son of God cometh in his glory, in his might,
majesty, power, and dominion. Yea, my beloved brethren, I say unto you, that the Spirit saith, Behold the
glory of the King of all the earth; and also the King of
heaven shall very soon shine forth among all the children of men;

51. And also the Spirit saith unto me, yea, crieth
unto me with a mighty voice, saying, Go forth and say
unto this people, Repent, for except ye repent ye can
in nowise inherit the kingdom of heaven.

52. And again I say unto you, the Spirit saith, Behold the axe is laid at the root of the tree; therefore
every tree that bringeth not forth good fruit, shall be
hewn down and cast into the fire; yea, a fire which
cannot be consumed; even an unquenchable fire. Behold, and remember, the Holy One hath spoken it.

Here, then, is but one of numerous passages, many of
far greater length, which show the empty loquaciousness of
the book, very contrary to the brevity of the Scriptures; and
at the same time we have here a book that is supposed to
have been written or spoken by "Alma the High Priest,"
centuries before the Christian era, but which contains passages obviously taken from the lips of John the Baptist as
recorded in the Gospels!

b) How is the following for "inspired" writing?

And it came to pass that he rent his coat; and he
took a piece thereof, and wrote upon it . . .; and he
fastened it upon the end of a pole *thereof*. (p. 370)

These our dearly beloved brethren, who have so dearly *beloved* us. (p. 311)

Yea, if my days could have been *in them days* . . .
But behold, I am *consigned* that these are my days.
(p. 449)

I say Jew, because I mean *them*, from whence I came.
(p. 127)

And they *having been waxed strong* in battle, that
they might not be destroyed. (p. 260)

We did *arrive* to the promised land. (p. 43)

Even until they had *arriven* to the land of Middoni.
(p. 297)

There were no robbers, nor murderers, neither were there Lamanites, nor any *manner of ites;* but they were *in one,* the children of Christ. (p. 545)

Now immediately when the Judge had been murdered; he being *stabbed* by his brother *by a garb of secrecy;* and he fled, and the servants ran and told the people. (p. 454)

Yet, a book containing such grammatical nonsense and rank crudities is perfected by a "Testimony of Three Witnesses," who "through the grace of God the Father, and our Lord Jesus Christ, have seen the plates which contain this record . . . and we also know that they have been translated by the gift and power of God, for his voice hath declared it unto us; wherefore we know of a surety that the work is true."

2. The book contains several so-called miracles, which are not miracles in any Biblical sense of the word, but stunts which God provides, often without any necessity, merely to favor his pets. Here are just a few samples:

a) Lehi has left Jerusalem upon command of the Lord, because the inhabitants, whom he has warned concerning their iniquity, seek his life. With him are his wife and four sons. Nephi, the youngest son, takes the others back to Jerusalem, to marry daughters of Ishmael. Afterward they travel again in the wilderness and suffer hardships. However, the Lord sees them through their difficulties as follows:

And it came to pass that the voice of the Lord spake unto my father by night, and commanded him that on the morrow he should take his journey into the wilderness. And it came to pass that as my father arose in the morning and went forth to the tent door, to his great astonishment he beheld upon the ground a round ball of curious workmanship, and it was of fine brass. And within the ball were two spindles; and the one pointed the way whither we should go into the wilderness. (p. 36)

b) This curious ball obviates much seeking and labor for food:

And I said unto my father, whither shall I go to obtain food. And it came to pass that he did inquire of the Lord . . . And it came to pass that the voice of the Lord said unto him, Look upon the ball, and behold the things which are written . . . And it came to pass that I, Nephi, beheld the pointers which were in the ball, that they did work according to the faith, and diligence, and heed which we did give unto them. And there was also written upon them, a new writing, which was plain to be read, which did give us understanding concerning the ways of the Lord; and it was written and changed from time to time, according to the faith and diligence which we gave unto it: And thus we see that, by small means, the Lord can bring about great things. And it came to pass that I, Nephi, did go forth up into the top of the mountain, according to the directions which were given upon the ball. And it came to pass that I did slay wild beasts, insomuch that I did obtain food for our families. (p. 38)

c) On the way to the Western continent, there was a mutiny against Nephi, which the inspired translation announces in the heading of the Book of Nephi as follows: "They come to the large waters. Nephi's brethren rebelleth against him [!]." Now God had prepared for them a compass, which refused to work when Nephi, the Lord's favorite, had been bound by his brothers. The result was a terrible storm. When Nephi had been released, he took the divinely wrought compass into his hands, and lo, it again pointed the way across the waters! (p. 46).

d) Jared's brother and his company have prepared eight barges, all "according to the instructions of the Lord"; but the opening for air and light has been forgotten. So the Lord bids him cut an opening in the roof for air, which he is to close when the waves go over the barges in a fierce storm. As to the lighting system, Jared's brother goes upon a very high mountain "and did moulten out of a rock sixteen small stones, and they were white and clear even as transparent glass." These sixteen stones he presents before the Lord, and says,

Therefore touch these stones, O Lord, with thy
finger, and prepare them that they may shine forth in
the darkness; and they shall shine forth unto us in
the vessels which we have prepared, that we may have
light while we shall cross the sea.

And the Lord did so, and the light-giving stones were
put two in each barge, one at each end. Incidently, Jared's
brother fell down with fear because he saw the Lord's finger
touch the stones. He is encouraged: he should not fear, for
the fact that he has seen the finger shows that he has great
faith. Wherefore, he is rewarded for this faith with the
sight of the entire body of the Lord, called "the body of my
spirit." And the Lord says to him:

Behold, I am he who was prepared from the foundation of the world to redeem my people. Behold, I am
Jesus Christ. I am the Father and the Son. In me shall
all mankind have light, and that eternally, even they
who shall believe on my name; and they shall become
my sons and my daughters. (p. 577)

e) Perhaps the silliest of all the "miracles" in this book
is the story that, when some twenty or thirty years after
Nephi has separated from his two brothers Laman and
Lemuel, and these two groups within those few years have
become two rival *nations* [!], God suddenly makes the entire group of Lamanites black lest they might become a
temptation to the Nephites: "Wherefore, as they were
white, and exceeding fair and delightsome, that they might
not be enticing unto my people, the Lord God did cause a
skin of blackness to come upon them." (p. 72).

Then, some five hundred years later, some of the descendants of these Lamanites united with the then Nephites, "And their curse was taken from them, and their
skin became white like unto the Nephites; and their young
men and their daughters became exceeding fair, and they
were numbered among the Nephites, and were called Nephites."(p. 480).

This, according to Mormons, explains the origin of
Black and "White" Indians!

3. To this must be added that the whole fantastic story of the Book of Mormon is contradicted on every point by careful scientific investigation of early American anthropology. According to the Mormon story there were two entirely different early American people, the first being the Jaredites, who came from the tower of Babel under Jared and his brother, crossing the Atlantic Ocean in 344 days in the above-named eight cigarshaped barges, and locating in Central America. They came to an end, after some 1600 years, about 600 B. C., as a result of dissensions and revolts. The second history described in the book is that of Lehi's four sons, Laman, Lemuel, Sam and Nephi, which Nephi left Jerusalem in the time of Zedekiah, and arrived "on the coast of Chili, not far from the thirtieth degree, south latitude." Nephi at once began to record the history of his people upon metal plates. His descendant Moroni, a prince of royal blood, finished the plates, and hid them in the hill Cumorah in New York in A.D. 420. That this entire fabrication, in its description of the American aborigines, their language and writing, and their names, contradicts in every detail what has become known of early American civilizations may be read in Charles A. Shook's *Cumorah Revisited,* and in M. T. Lamb's *The Mormons and Their Bible.*

4. The final test of the fraudulent character of the Book of Mormon may well be found in the fact that it postulates the necessity of further revelation in addition to the Bible, because the Bible is said to have been greatly marred by an apostate church, and was only meant for a certain generation anyhow. Consider this: An angel informs Nephi that the Bible has come out of the hands of the Jews and gone forth to the Gentiles pure and "according to the truth which is in God": but "a great and abominable church" of the Gentiles has so corrupted the Bible that further revelations and corrections through the golden plates have become necessary:

"And after they go forth by the hand of the twelve apostles of the Lamb, from the Jews unto the Gentiles, thou seest the foundation of a great and abominable church, which is most abominable above all churches; for behold, they have taken away from the gospel of the Lamb, many parts which are plain and most precious; and also many covenants of the Lord have they taken away; And all this have they done, that they might pervert the right ways of the Lord; that they might blind the eyes and harden the hearts of the children of men; Wherefore thou seest that after the book hath gone forth through the hands of the great and abominable church, that there are many plain and precious things taken away from the book, which is the book of the Lamb of God." (p. 27).

To this may be added the brazen statement by "Apostle" Pratt, "Indeed, no one, without further revelation, knows whether even one-hundredth part of the doctrines and ordinances of salvation are contained in the few books of Scripture which have descended to our times; how, then, can it be decided that they are a sufficient guide? . . ."

And yet, to quote the Rev. Mr. Lamb, "To the above specious question which has hid underneath it the boldest infidelity and the most wicked deception, it would be an all-sufficient answer to an honest Mormon, to reply as follows: 'The Book of Mormon itself is our proof that not only one verse but in the neighborhood of ten thousand verses in our Bible have escaped pollution, so that they convey the same sense now that they did in the original.' There are probably not less than ten thousand verses from our Bible found in the Book of Mormon and each of these verses is professedly translated by the gift and power of God from ancient Egyptian plates, professedly as pure as God first gave them. And yet each one of these verses is found in the Book of Mormon *precisely as we have them today in our English Bibles.*"

Mormonism and the Bible

Charles A. Shook, a thorough student of Mormonism, reminds us of Shakespeare's words,

In religion
What damned error but some sober brow
Will bless it and approve it with a text,
Hiding the grossness with fair ornament.

Very true; and eminently applicable to Mormonism. Well
I remember a former schoolmate of the Christian School
in my home town across the ocean who, with his wife, had
been "converted" by two Mormon missionaries. He had
swallowed the system, hook, line, and sinker. Both he and
his wife defended polygamy ardently. That the Bible predicted the arrival of the Book of Mormon he "proved" from
Ezekiel 37:16-19. "Is not the Bible the stick of Judah?" he
exclaimed triumphantly. "Then the Book of Mormon must
be the stick of Ephraim!" I have since read this astonishing bit of "exegesis" in Talmadge's standard book on Mormon doctrine.[16] It is merely another instance showing that
everything may be proved from isolated texts.

The Mormons "prove" polygamy from Isaiah 4:1, "And
seven women shall take hold of one man in that day, saying,
We will eat our own bread, and wear our own apparel [they
certainly applied that literally in Utah]: only let us be called
by thy name; take thou away our reproach." (Against
polygamy, see Matt. 19:4-6; Eph. 5:24-33).

Matthew 22:30, "For in the resurrection they neither
marry, nor are given in marriage," is explained to mean
that no new marriages will be made in the hereafter; hence
the "sealing" must be done in this life — as if the following
words, "but are as angels in heaven," do not exclude this
artificial exegesis.

It remains only to point to a few passages of Scripture
that seem peculiarly applicable to the system as a whole,
with its apostles and revelations and "corrected" Bible passages. Such references we find in:

Matthew 7:15, "Beware of false prophets, who come to
you in sheep's clothing, but inwardly are ravening wolves."

---

16. James E. Talmadge, *The Articles of Faith*, 5th ed.

II Corinthians 11:13, "For such men are false apostles, deceitful workers, fashioning themselves into apostles of Christ."

II Peter 3:16, "which the ignorant and unstedfast wrest, as they do also the other scriptures, unto their own destruction."

Revelation 2:2, "try them that call themselves apostles, and they are not."

Revelation 22:18, "I testify unto every man that heareth the words of the prophecy of this book, If any man shall add unto them, God shall add unto him the plagues which are written in this book."

We again close our chapter with quotations from accredited Mormon authors on various points of Christian teaching. These will show Mormonism to be a thoroughly antichristian cult.

Angels

"1. There are two kinds of being in heaven—viz., angels who are resurrected personages, having bodies of flesh and bones.

'2. For instance, Jesus said, 'Handle me and see, for a spirit hath not flesh and bones, as ye see me have.'

"3. The spirits of just men made perfect—they who are not resurrected, but inherit the same glory." — JOSEPH SMITH.[17]

Baptism

"Wherefore little children are whole, for they are not capable of committing sin; wherefore the curse of Adam is taken from them in me [Christ], that it hath no power over them; and the law of circumcision is done away in me . . . And their little children need no repentance, neither baptism . . . Behold, I say unto you, that he that supposeth little children need baptism, is in the gall of bitterness, and in the bonds of iniquity; . . . wherefore should he be cut off while in the thought, he must go down to hell."—BOOK OF MORMON.

---

17. *Doctrine and Covenants*, Section CXXXII.

"Millions of earth's sons and daughters have passed out of the body without obeying the law of baptism. Many of them will gladly accept the word and law of the Lord when it is proclaimed to them in the spirit world. But they cannot there attend to ordinances that belong to the sphere which they have left. Can nothing be done in their case? Must they forever be shut out of the kingdom of heaven? Both justice and mercy join in answering 'yes' to the first 'no' to the last question. What, then, is the way of their deliverance?

"The living may be baptized for the dead. Other essential ordinances may be attended to vicariously. This glorious truth, hid from human knowledge for centuries, has been made known in this greatest of all divine dispensations. . . . It gives men and women the power to become 'Saviours on Mount Zion,' Jesus being the great Captain in the army of redeemers."—C. PENROSE.[18]

Atonement

"It becomes evident that through the great atonement, the expiatory sacrifice of the Son of God, it is made possible that man can be redeemed, restored, resurrected and exalted to the elevated position designed for him in the creation as a Son of God.

"In the first place, according to justice, men could not have been redeemed from temporal death, except through the atonement of Jesus Christ; and in the second place, they could not be redeemed from spiritual death, only through obedience to His law. . . .

"Hence what was lost in Adam was restored in Jesus Christ, so far as all men are concerned in all ages, with some very slight exceptions arising from an abuse of privileges. Transgressions of the law brought death upon all the posterity of Adam, the restoration through the atonement restored all the human family to life . . . So that whatever was lost by Adam, was restored by Jesus Christ. The

18. *Mormon Doctrine*, p. 48.

penalty of the transgression of the law was the death of the body. The atonement made by Jesus Christ resulted in the resurrection of the human body. Its scope embraced all peoples, nations, and tongues."—JOHN TAYLOR.[19]

"The Church of Jesus Christ of Latter-Day Saints teaches as a doctrine founded on reason, justice, and Scripture, that all children are innocent in the sight of God, and that, until they reach an age of personal responsibility, baptism is not requisite or proper in their behalf; that, in short, they are saved through the atonement of Christ. To a degree, children are born heirs to the good or evil natures of their parents . . . but through Christ's atonement they are all re-deemed from the curse of this fallen state; the debt, which comes to them as a legacy, is paid for them, and thus are they left free . . . .

"The Special or Individual Effect of the Atonement makes it possible for any and every soul to obtain absolution from the dread effect of personal sins, through the mediation of Christ; but such saving intercession is to be invoked by individual effort as manifested through faith, repentance, and continued works of righteousness. The laws under which individual salvation is obtainable have been prescribed by Christ. . . . Now, that the blessing of redemption from individual sins, while free for all to attain, is nevertheless conditioned on individual effort, is as plainly declared as is the truth of unconditional redemption from the effects of the Fall. . . ."—JAMES E. TALMADGE.[20]

The Church

"From the facts already stated, it is evident that the Church was literally driven from the earth; in the first ten centuries immediately following the ministry of Christ, the authority of the priesthood was lost from among men, and no human power could restore it. But the Lord in His mercy provided for the re-establishment of His Church in

---

19. *The Mediation and Atonement*, pp. 170, 177, 178.
20. *Op. cit.*, pp. 90, 92.

the last days, and for the last time. . . . It has been already
shown that this restoration was effected by the Lord through
the Prophet Joseph Smith."—JAMES E. TALMADGE.[21]

"The departure from the order, doctrine, ordinances,
and spirit of primitive Christianity commenced at a very
early period. . . . The Church of Christ was gone, without
even a shadow of its presence to be seen upon the earth. . . .
After a time came the reformation. . . . Yet there was no
direct communication established between them and the
heavens. . . . There was no inspired prophet, no gifted seer,
no appointed revelator through whom the will of God could
be made known.   Therefore, the ordinances of the gospel
could not be administered acceptably to God, and all such
ceremonies as were established among the various sects
were of necessity void and without virtue in heaven. . . . Joseph Smith was the chosen instrument in the hands of God
to receive the glad message and direct its promulgation to
all the world."—C. PENROSE.[22]

The Fall

"Adam found himself in a position that impelled him to
disobey one of the requirements of God.   He and his wife
had been commanded to multiply and replenish the earth.
Adam was still immortal; Eve had come under the penalty
of mortality; and in such dissimilar conditions the two
could not remain together, and therefore could not fulfil the
Divine requirement.   On the other hand, Adam would be
disobeying another command by yielding to his wife's request.   He deliberately and wisely decided to stand by the
first and greater commandment; and, therefore, with a full
comprehension of the nature of his act, he also partook of
the fruit that grew on the tree of knowledge.   The fact that
Adam acted understandingly in this matter is affirmed by
the scriptures.   Paul in writing to Timothy, explained that
'Adam was not deceived; but the woman, being deceived,

21. *Op. cit.*, p. 68.
22. *Op. cit.*, pp. 33-38.

was in the transgression.' The prophet Lehi, in expounding the scriptures to his sons, declared, 'Adam fell that man might be, and men are that they might have joy.'"—JAMES E. TALMADGE.[23]

Fatherhood of God

"When our father Adam came into the garden of Eden, he came into it with a celestial body, and brought Eve, one of his wives, with him . . . He is our father and our God, and the only God with whom we have to do."—BRIGHAM YOUNG.[24]

God's Unity

"The passages are numerous in the inspired writings which indicate a plurality of God."—F. D. RICHARDS.[25]

"And they (the Gods) said: Let there be light and there was light. And they (the Gods) comprehended the light . . . and they divided the light."—JOSEPH SMITH.[26]

"Each of these Gods, including Jesus Christ and His Father, being in possession of not merely an organized spirit, but a glorious body of flesh and bones, is subject to the laws which govern, of necessity, even the most refined order of physical existence."—PARLEY PRATT.[27]

God's Trinity

"The Father has a body of flesh and bones as tangible as man's; the Son also; but the Holy Ghost has not a body of flesh and bones but is a personage of spirit. . . . Were it not so, the Holy Ghost could not dwell in us. A man may receive the Holy Ghost, and it may descend upon him, and not tarry with him."—JOSEPH SMITH.[28]

---

23. *Op. cit.*, p. 68.
24. *Journal of Discourses*, 1:50.
25. *Compendium*, p. 170.
26. *The Pearl of Great Price*, p. 67.
27. *Key to the Science of Theology*, p. 42.
28. *Doctrine and Covenants*, p. 462.

Good Works

"Abraham received concubines and they bare him children, and it was accounted unto him for righteousness. Go ye therefore and do the works of Abraham, enter ye into my law, and ye shall be saved. But if ye enter not into my law [of polygamy], ye cannot receive the promise of my Father, which he made unto Abraham."—JOSEPH SMITH.[29]

"Now, that the blessing of redemption from individual sins, while free for all to attain, is nevertheless conditioned on individual effort, is as plainly declared as is the truth of unconditional redemption from the effects of the Fall." —JAMES E. TALMADGE.[30]

Inspiration

"Thou fool, that shall say, A Bible, A Bible, we have got a Bible, and we need no more Bible. . . . Wherefore, murmur ye, because that ye shall receive more of my word?"— BOOK OF MORMAN.[31]

"And whatsoever they ['those ordained unto the priesthood'] shall speak when moved upon by the Holy Ghost, shall be scripture, shall be the will of the Lord, shall be the mind of the Lord, shall be the word of the Lord, shall be the voice of the Lord, and the power of God unto salvation." JOSEPH SMITH.[32]

"The written works adopted by the vote of the Church as authoritative guides in faith and doctrine are four — the Bible, the Book of Mormon, the Doctrine and Covenants, and the Pearl of Great Price."—JAMES E. TALMADGE.[33]

"We will first quote from the writings of the Old and New Testaments and, although we are informed by later revelations 'that many parts which are plain and most

29. *Celestial Marriage*, pars. 12, 14.
30. *Op. cit.*, p. 92.
31. Section CXXXII, 44.
32. *Doctrine and Covenants*, p. 248.
33. *Op. cit.*, p. 5.

precious' have been taken away therefrom, yet there is a
large amount of testimony left in this valuable and sacred
record."—JOHN TAYLOR.[34]

The Holy Scriptures. Translated and Corrected by the
Spirit of Revelation, by Joseph Smith, Jr., the Seer. 20th
Edition. Lamoni, Iowa. Published by the Reorganized
Church of Jesus Christ of Latter Day Saints. 1920.

"Wilfred Woodruff is a prophet, and he has a great many
prophets around him, and he can make scriptures as good
as those in the Bible."—JOHN TAYLOR.[35]

Justification

"The sectarian dogma of justification by faith alone has
exercised an influence for evil since the early days of Christianity."—JAMES E. TALMADGE.[36]

Priesthood

"But there are two divisions or grand heads — one is the
Melchizedek Priesthood, and the other is the Aaronic, or
Levitical priesthood. The office of an elder comes under the
Priesthood of Melchizedek. The Melchizedek Priesthood
holds the right of Presidency, and has power and authority
over all the offices in the church in all ages of the world, to
administer in spiritual things."—JOSEPH SMITH.[37]

"The Apostle was so overawed by his presence, that he
fell at his feet to worship him; whereas the angel said, 'See
that thou do it not; I am thy fellow servant . . .' (Rev. 19:
10). In other words, he had held the holy Priesthood on
the earth and had officiated therein; . . . But now the scene
was changed; he was officiating in another sphere, and was
revealing unto the apostle John. . . . All of these men, having held the everlasting Priesthood on earth, still retain
the power and authority conferred upon them, and stand

---

34. *Op. cit.,* p. 11.
35. Cf. Nutting, *Why I Could Never Be a Mormon,* p. 21.
36. *Op. cit.,* p. 120.
37. *Doctrine and Covenants,* p. 384.

forth as prominent examples of the perpetuity of the everlasting Priesthood, administering on the earth or in the
heavens, as the purposes of God . . . or the circumstances
require."—JOHN TAYLOR.[38]

Resurrection

"The statement that the heathen dead will have place in
the first resurrection is sustained by the word of scripture,
and by a consideration of the principles of true justice according to which humanity is to be judged. Man will be
accounted blameless or guilty, according to his deeds as interpreted in the light of the law under which he is required
to live . . . it is reasonable to believe that the plan of redemption will afford such benighted ones an opportunity of
learning the laws of God; and surely, as fast as they so
learn, will obedience be required on pain of the penalty."—
JAMES E. TALMADGE.[39]

Marriage

"In the case of a man marrying a wife in the everlasting
covenant who dies while he continues in the flesh and mar-
ries another by the same divine law, each wife will come
forth in her order and enter with him into his glory. Is
there any reason why this should not be so? Is not each of
these wives entitled to her position in eternity, by virtue of
the sealing power which made her part of the man? Why
should one enter into the exaltation of the celestial world
and the other be relegated to singleness and servitude?
They all become one in the patriarchal order of family
government. And if this be the case in heaven, why should
not similar conditions as far as possible exist on earth? Is
earth holier than heaven? If there were no law of the land
against it and a man received from the Lord more wives
than one under the sealing ordinances, where would be the
moral wrong? . . . Herein is our Eternal Father glorified
and His dominions extended."—C. PENROSE.[40]

38. *Op. cit.*, p. 161.
39. *Op. cit.*, p. 404.
40. *Op. cit.*, p. 66.

"Jesus Christ was a polygamist; Mary and Martha, the sisters of Lazarus, were his plural wives, and Mary Magdalene was another. Also, the bridal feast of Cana of Galilee, where Jesus turned the water into wine, was on the occasion of one of his own marriages."—BRIGHAM YOUNG[41]

"We say it was Jesus Christ who was married [at Cana, to Martha and Mary], whereby he could see his own seed before he was crucified. The reference is to Isaiah 53:10."—ORSON HYDE.[42]

Virgin Birth

"When the Virgin Mary conceived the child Jesus, the Father had begotten him in his own likeness. He was NOT begotten by the Holy Ghost. And who was the Father? He was the first of the human family . . . Jesus, our elder brother, was begotten in the flesh by the same character that was in the garden of Eden, and who is our Father in Heaven."—BRIGHAM YOUNG.[43]

For Reflection

1. Which books are considered divinely inspired by Mormons?

2. Which of these are considered most important? Does Revelation 22:18 apply here, or are Mormon missionaries right when they say, "That refers only to tampering with the Apocalypse"?

3. What brought on the split between the Utah and the Re-organized branches?

4. On which points do these two groups differ, and on which are they agreed?

5. What good things can you say about Mormonism? Are they also politically dangerous?

---

41. Quoted in Ann Eliza Young's *Wife No.* 19, Ch. XXXV.
42. Cf. C. A. Shook, *The True Origin of Mormon Polygamy*, p. 207.
43. *Journal of Discourses*, 1:50.

6. What do you think now of Dr. Kuizenga's statement that Mormonism has at any rate tried to bring sex under the aspect of religion? Should and can this be done?[44]

7. Explain the Mormon view of the origin of man, of Jesus Christ, of the fall of man, of the atonement by Christ, and of celestial marriage.

8. Is Mormonism a monotheistic religion? Is it Christian? Can one be a Mormon and a Christian at the same time?[45]

9. A minister had a suite of rooms for rent. Two men rang his door bell and said, "We are Christians. We'd like to rent your rooms." He discovered they were "Latter-Day Saints," and refused them, pointing to II John 10. Was the minister right?

---

44. Cf. here my chapter "The Service of Sex" in *Our Christian Heritage* (Grand Rapids: Eerdmans, 1948), pp. 301 ff.

45. Dr. Snowden wrote that if the Mormons would abandon their prophet and their book, they might well be accepted among the rest of Christian denominations; and Dr. Braden that "the plan of salvation does not, in its main outlines, differ essentially from the traditional orthodox view." Do you agree with these opinions?

,9

DESTINY OF AMERICA

Destiny of America! This cult is more generally known as British-Israelism, or Anglo-Israelism; but why not use the more fascinating of its names, Destiny of America. That name holds for the entire North-American continent; and the program can appropriately close its broadcasts with the one tune that to Canadians means, "God save the King," and to Americans, "My country, 'tis of thee." One program, and one melody for Dominion Day on July 1, and for Independence Day on July 4, one glorious, world-saving destiny indeed for all who have at one time or another emigrated to the North American continent; for Britain is Ephraim and the United States is Manasseh, and the throne of David is now the British throne.

With Mormonism, Anglo-Israelism has in common some wild speculations concerning the early inhabitants of America.

With Seventh-Day Adventism it has in common that it has some earnest Christians among its ranks, while both systems are vicious.

With the early Russellism it shares the intricate mathematical measurings of the Great Pyramid of Egypt from which "Pastor" Russell determined the date of Christ's return (afterward condemned by Rutherford) and Prof. G. P. Smith wrote *Our Inheritance in the Great Pyramid.*

On page 1 of the First Book of Nephi — (which also opens the Book of Mormon) we read: "I Nephi . . . make a record in the language of my father, which consists of the learning of the Jews, and the language of the Egyptians."

Not only were the "reformed Egyptian *caractors*" the product of a deceptive brain, but there never existed such a language.

On page 549 of the Book of Mormon we read: "And it came to pass that I Mormon, being eleven years old, was carried by my father into the land Zarahemla, the whole face of the land having become covered with buildings, and the people were as numerous almost, as it were the sand of the sea."

Now this boy Mormon, was one of the last descendants of the godly Nephi who had left Jerusalem in the days of Zedekiah. These Nephites had built a godly civilization during four hundred years. But they backslid, and were utterly destroyed in 384 A.D. by the descendants of Ishmael who had come from Jerusalem with Nephi. Israel's descendants, the blackskinned Lamanites, destroyed all vestiges of civilization in Central America. Mormon and his son Moroni fortunately recorded the entire story on golden plates, which were afterward hidden in the hill Cumorah in New York, until in 1827 they were revealed by Moroni, now an angel, to Joseph Smith Jr., the Prophet.

The Book of Mormon also tells of an earlier settlement in America, by the Jaredites, who had come in cigar-shaped boats to America after the Confusion of Tongues at Babylon. The Book of Mormon insists that between the Jaredites and the Nephites, Central America and Mexico lay idle for six hundred years, and the land was so desolate that it was named Zarahemla, the Land of Desolation.

According to such famous anthropologists and historians as Bancroft, Baldwin, and others, however, these lands have always had a dense population; and the inhabitants have always been copper-colored, that is, neither white Nephites nor black Lamanites; and they have ever been a gentle people.

Now when Christians refuse upon scientific grounds to accept these grotesque Mormon ethnological vagaries and fantasies, why should they accept the equally unattested Anglo-Israel fiction which traces America's white population to the Israelites of Zedekiah's time because "Saxon" is said to be really *Isaacson,* or son of Isaac; and "British" is alleged to be really a Hebrew word, derived from Hebrew *berith,* covenant, and *ish,* man, meaning therefore "the men of the covenant"?

At best, writes Dr. M. Wyngaarden, Professor of the Old Testament in Calvin Seminary, if the word "British" had aught to do with *bereth* and *ish,* it could not mean "men of the covenant," but only "covenant of man"; but besides, all scholars are agreed, and every seminary student discovers to his grief, that the Semetic and Anglo-Saxon tongues have nothing in common.[1] And so it is; and this is in keeping with the elaborate History of the English Language at the beginning of Webster's Dictionary, and also with the findings of the Oxford Dictionary. The only resemblance between Hebrew and English is to be found in a few words that have been taken over from the Old Testament.

Dr. Albertus Pieters, late professor in the Western Theological Seminary, Holland, Michigan, reminds us that the Anglo-Israelites have gone to such ridiculous lengths in this matter as to draw even the Japanese within the pale of ancient Israel; for, so they say, there is a remarkable similarity between the Japanese word *Samurai,* the name for the old Japanese military caste, and *Samaria,* the capital of the kingdom of Israel.

Not only so; they have even ventured to conclude that since the Hebrew word for a young bullock was *engle,* therefore the land of the "Anglosaxons" was called "England," and since these Isaac's sons no doubt, as good Israelites, sacrificed plenty of young bullocks or Hebrew *engles,* therefore England's inhabitants were called John Bull.[2]

1. "The British-Israel Movement" in The *Calvin Forum,* Dec. 1947.
2. *The Seed of Abraham.* (Grand Rapids: Eerdmans, 1950), p. 159. The author concludes "after careful study," "that it is one of the most baseless and absurd varieties of Bible study that the human mind has yet produced — which is saying a great deal!"

For all such palpable nonsense the movement keeps growing until it now claims some two million adherents scattered through many denominations.

In an article "Religion and Race" in *The Christian Century,* April 22, 1953, Ralph L. Roy writes: "Of the scores of Anglo-Israelite leaders in the United States a few are worthy of special note. Howard B. Rand of Haverhill, Massachusetts, 'dean' of the movement, led in the organization of the Anglo-Saxon Federation in 1930. Rand operates Destiny Publishers, the cult's central publishing house, and edits an expensive monthly magazine with 15,000 subscribers. James A. Lovell of Fort Worth, Texas, intermittently sponsors weekly broadcasts over 50 radio stations throughout North America. He edits a 70-page monthly, *Kingdom Digest,* and claims to distribute 300,000 pieces of literature annually. Wesley Swift of Lancaster, California, a loyal devotee of Gerald L. K. Smith, is regarded as the leading racist chieftain on the west coast. William L. Blessing, a lone-wolf Anglo-Israelite leader of Denver, Colorado, operates the House of Prayer for All People and publishes a monthly, *Showers of Blessing.* One of his novel fancies is that when Negroes become Christian, "God begins to remove the caste of color and to restore them into the White Israel race!" Interested parties will do well to order Mr. Roy's book on Protestant fringe groups, *Apostles of Discord,* (Boston: Beacon Press, 1953).

What, then, exactly, are the teachings of this bizarre system; and what, briefly, is the answer to its claims?

The theory is set forth clearly in the 52-page brochure *The Lost Tribes of Israel* by the late Reader Harris.[3]

This booklet opens with the incredible claim that when in Leviticus 26 God says that disobedient Israel will be punished "seven times more fiercely for your sins" (v. 18), and, "I will bring seven times more plagues upon you according to your sins" (v. 21), and, "I will also walk contrary unto you, and I will smite you, even I, seven times for your sins"

---

3. 10th ed., (Haverhill, Mass.: Destiny Publishers, 1941).

(v. 28), these words "seven times more fiercely" and "seven times more plagues" do not refer to the intensity of the punishment but must be understood as referring to time. "A time," Mr. Harris informs us, "is generally taken to mean 360 years"; seven times would therefore mean 2,500 years, "which if calculated from the captivity of Israel, would reach to about the beginning of the nineteenth century."

From this strange substitution of chronology for multiplication we are to infer that about the beginning of the nineteenth century we may look for the beginning of the end of Israel's afflictions; and, so we are told, with this agrees that just about that time some of God's people are awakened to "a spirit of enquiry as to the fate of the tribes with regard to their destiny."

The next link in the chain of reasoning is that until about a hundred years ago the great fault of Christians has been their refusal to distinguish and separate Judah and Israel. "The Bible, however, is perfectly plain. When it speaks of Israel in ninety-nine cases out of a hundred the ten tribes are meant." Judah and Israel always remained distinct after the latter had been carried captive in 721 B.C. and the former in 588 B.C.

Upon this distinction, of course, rest all of those modern theories which have identified the Lost Tribes with the Mormons, or which placed them in Arabia, or identified them with the Nestorians, or again re-discovered them in the Anglo-Saxons.[4]

Before we view the alleged results of these "facts," therefore, let us examine the Scriptural data. And when we do, this is what we find.

The Scriptures teach that all twelve tribes were under Babylonian and Persian dominion; and that the restoration was not a restoration of two tribes but of all twelve; and so indeed it had been predicted. Jeremiah (7th century B.C.) 3:18, "In those days the house of Judah shall walk with the house of Israel, and they shall come together out of the

---

4. A. Pieters, *op. cit.*, ch. IX.

land of the north to the land that I gave for an inheritance unto your fathers."

For Jeremiah had also stated definitely that Judah and Israel were together in Babylon as its fall drew near; and there was no hint at the tribes being lost: Jeremiah 50:33, "Thus saith Jehovah of hosts: The children of Israel and the children of Judah are oppressed together . . . Their Redeemer is strong. . ."

Similarly Isaiah (8th century) had predicted, 11:12, "And he will set up an ensign for the nations, and will assemble the outcasts of Israel, and gather together the dispersed of Judah from the four corners of the earth. (For the return of the ten tribes, see Isa. 10:20-23; 14:1).

Two other eighth-century prophets were Hosea and Micah. Said Hosea, "And the children of Judah and the children of Israel shall be gathered together, and they shall appoint themselves one head, and shall go up from the land; for great shall be the day of Jezreel (1:11).

And Micah's famous advent message, 5:2, stated that out of Bethlehem in the land of *Judah* the ruler of *Israel* would come forth.

Nowhere appears the arbitrary distinction between postexilic Judah and Israel which has given rise to Mormon and British-Israel fancies.

In harmony with the above, the prophet Daniel prayed for the restoration of all the tribes (Daniel 9:1, 7, 11, 15, 18).

Consequently, Ezra mentions among those who returned men from Bethel and Ai, centers of the idolatrous worship of the northern kingdom: Ezra 2:28, "The men of Beth-el and Ai, two hundred twenty and three."

And Ezra goes on to say (2:70), "So the priests and the Levites, and some of the people . . . dwelt in their cities, and all Israel in their cities.

Furthermore, Ezra offered a sacrifice for all Israel: "... and for a sin-offering for all Israel, twelve he-goats, according to the number of the tribes of Israel. . . . And the children of Israel that were come again out of the captivity, and all such as had separated themselves unto them from all the filthiness of the nations of the land, to seek Jehovah, the God of Israel, did eat . . ." (6:17-21).

The New Testament, following in the wake of the Old, knows of no lost tribes. Paul said, ". . . unto which promise our twelve tribes, earnestly seeking God night and day, hope to attain (Acts 26:7). Anna, the prophetess, was of the tribe of Asher (Luke 2:36).

Robert Moyer[5] states that the expression "house of Israel" is used fourteen times in the Old Testament before the nation was divided into two kingdoms, while the phrase "house of Judah" also occurs four times before the division. But the British-Israelites claim that after the division these two terms are strictly confined to the two kingdoms respectively. Why, then, if according to this theory only decendants of the two tribes returned, did Jesus say that His disciples should enter neither into homes of gentiles nor of Samaritans "but rather to the lost house of Israel" (Matt. 5:6)?

At the time when Jesus spoke, according to our opponents, the house of Israel was dwelling in Ireland and Scotland.

The above-quoted passages of Scripture, then, are in themselves sufficient to knock the foundation from under the entire Mormon as well as Anglo-Israel deductions concerning remote descendants of so-called Lost Tribes upon whom the Lord God should still look as upon His ancient Israel. It should be borne in mind that the group that returned from Judah and Benjamin was a small minority as well as those who returned from among the ten tribes; but these minorities are called Israel and the Jews; those that remained dropped out of the ranks, intermarried and were amalgamated among the nations. It would then be as logical and Scriptural to speak of the lost tribes of Judah and Benjamin as it is to refer to the lost ten tribes, but not more so.

5. *The British-Israel Delusion* p. 10.

Having thus rejected the foundation upon which this structure rests, let us trace to what fictitious and fantastic ideas this ill-based theory has given birth. Let us consider the things of which Reader Harris wrote, "The objection may again be raised that this is all very wonderful but that it rests to a large extent upon tradition. Tradition, however, is the basis of all earlier history."

Among these "wonderful" traditions, then, we meet with the following. British-Israelism does not abandon Scripture for tradition, but it takes such Scriptural passages as refer to pre- or post-exilic conditions of Israel and applies them, without further ado, to where they fit in with tradition.

Israel was to become "a company of nations," God said to Jacob; Joseph was to become "a fruitful bough; his branches run over the wall," Jacob added upon his deathbed. Israel was to be a maritime nation: "I will set his hand also on the sea" (Ps. 89) ; he was to possess the isles of the sea" (Isa. 24:15; 4:1; Jer. 31:10).

So, with the fiction of the Lost Tribes roaming the earth and with the centuries to work with, the British-Israelites move the descendants of the Ten Tribes over the map as the men upon a chessboard are moved. "His seed shall become a multitude of nations," said Jacob of Manasseh (Gen. 49: 19). It will at once be seen that this eminently fits that modern meltingpot, the United States.

The principle of British-Israel exegesis is to follow "the pattern of history." When certain features are predicted concerning Israel, look for the nation exhibiting those features, and, presto, you have found the Lost Tribes.

For instance, Israel was to be a Sabbath-keeping nation: that was to be "a sign between me and you throughout your generations," (Ex. 31:13). Great Britain and the United States "alone have observed the Christian sabbath" as over against the so-called Continental sabbath: Great Britain and the U. S. A. are Israel.

It was also said of Israel, "Thou shalt lend unto many nations, and thou shalt not borrow," (Deut. 28:12) ; Great

Britain and the United States have become the greatest money-lenders among the nations.

Similarly, Isaiah predicted that Israel would be an undefeated people (Isa. 54:17; 41:10).

But what of the United States? Isaiah prophesied that part of Israel was to split off from the mother country (49: 19, 20). Besides, already Jacob had predicted that while Ephraim was to be the greater, Manasseh also was to become a great people. "Where," exclaim British-Israelites rhetorically, "are the descendants of Manasseh?" And the answer is, "In Isaiah 49:20 we find these words, 'The place is too strait for me; give me place that I may dwell.'" Therefore, the descendants of Manasseh must be a great people, and "Many students of Scripture believe that in the U. S. A. we find the branch of Joseph that was to run over the wall. Manasseh was to be the thirteenth tribe, and the number thirteen plays an important part in much that pertains to the U. S. A. The original flag had thirteen stars for the thirteen states; 13 letters make up the American slogan E Pluribus Unum; the American dollar contains 13 stars and 13 letters on the scroll; the eagle on the reversed side has 13 wing feathers, 13 tail feathers, 13 arrow heads, 13 horizontal stripes, and 13 parallel lines."

The original white population of the United States came from England — but the Destiny Shapers of America fail to advise us how in the process of crossing the Atlantic these Ephraimites changed into children of Manasseh.

There is, of course, a great deal more, and it makes interesting reading; but it is all founded upon the same arbitrary method. And all of this pseudo-exegesis is backed up by equally precarious tradition.

Thus, beginning with Esdras, his second book in the Apocrypha, we know that "the ten tribes took this counsel among themselves that they should leave the multitude of the heathen and go forth into a further country, that there they might keep their law which they had never kept in their own land, and they passed by the way of the Euphrates." This is confirmed by Josephus who wrote A. D. 70:

"The ten tribes are now beyond the Euphrates and are an immense multitude." What became of them?

British Israelites have the answer. Past old gravestones in the Crimea and a town on the Danube near the Black Sea called Isacha — "evidently an Israelitish name" — they trace these tribes to Scandinavia and to western Europe. The Saxons, having come from the Black Sea, captured England from the original Britons, and divided the country into sections whose names all remind us of God's promise "In Isaac shall thy seed be called" (Gen. 21:12), for they are Sussex or South Saxon, Essex or East Saxon, Middlesex, and the like.

There is an Irish tradition that the prophet Jeremiah escaped from Egypt with a daughter of Zedekiah, the last (and by the way, illegally appointed) king of Judah. These two first reached Spain, and later Ireland. Here this female descendant of David — entitled to David's throne only by favor of Nebuchadnezzar — married an Irish tribal chief or king between B. C. 580 and 565. From then on the line of David has continued, first in Ireland, then in Scotland and England.

This feat, however, was by no means the only accomplishment of the aged prophet Jeremiah. He also succeeded in taking with him "the stone of destiny." It should be borne in mind, namely, that Jacob, when departing from Bethel, had taken with him the stone which he used for a pillow as a token of the Divine Presence, and on his deathbed had referred to it when according to Genesis 49:24 he said concerning Joseph, "From thence is the shepherd, the stone of Israel." This same stone went with the Israelites into the wilderness; Paul referred to it in I Corinthians 10:4, "the rock followed them" (just look that up in its context!).

Jeremiah, then, took this stone with him and it became the coronation stone of the kings of Argyle, then of the kings of Scotland, and until recently of the kings of England, resting as it did in Westminster Abbey. Small wonder the removal of this Stone of Scone, December 25, 1950, caused much consternation. The writer fears, however, that there is about as much historic evidence for all this as there is for the alleged story which claims that there is among Roman Catholic relics the stone upon which the rooster stood when he crowed at Peter's denial of his Lord; or, for that matter, for the feather that dropped from the wing of the angel Gabriel when he announced the Saviour's birth to Mary.[6]

Much after the same fashion great things were expected some years ago from the Prince of Wales, one of whose names was David, and who, reaching the age of 30 years in 1924, would duplicate his ancestor, the original King David. But Prince David, having become King Edward VIII, abdicated from the throne of Judah and Israel in favor of "the woman I love"; and the Duchess of Windsor proved a spoke in the wheels of Anglo-Israelitish exegesis.

It is impossible to look from the narrow confines of this brief chapter into various other angles of the strange theory which, as said before, is reported to have two million adherents; such as the fact that anthropological and racial studies and comparisons have refuted the British-Israel assertions concerning the racial peculiarities of the English and British as thoroughly as those of the Mormons that the American Indians are the Lamanite seed of Jacob. We refer the reader to the work of Dr. William Henry Smith for a knowledge of this and other features of the movement.

But, having given a brief description of the teachings and method of Destiny of America, let us ask in conclusion, Why should we concern ourselves about this cult? Why not let it alone. What is the harm it may do, the danger it may harbor?

The answer lies close to hand. Anglo-Israelites themselves reply to the question "What's the good of it?" by saying: first, it will make believers out of unbelievers.

6. Prof. A. C. Ramsey of the Dept. of Geology in London University submitted the stone to a chemical and to a microscopic examination, and pronounced it "calcareous sandstone of a reddish or purplish color with heterogeneous pebbles, and of Scottish origin." W. H. Smith, *The Ten Tribes of Israel Never Lost*, p. 91.

More men have remained unbelievers because in reading
the Bible and studying history they reached the conclusion
that God has failed to fulfill his promises in regard to Israel. But now, by studying the history of Britain and
North America, they see these promises taking shape and
being fulfilled.

And secondly, all these numerous material, national and
international, racial and economic blessings that have been
held out to the true Israel should be of great encouragement to us in these days of dire distress of the nations and
of great international fear.

It is all so very simple. "This is important to you, tre-
mendously important. Be not hasty in your judgment.
Let the overwhelming evidence *prove* to you that the Anglo-
Saxon-Celtic people of today are Israelites — and that their
nations form the nation of Israel.   Then if *you* are of
Anglo-Saxon-Celtic descent, you are an Israelite; or if *you*
are not of Anglo-Saxon-Celtic descent, but are a Christian,
then you are an Israelite by adoption! You are one of God's
chosen race: the Bible gives the story of your ancestors
and, importantly, the Bible shows the present, predicts the
future and declares the coming greatness of the Israel Kingdom. The Bible is, in fact, *your pattern of history!*"[7]

Observe, then, that British-Israel literature does not
bother with speaking of the deity of the Saviour or the
atonement for the sins of unworthy ones in His blood. It
speaks of the greatness of men, of some, nay, many men.
Their greatness is to be sought in physical descent or
adoption, as the Pharisees of old considered themselves
God's chosen people, and despised all others except those
drawn into their own circles as proselytes.

Surely, it is all very soothing, as long as it lasts. For the
Bible so read says of Great Britain, the Dominion and the
United States of America that they shall prosper; that they
shall be invincible; that their foot shall be upon the neck of

their enemies: "Israel is to be mistress of the ends, sides, and uttermost parts of the earth."[8]

We are even now accused of imperialism. What would it be if the Anglo-Israel ideas should become the prevailing view of prophetic Scripture? What if a future dictator, himself neither Anglo-Saxon-Celtic nor Christian, should decide that, the Christians themselves being witness, the Bible, that horrible, racial, material book, does indeed teach that all nations are to be subject to a fancied Israel with its numerous satellites? Surely, here lurks a danger. A political, an international peril.

The greater danger, however, lies elsewhere. The fundamental error of this cult lies in its positing another source of divine authority besides the inspired Bible. What to Roman Catholics is the ecclesiastical tradition, and to Spiritists the voices from departed spirits, that to British-Israelites is the Great Pyramid. All are condemned, together with Astrology, the voice of the planets, by Deuteronomy 18:9-15. For all substitute other sources of religious information for the God-appointed Christ.

The easy, superficial optimism of the cult is amazing. Before me lies a 40-page "Shopping Guide for Tourists," the page being 17 by 11½ inches. It is the Easter, 1954, edition of the *International Consumers Magazine*, left on my doorstep. Its subtitles are, "The King of King's Gazette," "The Universal Educator of the Sound Money Economic System Association."

Its pages are chiefly filled with advertisements by hundreds of business and professional people in Manitoba, Saskatchewan, Alberta, British Columbia, Washington, Idaho, Montana, North Dakota. The centers of the pages, however, contain such articles as: "Resurrection Life Brings Abundance of All Things"; "The Altar-Pillar in Egypt Speaks"; "King David Destroys the Lord's Enemies"; "A Sound Solid Money System Value for Value." Also, incidentally, "World News in Advance," predictive articles

8. *Ibid.*, p. 15.

concerning the future of Trans Canada Airlines and other big businesses. We learn that "A Man, a Great Engineer and a Master Mechanic . . . has built this earth . . . He has laid in it all materials needed for economic abundance. He has risen from the dead for this very purpose to make us understand that the Bible is 'God's lawbook of sound economics.' " Kingdoms that did not know this have been destroyed (Dan. 2). But now The Man proclaims abundance and prosperity to his own, "the fifth universal Stone Kingdom, made up of the British empire and the U. S. A. and Scandinavian people, who are all the same people of the Tribe of Judah, Christ's Kingdom now on earth." The Man now stands and proclaims "I am the resurrection and the life." But "no one can get these but through me from the Father." And to bring to pass all this economic abundance He has made known in these latter days "the four great powers made by the Great Engineer: steam, electricity, gasoline and oil."

Apparently, it is quite safe to trade with the advertisers, for the magazine proclaims (to the few favored nations), "The eternal gospel of abundance, peace, security coming for all."

Yes, indeed. *"And as it came to pass in the days of Noah, even so shall it be also in the days of the Son of man . . . Likewise even as it came to pass in the days of Lot they ate, they drank, they bought, they sold . . . but it rained fire and brimstone from heaven and destroyed them all. After the same manner shall it be in the day that the Son of man is revealed"* (Luke 17:26-37).

Thus Heedless was slain in Bunyan's allegory, while one Take-heed escaped. But Mr. Greatheart commented, "You cannot imagine how many are killed hereabouts, and yet men are so foolishly venturous as to set out lightly on pilgrimage, and to come without a guide!"

How About It?

1. Mention some of your objections to the theory of British-Israelism, and give reasons.

2. Why is it that these strange ideas appeal especially in our day and age?

3. Why does Satan conjure up before our eyes theories which have a following both among evangelical believers and among those who care only for the material blessings of God's promises?

4. If all Christian people had been grounded in the fundamental doctrines of Scripture, do you think Destiny of America would be able to boast as large a following as it does?

10

SEVENTH-DAY ADVENTISM

William Miller never dreamed that his name would be associated with a movement that denounces all Christians who observe the Sabbath on the first day of the week.

Miller, when he was converted from his deism, studied his Bible and Cruden's Concordance diligently for two years before he began to publish his findings. He was fifty years old when he began to preach, and even then he continued farming for some time. But he found himself led into preaching by divine providence, and yielded as opportunities to "lecture" on the prophecies forced themselves upon him. To the end of his days (Dec. 20, 1849, in the sixty-eighth year of his life), Miller remained a humble and devoted Christian. He and his followers were maligned and ridiculed; they were accused of cashing in on their preaching, and especially on those who expected the Lord to return in 1843 and, subsequently, in October 1844. The sober truth is, however, that Miller spent far more money on spreading his message than he got out of it; that he was as bitterly disappointed as any were when the Lord failed to return at the specified time; and that he remained a Bible-believing Christian who thought to the end that the Lord must come very soon.

Miller's strength lay in the fact that he preached the visible return of Christ to judge the world and to reward the faithful in an age when that cardinal Christian truth threatened to become a forgotten topic. His weakness was that he lacked theological training, and the early ministers who joined him were men of the same caliber.

It is true that a child may find the way of salvation in an emphasized Gospel of John: it is just as true that there are difficult portions in the Bible the interpretation of which a man should no more tackle without a solid theological education than one should begin to practice medicine or law without studying what medical science or jurisprudence has found in former generations.

Seventh-Day Adventists point to the fact that there have been theologians who held to the same views of prophecy which led Miller to his fundamental error, and that Miller was right when he held that any one can understand the Bible when he studies it earnestly; however, the outcome of Millerism has shown these theologians together with Miller to have been in error.

Miller's fundamental mistake was that he took the prophecy in Daniel 8:14 to refer to the end of time, and that he took the days there mentioned to mean years (one would think that "two thousand and three hundred evenings and mornings" is clear enough!). And when Miller found that his chronology had been somewhat off, it was Samuel S. Snow, one of Miller's followers, who changed the date, and first suggested the autumn of 1844.

Miller died in the Christian faith and in hope that he would soon be with the Lord.

It is here the place to remark that the book *The Midnight Cry* undoubtedly proves that most of the rumors about fanaticism in connection with the Miller movement were unfounded. (So was the rumor that the Millerites wore "ascension robes" on Oct. 22, 1844.[1])

It is a pity that Miller's followers failed to read aright the character of their mistake. When both 1843 and October 22, 1844, had gone by without the return of the Lord, they should have drawn the inference that it is wrong to figure from prophecy the time of the coming of Christ. Instead of doing this, however, Hiram Edson, a Millerite in the state of New York, saw a vision on the morning

---

1. This rumor has persisted a hundred years; it was printed even in the 11th edition of the *Encyclopedia Britannica;* also in previous editions of the present volume. Francis D. Nichol's scholarly and sober book, however, disproves these rumors as well as alleged cases of insanity as a result of the Miller movement.

after the "great disappointment." In this vision he saw
Christ standing at the altar in heaven, from which he concluded that Miller had been right as to the *time* mentioned
by Daniel, but wrong as to the *place*. The words, "Unto
two thousand and three hundred evenings and mornings;
then shall the sanctuary be cleansed," referred to a cleaning
of the heavenly sanctuary.[2]

This teaching was taken over by the later S.D.A. whose
beginning dates from this new interpretation, according to
Nichol.[3] Thus, "they have chosen to emphasize that the
'major mistake' of the Millerites was in their interpretation,
not in setting the time. Outsiders may pardonably continue to consider this as somewhat of a quibble."[4]

Elsewhere in this chapter we give what we consider the
obvious interpretation of Daniel 8:13, 14. Here we observe
that S.D.A., according to its own men, began with this
new interpretation of the 2300 days, and that this interpretation rests upon an alleged *vision* of one man.

Equally arbitrary is the choice of the second foundation
stone of S.D.A. According to Nichols it was "Father
Bates," one of the early converts to Millerism, and a captain at sea, whose "light was the seventh-day Sabbath."
Elder James White (the S.D.A. Church had been organized in 1860 and Elder White wrote this in 1868) endorsed
the view of Bates and others. To him the three angels mentioned in Revelation 14:6-11 in their "three messages sym-
bolize the three parts of the genuine movement," that is,
the genuine advent movement as begun by Miller.

Ellen G. White, who became the "prophetess" of S.D.A.,
wife of Elder James White, wrote in a similar vein. According to her, Miller and his associates "fulfilled prophecy." They had a clear understanding of the message of the
first two angels, but not of the third angel. Mrs. White
and others were willing to receive this also, and they did

2. Francis D. Nichol, *The Midnight Cry*, 3rd ed. p. 457.
3. *Op. cit.*, p. 457
4. Sidney E. Mead in reviewing Nichol's book in the *Christian
Century*, March 7, 1945.

receive it; and, says Nichols, "Seventh-Day Adventists believe that the third angel's message, when viewed in positive terms, is a call to men to honor the true Sabbath of
God, the 'seventh day' of the Decalogue, that is, the day
commonly known as Saturday. The preaching of the seventh-day Sabbath in the prophetic setting of the third angel
of Revelation 14, soon became a distinctive part of this
newly developing religious movement."[5]

And this conviction also rests, at least in part, upon an
alleged "vision" which was "revealed" to Mrs. White,[6] a
woman honored by S.D.A. as truly divinely inspired.

Peculiar Doctrines of S.D.A.

S.D.A. deviates from evangelical Christianity in four particulars. For this reason it will not be necessary to append a
list of statements by S.D.A. writers on various points of
doctrine. When we have considered these four points we
have discussed S.D.A.[7]

Moreover, two of the four points have been taken over by
Russell and are propagated by Jehovah's Witnesses with
added zest. Hence we shall discuss these in our next chapter. They are:

1. The doctrine of the *soul-sleep after death*. "The state
to which we are reduced by death is one of silence, inactivity
and entire unconsciousness," wrote Spicer; and he added,
"Between death and the resurrection the dead sleep." Suffice it here to say that we consider this teaching to be contrary to Luke 16:22-30; Philippians 1:23, 24 and II Corinthians 5:1-8; Psalm 73:24; Revelation 6:9, 10.

2. The doctrine of *annihilation of the wicked*. To quote
Spicer again: "The positive teaching of Holy Scripture is
that sin and sinners will be blotted out of existence. There

---

5. *Op. cit.*, p. 463.
6. Cf. *The Great Controversy*, by Mrs. White, p. 435. Cf. for other
"visions" and "revelations" of Mrs. White, her *Early Writings*, pp.
114, 115.
7. If we leave out of consideration that, like the Mormons, S.D.A.
are forbidden the use of tobacco, liquor, coffee, and tea. Pork and
pepper are also frowned upon.

will be a clean universe again when the great controversy between Christ and Satan is ended." In our discussion of Russellism we shall show why we consider this doctrine to be contrary to such passages as Romans 2:6-9, Revelation 20:13; also to John 3:26, Revelation 20:10.[8]

The third doctrine which is peculiar to S.D.A. is in reality their foremost and great point of doctrine. It has remained the private property of this sect. I refer to their view of the *atonement.* It is here that S.D.A. deviates most from Scriptural teaching. Before we enter into a discussion of this point we allow ourselves the following remark of a general nature.

It is evident that when we discuss Theosophy, Spiritism, and other cults which do not recognize the Bible as the inspired and final revelation from God, we can do little by citing Scripture. The Book has no authority to the mind of adherents of such cults. However, the matter becomes different when we review S.D.A. and Russellism since these systems claim to be based upon the Bible as the word of God. In such cases, therefore, it is sufficient to show that their teachings are contrary to Scripture, and are in many instances the result of hasty and superficial quoting from the Bible.

It is from their peculiar tenets concerning the atonement that this sect is named *Adventists.* Their deviation is in reference to the second coming or advent of our Lord.

1. Miller had inferred from Daniel 8:14 that Christ must return on October 22, 1844. And Mrs. White desired to vindicate the movement which Miller had inaugurated. Hence her predicament. She found a way out of the difficulty. Miller, so she maintained with a woman's love for the last word, had indeed been correct. If Daniel 8:14 showed that Christ must have returned in 1844, well, then

8. One of the most serious attempts to prove the doctrines of soul-sleep and annihilation from Scripture may be found in the two volumes, *Life and Immortality* and *Christ, the Firstfruits,* by Eric Lewis (Boston: Advent Christian Publishing Society, 1949). But see the present writer's review in *The Banner,* Grand Rapids, Mich., March 24, 1950.

He did return in 1844. And if He had not returned to this earth, well, then He had returned somewhere else. In other words, the sanctuary mentioned in Daniel 8:14 — "then shall the sanctuary be cleansed," was not on earth. Where was it then? In heaven, of course.[9]

Heaven, according to Mrs. White, is a counterpart of the typical sanctuary on earth with its two compartments, the holy place and the holy of holies. In the first apartment of the heavenly sanctuary Christ pleaded for eighteen centuries in behalf of penitent sinners. "Yet their sins re-

---

9. Both Wm. Miller and Ellen G. White were wrong. Miller's assertion that 2,300 days meant 2,300 years, these being "prophetic days" of one year each, is just as much gratuitous speculation as his statement that these "days" were to be reckoned from Artaxerxes' decree (Ezra's return to Palestine).

Verse 19 states that "the time of the end" refers to "the latter time of the indignation," God's indignation revealed in the Babylonian captivity. The vision therefore begins where the Babylonian captivity ends. Hence verse 20 speaks of the Medo-Persian power, which indeed destroyed the Babylonian empire.

In the vision it is therefore stated, verse 4, that the ram pushed westward, and northward, and southward; i.e., the Medo-Persian empire conquered Lydia (north, 564 B.C.), Babylon (west, ca. 554) and Egypt (south, another ten years later).

Then came the strong he-goat, verse 5, who is the king of Greece, verse 21. Greece defeated Persia in 490 and 480 B.C. When Alexander the Great "magnified himself exceedingly," verse 8, he suddenly died at the age of 33. His empire was divided into four parts, and out of one of these divisions came "a little horn," verse 9, "in the latter time of their kingdom," verse 23; that is, when the four divisions of Alexander's empire were going down, one by one, before the power of Rome. This little horn is Antiochus Epiphanes, who marched against "the glorious land" (Palestine, Dan. 11:16,41). He massacred 40,000 Jews in three days, entered the holy of holies of the Jerusalem temple, and offered a large sow on the altar of burnt-offering in the temple-court. This put a stop to the regular Mosaic burnt-offering. Now Daniel 8:14 states that this burnt-offering, which was rendered each evening and each morning, was to be omitted 2,300 times, in the evening and morning. That is to say, 1,150 days.

This prophecy was literally fulfilled: the first heathen sacrifice was offered on Dec. 25, 168 B.C. On Dec. 25, 165 B.C. the holy sacrifice was again offered on a newly erected altar. That is to say, the sanctuary was cleansed (I Maccabees 1:59 and 4:53). That makes exactly three years. Three years, however, equal 2,190 evenings and mornings. However, the divinely ordained regular burnt-offerings had been ordered stopped some time prior to the offering of the heathen sacrifices in their stead, which accounts for 2,300 evenings and mornings as stated in the text. —Cf. the Rev. Wm. Hendriksen in *The Banner*, March 20 and 27, 1942.

mained upon the book of records." Christ's atonement had remained unfinished. There was a task yet to be accomplished, to wit, the removal of sins from the sanctuary in heaven.

Now, as upon the great day of atonement the high priest entered into the inner sanctuary to complete, to add to the daily sacrifices for sin offered in the other part of the temple, so Christ began his work of completing His atonement for sin in the inner sanctuary of heaven in 1844. He thereby cleansed the sanctuary from sin.

And how did Christ do this? In 1844 He began His "investigative judgment." He examined all His people, and showed the Father those "who, through repentance of sin and faith in Christ, are entitled to the benefits of the atonement."

It remained only to draw the comparison between the earthly and the heavenly holy of holies still further. On the day of atonement there was a scapegoat who was burdened with the sins of the people and then sent into the wilderness. This scapegoat, so Mrs. White taught, typified Satan, the author of sin, "upon whom the sins of the truly penitent will finally be placed."

2. This speculation was duly rounded out with the assertion that when Christ had entered the heavenly sanctuary, *the door was closed.* After that no one could be saved except by receiving the heavenly sanctuary dogma. This, in other words, was a polite way of saying that which many sects have said: "Unless you accept our doctrine there is no hope for you. We alone have the truth."

Although the foregoing teaching is fundamental to S.D.A., it is not flung into our faces nearly as much as the doctrine from which the system derives the other half of its name. It is not *Adventism* pure and simple. It is *Seventh-Day* Adventism. This is the fourth point on which S.D.A. takes issue with all other Christian churches.

1. In one of her frequent visions Mrs. White saw the ark in heaven, for surely there must be an ark in heaven's coun-

terpart of the tabernacle. In the ark she saw the two tables of stone which contained the Ten Commandments; and as she looked, behold, the Fourth Commandment stood out above the others, for it was surrounded by a halo of light. With the incontrovertible logic of a woman, Mrs. White concluded that this commandment needed attention above its fellows. It had been neglected more than the other nine. How? It was evident. The Sabbath had not been kept holy. It had, in fact, been destroyed. A nasty Sunday, with wicked New England "blue laws," had been substituted for the Lord's Sabbath.

In her determination that Christians should return to the proper observance of Jehovah's Sabbath Mrs. White began to look into the history of the Sabbath in the Christian Church. She discovered that one of the popes had caused the change from Saturday to Sunday. Dr. Biederwolf tersely asks between parentheses: which pope? Now it happened that in the days of Mrs. White Christians were pretty well agreed that St. John the Divine spoke rather directly of "the pope." Mrs. White, therefore, duly concluded that Sunday observance is "the mark of the beast." The first beast in Revelation 13, so she added, is the papacy; the second beast is the United States government because this government "in spite of its youthfulness, innocence and gentleness" speaks "as a dragon" when it makes "Sunday laws." This present writer, who is an obedient subject of the United States Government, not by birth but by his own will and volition, humbly apologizes for this disrespectful reference to Uncle Sam as a beast. He disclaims all responsibility, and would not repeat it but for necessity.

Mrs. White identified this beast with the "little horn" in Daniel 7:25 and said that horn meant the papacy (see *The Great Controversy Between Christ and Satan, pp.* 51, 54, 446). In reality the little horn is said by Daniel to appear *after* the other ten horns that come out of the fourth (Roman) empire in the vision, and at the end of history, immediately before the final judgment (7:26, 27). The little horn refers to the Man of sin, described in II Thessalonians

2:4, Revelation 11:7; 13:7, cf. 20:7. See for detailed exegesis S. L. Morris, *The Drama of Christianity*, 1928; Charles R. Erdman, *The Revelation of John*, 1936; W. Hendrick-
sen, *More Than Conquerors*, 1939.

2.   S.D.A. stresses its view of the Sabbath far above its
other pecular doctrines. We are dealing here with an ag-
gressive system. There is nothing apologetic about these
people who call Uncle Sam a beast. They prefer to put the
churches on the defensive. They are forever attacking, and
their attack is almost invariably upon the wickedness of
Sunday worship.

The Atonement

1.   The sanctuary doctrine caused S.D.A. to say, "We
dissent from the view that the atonement was made upon
the cross, as is generally held." Mrs. White's writings on
the subject contain a mass of confused ideas. For instance:

"After his ascension, our Saviour was to begin his work
as our high priest. . . . The blood of Christ, while it was to
release the repentant sinner from the condemnation of the
law, was not to cancel sin; it would stand on record in the
sanctuary until the final atonement."—*Patriarchs and
Prophets*, 1908 ed., p. 357.

"We are now living in the great day of atonement. In
the typical service, while the high priest was making the
atonement for Israel, all were required to afflict their souls
by repentance of sin and humiliation before the Lord, lest
they be cut off from among the people. In like manner, all
who would have their names retained in the book of life,
should now, in the few remaining days of their probation,
afflict their souls before God by sorrow for sin and true repentance. . . . Now, while our great High Priest is making
the atonement for us, we should seek to become perfect in
Christ. . . . It is in this life that we are to separate sin from
us, through faith in the atoning blood of Christ. Our precious Saviour invites us to join ourselves to Him, to unite
our weakness to His strength, our ignorance to His wis-

dom, our unworthiness to His merits."—*Great Controversy,* pp. 489, 623.

These thoughts, scattered through many pages, first of all suggest a dangerous synergism or co-operation between man and Christ in effecting salvation. They are more briefly expressed in these words of the S.D.A. tract *Fundamental Principles of S. D. Adventists*: "He through the merits of His shed blood, secures the pardon and forgiveness of the sins of all those who penitently come to Him; and as the closing portion of His work as priest, before He takes His throne as king, He will make the great atonement for the sins of all such and their sins will be blotted out."

Another tract, *What Do S. D. Adventists Believe?*, contains this: "That by a life of perfect obedience and by His sacrificial death, He satisfied divine justice, and made *provision for atonement* for the sins of men . . . that in the final day of accounting He will formally blot out the sins of men, and they will be remembered no more for ever."

Regarding its theory of the atonement, Scripture clearly and unequivocally condemns this sect. For

a. Christ is respresented as the *ransom,* the *price for redemption* which pays for the freedom of those He represents. If Mrs. White wishes to point to the sacrifices of the Old Testament, she should have to read the book of Leviticus. Let the reader refer to Leviticus 1:4; 4:20, 31, 35; 5:10, 16; 6:7; 17:11. It is impossible to distil from these passages anything but what they plainly teach, namely, that the life of the animal is given in exchange for, as a redemption for, the life of the sinner. Thus the animal that is sacrificed atones for the sinner who goes free. Thus Christ is stated in the New Testament to be *lutron,* that is, *price of redemption* for those in Him. The word *lutron* in Matthew 20:28 and Mark 10:45 is the same word which the Septuagint has in Exodus 21:30 where it is clearly the price for freedom, that is, the atonement.

b. Consequently the New Testament is full of this teaching: namely, as the Passover lamb, or some other sin offering, took the place of the sinner, so Christ removes the *guilt*, or the *curse* from His people. For instance, John 1:29, "Behold the lamb of God, that taketh away the sin of the world." I Corinthians 5:7, "For our passover also hath been sacrificed even Christ." Several chapters of Hebrews compare Christ's sacrifice to atone for sin with the Old Testament sacrifices; see Hebrews 7:27; 9:7, 11, 14.

c. It is therefore stated that sin is removed, forgiven because of the blood of Christ; see Hebrews 9:22-26. The curse is removed by the cross, Galatians 3:13.

d. So complete is this atonement, that not only has the punishment of sin, which is death, been removed by it, but the opposite, that is life, has been gained by this cross; see I Peter 2:24.

e. Hence this atonement is described as, once for all, complete and finished. In Hebrews 9:11, 12 it is pointed out that the atonement of Christ did not need to be repeated because of imperfection, as did the atonement by goats and bullocks. On the contrary, "Christ . . . nor yet through the blood of goats and calves, but through his own blood entered in once for all into the holy place, having obtained eternal redemption" (*"lutrosis, liberatio a poenis peccatorum."* Grimm).

The latter passage is not only a sufficient answer to the supposed repitition of the sacrifice of Christ in the Romish mass; it is also a conclusive argument against Mrs. White's "The atonement was finished on the cross." Compare for the finality of Jesus' sacrifice also Hebrews 1:3; 10:12-14.

2. The teaching that the sins of Christ's people "still remained upon the record" in heaven after Christ's ascension is thus contrary to Scripture. But so is also this other tenet that the sins of the truly penitent will finally be laid upon Satan.

This entire heresy, that Christ did not fully atone for sin by His sacrifice upon the cross, is based upon another error. It may have been born of the "predicament" to interpret the cleansing of the sanctuary as occurring in heaven (contrary to Daniel 8:14, see above) ; it is bolstered up with a misinterpretation of Leviticus 16.

S.D.A., following Mrs. White, translates Leviticus 16:8, "And Aaron shall cast lots upon the two goats; one lot for Jehovah, and the other lot for Satan (Azazel).

The later S.D.A. quotes from many encyclopedias and dictionaries and thereby proves that many authorities understand the word "Azazel," which occurs only here in Scripture, to mean Satan or an evil spirit. There is no denying that they are right in this.

It is, however, just as true that other authorities still maintain that the word, "Azazel" cannot mean that in Leviticus 16:8 because that translation is contrary to the context. See for example, the *International Standard Bible Encyclopedia* under heading, "Azazel." The matter, then, remains unsettled.

But let us waive this important fact. Let us take for granted that the S.D.A. version of "Azazel" is correct beyond dispute: that does not prove what S.D.A. infers from it, namely, that the scapegoat is "for Satan" because the sins of God's people must be laid upon Satan in the judgment day in order to be removed.

This is first of all contrary to the plain sense of verses 20-22, the only passage that states what is to done with the scapegoat. After Aaron has made atonement for his own sins and for the sins of Israel, he must lay both his hands upon the living goat, and confess over him all the iniquities of the children of Israel; these are laid upon the head of this second goat. This goat is then sent into the wilderness never to return. The obvious meaning is that, since the death of the first goat has made a full atonement for the people's sins (typically, representing Christ), the curse owing to their sins is removed and can never reach them again.

This is in agreemeent with Isaiah 53:6 ". . . and Jehovah hath laid on him the iniquity of us all"; with II Corinthians 5:21, "Him who knew no sin he made to be sin on our behalf"; and with Galatians 3:13, "Christ redeemed us from the curse of the law, having become a curse for us."

To such plain language as these texts contain, S.D.A.'s statements concerning "Azazel" do gross injustice. They detract from Christ's saving work. And even if S.D.A. is correct in feeling irked when it is accused of making Satan a part-saviour (which they do not do), it has given occasion to this misinterpretation by belittling Christ's saving death and by its fantastic and unscriptural reference to the part of Satan.

3. Let S.D.A. cease from wondering when those who believe in Christ's saving work accuse them of splitting up the Christian Church on such flimsy grounds and of parading as "the only orthodox" church with a monopoly on the right interpretation of prophecy.

We now turn to the main plank in the S.D.A. platform, that of observance of the Sabbath on Saturday.

A Wrong Approach to the Sabbath Question

1. Many try to refute S.D.A. by denying the distinction between the *moral* law and the *ceremonial* law as given by Moses. They only know of one law, the law of Moses. This, they assert, belongs to the Old Testament, as it had been given to Israel. We Christians of the New Testament day have nothing to do with Moses' law. We are not under the law, but under grace. Hence the Sabbath has been abrogated. What we now have is the Lord's day, or Sunday, which we observe, not by command, but of our own volition to remember the resurrection of our Lord. It is evident that in this way important ground is yielded to the Seventh-Day Adventists. They can rightly accuse us of having destroyed the Sabbath. Moreover, Sunday observance becomes a matter not so much of duty as of choice. There is no such thing as Sabbath desecration.

2. Over against this erroneous view we hold with the Synod of Dordt of 1618-19 that there is in the Sabbath commandment something ceremonial as well as something ethical, that is, something that was temporary and something permanent. Mrs. White was correct in stating that

the Sabbath, as given by Moses, is the law of God, and no man has the right to change the law. But the form in which the law came contained temporary elements. We have no stranger within our gates, and most of us have no ass.

3. While it is true that Deuteronomy adds this reason for Sabbath observance, "And thou shalt remember that thou wast a servant in the land of Egypt, and Jehovah thy God brought thee out thence by a mighty hand and by an out-stretched arm: therefore Jehovah thy God commanded thee to keep the Sabbath day," this additional reason was given when a later generation was in danger of forgetting these things. We find the original form of the Ten Commandments in Exodus 20. And here Sabbath observance is said to be a duty because God kept the Sabbath after six days of labor. Man is to pattern his life after God's manner of working. The Sabbath goes back to creation, and is a perpetual institution.

It is for this reason also that we read of the Sabbath in Exodus 16. Before the law was given on Mt. Sinai, Israel was reminded to "remember" the Sabbath day. Since the Israelites had always had that creation commandment, they were not to gather manna on the seventh day.

It is therefore clear that Noah and Jacob counted time by weeks instead of days, Genesis 8:10-12; 29:27, 28, and that man, created after God's image, lived from Sabbath to Sabbath as did his God.

4. The objection that neither Christ nor Paul ever mentioned the Sabbath day is to no purpose. Jesus quoted from the second table of the law, and He did so at random; see Matthew 19:18, 19 and Mark 10:19. Did that mean that He changed the order, or that He abrogated those commandments He did not happen to quote? We should be careful with such arguments from silence. Certainly when Jesus said, "It is lawful to do good on the Sabbath," and, "My Father worketh until now and I work [namely, on the Sabbath]," He did not annul but recognized the Sabbath. And as to Paul, Dr. Warfield is right: We learn from Ephesians 6:2, first that obedience to parents is right. "The acknowl-

edged authority of the Fifth Commandment is simply taken
for granted. Observe, secondly, how the authority of the
Fifth Commandment, thus assumed as unquestionable, is
extended over the whole Decalogue. For this commandment is not adduced here as an isolated precept; it is brought
forward as one of a series, in which it stands on equal
ground with the other's, differing from them only in being
the first of them which has a promise attached to it. . . .
Observe, thirdly, how everything in the manner in which
the Fifth Commandment is enunciated in the Decalogue
that gives it a form and coloring adapting it specifically to
the Old Dispensation is quietly set aside and a universaliz-
ing mode of statement substituted for it: 'That it may be
well with thee, and thou mayest live long on the earth.' "

Paul showed with this quotation that the Ten Commandments were considered binding in the early Church, but the
people distinguished between what we have called the moral and the ceremonial, the abiding and the local or temporary aspects of these commandments.

And it is the same with James, as Dr. Warfield reminds
us. In the second chapter of James we are informed that
the law is a whole: we cannot break one commandment
without violating the entire law. "We might as well say,
if we have broken the handle or the lip or the pedestal of
some beautiful vase, that we have not broken the vase but
only the handle or the lip or the pedestal of it, as to say that
we have not broken the law when we have broken a single
one of its precepts." And this James illustrates from the
Ten Commandments. We must not commit adultery, but
we must not kill either. For if we keep one or nine of the
Ten Commandments and break one, we have transgressed
against the law of our God. The Ten Commandments are
a unit, and we are to keep them all, including, of course, the
Sabbath commandment.

The Right Approach

1. S.D.A. finds it impossible to keep the Sabbath day according to Old Testament specifications. What was possible

in certain regions to which the people of the Lord were limited of old, is not possible today. Thus Mrs. White began by keeping the Sabbath from six o'clock until the following day six P. M. S.D.A. practiced this for ten long years. Then Mrs. White discovered that this should have been from sunset to sunset. Was this change postponed, perhaps, because difficulties were anticipated as a result of the growth of the cult? Certainly it is Biblical to observe the seventh day from sunset to sunset. But how is this possible in lands where the sun sets once in six months? It appears, then, that the unbiblical "from six to six" is better adapted to the universal conditions of the New Testament Dispensation. However, as soon as we grant this, we have departed from the Old Testament, and conceded that a change may be introduced in the manner in which the time of the Sabbath day is determined.

2. Again, S.D.A. does not interpret the Fourth Commandment in the manner in which the "unchangeable law" demands it. On page 409 of *Patriarchs and Prophets* Mrs. White wrote: "One of the people, angry at being excluded from Canaan, and determined to show his defiance of God's law, ventured upon the open transgression of the fourth commandment, by going out to gather sticks upon the Sabbath. During the sojourn in the wilderness, the kindling of fires upon the seventh day had been strictly prohibited. The prohibition was not to extend to the land of Canaan, where the severity of the climate would often render fires a necessity; but in the wilderness fire was not needed for warmth." It is clear that the words in Exodus 35:2, 3. "Six days shall work be done; but on the seventh day . . . Ye shall kindle no fire throughout your habitations upon the sabbath day," do not refer to the wilderness journey alone, but are also for the time when the Israelites would indeed have habitations, that is, in Canaan. If S.D. A. wants to observe the Fourth Commandment as given in Exodus, let them try it, and not tamper with the literal meaning because they consider its plain language necessary

or not. The point is not that sometimes fires might be necessary on the Sabbath Day, and at other times not; but that provision should be made on the sixth day for the eventuality.

3. We have no choice left but to return to the statement that the Fourth Commandment contains something moral and abiding, as well as a ceremonial element which passed away in the transition from the Old into the New Dispensation. "The Sabbath," said Christ, "is for man," not for the Jew. But how much of it?

One might inquire why the New Testament contains no specific commandment as to how much should be kept and how much discarded or changed. The reply is that this was done in no case. The entire ceremonial law passed away; yet there is no series of injunctions as to how much of the Mosaic law may be disregarded. True, Paul fought against the necessity of circumcision in the case of Gentile converts. Circumcision in their case would have meant a denial of Christ's work which made works of the law unnecessary. Yet was there no injunction against circumcision in the case of Jewish converts. It was left to the guidance of the Holy Spirit to lead the Pentecostal church gradually into a consensus as to how much of the Old Testament law was to remain.

Thus, together with other Christians, S.D.A. does not observe the Passover; yet a Jew would have the same right to say to them, "Show me one text in the New Testament that the Passover has been annulled," as S.D.A. has to say, "Show me one text in the N. T. that says that the seventh day has been done away with"

4. Jesus, referring to what was to happen A. D. 70, evidently assumed that His disciples should at first observe the commandment of the seventh day: "And pray that your flight be not . . . on a Sabbath," Matthew 24:20. How could He refer to a future change as a result of that which they, as yet, did not understand, namely His resurrection?

5. It is futile even to attempt to refute the argument that a change slowly came upon the New Testament

Church. There is a gradual, almost imperceptible change
from the seventh day to the first day of the week. This
begins very early. The disciples are met by Christ on the
first day of the week, one week after His resurrection.[10]
At Troas Paul met the congregation "upon the first day of
the week to break bread," Acts 20:7. The church at Corinth
is advised to lay up their collections for Christian charity
on Sunday, I Corinthians 16:2. Why on earth should this
have been advised if Saturday had been still the official day
of worship? Imagine an Adventist laying aside his gifts to
the church on Sunday! To John the revelation on Patmos
came "on the Lord's Day." By that time the term had firmly
embedded itself in the Christian consciousness.[11]

6. *The* text for the change is therefore Colossians 2:16,
17. These verses do not totally abrogate the Sabbath day.
They put over against the disappearing, the *shadow,* that
which is abiding, *the body.* "The institutions of the law
which are referred to in verse 16 as foreshadowing in time

10. Seventh Dayists, holding that Scripture counts the day from
sunset to sunset, always, assert that Christ did not meet with the
disciples on the first day of the week, therefore, did not sanction that
day. He met on the second day of the week, for it was after sunset,
they claim. This is clearly contradicted by John 20:19: "When therefore it was evening, on that day, the first day of the week. . . ."
In verse 26 we read, "And after eight days again the disciples
were within . . . Jesus cometh . . ." Again the Adventists say: "That
was one day later, for after eight days is not the same as on the
eighth day." But once more they are refuted by Scripture: the Oriental way of counting time is by taking the day of departure as the
first day. One week after date, which we would call seven days
later, the Oriental calls eight days later. That "after eight days"
means the same as "on the eighth day" appears from Mark 8:31,
". . . and after three days rise again," and Mark 9:31, ". . . he shall
rise the third day" (A.V.).
It deserves attention, in this connection, that, while the women, still
under the O.T. dispensation, counted the day from sunset to sunset,
the N.T. immediately begins to count the day from midnight to midnight: Matthew 28:1.
11. The assertion of S.D.A. that "the Lord's Day" means Saturday
because Jesus said, "The Son of man is Lord even of the sabbath,"
Mark 2:28, refutes itself. Jesus said only this that, as David could
do certain things, under certain circumstances, that were contrary to
the commandment, so could He as Lord of all things including the
Sabbath day.
Already the *Didache* and Ignatius refer to Sunday as "the Lord's
Day."

of promise that which was to become real in time of fulfilment, i.e., the present time," says a commentator. So the
circumcision of the flesh was a "shadow," of which the circumcision of the heart is the "body," according to the context, verses 11-13. And this same thought is applied to the
Sabbath.

7. In accordance with this New Testament teaching and
example, S.D.A. has not an atom of evidence for calling
the Lord's Day "the pope's day." If some pope finally made
Sunday observance the legally recognized thing, this no
more proves that before this day the Sabbath was not kept
on Sunday than the formulation of the Church's faith at
Nicea in 325 proves that the Church did not believe in the
true deity of Christ until 325.

8. Consequently, the early writings of Church Fathers
contain a large number of references to Sunday as the
Sabbath day observed in their time. And these citations,
which one may find in many pamphlets dealing with the
issue, range all the way from *The Epistle of Barnabas* (100
A.D.) to Eusebius (A.D. 324). And these quotations show
that at first the Church observed both days, Saturday and
Sunday (just as at first the Jewish church kept circumcision and baptism), but gradually it was realized that the
one had come in the place of the other.

9. We confidently return, therefore, to the Synod of
Dordt. We are in great danger today of losing the Sabbath
which was made for man at the dawn of creation. Sports,
joy riding, and frivolity take the place of worship with increasing thousands. Churches stand desolate throughout
the country. Should we at such a time endeavor to divide
the Christian community even more than it already is
divided? As it is, there are only two things which all Christians reverence together, to wit, The Book and The Day.
Said the Synod of Dordt:

"There is in the Fourth Commandment of the Divine
Law a ceremonial and an ethical element. The ceremonial
element was the rest on the Seventh day after Creation,
and the strict observance of that day imposed especially

upon the Jewish people. The moral element lies in the fact that a certain definite day is appropriated for religion, and that for that purpose, as much rest as is needful for religion and its hallowed contemplation is demanded. The Sabbath of the Jews having been abolished, the Day of the Lord must be solemnly hallowed by the Christians. The day, since the times of the Apostles, has already been observed by the primitive Catholic Church."

Conclusion

S.D.A. has other strange teachings, such as the peculiar view that "during the whole period of the millennium the world is without inhabitants," and Satan will be "confined to a desolate earth for one thousand years." Such queer doctrines, like those of soulsleep and annihilation of the wicked, are arrived at by the simple process of quoting one or two texts without making the slightest effort to view them in the light of other passages; in other words are due to lack of systematic insight. But we prefer to pass by some of these things, and to give, by way of conclusion, an evaluation of S.D.A.

There is much in S.D.A. that is praiseworthy.

(1) Seventh-Day Adventists are doing a great work for the improvement of public health, through their magazine *Life and Health,* their sanatoria, and their medical missions throughout the world.

(2) They maintain free Christian schools in which they educate their children all the way from the kindergarten through college.

(3) They maintain and teach many cardinal Christian doctrines that are foreign to the other cults dealt with in this volume.

(4) They fight successfully for the sanctity of the home, the family, and marriage, and oppose worldliness in theater attendance, dancing, card-playing, and lodge membership.

(5) They put most, if not all, other Christians to shame by their very large per capita financial giving. Not only are

they all tithers (even the Mormons here put Christians to
shame), their tithes going toward the support of their own
churches, but on top of that they give huge sums of money
for missionary work.

In may therefore be asked (as Seventh-Day Adventists
ask) why this chapter should be included in a book dealing
with isms of a so much more serious nature?

To this the answer is twofold.

First, Seventh-Day Adventists are asking for it. They
are not as innocent as they want us to believe when they
complain because of our attack. *They* are the ones who began the attack upon all other churches.

Nor are they always consistent in their complaint. Thus
it will not do for officials of this church to invite the present
writer to forget about Mrs. White and to read current
S.D.A. publications, while these same current publications
state, "For her emphasis of Bible truth, for her application
of specific doctrines, for her simplification of the deep things
of God . . . the S.D.A. denomination and the world in general owe a great debt to Ellen G. White."

Moreover: look at the flimsy ground S.D.A. has for following Ellen G. White's hallucination of the Fourth Commandment surrounded by a halo of light, and building
upon that a system of theology and a church; compare with
that the firm basis for Sabbath observance on the first day
which the Church has always found in the New Testament
—then turn to the Venden brothers, S.D.A. evangelists,
unfolding their banners one after another, and arousing a
vast audience into a mob frenzy, repeating: "Is Sunday
worship from God?" "No-o-o-o!" "Is it from the pope?"
"Yeah!" "Is it of the devil?" "YEAH! !"

Are such methods of "evangelization" Christian? Do
they accord with the Godliness these "wonderful people"
(H. F. Brown) possess and desire to be credited with?

The methods whereby S.D.A. tries to gain adherents at
the expense of churches which hold to all the essentials of
Christianity to which S.D.A. confesses plus the ones they

deny or distort, are contrary to the many good points S.D.A. reveals.

Secondly: the sin of schism, of causing Christendom to lie divided before a paganizing world, is far from innocent Until recently the Christian Church has always had two things on which all agreed: the Book and the Day. S.D.A. wants to change all that. By its opposition to Sunday laws, and the like, it not only plays into the hands of the devil; it aids in breaking down the influence of the Church upon the world; it brings into disregard the very Sabbath for which it claims to have a respect that has not been shown these eighteen or nineteen hundred years. Surely, this is a zeal without knowledge. Let, therefore, S.D.A. abandon the rambling writings of a woman who suffered from a serious malady, and return to the voice of Barnabas, of Ignatius, of Augustine, of Luther, Calvin, Bunyan and all the other great Christians to which Ellen G. White so often refers in her books.

Above all, let them return to the New Testament, which states that:

1. Jesus rose from the dead on the first day of the week (John 20:1).

2. Jesus appeared to ten of His disciples on that first day of the week (John 20:19).

3. Jesus waited one week, and on the next first day of the week appeared to the eleven disciples (John 20:26).

4. The promised coming of the Holy Spirit was fulfilled on the first day of the week—on the day of Pentecost, which by law came on the first day of the week (Lev. 23:16).

5. On that same first day of the week the first gospel sermon on the death and resurrection of Jesus was preached by the apostle Peter (Acts 2:14).

6. On that first day of the week the three thousand converts were united into the first New Testament *ecclesia* (Acts 2:41).

7. On that same first day of the week the rite of Christian baptism in the Name of the Father, Son and Holy

Spirit was administered for the first time (Acts 2:41).

8. At Troas the Christians assembled for worship on the first day of the week (Acts 20:7).

9. At Troas Paul preached to the assembled Christians on the first day of the week (Acts 20:6, 7).

10. Paul instructed the Christians at Corinth to make contributions on the first day of the week (I Cor. 16:2).[12]

11. On the first day of the week Christ came to the apostle John on Patmos (Rev. 1:10).

A Dutch theologian has well expressed this truth as follows:

"Do you desire to know, O man, where the sabbath is, ask where Christ is; you will find him in the midst of Christians on the first day of the week, and not in the midst of Jews on the last. For where Christ is in the midst, there is the sabbath day. And this fact, that Christ is in the midst of His people on the sabbath, makes the day a day of spiritual rejoicing which leaves all the holydays and other days of the week far behind. Here all questions as to what we may do and what we must omit, those painful questions, drop away. Do we not limit ourselves upon a feast day to the most necessary labor? . . . Thus the commandment to rest becomes within us a desire to rest, and an example of the Sabbath of the age to come, a Sabbath that will be without evening."[13]

Finally: the writer regrets to state that a renewed study of the tenets and the methods of S.D.A. has accentuated rather than lessened his conviction that S.D.A. — although its adhrents are clearly sincere, and many Christians are among them — as a movement is dangerous.

This conclusion is based upon the following two facts:

___

12. Leaflet "Why We Observe the First Day of the Week for Worship." (Lord's Day Alliance of the United States, 156 Fifth Ave., New York, N. Y. 35c per hundred, $1.50 per 500).

It is noteworthy that the word *kuriake*, "Lord's," became the recognized word for Sunday in Christian Greek usage; and it is today, in modern Greek, the word for Sunday. —W. D. Chamberlain in *Presbyterian Life*, Vol. 6, No. 4.

13. J. Van Andel, *Vademecum Pastorale*, p. 175.

1. In its zeal for the seventh day S.D.A. goes far beyond the limits of sound and sober sense. Should, to put the matter in reverse, S.D.A. have remained satisfied to hold to its own peculiar view of the sabbath, we as fellow Christians would say, "We regret it, but the Lord will decide the matter. Salvation does not depend upon it." S.D.A., however, in its official periodicals denounces other Christians in language such as the following:

"But what the forces of tyranny really want in this country is religious favoritism and monopoly for a certain group of religionists. They would have their particular brand of religion taught in the public schools, regardless of the rights of other citizens. They would have their particular day of rest enforced upon the nation by State, Federal and municipal laws, instead of leaving the people free to rest in accordance with the dictates of their own consciences. Little by little ecclesiastical combines are bringing pressure to bear upon the powers that be to regulate the religious life of the American people in conformity to the dictates of a so-called religious majority.

"When the American patriots divorced church matters from civil government in this country, they planted the standard of religious freedom upon the solid rock of eternal truth. The majority of the people, in so far as religion is concerned, are not in the right. 'For wide is the gate, and broad is the way, that leadeth to destruction, and many there be which go in thereat: because strait is the gate and narrow the way, which leadeth unto life, and few there be that find it.' Matt. 7:13, 14."[14]

How can we escape the conclusion that these lines imply:

(a) That all who stood and stand for Sunday observance and "hallowing" of the day are tyrants and opponents of religious liberty, including those authors of liberty so much praised in this same paragraph (they certainly enforced Sabbath observance on Sunday) ;

---

14. *Liberty.* A Magazine of Religious Freedom. Vol. 41, No. 3. Third Quarter, 1946, p. 16.

(b) that as soon as there is a small minority with peculiar views of the Sabbath, the state must abandon all its
efforts altogether to make the national life at least outwardly Christian;

(c) that those who observe the Sabbath day on the first
day of the week are headed for destruction.

The latter opinion is expressed in many ways in many
S.D.A. publications. It is rather preposterous and arrogant.

But this is as nothing when compared with the following.

2. S.D.A., in making salvation dependent upon keeping
the law (especially, of course, its own interpretation of the
Fourth Commandment), returns to Judaism, not to the
pure Old Testament religion, but to that false religion of
autosoterism known as Judaism. S.D.A. wants to teach
salvation by divine grace apart from added works.[15] Like
all evangelical Christians Seventh-Day Adventists state
that God's saving grace renews man so as to write the law
upon his heart. Well and good. From it follows that the
keeping of the law is not necessary unto salvation, but
rather is an inevitable result of salvation. It follows also
that when two groups of Christians find themselves in dis-
agreement on a minor point of that law, they cannot be lost
when they live in accordance with the light that is theirs.
But S.D.A. reverses its professed faith in salvation without
works when it writes:

> "Sanctification is a definite and all-important part
> of redemption . . . God's true sabbath, the seventh day
> of the week, is declared to be the sign of sanctification
> in these words . . . Exodus 31:13 and Ezekiel 20:12."[16]
> "Yes, the test will come on the question of obedience
> to the commandments of God . . . What we need to re-
> member as we approach the final test is that God will
> mete out just rewards . . . Then if we are faithful to
> the end, even though we may have to make the supreme
> sacrifice in order to maintain our loyalty to God, we
> shall awake to hear His melodious voice saying: 'Well

done . . . enter thou into the joy of thy Lord.' Such will be the reward of all who successfully pass the final test."[17]

Evangelist D. E. Venden in his mimeographed lectures even refers to refusal to observe the seventh day as "the unpardonable sin," with reference to Matthew 12:32 and Hebrews 6:4.

From this wrong emphasis follow two things:

(a) that S.D.A. requires for baptism a confession that the S.D.A. Church "is the remnant Church" (excluding all others!) ; and

(b) That S.D.A. falls under the condemnation of Paul to the Galatians: "Behold, I Paul say unto you that, if ye receive circumcision, Christ will profit you nothing." With this last statement, however, we do not condemn individual men (we are not inspired as was Paul), but the system to which they adhere.

If, then, evangelical churches that do not observe the seventh day are "the false church";[18]

if Sunday observance is "the mark of the beast";[19]

if failure to observe the seventh day means appearing without a wedding garment (Matthew 22) ;[20]

if the Voice of Prophecy Radio Log now speaks over "Mutual System and 20 transcribed stations";[21] and

if *Signs of the Times* now boasts 27,000 copies with the promise that a new Goss rotary press will soon print more than half a million copies of this weekly —

can any earnest evangelical Christian wonder that we are

17. *Signs of the Times*, Dec. 24, 1946, p. 12.
18. "Are You on the Right Bus?" in *Signs of the Times*, the World's Prophetic Weekly, Nov. 20, 1945.
19. Mrs. White states that Sunday observance when we prefer it to Saturday observance after having heard the S.D.A. message, spells the mark of the beast, *Great Controversy*, 1911 ed., p. 449.
20. Lectures by D. E. Venden.
21. Jan. 14 and Jan. 21, 1947.

alarmed by this propaganda, and that we include a discussion of this cult in the volume *The Chaos of Cults?*[22]

Aids to Study

1. Where lies the origin of the entire Adventist error?

2. On which four points does S.D.A. differ from the accepted Christian teaching?

3. What is the correct interpretation of Daniel 8:14?

4. Whom did the two goats of Leviticus 16 represent, and how?

5. What is your understanding of the two beasts in Revelation 13? Does it accord with Mrs. White's ideas?

6. Point out the S.D.A. errors concerning the atonement. Reason from Scripture as to the real character of atonement. What do you think of the custom of reading it as "at-one-ment"? What sort of people do this?

7. What do you consider the best approach to the seventh-day position?

8. Does the Sabbath commandment belong to the ceremonial law or to the moral law? Has it been canceled for New Testament times?

9. Is S.D.A. consistent in applying the letter to the Fourth Commandment?

10. What does the New Testament mean by "the Lord's day"?

11. Is S.D.A. in line with other evangelical groups, or is it a divisive force?

12. What is your main objection to the propaganda of this group?

---

22. *The Christian Century*, Dec. 22, 1954, reports: "Seventh-day Adventists reported at their annual assembly, held in Takoma Park, that more than 83,000 converts were added during the past year, the largest number in any one year of their history. They expect to pass the million mark in membership during the coming year. Members now number 924,882. The denomination was called on 'in this midnight hour to place less emphasis upon the building of costly churches and the sponsoring of lucrative social occasions and look to the needs of the physically and spiritually poor and outcast.' The General Conference appropriated a total of $20.3 million for church projects around the world. Twelve million is definitely earmarked for foreign missions."

11

JEHOVAH'S WITNESSES

To the statement in our first chapter, that almost all cults today are more conciliatory than they were a generation ago, the Russellites are a notable exception, even though some of their literature is more sparing of violent language. They are the deadliest and most fierce enemies of the Christian religion extant today. Their zeal is in keeping with their hatred of all the evangelical doctrines, such as the Trinity, the Deity of Christ, and the true Biblical teaching concerning atonement; and they do not hesitate to denounce all others as enemies of Jehovah's kingdom on earth, grouping and labeling them the organization of "Satan the Devil."

Now here is a notable fact: Cults often put forth heroic efforts to hide the shame that attaches to their early origin.

Thus S.D.A. originated with a woman who, according to the most reputable physicians of her day, was a neurotic, suffering from mental or at least nervous disorder. With a subconscious desire to wipe the slate clean, S.D.A. has gone all out for physical health. It distributes health literature by the tons, promotes physical therapy, and has of late years its "health centers" in many cities.

Mormons, who were an illiterate group, have of late years invaded our universities and colleges with their "stakes" and educational centers; and they boast of the number of educated men and women in their ranks.

Similarly, Jehovah's Witnesses boast of their scholastic attainment in the realm of Bible study. It used to be, "Just look at your concordance, sir." Now they have graduated to, "If you will kindly consult your polyglot Bible, you will find. . . ." And they ignore all "manmade" translations of

231

the Scriptures except the *New World Translation of the Christian Greek Scriptures,* 1950, since followed by the *New World Translation of the Hebrew Scriptures* (Old Testament. Vol. I, 1953; Vol. II, 1955). These are said to be the work of "our scholars," and they ride roughshod over the conclusions of the most eminent students of Greek and Hebrew and the findings of the Church of the ages. That Arius was condemned at Nicaea in 325 A.D. simply proves to the Witnesses that as early as that the visible Church had degenerated into "the devil's organization."

Very few Witnesses have gone beyond high school. All study a few months in the Watchtower Bible School of Gilead, South Lansing, New York, and emerge as "ordained ministers," repeating the same Greek "findings" wherever they ring doorbells.

All of this goes back to Charles Taze Russell. There is no doubt that Russell was perturbed about his eternal state just about the time of the heyday of S.D.A., and he welcomed Adventism's assertions concerning soulsleep and annihilation of the wicked. That he went miles beyond S.D.A. in unchristian doctrine, we hereby state to the praise of the latter cult, which is infinitely superior to its more radical descendant.

The Beginnings

The unparalleled boldness of Russell, who founded Zion's Watchtower in 1879, and the Watchtower Bible and Tract Society at Pittsburgh in 1881, runs all through the man's life and religion. When Mr. Russell was asked in court to answer under oath the question, "Do you know Greek?", he replied, "Oh, yes." He was then handed a copy of the New Testament in Greek, by Westcott and Hort. When asked to read the letters of the alphabet on the top of the page he could not do so. Asked the attorney, "Now, are you familiar with the Greek language?" "No," said Mr. Russell, without a blush.

When in some other court Mrs. Russell sued her husband for divorce because of improper relationship with Rose

Ball, he denied the truth violently until, when cornered, he admitted embarrassing circumstances. His wife did not receive a divorce because of adultery but because his "conceit" and "domination" were such as to make life intolerable to any sensitive woman.

He then was dragged into court again because he practiced fraud upon his wife. He transferred his property to corporations and societies over which he himself had absolute control, and thus he tried to avoid paying his former wife alimony.

He was charged by *The Brooklyn Eagle* with causing "Miracle Wheat" to be sold at sixty dollars a bushel (in court he admitted that there was some element of truth in that"). He was also accused of inducing sick people to make over their fortunes to his organizations.[1]

Yet this man incessantly intimated that the churches were in the business for money, and he advertised "No Collection" meetings. And though, again under pressure, he admitted in court that he had never been ordained, this self-styled "pastor" replied to ministerial attacks upon his unscriptural teachings with the charge that the preachers did not like him because, "We have not ordained you."

He undertook a hurried trip to Japan and China, returned in a short while and called a mammoth meeting in the New York Hippodrome, where he denounced the work of "six hundred warring denominations" in China. When pressed hard he admitted that he had met neither missionaries nor prominent people in China.

And so it went continually. His boldness was so extraordinary that he calmly announced in the opening pages of his *Studies in the Scriptures* that it would be better to leave the Bible unread but to read his comments on it, than to omit the latter but read the Bible. And he stated without hesita-

1. Readers of earlier editions of this book have asked where the record of this court proceeding may be found. The answer is, in *Some Facts and More Facts About the Self-styled Pastor*, Charles T. Russell by the Rev. J. J. Ross, who quotes verbatim from the records of the High Court of Ontario and other court proceedings. Cf. also Marley Cole, *Jehovah's Witnesses. The New World Society.*

tion that no one ever understood the Book of Revelation until the "Pastor" came upon the scene, and that Jesus meant Russell alone when he spoke of "that faithful and wise servant whom his lord hath set over his household to give them their food in due season."

The "Pastor" died on board a transcontinental train in his sixty-fifth year, November 9, 1916. The belief that this unschooled, erstwhile haberdasher was something great was was kept up to the very end. His friend, Mr. Menta Sturgeon, called the conductor and porter of the train with the words, "We want you to see how a great man of God can die." But there was nothing on the sheet save an old man whose lips "did not complain, nor heave a sigh."

The funeral oration was delivered by "ex-judge" J. F. Rutherford, who proved himself worthy of the occasion. While the other mortals, according to Russellite doctrine, sleep in death until the resurrection, Rutherford prophesied concerning the great "Pastor": "Our dear brother sleeps not in death, but was instantly changed from the human to the Divine nature, and is now forever with the Lord."[2]

The "Judge" was properly rewarded for his bit of gratuitous prophetic utterance by having the cloak of leadership transferred to his own shoulders. The "Judge" became the spokesman of the "International Bible Students." In boldness the "Judge" did not yield to his master. To him the Church was *Babylon, the devil's organization.* And with an air of finality "His Honor" informed us that "preachers are dumb dogs that cannot speak for their Master (D. D.)."

In July, 1927, the "Judge," towering high above his fellowmen, thundered his challenge, "I dare you to let me

---

2. Under date July 19, 1946, the Rev. J. B. Sims, Baptist pastor, informs me from Fillmore, Calif., that he was born in the same community with J. F. Rutherford, not far from Versailles, Mo., in Morgan County. "Our mothers," writes Mr. Sims, "were very close friends." There were five girls and three boys in the Rutherford family. J. F. was an attorney, but he was never a judge of any court. "That honor he assumed, as Russell did that of PASTOR." Braden says, "He was not really a judge but a lawyer who did now and then serve as a judge on a traveling circuit in Missouri." *These Also Believe,* p. 362.

speak," and *The Messenger* could boast that our Judge had spoken over fifty Canadian and American radio stations, "a hook-up unparalleled in radio history." All that the "Judge" requested was that we give him five minutes ("Five Minutes, That's All. You Can Spare That Much, Can't You?") some time on Sunday, to hear one of his "new, clear-cut and comforting talks on 'Where are the dead?' 'Which is the true church?' and 'hundreds of others.' " For those who were so behind the time as not to possess a radio set, or who loved to hear the "Judge's" voice again, "These talks by Judge Rutherford are recorded on phonograph records. You may hear them, without obligation, right in your own home. Send a post card saying you desire this service . . . and one of Jehovah's witnesses will bring these records with a phonograph and play them for you and any friends or relatives whom you may invite. Address: Watch Tower, Brooklyn."[3]

Surely, "the Judge and Jehovah's Witnesses" knew how to gain access. The name "Jehovah's Witnesses," by the way, was adopted in 1931 at Columbus, Ohio, to distinguish the main body from a smaller group which seceded. This group has called itself at various times, "Bible Students," "Associated Bible Students," "Russellites teaching the truth as expounded by Pastor Russell," "Stand-Fasters," and other names. All are agreed, however, that when Charles Taze Russell began his teachings in 1874 it meant the coming of the Lord to prepare the world for the end.

Thus the system is based upon a bold assertion, akin to that of Joseph Smith, that there was no truth on earth until the "Pastor" came. For all that, one cannot escape from the impression that the deluge of abuse heaped upon all but Russellites serves the purpose of covering up the system's poverty of constructive thought. Someone has said, "Mr. Russell takes a drop of an idea and diffuses it into an ocean of verbosity." The system appeals to unschooled men who

---

3. These record players and the subsequent noisy sound trucks, however, have since been abandoned.

will refer you to your "concordance" to see for yourself
that "the Greek word is here *kolasin,* not *basinos,*" and
that, "It seems that the translators deliberately changed
the text here."

As the Seventh-Day Adventists conjure with the books of
George McCready Price against Evolution, so their Russellite cousins deliver lectures or vituperations against this
theory.   Evolution does not harmonize with the findings
of Jehovah's Witnesses.   It is impossible in our age to
propagate a "new" religious system without in some way
acknowledging the Bible. This was well understood by Russell. In his bold way he vehemently denounced evolution-
ists and "higher critics." But Russell's professed champion-
ship of the Scriptures hides a thorough-going rationalism.

Russellism and the Supernatural Character of the Bible

Always what appears reasonable to the Russellite mind
is of greater importance than Biblical teaching. In a pamphlet by J. F. Rutherford the doctrine of eternal torment is
said to be impossible because (1) it is unreasonable, (2) it
is repugnant to justice, (3) it is contrary to the principle
of love, (4) it is wholly unscriptural. This means, of course,
that the author's sense of justice and conception of love are
determined by his reason, and that the Scriptures are made
to coincide with the pre-established findings of his reason.
That this rationalism is fundamental to the system appears
from the opening pages of the six volumes that boldly claim
to be a better key to the Scriptures than "the testimony of
modern theologians and that of the so-called Early Fathers." We read there, "Since skepticism is rife, the very
foundation of true religion, and the foundation of truth is
questioned often, even by the sincere. We have endeavored
to uncover enough of the foundation upon which all faith
should be built — the Word of God — to give confidence
and assurance in its testimony, even to the unbeliever. And
we have endeavored to do this in a manner that will appeal
to and can be accepted by reason as a foundation. Then we

have endeavored to build upon that foundation the teachings of Scripture in such a manner that, so far as possible,
purely human judgment may try its squares and angles
by the most exacting rules of justice which it can command."

"There is a little vagueness, and a good deal of confusion
in this passage, hovering about the word 'foundation.' For
instance, there seems to be some little mixing of ideas that
are in their nature incompatible in the statement that the
word of God is 'the foundation *upon which all faith should
be built,'* and yet the writer has uncovered enough of this
foundation to give confidence and assurance in its testimony,
even to the unbeliever — that is the man who has no faith!
How can a man get 'confidence and assurance' from what
he does not believe? But one thing is clear in the passage,
namely, the writer builds his teachings of Scripture on the
foundation of reason, and endeavors to make it possible for
'purely human judgment' to try its squares and angles.
Human reason is his guide, not the Spirit of God. He sets
out with the intention of making Scripture square with human reason. The ordinary rationalist, because he cannot
square the word of God with human reason, rejects it; but
here we have a rationalist who undertakes to make the
word of God acceptable to human reason — to the minds of
fallen man, the 'unbeliever.' "

In these words J. H. Burridge has ably summed up the
situation. From Russell's introductory words we may learn
why translations are arbitrarily changed, why words are
put into our Lord's mouth that are glaringly contradictory
to anything ever spoken by Him;[4] why Russell, after stating that the Bible is a revelation from God, says, "Let us
examine the character of the writings claimed as inspired,
to see whether their teachings correspond with the character *we have reasonably imputed to God."* To quote J. H.
Burridge again, "It is quite true that a revelation from God

---

4. See, for instance, the imaginary discourse between Jesus and
Nicodemus in *Studies in the Scriptures*, I. 277-282.

to His intelligent and responsible creatures might be expected, and we can scarcely conceive aught else. But to suppose that such revelation would justify, by its nature and contents, and be in accord with the anticipations of human reason, is to deny the depravity of human nature; it supposes the mind of man of paramount authority with the word of God, and renders such a revelation unnecessary. For if it were possible for man to anticipate what is revealed, the need of revelation would be much less, if needed at all. As another has said, 'the very idea of revelation supposes that it would contain things that the human mind could not conceive without it'; but it is these very things that men object to, if they do not positively reject them. Such is the rationalism of unbelief."

Russellism, then, destroys the supernatural character of God's revelation. In this it stands with all pagan religions in opposition to the united testimony of Christendom. That it loudly speaks of the Bible as the Word of God cannot blind us to this fact: it boldly condemns those who have studied Hebrew and Greek for believing that the congruent versions of the Scriptures in all modern languages are true to the original, and substitutes as inspired a Bible that has been first submitted to the opinions of "we who have the light." Let us be as charitable as possible, and not ascribe this attitude to willful deception on the part of the system's leaders: we shall at least have to acknowledge the terrible pride of the natural mind which asserts that the Bible must teach doctrines that are in agreement with "the character we have reasonably imputed to God"; and which, without knowledge of the original languages, proceeds to label "hypocrite" whoever refuses to bow before the authority of a given Russellite's "Concordance," or "Polyglot Bible" to which they have now advanced.

Russellism and the Supernatural Saviour

Like Arianism in the fourth century, Russellism states that the Son of God is a created being. To Russellism he was Michael the archangel. This archangel became a man at the birth of Jesus, thus losing his angelic nature completely. Thus Russellism rejects the divine nature of Jesus Christ. He may have been a secondary God, but "he was not Jehovah God," as a favorite Russellite saying has it. That even a Harnack has stated, "Had the Arian doctrine gained the victory, it would in all probability have ruined Christianity," means nothing to men who brush aside the entire development of Christian theology with one easy sweep.

Russellism does maintain, however, that it bows before Scripture. But let the reader convince himself of the evasive and superficial manner in which Russell disposed of the Scriptural teaching concerning the deity of our Lord. His refutation of a mere reference to such texts as John 5:30, and John 14:28, in which Christ speaks of His human nature as subordinate to God, followed by a most arbitrary exegesis of such passages as Jeremiah 23:5, 6; I Corinthians 2:8 and the like. Let this one sample suffice here: Of the words in Micah 5:2, Russell says, "They can be well understood thus, 'Whose goings forth have been (foretold) from of old, from everlasting (his coming and Messiahship were purposed and provided for in the divine plan).' "

Meanwhile Russellism is strangely silent on such passages as Romans 9:5, ". . . of whom is Christ as concerning the flesh, who is over all, God blessed for ever"; I John 5:20, " . . . and we are in him that is true, even in his son Jesus Christ. This is the true God, and eternal life." There is but one God according to the Old and New Testament alike; if Jesus is called the true God, who could He have been but this one God, even Jehovah? As to the alleged assertion that Jesus Christ is not called Jehovah, Isaiah saw the glory of Jehovah, (Isa. 6:1-3). John states that Isaiah spoke because he saw the glory of Jesus (John 12:41) ; and of the "voice of the Lord" in Isaiah 6:9, 10, it is said in Acts 28:25, "Well spake the Holy Spirit." Again,

Peter substitutes Christ for Jehovah. "Jehovah of hosts him shall ye sanctify," said Isaiah (8:13). Peter says, "But sanctify in your hearts Christ as Lord," (I Peter 3:15). Reminding us that "Christ" is here the correct reading, good old Dr. Alexander McLaren said, "We have first to note the substitution, as a matter of course, without any need for explanation or vindication, of Jesus Christ in place of the Jehovah of the Old Testament."

Jehovah's Witnesses, then, would do well to bear in mind that Christ is substituted for Jehovah; and also that Scripture knows but one God. The subterfuge that we may call Jesus God now, but "He was not Jehovah-God," runs contrary to Scripture.

From this fundamental error concerning the Person of Christ, other errors follow:

1. Certainly, if Russellites do not believe the doctrine of the Trinity which is involved, they need not distort that great doctrine as did H. E. Pennock of New York City, "regularly assigned to the staff of I.B.S.A. (International Bible Students Association) Lecturers," whose lecture on "Things the Clergy Never Tells" was advertised on a sheet as follows: "There are some clergymen, no doubt, who are really sincere in thinking that Jesus was his own father, and the Almighty is the son of Himself; and that each of these is a third person who is the same as the other two, and yet different from them." We deem comment superfluous. It is well-nigh impossible to argue with men who are not only prejudiced but who deliberately fly in the face of all historical facts, as do these Witnesses, who connect themselves with early Christianity via Russell, Luther, the Lollards, the Waldenses (without sufficient proof to establish the connection), and at the same time speak of "that notorious pagan doctrine, the Trinity."

2. It will appear below to what deviating views of the atonement, salvation, and retribution this fundamental error has led Russellism.

Russellism and the Supernatural Work of Salvation

1. If the Mediator was not a divine person it must follow that his mediatorial work is of less than infinite value.

2. If God has not provided a supernatural Saviour for the fallen race it must be that man was not so utterly sinful that, given certain conditions, he could not be saved by a natural process (autosoterism).

3. If Jesus Christ is not a divine Redeemer, and if man has not fallen beyond repair (apart from a supernatural saving work), it follows that an eternal torment would be unjust retribution for rejecting the work of Jesus and also too severe a punishment for the not deadly character of sin.

Now all this is exactly what Russellism teaches, as we proceed to show.

1. *Atonement*

Like Christian Science, Russelism ignores the Hebrew and Greek meaning of the word "atonement," splitting it into three words, and arguing from the idea it puts into these three Anglo-Saxon words. "Pastor" Russell wrote a volume of five hundred pages entitled, *At-One-Ment Between God and Man.* Like his other writings, the book does not limit itself to the question in hand (on which Russell had little to say), but brings every Russellite hobby into direct or remote relation to the title. The first chapter on "The Fact and Philosophy of the Atonement" makes sorry reading. Not only is it disproportionately brief, and unphilosophical, and not only does it dwell at length on the theory of evolution — something that should have been done in another connection — but what little "philosophy" there is, is unscriptural. According to Russell the atonement consists of two parts, a divine and a human. But the Scriptures speak of the atonement as being so complete in the sacrificial work of Christ — see, for example, Romans 5:10, 11 — that man's part is not the establishing of the atonement or some part thereof, but the

mere entering into the atonement perfected by Christ —
see, for example, the passive form, "Be ye reconciled to
God" in II Corinthians 5:20: all that man is to do is to receive by faith, to embrace, the redemption in Christ and
thus to have himself reconciled.

But Russell conceives of the two parts of "at-one-ment"
as:

a) a work of reconciliation by the man Jesus, and

b) man's returning to God by his own free will, the condition for such returning having been made by the
part of Jesus.

(a) Not unlike the Mormons, Russell conceives of Jesus'
work as having removed the penalty of death which resulted from Adam's sin. Here again we meet with an inconsistency inasmuch as Jesus is only one man, although a
perfect man. How the death of Jesus, even though volun-
tary and not a penalty for sin in His case, could serve to
remove death not only from the one man Adam, but also
from all his posterity, neither Russell nor Rutherford as
much as attempt to explain. These men merely assert it;
and this inconsistency is all the more glaring since Russell
denies that Jesus in His human nature was the second
Adam, the new head of the human race. All that Russell
needs in order to crowd this into his system is a reference
to I Timothy 2:6, "a ransom for all." That it does not fit
into the rest of his system does not bother him one whit.

b) Russell teaches that the great work of atonement has
not been completed by the death of Christ, the latter being
merely the ransom, the price that set free from death.
Atonement is also "the bringing into harmony or 'at-one-
ment' with God of so many of his creatures as under full
light and knowledge shall avail themselves of the privileges
and opportunities of the New Covenant." And this work
of atonement "will be completed with the close of the Millennial Age." Yes, Russellism with its merely human
Jesus destroys the character of Christ's mediatorial office

to such an extent as to include the church, with Jesus, in
the name "Mediator"; the "little flock" "are privileged
to be reckoned as joint sacrificers, joint mediators, joint
reconcilers, joint at-one-ers"; "willing to lay down their
lives in God's service; who, because thus copies of their
Saviour, shall by divine arrangement be privileged to be
his joint-heirs in the Millennial Kingdom and partakers
of his divine nature."

2. *Autosoteric Utterances*

It will have become evident from the above that the
autosoteric character of man's salvation is given with the
denial of the divine character of the Mediator and the
infinite value of His mediatorial work. We shall therefore
limit ourselves at this point to one or two brief citations.

Romans 5:18 is thus quoted by "the great Paraphraser"
Russell: "For as through the disobedience of one man
(Adam) many were made sinners (all who were in him),
so by the obedience of one man (Jesus) many (all who
ultimately shall avail themselves of the privileges and
opportunities of the New Covenant) shall be constituted
righteous." He speaks of "the Church which already has
received the atonement (accepted the divine arrangement) and come into harmony with God, and . . . nevertheless . . . waits for her share of the completed work of
the Atonement, in her complete reception to the divine
favor." And he states "that this offer of salvation is a
great boon and should be promptly accepted and that
its terms are but a reasonable service."

In the same manner J. F. Rutherford describes the process of man's salvation in a genuinely autosoteric manner.
It is always man who acts first, and God who accepts
man's efforts. Even such passages as John 6:44 and John
3:7 which lay emphasis upon the work of God are twisted
into their autosoteric opposite. Thus the first named passage — "No man can come to me, except the Father that
sent me draw him"—follows the discussion of man's giving

his heart to the Lord. "It has pleased Jehovah, then, during the gospel age to draw to Jesus, great Redeemer and Deliverer, those who have the desire to come into harmony with him . . . The man now (after repentance) is drawn to Jesus by what he learns of Jesus, what Jesus has done for him, and by his own desire to follow a different course." For reasons we do not desire to investigate, this plain and unadulterated self-salvation is mixed with pages and lengthy quotations from Scripture which seem to teach the opposite doctrine from that held by the Church universal. It is the admitted *universalism* of Russellism that leads to this autosoterism, as universalism ever tends to do.

Russellism and Divine Retribution

We have now arrived at our fourth point. Russell's denial of the supernatural revelation in Scripture (in fact, though not acknowledged), his denial of the supernatural Saviour, and his denial of the supernatural character of the work of salvation, these three, lead inevitably to the denial of the doctrine of divine retribution upon those who reject God's divine plan for redemption. This point in turn contains two elements:

(a) Russellism denies that man is so constituted as to be able to suffer such punishment.

(b) It denies that Scripture teaches the existence of a place of torment.

Perhaps the last named doctrine was the original rock of defense to Russell, for from this denial he reasoned back to the points already discussed. It would seem that way when we consider the undue prominence given in all Russellite literature to "Satan's lie." Certainly Dr. Gray was right in stating that "its theory of the future life" is "that which chiefly gives 'Millennial Dawnism' its popularity with the natural heart, and constitutes its greatest harm"; just as Dr. Haldeman was correct when stating "Russellism puts a premium on wickedness." Of what was first in Russell's mind, however, we need not judge. Logically, inadequate views of the Scriptures, of the Saviour, and of the work of salvation must lead to erroneous views of the sinner.

(a) In order to make man incapable of endless suffering Russellism has invented two arbitrary definitions. The first one is that *man is a soul, but does not have a soul;* the second, that *death means destruction,* an absolute non-existence. Both are hobbies Russellites do not weary to ride. Rutherford states that "the reason the Scriptures designate animals as souls is that they are all breathing creatures. Man is the highest order of animal." He then continues in this quasi-witty manner: "The proper definition of soul is, then, any creature that breathes and possesses the sense of sight, smell, etc., and uses them. Man is a soul. Man does not possess a soul. For instance, we say a man has a cow; not that man is a cow." The "Scriptural proof" for this remarkable ingenuity is Genesis 2:7, ". . . and breathed into his nostrils the breath of life; and man became a living soul." A single text, quoted regardless of other texts, it will be noted. Why did not Rutherford read Numbers 21:4, "and the soul of the people was much discouraged because of the way"; or Matthew 26:38, "Then saith he unto them, My soul is exceedingly sorrowful and sore troubled"? Why did he not quote Ecclesiastes 12:7, where the body and the spirit are referred to as the two distinct component parts of man? He might then have learned that the soul is indeed in the cow-class; that is, it may be spoken of with a possessive pronoun: the man has a soul! Russellites as a class have not heard of a figure of speech that is called *a part of the whole.* Tell them that you saw two hundred heads of sheep in a pasture; they will conclude that the heads of sheep had been cut off and thrown on a heap; inform them that a farmer had twenty hands working for him on threshing day; they will at once (notwithstanding the Russellite pamphlet *Spiritism? Proof that it is Demonism*) have a doleful vision of hands floating through space; for man is called a soul, and that means he is all soul.

The second arbitrary definition is that of death. "The penalty is death, not dying; and death is the absence of life, destruction." To prove this definition Russell made a very poor choice when he quoted, "Had it not been for the redemption, Adamic death would have been what the Second Death is to be, namely,'everlasting destruction from the presence of the Lord and from the glory of his power.'" For there is a marked difference between total destruction and destruction from the presence of the Lord and from the glory of His power.

That "destruction" does not necessarily mean annihilation, Russell might have learned from Deuteronomy 28: 15-20, 61-64; 30:1-4. Russell did not distinguish very well when stating that absence of life means absence of existence. Why did not our Bible student refer to Matthew 22: 32, "I am the God of Abraham, and the God of Isaac, and the God of Jacob. God is not the God of the dead, but of the living"? Jesus here refers to the resurrection of the body, the plain implication being that since the patriarchs are *not dead as to the soul*, their *dead bodies* must needs be raised in order that the patriarchs may again live as men, that is, souls in bodies.

(b) Russellites become eloquent to the breaking point when speaking of "the nightmare of eternal torture." Consult among many similar utterances an anonymous pamphlet copyrighted in 1924 by the I.B.S.A. "Sheol," or "Hades," according to *Hell. What Is It?, Etc.*, should have been invariably translated "grave," while "Gehenna" means destruction, annihilation. Since the valley of Hinnom was a place where refuse was destroyed by fire, and this valley stands metaphorically for Gehenna, the fire of Gehenna is an emblem of annihilation. There is an eternal punishment, but not eternal damnation, far less eternal torment. The punishment consists of quietly going out of

existence. The dead — those not existing! — will be raised
with the same thoughts they had before their destruction,
and those who have not had an opportunity to hear or to
appreciate the (Russellite) gospel, will live again, namely, during the Millennium. If then, following their former bitter experience of the result of evil (death, destruction), they fulfil the Christian's part of the atonement,
they will enter life eternal. Should they, however, choose
to live in sin once more, their "punishment" will con-
sist of "everlasting cutting off." Where this interpretation does not fit in, as for instance, John 5:29, we are
dogmatically informed, "this word 'judgment' is mis-
translated in our Bible 'damnation.'" This, of course,
settles the matter.

While this travesty upon Holy Writ may appear conclusive to those who fall before the Russellite manner of
parading Greek words such as 'kolasis, not basinos, punishment, not torment," the truth is that here again Russellism contradicts itself. There can be no suffering in
Sheol, Hades, or the grave, since Ecclesiastes 3:19 and
9:5, 10 declare that man in death is like the beasts, without knowledge. And yet Russellites in a far-fetched
paraphrase of Luke 16:19-31 state that the rich man in
Hades represents the Jewish nation "in a condition of
torment ever since the destruction of Jerusalem; for they
have been hunted like wild animals hunted to their dens.
They have been persecuted for centuries."[5] How this state

5. Seventh-Day Adventists follow the same exegesis. In his lecture
The Rich Man and Lazarus D. E. Venden says: "The rich man who
lived sumptuously represents Israel. They were the ones who were
blessed of heaven. As far as the truths of the gospel were concerned
they had everything. . . . The Jews looked upon the Gentiles as bar-
barians and dogs. . . . In the parable it mentions Lazarus as classed
with the dogs. But a great change was brought about by the death
and resurrection of Christ . . . The beggar (Gentile), after Calvary,
awoke to find himself in the position formerly occupied by the sump-
tuous Jew, for he is now privileged through Christ to be adopted into
the family of Abraham. . . . Jesus Christ foresaw and foretold the rejection of the Jews and the long night of wandering in unbelief that
would follow, Matt. 23:37, 38." (*Continued next page*)

of torment could possibly be called being in Hades, when, according to Russellites, Hades, denotes a condition of non-existence, we do not learn. But there is more we try to find out in vain. Of Mark 9:47, 48 it is said, "This text has long been a favorite with the hell-fire screechers"— an amiable likeness of a "screecher" in the pulpit adds to the zest of what is about to be dished up — and the argument proceeds as follows: "In it they think they have conclusive proof that the sinners are punished by torment in a fire which is never quenched. They argue with great warmth that the worms die not. But be it noted that the only thing mentioned as dying not are worms. Therefore,

---

It is interesting that Jehovah's Witnesses have exchanged this earlier interpretation for another. "By this parable Jesus uttered a prophecy which undergoes fulfillment in its modern setting since A.D. 1918. It has its application to two classes existing on earth today. The rich man represents the ultraselfish class of the clergy of 'Christendom,' who are now alienated from God and dead to his favor and tormented by the truth proclaimed. Lazarus depicts the remnant of the 'body of Christ' and also that class of persons who are of good-will. These, on abandoning religion, receive God's favor and comfort through his Word." (Let God Be True, 1946, p. 79).

Both interpretations have in common that the "parable" is said to have nothing to do with conditions after life on earth. It is no sin to be rich, and it is "contrary to reason" to suppose that one should go to heaven merely for having been poor.

It is passing strange that neither Adventists nor Russellites have realized the utter impossibility of their so-called exegesis. Suppose, for argument's sake, that we fully grant that Jesus in this "parable" was referring to Gentiles and Israel or to modern preachers, would He have made their plight clear by comparing it to something which is not only non-existent, but the description of which is contrary to Biblical teaching, namely, that the dead do suffer in Sheol? It is natural and true to compare the kingdom with a mustard seed in its growth, but would Jesus have said that the kingdom is like a pebble which a man sowed in his ground and it became the greatest of herbs? Or, that it is like sand which a woman mixed with dough until the whole lump became leavened? It were just as foolish to say that Jews or modern preachers suffer as Dives did in Sheol after death if there be no Sheol where the departed suffer. Moreover, our Lord, by such careless language, would have laid Himself open to the accusation of having suggested, at least, erroneous doctrine concerning the hereafter.

The truth is that this is not a parable, but a sample case. Dives is merely one of a class. And when the story is read in its connection, Dives did not suffer torments because he had been rich, but callous, covetous, and lacking in love; see verses 14, 15. He represents the self-contained Pharisees, proudly disregarding the "accursed" masses.

it is worms that are immortal, from their viewpoint. Nothing is said about human beings as alive and conscious in that fire."

All this is no doubt very humorous — to Russellites. But this position can only be maintained by placing *the judgment before* the Millennium (in the case of believers), or *during* the Millennium (unbelievers), and by changing the meaning of the word "judgment" into "trial," or, "an honest chance." That this is contradictory to Matthew 13:42, 50, and to Revelation 20:11-15 may be considered self-evident. And this is true regardless of the question of whether these texts are to be understood in the pre-millennial or in non-millennial sense. Then there remains the conundrum as to how Russellism can admit that the wicked shall go into *everlasting punishment* and assert that this means annihilation. For the word "punishment" certainly denotes an unpleasant experience. If, then, this punishment is admitted to be everlasting, what becomes of the objection to the word "torment?" And what is more, if the punishment consists of annihilation, how can it be an everlasting punishment? How can a non-existing, annihilated non-entity continue to be everlastingly punished? But such minor contradictions in terms do not trouble Russellites.[6]

The Truth About Hades

Not a little confusion surrounds this matter, for which the old version of the Bible is somewhat responsible, and we shall therefore state the truth concerning these terms. Had the King James Version left the words "Sheol" and "Hades" untranslated, instead of rendering by "hell," there would probably not have been so much haziness on this point, and Russellites would not have been able to im-

---

6. Here also Russell-Rutherford have further corrupted the error of S.D.A. Mrs. White taught that the wicked shall suffer prior to being destroyed, some more, others less, and Satan worst of all. After suffering they are to be annihilated; see *The Great Controversy*, p. 673. Russell believes in a punishment without any suffering.

prove this confusion for their nefarious doctrine. Gehenna
means *hell;* and this is the final abode of the devil, his
angels, and the wicked. This is the place of eternal torment. Sheol, however, or Hades, is the *state of separation,*
the condition of the soul after corporeal death. Here all
the dead are alike in these two particulars: they are without the body, and they are cut off from communication
with our world. Now the Bible compares this state of
separation from the body and from the land of the living
with a local abode that is surrounded by a wall that is
locked and unlocked with a key. But even in the Old Testament dispensation, God's people, owing to God's special
revelation, understood to an extent (not as clearly as those
of the New Testament period) that this one great realm
of the dead is divided into two parts. In one of these the
initial bliss is experienced; in the other the initial doom.
The first, therefore, is the heaven of the soul, or paradise;
the second, the initial hell of the soul before body and soul
together are cast into Gehenna. This view will be found
to cover such New Testament passages as Luke 16:26:
23:43, and Revelation 1:18. That paradise is the same as
heaven, where God dwells, appears from I Corinthians
12:2 and 4. Being caught up into paradise is the same as
being caught up into the third heaven, the place where
neither unconsciousness nor unhappiness can exist, but
unspeakable words are heard. However, if the soul exists
after death in a condition of separation from the body,
the body also is separate from the soul. For this reason
"Sheol" is sometimes used of the dead body, for example,
Genesis 42:38; Ecclesiastes 9:10. At other times the word
is used of the soul, which is conscious in *Sheol;* see Ezekie¹
32:21.

The Truth About Gehenna[7]

Ge-henna is merely the Greek or New Testament expression or pronunciation for the Hebrew or Old Testament

---

7. The author acknowledges his indebtedness for this section to
Wat Is de Hel? by K. Schilder, Kampen, 1920, pp. 29 ff.

Gehinnom. Originally the vale of Hinnom, also called the Valley of the Sons of Hinnom, was an attractive spot. It was situated to the southeast of Jerusalem.

In this beautiful valley the Israelites had killed and burned their own children for the Ammonite idol Moloch. This was contrary to God's express command; see Leviticus 18:21 and Deuteronomy 18:10. Ahaz had done so (see II Kings 16:3 and II Chronicles 33:6). In Jeremiah's day the Israelites even had systematic child-sacrificing there. In this way they began to call the Valley of Hinnom *Tofeth,* that is, *place of burning;* see Jeremiah 7:31, 32; 19:6, 14; also Isaiah 30:33.

Josiah tried to destroy this Tofeth at Hinnom; see II Kings 23:10. However, his efforts were of no avail. The child-sacrifices began anew under Jehoiachin. This time the sin was that much greater because Josiah had warned against it. For this reason the prophets announced that the Valley of Hinnom would no longer be a place of burning, a Tofeth, but a place of slaughter where they would be forced to bury their dead in large numbers: see Jeremiah 7:32-34. Isaiah refers to this as to a place where "their worm shall not die, neither shall their fire be quenched," Isaiah 66:24.

This then became the irony of history, to borrow Dr. Schilder's phrase, that the former sanctuary of idolatry became the dumping ground, the sewage plant of Jerusalem, where the fire smouldered continually. The worm that always gnawed there at the corpses of the dead, and the fire that was never quenched, became the mockery of the former burnt offering in honor of the Ammonite abomination, Moloch.

Thus slowly arose the idea that this Valley of Hinnom, this Gehinnom or Geēnna, was a picture of the place of punishment of the wicked; and this idea was elaborated upon in the apocryphal literature; see Enoch 26:1-27:3.[8]

---

8. And compare Kœnig, *Geschichte der A. T. Religion,* p. 502.

In Jesus' day the idea of Geênna as a picture of eternal punishment had firmly embedded itself in the public mind, and our Lord took the thing for granted, as appears from Matthew 5:22, 29, 30; 10:28; 18:9; 23:15, 33; Mark 9:43, 45, 47; Luke 12:5. See the margin in the American Standard Version.

Gehenna, then, became the name for the abode of eternal punishment. Here the worm does not die and the fire is not quenched; that is to say, the doomed will be tortured continually. That Russellism denies, hates, and continually repudiates this Scriptural doctrine, is only due to its self-righteous exaltation of man and its belittling of the holiness, the divine majesty, and the retributive justice of God. Yet all the conceited hatred of Russell-Rutherford and the rationalism of Mrs. White cannot efface from the divine record such words as, Revelation 14:9, "If any man worshippeth the beast and his image, and receiveth a mark . . . he also shall drink of the wine of the wrath of God, which is prepared unmixed in the cup of his anger; and he shall be tormented with fire and brimstone in the presence of the holy angels, and in the presence of the Lamb: and the smoke of their torment goeth up for ever and ever; and they have no rest day and night, they that worship the beast and his image . . ." Certainly, this means more than annihilation, which is a sort of euthanasia-idea, formed to please the pleasure-and-sin-loving generation of this day and age.

Meanwhile it is well to bear in mind that there will be degrees of torment in hell: a Russellite who deliberately refuses to bow before Scripture, substituting his impertinent, "Is it reasonable?" will receive far more stripes (to borrow another Biblical metaphor) than a poor heathen who has only known the law of conscience. So we read in Luke 12:47, 48. Likewise, Paul says that judgment will be meted out to each one "according to what he hath done, whether it be good or bad," II Corinthians 5:10 and Christ said that "it will be more tolerable for the land of Sodom and Gomorrah in the day of judgment than for

that city," Matthew 10:15. Surely, this does not indicate
that sinners shall all quietly and in the same manner go
to sleep or out of existence.

The Resurrection

Most antiscriptural is also the Witnesses' doctrine of
the resurrection of Christ and, with that, of the "first
resurrection" of the 144,000 (see below).

Some years ago Russellites were significantly absent from
street corners around the time of Easter: not believing in
the resurrection they passed by that great Christian fes-
tival in silence. But that, too, has changed. A doctrine of
a 'spiritual resurrection" is being taught. That this is
something kindred to the rationalism of some Modernists
(others only teach immortality) deserves attention.

In support of this teaching witnesses will refer to I
Peter 3:8, ". . . being put to death in the flesh ["in physical form," they read] but made alive in the spirit."

Furthermore, they quote I Corinthians 15:45, where
Christ is said to have become after His resurrection "a
quickening spirit." A spirit, so is the argument, has no
flesh or blood, which are essential to the human body.
Moreover, the life is in the blood: Christ gave His life in
the shedding of His blood; therefore He cannot live with
blood and body as a human being again. When it is said
in Acts 10:40, 41, "Him God raised up the third day, and
gave him to be made manifest . . . unto witnesses," it is
asserted that Christ "took on different materialized forms,"
not having a human body, in order to show Himself alive
in the spirit.

All of which references are flatly contradictory to Jesus'
own words on Easter day and on the following Sabbath;
namely, that He was not a ghost, or spirit, but had a body
of flesh and bones, one with the spear wound still in it,
and one that could eat bread and honey. This Witness doctrine is also contradictory to Paul's words in I Corinthians
15:35ff. For Paul did not say in verse 44 that *no body* was

raised, but a body different from the first: the first being *psychical*, under the control of the lower passions, the latter *pneumatic*, that is, under the control of the higher spiritual element in man. But a body!

Doctrine in the Light of History

Unlike the followers of Miller-White, who changed their emphasis from the return of the Lord to the observance of the seventh day, the Russellites are laying ever greater stress upon eschatology. This is undoubtedly in a large measure due to recent world events.

The present arrangement, according to Jehovah's Witnesses, is as follows: "The great 'day of Jehovah' began in A.D. 1914, when he set his Beloved One, Christ Jesus, upon his throne and sent him forth to rule in the midst of his enemies, including both 'the king of the north' and 'the king of the south.' Both these kings, under demon influence, became angry and engaged in the first world war.

"The way having been prepared before the Lord, then Jehovah's 'Messenger of the Covenant,' the Lord Jesus, straight-way came to his temple, in 1918, and with that event the 'day of our Lord Jesus Christ' began. There also the judgment began at the house of God (I Peter 4:17). The approved remnant the Lord anointed, and commissioned them and sent them forth to bear testimony to the name of Jehovah and to his Theocratic Government by Christ Jesus.

"By the proclamation of the Kingdom message all nations are gathered before Jehovah's Judge on his throne, and the Lord Jesus judges them and separates them as sheep from goats. He puts the 'sheep' on his right hand and makes them the earthly companions of the faithful remnant and graciously invites them to participate with the remnant in declaring Jehovah's name throughout the earth and the establishment of his Righteous Government."

There were in 1941 "really three Great Organizations" in the world. The Nazis, who are identified with the king of the north in Daniel 11; the democracies, the king of the south of the same chapter; and the true remnant proclaiming over against both the Theocracy. The latter are "Jehovah's witnesses." They represent "the great Star and Light of Brilliancy," that stands out over the entire universe and causes "the king of the north and the king of the south to fade into insignificance."

The issue at stake was "World Domination," toward which all these three forces aspired. Our Russellites gave the democracies credit for good intentions, but they were in reality as demon-controlled as the axis powers. "The liberty-loving people, desiring peace, joy, and righteousness have operated the nations of the earth under the name and title of 'democracies.' Their purpose was good, but the demons, Satan being their chief, overreached them, and the consequences are that now in these last days the demons stand in control of all worldly governments on earth, and no human government is operating without demon control and without religion."

The last words in this citation are important. "Religion," meaning every religious force but Russellism, is one of the greatest forces for evil. Churches, labor unions, the American Legion, all fall under the term "the Devil's organizations." The Church of Rome seems to be the *bête noire*: "The Roman Hierarchy, those children of Satan," "the greatest racket ever in operation, the Catholic Hierarchy."

When therefore "the king of the north and the king of the south" made war against each other, it did not move Jehovah's Witnesses. They "hold themselves aloof from the warring nations." "If the nations of this world see fit to engage in war, that is for the nations themselves to determine and it is their responsibility."

Consequently, our Russellite friends were conscientious objectors, and they taught their children refusal to salute the flag of the United States. Their hand was against all, and the hand of all was against them.

This, in the nature of the case, led to serious frictions, and Jehovah's Witnesses have developed that comfortable martyr complex which has convinced so many fanatics of the rightness of their cause.

The 1942 *Yearbook of Jehovah's Witnesses* states that during 1941 "three thousand-odd arrests" have been made in the United States in the name of the Devil's organization among those persecuted for the name of Jesus and his Theocracy. These arrests "have been vigorously pushed with demon-controlled cunning, in localities where officials continue to yield themselves to anarchy influence of the Roman Catholic Hierarchy, the American Legion, and other law violators." Many cases in the trial courts "have been summarily dismissed without trial since the Supreme Court has said that the Constitution guarantees to Jehovah's Witnesses their rights freely exercised in doing good to the people by publishing the Kingdom messages." A booklet, *Advice for Kingdom Publishers*, has been circulated to advise Russellites how to proceed when molested by the authorities.

Literally hundreds of such cases have occupied American and Canadian courts since then. The lawyer's mantle of "Judge" Rutherford has fallen upon Hayden C. Covington, as the administrative work of Rutherford has passed on to Nathan Homer Knorr (1942). Writing books is now said to be the result of the joint efforts of many men, so that books are rolling off the presses without the imprint of an author's name.

We may here state that the cause of individual liberty, of the right to exercise one's personal religious convictions, has been served well by the Witnesses. Case after case where the lower courts had condemned the Witnesses for refusal to salute the flag or to participate in military service has been appealed to the Supreme Court and there won by the Witnesses.

The Witnesses do not assert to be pacifists; in fact, they repudiate such cataloging. Taking the Bible as their guide, they say that active participation in any "theocratic war" would be a duty. However, they know of no theocratic wars since God led Israel's hosts against the enemies of Jehovah. Active participation in wars between Devil-inspired nations is a different matter. So the Witnesses are not pacifists, but they are conscientious objectors. Moreover, virtually all of them are "ordained ministers of religion," and many have gotten free from service on that account.[9]

In the forthcoming Battle of Armageddon the Witnesses will not have to fight with carnal weapons. The nations will destroy one another, and the true servants of Jehovah will survive or be resurrected. Already the rumblings of the great battle and the surviving millennial reign of Jehovah under Christ are being heard. As Mr. Fillmore of Unity did not expect to die physically, and as the followers of Father Divine in Harlem and Philadelphia could not conceive of their leader succumbint to death, so the Witnesses are confidently looking forward to seeing their bodies renewed like the eagle's youth during a millennium in our own lifetime. The future is theirs, and it is a rosy future. Marley Cole concludes his recent volume, *Jehovah's Witnesses, The New World Society* (the most complete history of the movement) as follows: "I know of no more apt words to describe them in than those of the prophet in Joel 2:3: 'The land is as the garden of Eden before them, and behind them a desolate wilderness.'"

This is worth all the efforts, the self-denial of taking time off to sell *Awake* and *Consolation* to an unwilling public in all sorts of weather on street corners in every town and hamlet. This vision inspired the coming of 165,829 people to New York for the New World Society Assembly in 1953. This inspired the Gilead School (estab-

---

9. See, for example, the article "Jehovah's Witnesses Recognized as Conscientious Objectors. U.S. Supreme Court hands down important decisions," in *Awake*, June 22, 1955.

lished in 1942) to minister in 1942 to eleven lands by 10,-070 "ministers," and in 1953 to 143 lands by 519,982 "ministers."[10]

Source of Inspiration

Given the beliefs of Jehovah's Witnesses, it is to be understood that they should be zealous and without regard for the opinion of men. For the Russellites are convinced that the millennium is around the corner. Since Christ returned to the earth in 1874, and came to His temple in 1918, He is with us now. His return has been secret, invisible as might be expected, since He is a spirit being without a material body. If the Devil has been here all these ages without being seen, why could not Christ be here? The words of Matthew 24:36, "Of that day and hour knoweth no one," were meant for that day, but not for the time after Christ's glorification.

In series 3 of *Studies in the Scriptures* (1916) Russell reached the year 1874 as marking the beginning of Christ's progressive return through an intricate and ingenious measuring of dimensions and distances in the great pyramid of Egypt. Rather, he found in it "The Corroborative Testimony of God's Stone Witness and Prophet." It is an interesting but highly imaginative study.

These speculations were condemned by "Judge" Rutherford, who rested faith upon the Bible alone and not

10. The 1951 *Yearbook* reports on propaganda in 115 lands, islands, territories by 14,093 *full-time* workers. In all, in 1950 a total of 121,281,123 copies of "miscellaneous printing material" was distributed as compared with 100,200,094 in 1949; 622,094 new subscriptions to *Watchtower* and *Awake* were entered; a new, eight-floor "factory" was completed with a press capable of producing 29,000 magazines per hour, indicating a coming increase in printed propaganda; 49,151 more people "proclaimed the message of the Kingdom in 1950 than in 1949, an increase of 18%." And all this "means liberty for the prisoners held in ignorance and superstition in the Devil's organization and its religious prison-houses."

In a National Report by Fred Bodsworth in *MacLean's Magazine*, Dec. 15, 1953, it is stated that according to the census figures in Canada "the greatest gains, by far, are made by Jehovah's Witnesses. There are nearly five in Canada today for every one the canvass shows for 1941." The Witnesses now are represented in 160 countries (1956).

upon a pyramid. His speculation on Scriptural data is reminiscent of William Miller's ideas concerning Daniel 7:25 and 8:14.

A brief exposition of the Witness theory regarding the return of Christ may be found in Rutherford's *Creation* (1927), pp. 288-313. It begins with the following typical tirade: "It is equally certain that the clergy would not understand these times and seasons, because they form a part of Satan's organization, to wit, the ecclesiastical part. They love the plaudits and approval of men and give themselves titles, such as D.D. God foreknew and foretold through his prophet that they would thus do, and that they would be so concerned with these worldly things that they could not understand (Isa. 56:10, 11) . . . To understand the events concerning the Lord's second presence from 1874 to 1914 requires one to be spiritually-minded; and the clergy are not spiritually-minded—I Cor. 2:10-14."

Rutherford then refers to Daniel 11:40, 41. In reality these verses mean that "at the time of the end " of Antiochus Epiphanes the king of the south (Egypt) shall contend with him (Antiochus), and the king of the north (Antiochus, Syria) shall come against him (the king of Egypt), as narrated by Porphyry (whose books are lost, but who is quoted as such by Jerome). Rutherford, however, simply decrees, "Here the time of the end means that period of time in which God is shaping the affairs for the overthrow of unrighteousness by and through his beloved Son." The king of the south means Egypt, and the king of the north, says Rutherford, means Great Britain, which was then an integral part of the Roman Empire. Therefore "the campaign of that great warrior, Napoleon Bonaparte, is clearly a fulfilment of this prophecy, as reference to the historical facts concerning his campaign plainly shows."

Given this much to start with, the rest follows easily. Napoleon's Egyptian campaign began in 1798 and ended October 1, 1799. Therefore 1799 marks, "according to the prophet's own words, the beginning of 'the time of the end.' "

Applying the "rule of a day for a year" to Daniel, Rutherford has a second argument: "A time" means a year of
twelve months of thirty days each, or 360 days. This gen-
eralization is inferred from the specific instance of Ezekiel
4:6. Consequently, the "time, times and a half" of Daniel
12:5-7 are three and a half times 360 prophetic days or a
total of 1260 years. Now 539 A.D. is the year in which "we
see the Papacy, the ecclesiastical element of the unholy
Trinity ["professional politicians, great financiers and ecclesiastical leaders"] in the saddle, riding and directing
everything." Add 1260 to 539, and again we arrive at
A.D. 1799!

"In 1799 the beastly power of Rome, predominated by
the Papal system, received a deadly wound: Napoleon took
the pope a prisoner, carried him away to France, and later
refused to permit the pope to crown him as king, thus disproving the divine right of the Papacy."

A short time thereafter the first Bible Societies were organized (British and Foreign Bible Society, 1803; New
York Bible Society, 1804, and others). In 1874, the date of
our Lord's second presence, the first labor organization in
the world was created. From that time on there has been
a marvelous increase in light: inventions, discoveries, and
the like. This is in fulfillment of Daniel 12:4. And this
tallies with Daniel 12:12: 1335 days means 1335 years,
which must be added to A.D. 539, and brings us to A.D.
1874, "at which time, according to Biblical chronology, the
Lord's second presence was due." The evidence of it is
found in the beginnings of Russellism in 1874.

We are then simply asked to believe that "1914 marked
the end of the Gentile times and therefore the end of the
world," because "the facts show it." For "in all the history
of man the World War, which began Aug. 1, 1914, was the
only war of 'nation against nation and kingdom against
kingdom.'" Therefore, this marks the beginning of the
end according to Matthew 24:7, 8.

At that time also the afflictions of the disciples were to
begin, Matthew 24:9, which is being fulfilled in Christians

betraying and hating one another.   All this arbitrary exegesis should be brought up to date in the interest of Russellism: Rutherford states that Luke 21:24 contains the additional proof of the end of the world, that the Jews will be favored of Jehovah at that time; and that has happened, so he states, in the British promise of 1918 to establish a Jewish government of Palestine.

Here, of course, history has contradicted Rutherford. But the theory is changed to fit the facts; and we are now told that "the natural Jews will never again be a chosen, regathered people." Nazis have come and gone, but "Catholic Action is the chief weapon used by Satan the Devil to assault Jehovah's ancient chosen people as well as to assault the present-day anti-typical chosen people, namely, Jehovah's witnesses."[11]

Finally, since Christ took His power to reign in 1914, at which time the nations would be angry (Rev. 11:12, 13), there must be a parallel between Christ's earthly ministry and His present reign [Why?].   Therefore, as Jesus came to His temple the first time three and a half years after the beginning of His ministry, He came to His temple the second time three and a half years after 1914.   However, the "temple" now means Jehovah's Witnesses, since Christ's people are called "temple" (II Cor. 6:16, Eph. 2:18-22, I Pet. 2:5).   Hence the conclusion is drawn that in 1918 Christ came to His temple, meaning to the Witnesses, in order to test them and to put them to trial in accordance with Malachi 3:2, 3.

There are, then, two sections to the Kingdom, the heavenly part and the New World Order on earth.   Since 1914 Christ rules in His heavenly Kingdom, and He has caused to reign there with Him the "mystery class," also called "the bride class," or "the anointed class."   This is "Christ, the body," Christ Himself being "the head."   These are to number ultimately 144,000, all resurrected since 1918.   Rutherford thought in 1926 that perhaps some 50,000 of the final

11. *Let God Be True*, p. 207.

144,000 had not yet died. There will be a few tarrying when the battle of Armageddon will be fought against all the earthly forces of Satan by Christ and His spiritual forces. These few Christians (Witnesses) on earth will see the terrible onslaught without partaking themselves in the fight except by prayer and encouraging the spiritual soldiers of Christ the Captain.

After Armageddon the millennium will begin. It will be a period of cleansing from the pre-Armageddon spiritual and physical evils. There will be no instantaneous perfection, but a gradual increase in grace. And it will be a period of great happiness.

Then the Lord will come with such saints as Abraham, Isaac, Jacob, Jephtha, David, and others, in order to judge the living and the dead. First the living. Millions now living, who have an earnest desire for righteousness, but know not the way out of the world's troubles, will be given a chance. The blind, the deaf, dumb, crippled, will "develop new arms, legs, eyes, be given power of speech, and gradually develop a sound body." "Then the most skeptical, it is to be hoped, will believe that the Lord Jesus reigns." Restoration will then continue with the resurrection of those who have died without knowledge of Christ. For it is "not reasonable" that they should be judged without a trial. The trial period of each individual will be at least a hundred years (for which Isaiah 65:20 is quoted). All must have a change.

Until 1948 Rutherford and his successors maintained a "House for King David" (*Beth Sarim*, meaning "house of the princes"), equipped and kept for the reception of the ancient worthies whose arrival was expected at any moment. This house was kept also as a testimony to the world of the faith of the Witnesses in the imminent establishment of the heavenly Kingdom on earth. But in 1948 this estate was sold, although the arrival of Abraham, and others, is fully as much anticipated today.

Fifty billion people, so already Russell figured, could easily live on the earth at the same time, especially under millennial conditions, for "that number of people could be placed in the state of Texas alone, giving each one about 146 square feet of land upon which to stand."

At the end of the trial period the disobedient will be destroyed. Of these there will be exceedingly few, the theory being that during the millennial trial period most everybody will have realized the folly of his former sin, and the desirability of sharing in the life offered. Satan himself will be destroyed together with those who have chosen to throw in their lot with him. Their fate, following the final judgment, will not be a suffering in purgatory, nor in a fire and brimstone hell, but they will be annihilated and cease to exist.

But the "other sheep" of our Lord, they who did not belong to the 144,000, but got safely through Armageddon and the millennium, will continue in God's everlasting Kingdom: "Millions now living will never die."

Thus "the golden age," or millennium, will be superseded by universal Edenic conditions. Then will follow "the great Hallelujah chorus. . . . It is an entrancing scene."[12]

Russellism and Scriptural Doctrine
The Person of Christ

(a) NATURES.

"Our Redeemer existed as a spirit being before he was made flesh and dwelt amongst men. At that time, as well as subsequently, he was properly known as 'a god' — a mighty one. As chief of the angels and next to the Father he was known as the Archangel (highest angel or

---

12. Rutherford, *The Harp of God*, pp. 211-358. It is quite interesting to observe that, whereas according to this book, published in 1921, p. 228, "The king of the south mentioned in the prophecy [Dan. 11:40, 41] refers to Egypt; the king of the north means Great Britain, which was then an integral part of the Roman empire"; the 1942 *Yearbook* says, "So there are . . . the democracies, the Nazis, the first called 'the king of the south,' the next being called 'the king of the north,'" so Britain has changed from being the king of the north to the role of king of the south. Strange exegesis indeed! And look how much is inferred from such arbitrary exegesis.

messenger), whose name, Michael, signifies, 'Who as God', or God's representative. As he was the highest of all Jehovah's creation, so also he was the first, the direct creation of God, the 'only Begotten,' and then he, as Jehovah's power, and in his name, created all things, — angels, principalities and powers, as well as the earthly creation."—C. T. RUSSELL."[13]

"It is a great mistake of some to suppose that 'the man Christ Jesus' was the Second Adam. Oh, no! As the Apostle declares (I Cor. 15:47) the second Adam is the Lord from heaven — the Lord who will come from heaven, and at his second advent assume the office and duties of a father to the race of Adam."—RUSSELL.[14]

"Some insist that Jesus when on earth was both God and man in completeness. This theory is wrong, however. . . . It is also easy to be seen that Jesus could not be part God and part man, because that would be more than the law required; hence divine justice could not accept such a ransom."—J. F. RUTHERFORD.[15]

"Neither was Jesus a combination of the two natures, human and spiritual. The blending of two natures, human and spiritual. The blending of two natures produces neither the one nor the other, but an imperfect, hybrid thing, which is obnoxious to the divine arrangement."—C. T. RUSSELL.[16]

"Our Lord Jesus, who is now exalted to the divine nature, and who is not only a moral likeness of God, but in fact, 'the express image of the Father's person,' is no longer a man but a spirit being, whom no man hath seen nor can see without a miracle."—C. T. RUSSELL.[17]

(b) OFFICES.

"The Lord Jesus and his Bride (the Christ, Head and Body)."—C. T. RUSSELL.[18]

---

13. *Studies in The Scriptures*, V, p. 84.
14. *Ibid.*, V, pp. 137, 453.
15. *The Harp of God*, pp. 101, 128.
16. *Op. cit.*, I, p. 179.
17. *Ibid.*, II, p. 131.
18. *Ibid.*, I, p. 181.

"The word Christ signifies anointed. Anointing means designation to official position in God's arrangement. The Christ is the instrument or channel for the blessing of mankind. The Christ is composed of Jesus, the great and mighty head, and 144,000 members (Rev. 7:4) . . . The apostle Paul uses a human body to illustrate the Christ, the great mystery class."—J. F. RUTHERFORD.[19]

"The Scriptures refer to THE Christ as 'a holy nation' (I Peter 2:9)."—J. F. RUTHERFORD.[20]

(c) RESURRECTION.

"He was put to death *a man*, but was raised from the dead a *spirit being* of the highest order of the divine nature . . . For our Lord Jesus to have been raised a man would have implied two evils: (1) It would have implied the taking back of our ransom, which would have left us as much under sentence of death as before. (2) It would have implied to him an everlasting loss of the higher nature which he had left in order to become a man and to be our Redeemer. . . . The *man* Jesus is dead, forever dead." — C. T. RUSSELL.[21]

"Our Lord's human body was, however, supernaturally removed from the tomb; because had it remained there it would have been an insurmountable obstacle to the faith of the disciples, who were not yet instructed in spiritual things —for 'the spirit was not yet given' (John 7:39). We know nothing of what became of it, except that it did not decay or corrupt (Acts 2:27, 31). Whether it was dissolved into gases or whether it is still preserved somewhere as the grand memorial of God's love, of Christ's obedience, and of our redemption, no one knows." — C. T. RUSSELL.[22]

"Our Lord's human body, the one crucified, was removed from the tomb by the power of God . . . The Scriptures do not reveal what became of that body, except that

19. *Op. cit.*, p. 187.
20. *Deliverance*, p. 235.
21. *Op. cit.*, V, pp. 453, 454.
22. *Ibid.*, II, p. 129.

it did not decay or corrupt (Acts 2:27, 31). We can only surmise that the Lord may have preserved it somewhere to exhibit to the people in the Millennial age. The Scriptures tell us that God miraculously hid the body of Moses (Deut. 34:6; Jude 9); and Jehovah could just as easily have preserved and hid away the body of Jesus."—J. F. RUTHERFORD.[23]

"The human body of flesh and bones, etc., and its clothing, which *appeared* suddenly while the doors were shut, did not go out of the door, but simply *disappeared* or dissolved into the same elements from which he had created them a few moments before."—C. T. RUSSELL.[24]

"We have no more reason to suppose that our Lord's spirit body since his resurrection, is a human body than we have for supposing that his spirit body prior to his first advent was human, or that other spirit beings have human bodies; for a spirit hath not flesh and bones; and, says the Apostle Peter, our Lord was 'put to death in the flesh but made alive in spirit.' "—C. T. RUSSELL.[25]

Atonement

"The 'ransom for all' given by 'the man Christ Jesus' does not give or guarantee everlasting life or blessing to any man; but it does guarantee to every man another opportunity or trial for life everlasting."—C. T. RUSSELL.[26]

"And having had such a long experience with evil, those who hate evil and love righteousness will gradually be brought back by restitution process to perfection of body and mind and heart. And this restitution process will continue for a period of a thousand years, viz., the period of the reign of Messiah, during which time every one of Adam's stock, including Adam himself, will have a fair and impartial trial for life under favorable conditions." — J. F. RUTHERFORD.[27]

---

23. *The Harp of God*, p. 170.
24. *Op. cit.*, II, p. 127 (1916 Edition).
25. *Ibid.*, II, p. 129.
26. *Ibid.*, I, p. 150.
27. *World Distress*, p. 9.

"The Lord . . . does not immediately destroy all such ["stubborn, proud, disobedient ones"] . . . but gives each one a full and fair opportunity, the Prophet showing that each one shall have at least a hundred years of trial."

"But as he strives to cleanse himself [the unclean] and be obedient to the Lord, he will be helped. There shall be nothing to hinder him, because Satan's influence will be restrained (Rev. 20:1-4). The way shall be so plain and clear, that any and all may see it." —J. F. RUTHERFORD.[28]

Salvation

"Some have been blind in part, and some completely, by the god of this world, and they must be recovered from blindness as well as from death, that they, *each for himself*, may have a full chance to prove, by obedience or disobedience, their worthiness of life eternal."—C. T. RUSSELL.[29]

"The fact that God asked man to reason with him shows that he is not going to arbitrarily deliver man and give to him blessings without man's consent. If the destiny of man is fixed, without regard to whether he accepts or rejects the provision made for him, then there would be no occasion for him to reason with the Lord. This for ever puts to silence the theory of predestination of every creature." — J. F. RUTHERFORD.[30]

The Church

"These facts are set forth here, not for the purpose of holding men up to ridicule, but for the purpose of informing the people that the ecclesiastical systems, Catholics and Protestant, are under supervision and control of the Devil, and form a part of his visible organization, and therefore constitute the antichrist . . . Why do true Christians suffer? Because God has chosen them out of the world and because they refuse to show allegiance unto the Devil's organization.

28. *Harp of God*, pp. 336, 339.
29. *Op. cit.*, I, p. 158
30. *Deliverance*, p. 102.

. . . The Devil's organization is designated in the prophecies under the symbol of a 'beast' and also as 'an image of the beast.' "—J. F. RUTHERFORD.[31]

"The clergy met the conditions and they have failed. They have worshiped the Devil, sanctified war, for pay have acted as military recruiting officers, and have resorted to other devilish methods to gain their selfish and ambitious ends. They have ignored God and the Lord Jesus, and have waxed rich and powerful, while associated with their allies and under the direction of the super-mind of the god of this world. . . . They stand self-confessedly guilty before God and man."—J. F. RUTHERFORD.[32]

Hades and Gehenna

"Our Lord did not go to everlasting torment, hence we have this indisputable testimony that everlasting torment is not the wages of sin." —C. T. RUSSELL.[33]

"It was written of him that he went to hell. 'Thou wilt not leave my soul in hell' (Psalm 16:10). If hell is a place of endless torment and Jesus went there, he could not have been released. The fact that he did not remain in hell is proof conclusive that hell is not a place of eternal torment. —J. F. RUTHERFORD.[34]

"Punishment does not mean torture. . . . So those who go into destruction suffer a punishment that is everlasting; therefore everlasting punishment."

"Eternal torture is void of the principle of love. 'God is love.' A Creator that would torture his creatures eternally would be a fiend, and not a God of love."—J. F. RUTHERFORD.[35]

For Deliberation

1. Show that Jehovah's Witnesses are rationalists; and prove that rationalism and the Christian faith are mutually exclusive.

---

31. *Ibid.*, pp. 222, 226, 230.
32. *Ibid.*, p. 213
33. *Op. cit.*, V, p. 441
34. *Harp of God*, p. 53.
35. *World Distress*, p. 40.

2. In view of Russellism's rationalism, can you discover a hidden reason for its continuous attack upon all churches alike?

3. Jehovah's Witnesses are outspoken Arians (though with slight modifications). What was wrong with Arianism? When and how was it condemned by the Church?

4. Show from Scripture what is wrong with the Russellite doctrines of (1) the atonement; (2) man's efforts in salvation; (3) annihilation vs. judgment; (4) attitude toward hell.

5. Why is it said that "the day of Jehovah" began in 1914? Or is this a dogma of the Witnesses?

6. State the Rutherford exegesis of Daniel 11:40, 41; 12:5-7. Compare with these passages Revelation 13:5 and place over against the explanation of the Witnesses your own interpretation.

7. How do the Witnesses vary from the Christian interpretation of Armageddon, and of "the new heaven and the new earth"?

8. How much do you know of the vast organization and publicity of this cult?

9. Do Jehovah's Witnesses have a right to assume a mien as though they were being persecuted or discriminated against?

12

BUCHMANISM

As long ago as 1946 *Newsweek* Magazine called Buchmanism "a cat with nine lives." Many a time the movement has been written off as defunct; but always it has been revived. Indeed, what is perhaps the most exhaustive critique written by an outsider from within, appeared in 1955. It is the book of the English journalist Geoffrey Williamson, *Inside Buchmanism,* An independent inquiry into the Oxford Group Movement and Moral Re-Armament. The book is truly exhaustive, not from a historical point of view, but from a reporter's standpoint who has visited and lived with the Groupers in their Caux, Switzerland, elaborate headquarters, asked questions, and has even submitted his findings to their leading men.

The mountain house at Caux was bought, with all its towers and minarets, after World War II, from the Swiss government for the "bargain price" of 80,000 pounds, less than a French company had offered in the hope of securing the fittings and furniture for resale in France.

One of the abiding mysteries is whence all the money; however, this case is not unlike that of Father Divine, whose devotees give their capital to the cause for the privilege of serving and being provided for from a general fund: there is a sort of communism in these movements that is born of a great love for a cause.

There is no organization, no membership; there is only an organism. Buchmanism is registered in Britain as the Oxford Group (for historical reasons, no doubt), but in Switzerland as Moral Re-Armament (MRA).

The movement is still evangelistic, as it was when it originated around 1910; only its emphasis changes from time to time.

With their highly trained Macinac singers Buchmanites outdo the standard evangelistic campaigners in creating emotional pitch at the beginning of their meetings. MRA women do not use cosmetics, but good food and elaborate dinners are appreciated at Caux. One marvels at the number of men and women who work without salary. Some throw in their substance, while others donate their time and energy and are rewarded with extravagant living when on tour, because "where God guides He provides."

From the First Century Christian Fellowship, through The Oxford Group Buchmanism has arrived at Fondation du Re-armament Morale, which held its first international convention, called modestly the First World Assembly, in 1947 at Caux.

The movement is as pretentious as ever: it bids to change effectively the thinking and living of nations and their leaders before it is too late and a third world war destroys us all. And this change it expects to effect by the simple process of changing individual lives by means of its *Four Absolutes*: Absolute Honesty, Absolute Purity, Absolute Self-Sacrifice, Absolute Love.

In the most fundamentalist style the followers of Frank Buchman believe that if we change enough individuals, society and international conditions will change: "Make the man good and the world will be good."

As a result, perhaps, of the tremendous impact of two world wars and the spread of Communism Buchmanites have changed their emphasis. They now lay stress upon social and economic changes, whereas thirty years ago they planned to change the world by ridding youths of their sex-sins and later South Africa of its racial antagonism. But fundamentally the movement has remained true to itself: change the man by a *washout;* let him confess his sins before his fellow and so rid himself of his hidden obsessions; then let him begin each day with a silent period during which he listens in for divine *guidance,* and his life will be renewed and become an influence to renew the world round about him.

Historical

*Died in germa[?]
aug. 7, 1961*

Frank Daniel Buchman, of German-Swiss/Lutheran descent, was born in Pennsburg, Pennsylvania, in 1878. He studied at Muhlenberg College and Mt. Airy Seminary. Ordained to the ministry, he looked for a difficult field, trying to offset the accusation of a friend that he, Frank, suffered from an overdose of personal ambition. At Overbrook, Pennsylvania, Buchman accepted the call of a church in poor condition, and out of his labors there grew a settlement house for boys. "Frank" — as his followers familiarly called him — had a clash with some of the board members, resigned, left, toured Italy, landed in England, and had his first heart-changing experience as a result of an address by a woman whom he heard speak at Keswick on the subject of the Cross.

Having been converted, he at once wrote six letters to as many board members. These were meant as an apology, but remained one and all unacknowledged. Nevertheless, there was a new and complete friendliness when he met the addressees later on.

His mind having been completely healed by a decision to submit his will entirely to the will of God, Buchman decided that religion is not so much a matter of emotion, nor of doctrine, as of the will. His task now became twofold: to be led by God's will, and to induce others to be led by God's will.

Pondering still further the problem of sin, having seen his own sin at the Cross and surrendered his pride, he reached this conclusion: "The degree of our freedom from sin is the degree of our desire to be free." "Further," says Russell, "he believes that wherever possible one should not only hate sin, but confess sin and forsake sin, making restitution to the person sinned against."[1]

"Frank"—for some reason or other the members of the cult all prefer their own and each other's given names— went to Cambridge, where he spent a short time only. At

---

1. A. J. Russell, *For Sinners Only.*

the request of a bishop he went to Oxford, "guided to put his challenging convictions into operation in the intellectual center of England." In untheological language he spoke to university men about changed lives. The following year, which was 1909, he returned to America, where, at the request of Dr. John R. Mot, he cleaned up Pennsylvania State College in three years' time.

In 1945 Buchman went through India, Korea, and Japan. In 1916 we find him teaching in an American theological seminary. From 1917 to 1918 he was again in the Orient, where he became clear as to his convictions, method of work, and so forth.

The first house party was held in Kuling, China, in the summer of 1918, at the summer home of an important lawyer, with one hundred guests attending.

In 1921 Harold Begbie was "changed" at a Cambridge house party. He afterward wrote *Life Changers,* published in America under the title, *More Twice-Born Men.* Buchman continued traveling from one part of the world to another. His movement spread from England to South Africa. In England the leadership of the movement passed into the hands of Louden Hamilton; in the United States into those of New York's Rector of Calvary Church, Samuel M. Shoemaker, Jr.

Shoemaker abandoned the movement in October, 1941, saying: "Be kind and good — the people who do that are Christians. The people who try to act like Jesus and go about doing good — they are the Christians. 'Be like Jesus' that is Christianity. Is that Christianity? Is the poor effort of any man to approach perfection Christianity? Is my attempt to find my way back to God Christianity? . . . I know it is not, and so do you."

"I am sick of all this talk about the Golden Rule. . . . Some of us have never caught original Christianity by the hem. For original Christianity began with the announcement of something that God had done, something that God had given. It was wholly supernatural, not so much in the sense of the miraculous accompaniments of it, but in the sense that it was itself a great miracle, because only God Himself could have created it. Original Christianity, true Christianity for all time, is not a matter of man reaching up to find God, but of God reaching down to find man; not a matter of man trying to live up to a moral code, but of man responding with his whole nature to the mercy and kindness of God."[2]

Buchman himself for many years remained a sort of international supervisor, now in Africa, now in Europe, then in America. Since 1946, however, he has had his headquarters in London, and his personal abode since the First World Assembly in 1947 at Caux, Switzerland. In 1951 he revisited America, perhaps for the last time, for the World Assembly at Mackinac Island, Michigan. In 1953 he visited India with a "world team." Since that the aged leader has lived at Caux. There Mr. Williamson had occasion to wonder whether the leadership has not already been taken out of his hands by younger men, while the founder confines himself much to his room and, when attending meetings, limits his remarks to, "Close that window: too much air!" and similar expostulations.

For the sake of completeness it might be added that the names "Oxford Group" and "Oxford Movement," still in use in Britain for obvious reasons, were first coined in South Africa in 1929, while "Moral Re-Armament" was first used in 1938 in East-Ham when Buchman was 60 years of age.

Appraisal

From the beginning Buchmanism has evoked both favorable and adverse comment, often from similar quarters. When in 1924 President Hibben of Princeton University had banished Buchman from the campus, Dr. Stevenson, President of Princeton Seminary, presided at a house party in New York. Perhaps Ferguson was right when he stated that President Hibben resented Buchman's

---

2. *Moody Monthly*, Jan., 1942,

statement that eighty-five percent of Princeton's students
were sex perverts.

Even since that day liberal ministers have condemned
Buchmanism for its orthodox theology, while evangelicals
have repudiated the movement because of its liberalism
and lack of doctrine. Buchmanism has no organization
and is not interested in denominations; it urges its adherents to improve conditions wherever they are.

(A) *Good Points*

1. Buchmanism is a reaction against mass revivalism
gone to seed. Clover C. Loud has been refuted by today's
developments (he said that Moody was the last bona-fide
evangelist in America) ; yet there is truth in the assertion
that increased commercialism, together with a demand for
statistics and numbers, has spoiled revivalism in America.
Buchman's emphasis upon individual changed lives is a
wholesome thing. It is in line with Homrighausen's celebrated small volume written for the Federal Council of
Churches in 1943, *Choose Ye This Day,* Philadelphia (The
Westminster Press). We need individual conversions, decisions and commitment rather than mass hysteria and
mob psychology.

2. The fact that Buchmanism labors mostly (not exclusively!) among the educated and the rich, should not, in the
writer's opinion, be held against it. It is an undeniable fact
that generally the Church has greatly neglected the upper
classes, and has seemed rather afraid of them. It is high
time that, beside the many and costly efforts to win "the
down and outs," someone should have started something to
reach "the up and outs."

3. Buchmanism challenges our dead or lukewarm
churches. With its demands for a *testimony* and a *surrendered* life, it throws down the gauntlet to churches whose
members have merely "joined a church and sat in a pew,"
to borrow a witticism of Salvation Army origin and have
brought only their leavings to the collection plate on Sun-

day. Any Buchmanite knows that he may be guided at any time to leave home and to "change" those nearby or far away.

4. There is an element of truth in what the Primate of Denmark said at Berlin, Germany: "We never realized how unintelligible our language was until we heard the Oxford Group . . . The old language may suit conventional Christians, who probably have been familiar all their lives with the Bible and with Christian phraseology and customs. But we must talk differently to pagans and atheists, skeptics and critics, the wanton, the vicious, the scoffer, and even to those who are in doubt, but are earnestly striving to find the Truth." However, though we admit this need for reaching people by beginning just where they are, and though we confess that the Church has often failed to do this, there remains a difference between dragging the Bible down to the low level of the people and beginning on the low level in order to lift the people to the level of the Bible and the Church. The old terms, such as regeneration, conversion, justification by faith, are not above the capacity of a man with average mentality; and there is a danger lest, in discarding these technical terms, we also lose the ideas they represent.

5. We may wholeheartedly welcome Buchmanism's emphasis upon life as over against dogma accepted by the intellect. It should be added, however, that life without doctrine is just as futile as doctrine apart from life.

6. It may be added that Buchmanism has stressed again something that modern Protestantism had lost. Luther kept the confessional; the Calvinistic branch of Protestantism substituted for it the official family visiting by the elders of the church. Family visitation has the inherent weakness that adolescents in particular hesitate to speak of their sins in the presence of their elders, parents, brothers, and sisters. And thus James 5:16 has gone largely by the board. Buchman has again called attention to the fact that confession is good for the soul: it is that even from a psychological point of view. And truly, many of the Buchmanite "soul-

surgeons" have proved no mean doctors. Some of these men have acquired remarkable skill. When a prospect is reticent, the surgeon begins to take him into his confidence by telling the surgeon's own experience with sin and cleansing. This opens the way to confession, which is to be done in the face of the Four Absolutes: Absolute Honesty, Absolute Purity, Absolute Self-Sacrifice, Absolute Love. This is called sharing. But sharing is also the rehearsal of one's experience in confession and release. This occurs sometimes before one person and at other times before an applauding crowd met for the purpose of exchanges. This then takes the place of the old-fashioned testimonial meeting.

(B) *Weaknesses*

1. The Buchmanites put the cart before the horse when they say that doctrine is based upon experience. My own experience with the Groupers here tallies with that of other evangelical writers. I met with a strange unwillingness to state any doctrinal convictions. "As a Group we do not put theology before experience. If I know anything about the development of theology, it came from the experience of men. It is merely a statement of an experience which has come to men; therefore, you and I have no right to say to people, 'You must believe a set of dogma if you are to be saved.' In the first place, there is nothing magical about a belief, and in the second place, if there is no real genuine experience combined with the belief, it is hollow and unreal. I can say from my own experience that in the five years during which I have lived this life, I have learned more theology than I ever did in my whole seminary career. It is a theology that has grown out of my growing experience of God."

This citation from a letter by one of the leaders presents the dominant view. It is essentially and fundamentally erroneous. It is the view held by all the false mystics. Theology is bound to the inspired Word of God. So is experience. Theology is the formulation of what Scripture tells us about the works of God for us, in us, and through us. Scriptural teaching is to be accepted with the head and the heart; and life is to be based upon it and regulated by it. "To the law and to the testimony! if they speak not according to this word, surely there is no morning for them." Isaiah 8:20.

2. From this fundamental error of Buchmanism follows a neglect of Christian doctrine which makes the entire movement look suspicious. This may be seen from the following facts:

a. A. J. Russell's *For Sinners Only*, one of the chief, older works of the cult, contains no reference to the saving blood of Christ. The same holds true of the "Layman's" *What is the Oxford Group?*

b. There is a general disregard of doctrine. Shoemaker says, "I have not time to align myself with any group who think that by the promulgation of a point of view they are going to save the world." We might well ask if insisting upon Sharing, Surrender, Changing and Guidance is not a point of view which they promulgate.

c. This undoctrinal and antidoctrinal point of departure results in faulty and totally inadequate definitions. Thus Dr. G. T. Lee, Editor of the *Lutheran Herald*, points out that there no no proper sense of the awfulness of sin. One looks in vain for a statement concerning the *guilt* of sin. Dr. T. T. Shields, who has had considerable experience with the Groups, has never heard them repudiate the most modernistic tenets held by some of the members. Sin, according to Russell, is "anything in my life which keeps me from God and from other people."

Similarly, "Surrender" is described by the Layman as "a simple decision put into simple language, spoken aloud to God, in front of a witness, at any time and in any place, that we have decided to forget the past in God and to give our future into His keeping."

d. At times this inadequate respect for wholesome doctrine degenerates into a positive dislike for fundamental doctrines. Thus when a Group convert wrote in *The Church*

of England Newspaper, July 29, 1932, "I have lived without
God all my life . . . I came into touch with the Oxford Group,
and life has been transformed for me, I have found a happiness and a peace that I never suspected the existence of. But
I feel this difficulty: The Church requires me to stand in the
presence of that Baby in the manger and say: 'Lo, there
lies God,' and I cannot do it. I feel that He is unique . . .
yet, to say straight out, 'There lies God,' is more than I can
manage . . ."

e. In view of such statements, what becomes of Buchman's own conversion which is described as "an experience
of the Cross of Christ?" What does it mean? And why did
not Shoemaker realize when commenting on Acts 2:42-47,
on page 88 of *The Conversion of the Church*, that it is inadequate to say, "Not only was this an experience of fellowship between individuals, but groups in different localities
were in touch with groups in other places"? He should have
marked the words, And with great power gave the apostles
witness of the resurrection of the Lord Jesus; and great
grace was upon them all. Dr. Machen said of Peter's Pentecostal sermon, "There was nothing about Peter's experience, but a great deal about Christ."

(3) In close connection with this is the refusal of Dr.
Buchman and others to discuss, or to listen to criticism.
There is too much pragmatism. The question, "Does it
work?" is insufficient. Changed lives, improved lives, are
not necessarily the fruit of regeneration.

4. Rom Landau discovered that the "Sharing" of Buchmanites is not always honest. Stories were repeated and
changed from time to time. Moreover, many visitors have
remarked that the stories rehashed at the hilarious meetings
at house parties were an insult to the majesty of God.

5. To dwell upon sins formerly committed, and to tell
them with gusto, as is undoubtedly done at the house parties, often creates the impression of boasting in one's shame.
Some critics could not escape the conviction that the Buchmanites enjoyed each other's filth with a vicarious taste of
the sin described. True repentance results in the language

of Psalm 51 or Psalm 32. Can we imagine David recounting
his sin under applause?

6. "Guidance," with the mind entirely relaxed and surrendered, is dangerous. Such ludicrous and silly suggestions as, "You must eat porridge in the morning," or: "sau-
sage," do not proceed from God as guidance for breakfast
or dinner. Buchman's definition that religion is a matter
of the will is wrong. When God renews man, He renews
his intellect as well as his emotional life and his will. Nor
has God given us our intellect to set it aside. The quiet
"listening in" must again give way to speaking to God and
letting the Bible-saturated mind decide for itself after
prayer. Dr. G. H. Stevenson, a Toronto physician, wrote in
The New Outlook, "The hallucinatory *'voices'* of the mentally ill, the spirit voices of our spiritualist friends, the
'guidance' of the Oxford Group, are as closely related as
children of the same parents, and the parents of these three
unusual children are a sensitive, emotionally unstable personality in union with the longing for happiness in some
other world than the one God has given us."[3]

7. Closely related to this puerile conception of prayer as
a one-sided "listening in," with a pad and pencil, are some
of the little things wherewith "Frank" amuses his followers. P, R, A, Y, he tells them, means "Powerful Radiograms
Always Yours." J, E, S, U, S, means, "Just Exactly Suits
Us Sinners."

It is rather interesting to hear Dr. Buchman relate that
the totality of Christian experience consists in *The Five
C's*: Conviction, Contrition, Confession, Conversion, Con-
tinuance. But the terms are insufficiently defined, and there
is not enough of Christ according to the Scriptures in them.

8. In regard to "Sharing" in the sense of confession: It
may be true that our Protestant reaction against the confessional has gone quite far. It certainly is true that when
we become aware of a sin committed against our fellow

---

3. Similarly, Dr. Leslie Weatherhead. Cf. *Religious Digest*, Feb.,
1938.

men, we should confess to them as well as to God. It is also
laudable that the necessity of restitution is stressed. We
are willing to go beyond this. We can agree with Shoemaker's words, "Of course, confession, in the absolute sense,
is to God alone: but where there is a human listener, confession is found to be both more difficult and more efficacious. It is, as a matter of fact and experience, a relatively
uncostly thing to fall on our knees and confess our sins
to God — it should not be, and perhaps would not be if we
were closer to God and more sensitive to His will; but it is a
very costly thing to say these things out in the presence even
of a human being we can trust; and, as a matter of fact, this
is extraordinarily effective in making the first break to get
away from sins." Dr. Shoemaker points to John Wesley's
elaborate rules in 1748 "to meet once a week at the least"
to "speak each of us in order, freely and plainly, the true
state of our soul, with the faults we have committed in
thought, word, or deed: and the temptations we have felt
since our last meeting."[4]

But when the same truth is expressed as follows by Mr.
Day, "Confession to God alone is often not good enough in
that it may cost nothing and may be merely the confession
to a subjective picture of God which the person has built
up for him or herself. In such a case, what actually happens is that the person does not confess at all — there is
no real pain and repentance — It is an easy way of trying to ease one's conscience. Confessing to another person
always costs and is thus a test of our honesty in hating
sin"; we feel how easily the same truth may be misused
and we incline to exclaim with Dr. Shields, "As though
man were more real than God!" Surely, if Buchmanites
have only a subjective picture of God, the remedy lies not
in confessing to men, but in first getting the right conception of this Holy God against whom we have sinned; and
this is done by prayerful study of the Word of God, and

---

4. *The Conversion of the Church*, pp. 36, 37.

by humble acceptance of the picture of Himself He has revealed to us.

9. Our criticism may return to an earlier remark that
the favorite name of "First Century Christian Fellowship"
is significant for a proper understanding of Buchmanism.
One might subsume one's critique of the movement under
this one heading.   For:

a. That is an impossibility in the twentieth century. We
cannot go back to one o'clock in the morning at eleven
o'clock in the evening of the same day. The "guidance" of
the Holy Spirit certainly did not begin with Dr. Frank
Buchman.   Through toil and strife, attacks from within
and without, God has guided His Church through nineteen
centuries. She has been rent apart by schisms. She has
suffered from character faults. Yet she has kept the faith
to which all Christians have at all times subscribed. And
that faith has been expressed in the great historic creeds of
Christendom. To ignore all this, and try to start as though
nothing had happened since the first century, is Buchmanism's fundamental mistake. It cannot be done without sur-
rendering vital truths of the Christian religion. It is a denial of the historic *guidance* of the Holy Spirit in the name
of spontaneous guidance.

b. And this is all the worse since Buchmanism, as Dr.
E. D. Kraan has pointed out, misrepresents first-century
Christianity.   The early Christians did not form groups
for the exchange of experience. In the apostolic age they
formed churches. The apostles appointed elders in every
church. They laid great stress upon the duty of the pastors
to preach and teach, and upon the task of the elders to rule
and to discipline.

c. Buchmanism, reading its favorite book of the Bible,
The Acts, in this erroneous manner, underestimates the
church. This the great reformers of the Church, Martin
Luther, John Calvin, John Wesley, did not do.

10. Buchmanism has changed, in practice if not in theory (there is little theory at best, the movement being
pragmatic to the core), from evangelism to a wholesale

plea for democracy as the panacea for the nations. Buchman is the recipient of many honors from many governments. However, the endless repetition of such slogans as "Sorry is a magic word," "Families can be fun," and the showing of "films to change the world" and plays of a similar order, such as *The Good Road,* may well be found in the end to be ignored when the international "warmongers" feel the time ripe to strike for world power.

A two-page advertisement in *Time* for January 9, 1956, may serve as proof of this contention. The title of the ad, reads, "An Idea to Win the World: Moral Re-Armament, a Statesmanship that Works." Statesmen from many lands are quoted in favor of the "MRA World Mission," which is said to be "For All Men Everywhere." The means advertised are such plays as *The Vanishing Island.* From London Beverly Baxter condemns this as an "oversimplification" which "rules out the intellect and appears purely to the spirit." He further illustrates this with a reference to "a very nice Canadian woman," who said that the town in which she lives has two cinemas; when she wants to decide which motion picture to see, she depends upon "divine guidance." Baxter calls this "the climax of absurdity." He adds that the British press resents the secrecy on the part of Buchmanism as to the source and the expenditure of vast sums of money.[5]

11. Williamson's chapter "Tears in the Morning" is worth reading. A young girl, amidst the peaceful surroundings of Caux Mountain House, was overheard sobbing as she struggled against the attempts by Buchmanites to make her surrender her own personal convictions to the spirit that brooks no opposition, no criticism of any kind: Buchmanism alone has the key to the solution of the world's problems!

Any movement or group that feels that way in the complicated world situation of today, stands condemned, as suf-

5. *Maclean's.* Canada's National Magazine, May 26, 1956.

fering either from an excess of naiveté or of something
less excusable.

For You to Ponder

1. Why are such names as *First Century Christian Fellowship* to be condemned?

2. Which principle, overdone by the Church of Rome,
neglected by Protestantism, has been re-emphasized by
Buchmanism? Has it done justice to this principle?

3. Is it easier to make confession before God or to do so
before man? Should both be done? Have you ever confessed your sins to your fellow men? If not, why not? Is
it sufficient to confess our sins before God in general terms,
without mentioning specific faults?

4. What does Buchman mean by the Four Absolutes?
What are the Five C's?

5. What is your main objection to Buchmanism?

6. Why has the original Buchmanism changed its emphasis to Moral Re-Armament?

7. Is it correct to say that a mere listening to the inner
voice will reveal God's will to us? Do you know of other
Christian groups which are in danger of falling into this
error?

8. To what danger do we lay ourselves open when we
neglect Scripture at the expense of the "inner voice"?

13

UNITARIANISM-MODERNISM

Perhaps the Modernist would frown at being classified or even discussed together with Spiritism and Unity. There is indeed a marked difference. In fact there is so much that is good and noble in Modernism that at times it seems rather difficult to classify the movement as anti-christian. Are the morals of American youth systematically corrupted by moving pictures portraying the sex- and the crime-life of society? *The Christian Century* fights tooth and nail the evils of block-booking and blindselling. Is the hire of those who labored for the rich kept back? It is the Modernist who openly denounces the greed of the great industrialist and points him to the Golden Rule of Jesus.

Surely, there is much that is good here. In correcting social evils our modernist friends are far more active than many orthodox. The latter fail to realize that condemnation of the world is not sufficient since Christians must let their light so shine before men that they will glorify the Father in heaven. We who are to be the salt and the leaven are not fulfilling our duty when we assign the world to the Devil. Neither may the Church tolerate evil for fear that its revenues will be cut off.[1]

And yet we must condemn Modernism as one more ism. Why? Because of the fundamental difference between the assertion that man in his own strength can do the Father's will, and the Christian doctrine that without the regenerating power of the Holy Spirit "ye can do nothing."

Moral good of a kind is excellent. Civic righteousness exalteth a nation. But of those who deny the necessity of

1. Cf. my *Kagawa, the Christian*, pp. 91 ff.

Jesus' death to propitiate for our sins, though we may stand shoulder to shoulder with them in fighting tuberculosis and alcoholism, we must, with the inspired apostle Paul, "tell you even weeping that they are the enemies of the cross of Christ."

Our supreme loyalty must, in the final analysis, be to the Christ of the Scriptures. We need not narrowly condemn those who disagree with us on many points. But when the supernatural character of Jesus Christ and His salvation are questioned and even openly denied, we must draw the line, across which we write, *Non possumus*. Ethics is not necessarily religion, and religion is not the same as Christianity.

The term "Modernism" is used somewhat loosely in our country. "Modernism," says Dr. E. E. Aubrey of the Divinity School of the University of Chicago, "is a method, not a creed. Modernists are unified by their approach to theology, not by their theological conclusions." Just like Buchmanism, in other words: a method, not a creed. "The message is the method, and the method is the message." You can believe pretty well whatever you desire, just so you are of a certain mentality. This is why it is difficult to say, "Modernism teaches this or that"; we should rather say, "This Modernist holds to such a view."

For historic reasons, as well as to limit the term Modernism, we speak of Unitarianism-Modernism.

A Hint from History

When the eminent revivalist, Charles G. Finney, arrived in Boston in 1843, Dr. Lyman Beecher said to him, "Mr. Finney, you cannot labor here as you do anywhere else. You have got to pursue a different course of instruction, and begin at the foundation; for Unitarianism is a system of denials, and under its teaching, the foundations of Christianity are fallen away. You cannot take anything for granted; for the Unitarians and the Universalists have destroyed the foundation, and the people are all afloat. The masses have no settled opinions, and every 'lo here,' or 'lo there,' finds a hearing; and almost any conceivable form of error may get a footing." And more than thirty years later Mr. Finney stated, "I have since found this to be true, to a greater extent than in any other field in which I have labored. The mass of people in Boston are more unsettled in their religious convictions than in any other place that I have ever labored in, notwithstanding their intelligence; for they are surely a very intelligent people, on all questions but that of religion. It is extremely difficult to make religious truths lodge in their minds, because the influence of Unitarian teaching has been to lead them to call in question all the principal doctrines of the Bible. Their system is one of denials. Their theology is negative. They deny almost everything, and affirm almost nothing. In such a field, error finds the ears of the people open; and the most irrational views, on religious subjects, come to be held by a great many people."

Such scathing verdicts by men like Beecher, who lived and labored in that hotbed of Unitarianism, and by Finney, who had wide experience in evangelistic work on the Continent, are worthy of attention. But besides, after half a century more of untiring Unitarian propaganda throughout the country, we can corroborate these condemnatory statements ourselves. That "the Unitarians and the Universalists have destroyed the foundations, and the people are all afloat," was meant as the statement of a historical fact in 1843. It has since proved a prophecy. It was Unitarian Boston that became the nursery of Eddyism. Thousands of well-meaning folk have fallen a ready prey to the various antichristian cults of the day, and that without even suspecting that they have abandoned the Christian faith, as the result of the work of Unitarian preachers who had "destroyed the foundations" with their empty denials. Nor is it amazing that this same Boston, at first Puritan, later Unitarian, then nothing in religious convictions, has become the happy hunting ground of that strange and un-American mixture of Christianity, paganism and corrupt politics that goes by the name of Roman Catholicism.

Unitarianism and Modernism Are One

Denying the fundamentals of the Christian religion is like putting one's feet upon a declining slope. Unitarianism in its beginning was not nearly as radical as it has since become. Gradually, however, it has drifted into a dull pantheism with no hope beyond a universal evolution. The history of the movement in the United States makes sad reading.[2] When we learn of the manner in which Unitarians wrested church buildings and property from orthodox congregations; of how little they spend for missionary work, even after a continued existence of one hundred years, and notwithstanding their great wealth; of the early opposition of most of the Unitarians to the anti-slavery movement; of the Harvard defense of alcoholism; we cannot help but think of the words of Jude, "clouds without water, carried along by winds; autumn trees without fruit, twice dead, plucked up by the roots." One thing they do engage in: they conduct a vigorous propaganda among evangelicals by means of advertising free literature in various periodicals.[3] "Some years a million pamphlets go out from the American Unitarian Association. Local parishes also send them out continually by the thousands."

Of late years Unitarian tactics have changed somewhat. Ministers with Unitarian convictions are now advised to stay in the orthodox churches, and work "from within." This procedure is called "strategic" by Dr. Slaten of the West Side Unitarian Church, New York; it is recommended

2. The scope of our work does not allow a comparison between Unitarianism and European Modernism of the last century. The intimate resemblance between them is clearly borne out not merely by their theology, but also by the hateful tactics employed against those who dissented from their views.

3. Of Mormonism, which follows similar tactics, E. L. Mills writes in (modernist) *Christian Century*: "It is a parasitic religion, living off Christianity. It does not seek to convert sinners, but to make 'saints' out of church members who already have a fair degree of saintliness."

by Dr. Palmer, the editor of the *Harvard Theological Review;* while Dr. J. W. Day, a leading Unitarian minister, writes, "A good many Unitarians are doing more good where they are than they could do anywhere else. They are undoubtedly capturing strongholds that we could never carry by direct attack. They are the Modernists of Protestantism who are working from within the fold. . . . We want more of them and we want them where they are." Consequently we should not be lulled to sleep when we read that between the years 1916 and 1926 "among the Protestant bodies the two liberal denominations, the Unitarians and the Universalists, suffered a decrease in membership, the former by more than 22,000." Unitarians, after appropriating universities and divinity schools that had been founded and endowed for the express purpose of propagating Calvinism only, now advise "liberal" ministers in evangelical denominations to use the property of their churches in order to undermine those churches "from within," that ultimately "all may be one," when the unnerved denominations shall come over in bulk.

Aversion to Creeds

This, of course, is not saying that all Modernists and all Unitarians think alike on every point of religion. If anything is characteristic of present-day liberals, it is their profound aversion to fixed doctrine. In this, as also in other points of similarity, they do not yield an inch to the stoutest Ritschlian. "Free-thinkers" is a title these men are proud of. It may, perhaps, be said that, on the whole, the Unitarian of today is somewhat more outspoken than is the average Modernist in an evangelical church; and denominational "fetters" may well account for the latter's more guarded language. The general feeling on the subject is typically expressed by Dr. C. S. Wicks, for more than twenty-five years minister to the All Souls Unitarian Church, Indianapolis. Says Dr. Wicks, "We have no creed of any kind. Is it because we believe nothing or so little?

No; it is because we believe so much we can find no formula to express our beliefs. To us Truth is infinite and cannot be enclosed in any statement of belief . . . Each one of us should have his own creed, the result of his own best thinking, but he has no desire to fix that creed upon any one else. The nearest we have ever come to a creed is the Bond of Union of our former General Conference now merged into the American Unitarian Association, reading, 'These churches accept the religion of Jesus, holding in accordance with his teachings, that practical religion is summed up in love to God and love to man.' "

So much for Unitarianism. What about Modernism? Let Dr. Shailer Mathews, Dean of the Divinity School, University of Chicago, speak for Modernism. Said the Dean in an interview to Winfred Ernest Garrison of the *Christian Century* staff: "The modernist's objection to creeds is not that they formulate the intellectual aspects of a religious experience, but that they are made authoritative and final tests of such experience . . . Most assuredly I believe that religious thinking must be clearly kept within the limits of what may be called personalism."

It follows that it would be difficult to define the theological system of Unitarian and modernist preachers in such a manner that they would agree. They have no authoritative or representative statement. Their theology is admittedly the reflection of their religious experience, and the latter varies and changes with time, personality, and the dictates of "science."

Basic Principles

Still, there are some thoughts that may be considered the *communis opinio.* "There is no answer to the question: What do Unitarians believe? I can only say that there are certain things commonly believed among us. So far as I know, all Unitarians affirm:

    (1) The divineness of all life.

    (2) The oneness of man with the Eternal.

(3) The essential goodness of human nature.

(4) The Rise of Man through a process of evolution.

(5) The universality of Revelation; not to one race or one nation have come glimpses of truth divine.

(6) The reign of Natural Law.

(7) Heaven and Hell not as places but as conditions of the soul.

(8) The primacy of reason in the search for truth.

(9) Character the aim of religion.

(10) There is but one principle in the universe, and that principle makes for good."

This creed (the personal creed of most Unitarians, according to Dr. Wicks) is rather pantheistic, it will be observed. An even smaller number of articles of faith has been kept by some modernists. Bruce Barton, the celebrated author of *The Man Nobody Knows*, and *The Book Nobody Knows*, offers these "few simple things":

1. *I believe in myself*, i. e., I know that I am.

2. *I know that I am intelligent* . . . I know that my intelligence (and by *me* I mean, of course, mankind) is the highest and most powerful thing in the natural universe.

3. *Because I am, I believe God is.* A Divine Intelligence is beyond my meager comprehension . . . but I know that men and women are intelligent, and to believe that an unintelligent universe produced something greater than itself . . . this is an absurdity.

4. *He must be* at least as *good* as I am, for He created me, and my intelligence is a tiny fragment of His own.

Methods of Denial

This Unitarian-Modernism with its few articles of faith, when at its worst, simply brushes aside whoever holds that the Christan faith needs more, and more solid, foundations. With Dr. Wicks it says, "Already the Fundamentalists have drawn the line. On one side, all the intelligence, all modern learning; on the other, sincerity, yes, but ignorance and superstition." It sweeps past the serious work of such scholars as Dr. James Orr, Prof. J. G. Machen, Bishop R. J. Cooke, and announces that "everyone who had studied and thought knows that there is not the faintest evidence." of Jesus' virgin birth. Or, it reasons the miraculous element out of the gospel by stating that "the leprosy which Jesus healed was presumably a curable skin-disease"; the words, 'Peace, be still' were presumably directed to the disciples, "but the wind, as so often happens there, subsided as quickly as it had risen . . . the disciples thought that the blowing had ceased in obedience to their master's command."

But when Unitarianism-Modernism is more carefully viewed, the question arises as to how this denying spirit reveals itself. Consider the following. On my desk lies a sermon, entitled Easter Inevitable, written by Charles Clayton Morrison, former editor of the *Christian Century*.[4] The Introduction dwells upon the thought that Jesus was a true man; not a recluse, but "a man indeed." The first part of the sermon begins with stating, "Our hearts wish to be assured of an event so wonderful as the resurrection of Jesus. Where shall we look for our proof?" It continues by asserting that there are two kinds of evidence, even in a common law court, namely direct and presumptive. Modernistically, the "direct evidence" is disparaged. "If we examine the resurrection narratives we are almost dismayed at their fragmentariness, their doubtful consistency, and the possibilities by which psychology might explain them away." Nevertheless, we are assured, there is plenty of "presumptive evidence." Such a person as Christ could not but have risen. If there is therefore any guarantee of the resurrection, Christ is himself that guarantee. The more we know of him, the further we enter into his experience of life and sense the power of his personality, the greater miracle we feel would be wrought if he had not risen. His rising from the dead was no miracle but the prevention of a miracle." With enhanced interest we read on. If we regret the

---

4. *The Christian Century*, April 14, 1927.

writer's light esteem for Scriptural evidence, we are glad that, after all, his religious heart forces him to admit that all-important fact of the Christian religion, concerning which Paul wrote: "If Christ hath not been raised, your faith is vain; ye are yet in your sins." But alas, we are immediately robbed of our sense of joy. As soon as the former editor of the *Christian Century* has informed us that Christ must have risen, that it would have been a greater miracle had He not risen, he continues as follows: "I would not divert your thought from the essential faith of Easter to dwell upon the mere physical details of this supreme event. I confess that my own interest in the physical details is so slight that I have hardly so much as a tentative opinion of my own. Whether, for instance, the body of Jesus literally came from the tomb, whether his appearances to his disciples were objective materializations in space and time, whether his ascension from Olivet in which it is said a cloud received him out of the sight was physical — whether these and other such apparent statements of fact are intended to be taken as real statements of fact, or are themselves symbols of an experience impregnated with a vast faith, I leave to those who are interested in such questions to form their own opinions. To me the essential Easter event was not the upstanding of a dead body from the tomb, but the breaking of the fact upon the minds of these disciples that there was something about their Master which death could not touch, which not only survived death, but transcended death and conquered it, and that there was such connection between their world and the world to which death is an open gate that his living presence could still abide with them and guide their thoughts and plans. Stripping off the inconsequent details of the story, we have left this pith of faith which was not alone for the first disciples the great reality, but has been the great reality for those who through all the centuries have worn the name of Christ."

The sermon then continues to expatiate on the thought that it was not possible *for Him* to be holden by death —

the text is Acts 2:24 — since it was a moral demand that
He should rise; and it concludes by giving this hope for
eternal life that one may and should "accept his human
life as your life, his way of thinking about God and man
as your way of thinking. To accept Christ is not to believe
any doctrine, but to commit yourself to his way of life, to
accept his way of life as your way of life, to go with him on
the paths of service and self-denial and temptation."

This is a true sample of modernist preaching. There is
no telling what the preacher means by a resurrection without "physical details," and it is perhaps as well for himself
that he has not attempted to inform us; there is no telling
whether the "essential Easter event" of a living presence
that could still abide with the disciples in their world, must
be understood after the manner of our friends the Spiritists
(what is the difference, just what there is and how it is, as
long as you are informed that there is "something"?) ; and
you should not probe the truth of the assertion that this un-
named "something" with or without "the upstanding of a
dead body" (?!) has indeed been "the great reality" of
Christians "through all the centuries" (they are dead and
gone anyhow, and have only left a few worthless doctrinal
treatises on the subject!). This, we repeat, is a typical
sample. Thus playing with words — akin to the Glossary
of *Science and Health,* and born of aversion to doctrine —
might be multiplied from sermons by Paul Hutchinson,
Alfred Wesley Wishart, and others. But to what end? The
sample we gave is by a recognized "liberal" leader. It came
after two series of sermons, one by America's twenty-five
"Peers of the Pulpit," the other by representative British
pulpiteers. Then someone raised the cry, And now, let us
see what the editors can do themselves in that line. Dr.
Morrison's sermon may be considered to be as good a speci-
men as Modernism has to offer. Meager Unitarian-Modernism! we are forced to exclaim; and poor people who are
thus deluded!

And let us observe right here that, no matter what
changes Modernism may have undergone of late years, there

is no change as to this loose usage of doctrinal terms, this complete denial of the fundamental doctrines upon which Christianity has been built. When Dr. Morrison continued to write of Christ's resurrection, a Methodist minister, as late as 1946, asked him what he meant by the term, saying, "Do you mean the physical reanimation of Jesus in either his natural or some 'supernatural' body. Or do you mean, as do some theologians, 'the process whereby the Jesus of history becomes the Christ of the Church?' I write because I have nearly a dozen research scientists in my church, devoutly Christian, who would challenge any use of the term at all."

The answer — and this is *The Christian Century* of July 10, 1946 — was as follows:

"I do not pretend to know the precise nature of the resurrection fact, nor am I concerned to know — whether the physical body of Jesus was resuscitated or whether he appeared in some other form. On the whole, I am inclined to stand with Paul, who denied the resuscitation concept and based his argument upon the concept of a 'spiritual body.' Paul's statement is earlier than the date of our earliest Gospel. The manner of the resurrection is not important. But the fact of the resurrection is supremely important. Christianity cannot be understood without it."

One may well ask whatever the meaning might be of a historical fact that eludes all definition and which yet is said to be *sine qua non* of the Christian religion?[5]

Nor is this by any means the only evidence that Modernism is not defunct, and does not change its attitude toward Christ's resurrection. The late Dr. Biederwolf expressed the entire matter in these words, "We are referring, of course, to the resurrection of His body. Who ever heard of a spirit being buried?" But as late as the March, 1952, *Pulpit*, Dr. Morrison wrote, "I have long ago ceased to be concerned about the physical details of the resurrection."

---

5. From a popular apologetic standpoint the physical resurrection of Christ is dealt with in an excellent manner by Dr. A. Pieters in *Facts and Mysteries of the Christian Faith*, Eerdmans, 1933.

And Dr. Robert J. McCracken, Fosdick's successor as minister of the Riverside Church, wrote in the *Christian Century*, April 9, 1952, "In the thought of Greece the keyword is immortality. In the New Testament the keyword is resurrection — not a bare dogma of the survival of some vague and intangible essence, but the re-establishment of personal life on the farther side of the grave, the conviction that the total personality, invested by God's gift with a perfect organism, passes on and encounters God. This is the substance of the Easter faith." How unlike Luke 24:39, 40, and I Corinthians 15:35ff.[6]

Dr. Reinhold Niebuhr, chief exponent upon this continent of dialectical theology, either goes beyond Dr. Morrison, or, perhaps, uses more honest speech. He does not hesitate to call the resurrection "a myth." The creation story in Genesis is also "a myth." God's eternal wrath is "a symbol of the unpredictable possibilities of eternity which may appear in time." Jesus' incarnation, in Niebuhr's opinion, is "an offense to reason." The Chalcedon doctrine of the two natures is the "wooden-headed literalism of orthodoxy." Jesus not only was at times in error, but could not have been tempted had He not first sinned. Jesus is not the Christ, but created the ideal of Christ, an ideal larger than His own possibilities. There was no historic Adam who fell from original righteousness. Every born man is Adam, and the fall of man is an inward conflict "between the *is* and the *ought* of life, between the ideal possibilities to which freedom encourages man and the drive of egoism, which reason sharpens rather than assuages."

Small wonder, then, that Niebuhr does not refer to the atoning blood of Christ, but to "the Cross," which to him is "the defeat of love." The second coming of Christ (the

---

6. See also J. H. Skilton's review of the *Interpreter's Bible*, vol. VII, in the *Westminster Theological Journal*, May, 1952.

To this may be added that Dr. Wilbur M. Smith stated in the *Moody Monthly*, copied in *Action* (N.E.A. organ) for Feb. 1, 1954, that it made his temperature rise when he read in the *Interpreter's Bible* the statement by Dr. J. Edgar Parkes that the demand for an infallible book "is one of the relics of our heathenism."

"ideal") becomes with Niebuhr a mythical symbol. Science teaches that the human body cannot possibly be raised from death. Immortality of the soul is what we now believe in rather than the resurrection of the body.

The power of the Cross lies exclusively in the "conversion" of the sinner, which means a confession of the fact that there is no salvation apart from the intrusion of divine grace into the life with a new power. Repentance and conversion are followed by a sense of relief, as man, who remains imperfect, is judged by God according to "the Christ in us," who is "not a possession but a hope."

And all of this is, of course, the result of Niebuhr's refusal to acknowledge the Bible as containing the objective, God-given and normative truth.[7]

Nothing New in Modernism

These writers love to refer to "the modern mind" as if it were something altogether novel and superior to the unscientific mind of the barbarous age just concluded. The truth is that their entire system is hoary with age. The *Aufklärung* in the eighteenth century may not have a phraseology as replete with terms borrowed from the dogma of evolution, but its ideas on all points of weight were substantially the same. Ernest Gordon in his chapter *"Modernist Antiques, or The Old and the New Enlightenment" (The Lesson of the Sadducees)* has gone to the trouble of putting side by side citations from the eighteenth century liberal and from twentieth-century Modernists: The similarity is more than accidental. And Dr. Dowkontt has given page after page of parallel quotations from *The Age of Reason* by the American deist Thomas Paine (1793) and from Harry Emerson Fosdick's *The Modern Use of the Bible* (1924) — and the two are as similar as two

7. Cf. E. J. Carnell, *The Theology of Reinhold Niebuhr.* Eerdmans. 1951. The author gives numerous citations, some of which (with others) may be found at the close of this chapter. They should fully warrant the conclusions of Van Til, Morrison, and Carnell that "neoorthodoxy" is in reality "neo-liberalism."

books by different authors could well be expected to be.[8]

Nor is this all there is to be said. Unitarians, according to the church historian Prof. Walker, are "of a decidedly Arian tendency"; and that Modernists are Arians the present writer has shown in another connection.[9] As such they are related to Russellism as two branches growing out of the same trunk. Russellism is the type of Arianism that claims to believe in the inspiration of Scripture, and proceeds to twist its teachings into the opposite; Unitarian is that form of Arianism that comes out in the open and denies the inspiration of Scripture.

An Insufficient Change

True, Modernism has changed somewhat during the last three decades. The superficial optimism which formerly characterized the movement has given way to a more sober outlook on life. Two world wars with the amazing bestiality of man toward men, plus an in-between, world-wide "depression" have sobered even "liberal theologians." Wilhelm Pauck, H. Richard Niebuhr, Reinhold Niebuhr, H. P. Van Dusen, and many others have revolted against "the superficial optimism" of the Coolidge era. The hour of repentance and of realizing the sinfulness of man has arrived. And they now couch their liberalism-with-alterations in terms largely borrowed from the old orthodoxy.

"Rousseau's doctrine of man is the curse of the age in which we live. It has become a curse because it has been accepted as true, whereas it is palpably false . . . The greatest evils which harass the modern world and which threaten it with destruction are the lineal descendants of the doctrine that man is naturally good. It is that false doctrine which has made man himself the end-all and be-all of existence, and which has filled the world with the cults of

8. Dowkontt, *The Deadly Parallel.*
9. See my articles on "The Ritschlians and the Pre-existence of Christ" in *The Princeton Theological Review* of July and October, 1920; and compare my "The Pre-Existence of Christ and (revised) Arianism," in *Religion and Culture*, Grand Rapids, Mich., May and August, 1920.

blood and race and nation. And in so far as that doctrine continues to dominate Western thought we may expect the recurring horrors of war and revolution, because it is a doctrine whose logic deprives mankind of a common frame of reverence and in the end sets every man against every other man."

These words of F. P. Miller are paralleled in the same volume by those of H. R. Niebuhr: "Modernism has attempted to interpret religion in all its aspects — philosophical, historical, psychological, doctrinal and practical — from the point of view of anthropology. In spite of all its theoretical and practical knowledge of religion, it has lost God. Hence it is drawn into the conflicts of human life to such a degree that it can no longer speak with that authority or objectivity which ought to be expected of those who believe in God. It is this aspect of Modernism which brings it so dangerously close to the heresy of Humanism."

"From the very start," so Dr. Niebuhr continues, "Modernism has taken Christianity for granted. It has always thought and acted on the basis of the existent church. As a matter of fact, its chief purpose was and is a defense of the church. Modernism is an apologetic movement . . . But in spite of all this, two questions were very persistently raised: What is Christianity? and, What is the church? The answer which Harnack gave with such scholarly confidence and gentlemanly self-assurance has long been deemed insufficient. But the questions persist. And who among the Modernists can be said to have given them a cogent answer?"

One readily sees from such citations that there is less optimism among Modernists than there was a generation ago. And they are less satisfied with their own achievements than their hopeful outlook would have warranted.

From the evangelical standpoint one can only rejoice at this change. However, when we look somewhat more closely, we are disappointed. The change is not a radical change. It does not go down to the bottom of things. The modernist outlook is less roseate because men have been disappointed.

The return to God which is advocated is not a return to the
God of the Scriptures. The repentance that is spoken of
does not go far enough. Modernism still trusts in its own
arm. The result is often a pessimism that is as thorough-
going as the optimism of yesterday. Edward J. Carnell
aptly remarks: "Neo-orthodoxy is the construction of the
minds of erstwhile liberals. Barth, Brunner and Niebuhr
were all schooled as liberals. And the tragic events of history, together with a discovery of Kierkegaard, have forced
them from immanence to transcendence. But one of the liberal presuppositions which no member of this school has
been able to slough off is the hypothesis that science and
higher criticism have forever smashed the doctrine of the
plenary inspiration of the Bible."[10]

"The Christian analysis of life," states Reinhold Niebuhr
in his *An Interpretation of Christian Ethics*, "leads to conclusions which will seem morbidly pessimistic to moderns,
still steeped as they are in their evolutionary optimism."

"Beneath the thin veneer of satisfied self-assurance," accordingly to Dr. Van Dusen, "the man of today is a strangely bewildered, profoundly, unhappy mortal . . . Today [1935],
we confront a generation shorn of self-confidence — disillusioned of its leadership, disillusioned as to the significance
of its own achievement, disillusioned of its ability to save
the crumbling remnants of its proud domain. The florid
optimism of yesterday has evaporated overnight."[11]

But what is the remedy these dissatisfied men offer?

To begin with they expect to heal the individual through
healing the mass. That old cure-all has not been abandoned.
"The social gospel" remains the great hope. Thus Van
Dusen acclaims first of all that history teaches: *"The ultimate outcome of history is within God's control."* The
second thing we are to learn, so he states, is *"the moral
determination of history."* God's influence upon society is

10. *Op. cit.*, p. 138.
11. For the same vague dissatisfaction with Modernism, see Dr.
Fosdick's article, "Beyond Modernism," in the *Christian Century*,
Dec. 4, 1935, and Dr. Morrison's "The New Modernism" in the same
weekly for March 4, 1936.

continuous, unwearying; and it is for good. Thirdly, we learn that *"God's influence upon society is most easily discerned as judgment and as discipline."* History teaches, even today, that the wages of sin is death. And fourthly we discover that "the Christian understanding of history declares *the only ways by which social ills can be soundly and permanently rectified.* It dictates the conditions of effective social change, the methods in the social struggle to which Christians can give ready support." In brief, then, this is "The Message in Society's Crisis."

It will be observed that both the disease and the remedy are described as social. Is there no message, then, for the individual? Yes, there are "Gifts of Personal Religion." These are said to be: "1. Vision; 2. Insight; 3. Radicalism; 4. Faith." When it is asked, what is meant by faith, we reply in Dr. Van Dusen's own words: "If one were asked what it is which these times will most urgently need, the answer would be unhesitating — *men and women with sticking power."*

Dr. E. E. Aubrey informs us, "The new social psychology has brought about an important modification of individualism by pointing out that individual personality is a social product. This gives a new setting to any discussion of individualism."

And a few lines further he states, "This serves to explain the interpretation of Christianity in terms of individual worth and the testing of authority and doctrine by individual experience — two emphases in modern preaching." This means that the individual is reached as a unit of society, and so the individual's experience accounts for whatever doctrine he holds. The reason that Buchmanism, with a similar emphasis upon doctrine as the fruit of experience, is severely criticized in modernist circles lies not, of course, in this fundamental concept the two hold in common, but rather in what Modernists term Buchmanism's "pietism": its emphasis upon the personal change at the expense of proper stress on the "social gospel."

Dr. Wilhelm Pauck, be it observed, has no solution to offer. Writing on "The Crisis of the Church," he concludes, "The considerations of these pages . . . do not offer a solution to the problem to which they are addressed . . . But they hint at the solution in so far as they contain the observation that an age which has attained more power of world control than any other longs for sanctification by a new sense of God. The spirit of secularism has brought about the crisis of the old and contemporary religion. A new religious sense, built upon a new certainty of God, must bring the spirit of secularism into a crisis. When the event occurs we shall be saved. Perhaps the time is not far distant when a prophet will arise among us who, fully imbued with the mood and spirit of our era, will speak to us in the name of the living God with such power and authority that all who long for salvation will be compelled to listen. In the meantime, we must learn to be humble in the awareness that it is God, the Lord of all life, who has laid his hand upon us in this crisis. And we must learn to pray: We believe, O Lord, help thou our unbelief. He who will have authority to declare that this prayer has been heard will be the leader of the movement by which the crisis will be overcome."

Very true. But the man with that authority will point back to "the faith which was once for all delivered unto the saints." Jesus Christ came to lay down His life a ransom for many. God did not intend that man should be saved through His blood in the first century, and by an easier, less costly way in the twentieth.

And so the vagueness, rather the absolute lack of doctrinal content of the most modern Modernists, as well as the outspoken aversion to Scriptural and creedal doctrine of the earlier Unitarians, cause us to maintain the verdict of one modernist as over against that of another.

Dr. Aubrey stated, "The modernist is able to co-operate with any man who is honestly seeking light, be he archconservative or humanist, because they both have the same objective."

That may be true when it comes to closing beer gardens before midnight and fighting prostitution. But when it comes to the service of the "Lord of all life" we remind all Modernists that Dr. Morrison of *The Christian Century* wrote a true word in the January 3, 1924, issue of that paper. As a rule Dr. Morrison is far more clear when he writes on sociological matters than when he trespasses upon the field of theology. But in that lucid hour he caused something of a stir with the editorial *Fundamentalism and Modernism: Two Religions.* "'Blest be the tie' may be sung until doomsday, but it cannot bind these two worlds together. The God of the fundamentalist is one God; the God of the modernist another. The Christ of the fundamentalist is one Christ; the Christ of modernism is another. The Bible of fundamentalism is one Bible; the Bible of modernism is another. The church, the kingdom, the salvation, the consummation of all things — these are one thing to fundamentalists and another to modernists. Which God is the Christian God, which Christ is the Christian Christ, which Bible is the Christian Bible, which church, which kingdom, which salvation, which consummaton are the Christian church, the Christian kingdom, the Christian salvation, the Christian consummation? The future will tell."

We are grateful for the candid admission in the first part of this citation. We cannot agree with the thesis on the latter part. With Dr. Morrison himself stating, "There is a clash here as profound and as grim as that between Christianity and Confucianism," there is no need to wait for the future to tell us which of these two religions is the Christian religion. The Christian religion is as much and as definitely a historical phenomenon as is Confucianism, or Taoism. What the Christian religion is, historical investigation will show undeniably. And such historical investigation will bring to light that the Christian religion has ever held to the God, the Christ, the Bible, and the salvation of supernaturalism, and these are exactly the God, the Christ, the Bible and the salvation that are denied by Mod-

ernism.   When the *Christian Century* stated editorially,
"Christianity according to fundamentalism is another religion," the most popular modernist religious weekly in the
country signed its own death-warrant.   The editors on
Dearborn Street should have the courage of their conviction.   The sub-title of their admirably edited paper reads, *A
Journal of Religion.*   That is correct.   The main heading,
however, should be changed from The *Christian* Century to
The *Modernist* Century!   And the puzzle that confronts us
is this : Why are men so eager to maintain the name Christian when everything Christian is admittedly rejected by
them?

Entered World War II.   As long as the United States was
not a participant, American Modernism stuck to its position.   But when our own nation suddenly became involved
by the Japanese attack upon Pearl Harbor on December 7,
1941, the modernist dream went to pieces.   Dr. Morrison,
sponsor of "the outlawry of war," frankly abandoned his
pacifism, and wrote on war as "An Unnecessary Necessity."
General Sherman, so he stated, had uttered a far more theological truth than he realized when he defined war as hell.

It was an adroit move.   For it took war out of the category of moral good or evil, and made the killing of their
fellow men by men who had asserted that under no condition would they again obey the government to the point of
killing, an "amoral act."

"Nobody in hell calls hell a sin.   By the same token war
cannot be called a sin.   Nobody imagines that it is his 'duty'
to 'renounce' hell, once he is in it.   Likewise war can be renounced only before we get into it, that is, while there is
peace.   No one in hell thinks of 'bearing witness' against
hell, by refusing to take part in *some* of its functions.   No
one in hell thinks it necessary to call certain of its functions
'righteous' in order to engage in them.   And certainly no one
in hell imagines that he must justify any of his selfish activities by getting the approval of God.

"The only sin against which a soul in hell can bear witness is the sin that brought him there.   The only righteous-

ness to which he can bear witness is the righteousness of God's judgment in condemning him to the hell in which he now finds himself. Hell is that realm or condition or situation — call it what you will — where good and evil have lost their distinction, where evil is good and good is evil. This is precisely what war is, and total war answers this description in amazing full details."[12]

So wrote Dr. Morrison. What is wrong with this?

It is not what Dr. Albert Edward Day, vice-president of the Federal Council of Churches of Christ in America, alleges against this view. Wrote Dr. Day:

"Hell is not external circumstances. Hell is internal corruption. One is never *in* hell; one *is* hell. Hell is not anything done to a man by events or people; hell is disintegration within a man. It is not something to which God condemns a man. It is separation from God by an atrophy or suicide of the faculties whereby God gets a man or man holds fellowship with God. One repents of *nothing* in hell, neither of hell itself, nor of the sins that have made hell. One has lost all capacity for repentance for he has shut out the God who alone can evoke repentance. One does not have a tormenting conscience. One has only the torment of absence of conscience. One then makes no moral choices of any kind; one has become hell, the paralysis of moral choice. War is not hell."[13]

Thus these rationalists continue to borrow the terminology of Scripture, to pour into it their own conceptions, and, incidentally, to contradict one another.

If they would but turn to the inspired Scriptures, and inquire into the meaning of the words "repentance," "judgment," "hell," they would not have to change their stand so often.

The dramatic book of Revelation, with its returning cycles of sin, judgments and apothesis, presents a clear and different picture.

---

12. *The Christian Century*, Jan. 21, 1942.
13. *The Christian Century*, March 18, 1942.

Take, for instance, the third cycle, that of the seven angels sounding the seven trumpets (Chs. 8 and 9). Here the
sins of the apostate nations are visited by judgments in nature: upon the land (8:7), on the sea (8:8, 9) and the
rivers (8:10, 11), in the heavens (8:12). All of these are
in symbolic language, reminding us of the Old Testament
calamities in nature with added features to augment their
horror.

Then, because there is no return to God as a result of
these, an angel announces that another three trumpets will
introduce three more judgments which far surpass any divine judgments so far experienced upon the earth (8:13).
They are therefore called "woes."

Two of these woes are described in picturesque language.
The fifth trumpet inaugurates the increasing influence of
demons, let loose to torment men with the removal of all
light of righteousness and holiness (9:1-11).

The sixth trumpet introduces a picture of ever larger
wars as the most terrible of divine judgments upon earth
(9:13-19).

Then follows this terrible indictment, "And the rest of
mankind, who were not killed with these plagues, repented
not of the works of their hands, that they should not worship demons, and the idols of gold and silver, and of brass,
and of stone, and of wood; which can neither see, nor hear
nor walk: and they repented not of their murders, nor of
their sorceries, nor of their fornication, nor of their thefts."

This should logically be followed by the sounding of the
seventh trumpet. But the dramatic action is interrupted
and a comforting interlude is introduced (10:1 to 11:14).

When the seventh trumpet sounds, we are given a view
of eternal bliss *after* the final judgment. The final judgment is not described until the end of the last cycle (20:
11-15). At that point we are told *what hell is*. Hell is the
state of final judgment to which all those will be condemned
who have not repented as a result of previous divine judgments, which had been so many warnings to seek redemption from the wrath to come in "the blood of the Lamb."

War, therefore, is not hell. Neither is man hell. Hell is God's final answer to a world that refuses the saving gift of His Son. War is only a warning, a precursor of hell.

Nor was the late war the final calamity prior to the return of Christ. The King of kings and Lord of lords continues to gather "a great multitude, which no man could number, out of every nation and of all tribes and peoples and tongues" which John saw "standing before the throne and the Lamb" (7:9) at the close of an earlier cycle.

In his boyhood years the present writer wondered how destruction could strike against all nations at once. The latest inventions and discoveries of an apostate world have made that clear. Yet even World War II did not strike everywhere at once; large continents, the resources of which have hardly been tapped, are isolated. When, in a future war, bombs will sail through the stratosphere, and one continent will, from its home base, destroy metropolitan areas upon another continent, the words of Christ will be fulfilled, "And except those days had been shortened, no flesh would have been saved: but for the elect's sake those days shall be shortened" (Matt. 24:22).

In those days of the end, false Christs and false prophets will arise, as have already arisen today, and have been described in this volume.

Then, when the humanistic dream of a man-made gospel of tolerance, goodwill, brotherhood and democracy will have ended in the total collapse of a civilization that owed its rise and development to the light of Christ but used it in the pursuit of sinful and ungodly ends, then, "as the lightning cometh forth from the east, and is seen even unto the west; so shall be the coming of the Son of Man" (Matt. 24:27).

Then shall be the final judgment.

Then shall the unrepentant be consigned to "his portion with the hypocrites: there shall be the weeping and the gnashing of teeth" (Matt. 24:51).

"But according to his promise, we look for new heavens and a new earth, wherein dwelleth righteousness" (II Peter 3:13).

It is for us to answer our Lord's question: "Nevertheless, when the Son of man cometh, shall he find faith on the earth?" (Luke 18:8).

Humanism

There are those among the more recent Modernists who resent the name "Humanism" as applied to Modernism, preferring the statement that Modernism is "anthropocentric." But is not this just a different name for the same thing? Dr. Walker has written of the Italian Renaissance, the forerunner of medieval Humanism, "Yet, when all these elements are recognized, it remains true that the Renaissance involved an essentially new outlook on the world, in which emphasis was laid on its present life, beauty, and satisfaction — on man as man — rather than on a future heaven and hell, and on man as an object of salvation or loss. The means by which this transformation was wrought was a reappreciation of the spirit of classical antiquity, especially as manifested in its great literary monuments." Substitute "science" for "the classics," and this sentence applies verbatim to Unitarianism and Modernism.

This Humanism is observed even in the strictly Unitarian hymns to which we have been treated of late years. Our modernist friends have at last awakened to the incongruity of closing a service in which the resurrection of Christ is denied with a hymn asserting, "Hallelujah, Christ arose." It was this situation which caused the late Dr. Francis L. Patton to say, with a twinkle in his eye, "Well, they have left us the choir, anyhow." The much advertised and much used volume, *Hymns of the United Church*, with its companion volume, *Hymns for American Youth*, contains a liberal mixture of both orthodox and unorthodox materials. The following "hymn" however, has been advertised most widely as "a typical page from this hymnal":

1. *My Master was a worker,*
   With daily work to do,
   And he who would be like him
   Must be a worker, too;

   Then welcome honest labor,
   And honest labor's fare,
   For where there is a worker,
   The Master's man is there.

2. *My Master was a comrade,*
   A trusty friend and true,
   And he who would be like him
   Must be a comrade, too;
   In happy hours of singing,
   In silent hours of care,
   Where goes a loyal comrade,
   The Master's man is there.

3. *My Master was a helper,*
   The woes of life he knew,
   And he who would be like him
   Must be a helper, too;
   The burden will grow lighter,
   If each will take a share,
   And where there is a helper
   The Master's man is there.

4. *Then, brothers brave and manly*
   Together let us be,
   For he who is our Master,
   The Man of men was he;
   The men who would be like him
   Are wanted ev'rywhere,
   And where they love each other
   The Master's men are there.

The beauty of a product like that lies in the first place in the melody, which is "arranged from Mendelssohn," and further in the almost universal use that may be made of the hymn. If we should ever have to face an audience made up of Spiritists, Theosophists, Freemasons, Russellites, Mormons, and Baha'ists, with a generous sprinkling of Unitarians and Modernists, we could think of no song that might prove more acceptable to that motley crowd than this "typical page from this hymnal." They could all heed our request, "Everybody sing, please." Not only that, but this typical song could also *mutatis mutandis* be recommended to adherents of other religions, provided their prophet had a name not exceeding three syllables. Thus, "Mohammed was a worker, With daily work to do," would not sound bad at all. As a sort of international national anthem this "hymn" could be made to render excellent service with only very slight alterations. Thus the Germans might be asked to sing, "Old Bismarck was a worker, With daily work to do, And where there is a worker, Count Bismark's man is there." Likewise an American can scarcely be expected to object to the paraphrase, "Our Lincoln was a helper, The woes of life he knew, And he who would be like him, Must be a helper, too." The song, then, is indeed of wide usefulness. The only difficulty is to discover why it should be called a hymn. Hymnals usually contain religious songs, while this "typical page" contains no religion, except it be the worship of man.

This chapter would become too long if we tried to take cognizance of the ever-shifting opinions within the ranks of a system whose adherents lay more stress upon the method than upon the content of their message, and who write books on such subjects as "One Man's Religion."

Since, however, *The Christian Century* continues to be the most popular and widely read organ of Modernism, we include the following few observations on Dr. Morrison's provoking series of thirteen articles, *Can Protestantism Win America?*[14] For even if it is impossible to deal exhaustively with the thrust of these articles (which is a plea for an undenominational and nondoctrinal "ecumenicity," that is, a unity of effort under the "Lordship of Christ" over against the Catholic unity of effort under the pope),

---

14. *The Christian Century*, April 3, 1946 to July 5, 1946.

it will be possible to make a few remarks that will cast light upon this latest effort of Modernism.[15]

Our first remark, then, concerns the article "The Wasted Power of Protestantism." While it remains true and needs to be emphasized more today than ever before that the endless splits from ten to twenty struggling and overlapping churches and Sunday Schools in the average American town of from five to ten thousand population is a "scandal," and a sad waste of money and energy,[16] the solution of the problem can never be found in the method of the *Christian Century*, which fails to reckon with sin as the cause of the present division. "Sin on the one hand and grace on the other account for the distinction between believers and unbelievers and make the universal brotherhood of man, of which the modernists love to speak, an utter impossibility. The difference between the friends and the enemies of the Christ of the Scripture is found not only in the world but in the Church as well. In short, there is truth and error in the Visible Church; there is a true Church but also a false Church. There are synagogues of Satan which call themselves by the name of Christ. There is no recognition of these distinctions, by so much as a syllable, in the series of Dr. Morrison. His entire plea for the union of all Protestant churches is based on the assumption that all Churches, at least those called Protestant, belong to the body of Christ, and that no Church has the right to refuse to fellowship with them as spiritual brethren."[17]

Our second major objection is against the thesis advocated by Dr. Morrison that ecumenicity should be based upon "the Lordship of Christ." This is not a Christian ecumenicity (though it may be one of high ethical ideas) because it fails to be based upon revealed truth. Evangelicals will never be able to recognize as Christian a conception of the Lordship

15. A good and more detailed criticism has been given by the Rev. H. J. Kuiper, editor of *The Banner*, in the July to Sept. 1946 issues of that weekly.
16. Cf. my *Our Christian Heritage*. (Grand Rapids: Wm. B. Eerdmans Publishing Co., 1948).
17. H. J. Kuiper, *The Banner*, Aug. 30, 1946.

of Christ that is not based upon an objective, God-given standard, but upon "the dignity of the individual man whose capacity to answer for himself directly to God" is considered apart from the infallible Scriptures.

In close connection with this we list as a third objection to Morrison's plea for an ecumenical Protestantism his gross historical inaccuracy on a basic point. We refer to the fact that Dr. Morrison in order to clinch his position for a unified Protestantism, asserts in "Protestant Misuse of the Bible" that later Protestantism has erred in viewing the Bible as the inspired Word of God, and the final arbiter and authority of religious opinion. This view is said to have given birth to denominations. For it has substituted a book for a man, but the principle remains the same. "Rome can point to its [Protestantism's] more than 200 denominational 'churches' and, looking Protestantism fairly in the eye, can scornfully say: 'These churches belie your claim to be ecumenical. Your denominational 'churches' are, every one of them, little counterfeit imitations of Rome, resting upon the same kind of basis as that which you say caused you to leave the Roman Catholic Church, namely, an infallible interpretation of an infallible Bible. We have one vice-regent of Christ; you have more than one hundred.' Every word of this indictment would be true; and the scorn with which it was spoken would be fully warranted."

This presentation is palpably inaccurate. In the first place, no Protestant church has ever claimed infallibility for its own interpretation of the Bible. But secondly, and this is more pertinent, Morrison enforces his view with the startling claim that it was Calvin who was to blame for this conception of an authoritative Bible. "Calvin was originally a lawyer, and he interpreted the Bible as if it were a book of law, infallibly and equally authoritative in all its parts and in every word." Of Luther he says that Luther considered not the Bible but Christ as the Word of God.

This view, which discriminates between the Reformers and states that Luther found Christ "where the Book says he is to be found, namely, in the living community of believers from which he has never withdrawn his living presence," and that to Calvin "the Bible was itself the divine revelation," is untenable for two reasons. The first is the historical fact that to all the Reformers Christ was the incarnate Word of God and the Bible the written Word of God, and to the entire Reformation movement the principle of authority was the Bible as distinct from the Church (Rome) or human reason (Modernism).[18] That in this respect Luther was in agreement with Calvin, not with Morrison see the article "The Place of the Bible in Protestantism" by Dr. Theodore Graebner in *The Lutheran Witness,* July 2, 1946.[19]

The second reason is that when Dr. Morrison states, "The Protestant mind has not allowed Christ to be the interpreter of the Bible; it has used the Bible as a realistic and literalistic interpreter of Christ", the question immediately arises, Which Christ are you referring to? Do you mean the "resurrection" Christ of Dr. Morrison, or the Christ who said, "The scripture cannot be broken" (John 10:35), and, "Till heaven and earth pass away, one jot or one title shall in no wise pass away from the law" (Matt. 5:18)?

For the rest, we may remind the reader to make this brief survey somewhat less incomplete, that Prof. L. Berkhof divides the more recent Modernists into two groups, "the social theologians or meliorists," among whom he counts the men of the Divinity School of Chicago, and the "new theists" among whom he numbers Wobbermin, Hocking and Fosdick, the Fosdick since *Beyond Modernism.* The latter lay greater emphasis upon the personality of God, and to them He is both transcendent and immanent.

When Barthianism at first took the theological world by storm, it was believed for a while that Modernism had virtually died of old age. Then came Dr. C. Van Til's book *The*

---

18. Cf. G. H. Hospers, *The Reformed Principle of Authority.*
19. Dr. Graebner states, "One need only consult the hundreds of references by which the late Dr. M. Reu in his *Luther and the Scriptures* (1944) proves his proposition that the Scripture was Luther's sole authority."

New Modernism, in which he placed Barthianism in the camp with Modernism. This was followed by Charles Clayton Morrison's keen analysis, "The Liberalism of Neo-Orthodoxy" in *The Christian Century,* June 7, 14, 21, 1950. And now comes Dr. Wilhelm Pauck's chapter "A Defense of Liberalism" in his book *The Heritage of the Reformation* (Boston: Beacon Press, 1950). But with these, one interested in forming a studied opinion should also read *The Triumph of Grace in the Theology of Karl Barth,* by G. C. Berkouwer (Grand Rapids: Wm. B. Eerdmans Publishing Co., 1956).

That the same old Modernism with its denials of the virgin birth, the bodily resurrection of Christ, the inspiration of Scripture, and the like, has by no means abdicated is further evident from such facts as these: In the Netherlands L. Praamsma has argued at some length that the situation has changed but little ("Zijn Er Nog Vrijzinnigen?" in *Gereformeerd Weekblad,* Oct. & Nov., 1950). In China Machen's old book *Christianity and Liberalism* was translated into Chinese in 1950. In the United States Chester A. Tulga argues that the missionaries in Asia are removing from "the gospel" whatever may appear distasteful to the pagan mind. (*The Case Against Modernism in Foreign Missions.* Chicago: Conservative Baptist Fellowship, 1950).[20]

---

20. It is difficult to refrain from quoting the following apt and eloquent words:

"Does not the modernist know Christ after the flesh, as the man of Galilee? as the beautiful Master, the uncrucified Teacher? Listen to Paul: 'Henceforth know we no man after the flesh: yea, though we have known Christ after the flesh, yet now henceforth know we Him no more' (II Cor. 5:16). These modernists have taken away our crucified Lord and know where they have laid Him; they have smothered Him with flowers. And does not the ritualist have a cross? a gold cross, a white cross, or a brass cross? (A number of years ago it was said there were enough crucifixes in the United States to fence in the state of Kentucky; ere long the whole nation may be fenced in.) The ritualists too have taken away the Crucified; they have buried Him beneath some Christless cross. Both of these extremes are, "after the flesh." What a relief then to sing: (*Cont. on p.* 315)

The few quotations, below, from the latest modernist works will reveal, we regretfully note, that many men who would seriously object to being classed with Modernism, foster the same attitude toward Scripture as that of the old-time Unitarians and Modernists. The truth of Scripture becomes subjective and dependent upon the reader's reaction to what is written; one does not find in the Scriptures an objective and authoritative statement of truth.

Modernism and Christian Doctrine

That Unitarianism and Modernism are firmly opposed to the essentials of Christianity may be gathered from the following quotations which are taken almost at random. As in later Spiritism, so here, we find a swing toward a more suave and less hateful expression. This is not due, it would seem, to greater tolerance, but rather to a larger measure of indifference to all doctrinal teaching, the logical outcome of pragmatism. It will be observed, however, that the cardinal teachings and the great redemptive facts of the Christian religion are just as decidedly rejected in the latest works.

The Bible

UNITARIANISM:

"We no longer depend for salvation upon either a man or a book. Men help us; books help us; but back of all stands our divine reason."—CHARLES W. ELIOT (late president of Harvard).[21]

"The Old Testament is a narrative of the early life and thought and struggle of the Jewish people, perhaps the most remarkable and, on the whole, admirable people of whom there is any record. The New Testament is made up of accounts of the life and work of Jesus, accounts given long after His death by persons who had never seen

---

A Christless cross no refuge were for me;
A crossless Christ my Saviour could not be.
But O Christ crucified, I rest in Thee!

L. E. Maxwell, *Crowded to Christ* (Grand Rapids: Wm. B. Eerdmans Publishing Co., 1950), p. 203.
21. *The Indianapolis Unitarian Bulletin*, 3, 5, 1927.

or heard Him, but were profoundly moved by reports concerning Him, reports more or less colored by the fact that
they were formulated in a very credulous age by simple
and, for the most part, unlettered men. In spite of these
drawbacks, the really beautiful and divinely human character of Jesus shines forth, and increasing numbers of
men are catching His spirit and following, though afar
off and with halting steps, His glorious example." —
GRACE JULIAN CLARKE.[22]

MODERNISM:

"Men can get on without the Bible, they can live good
and religious lives without it, or without any sacred book.
The man who does not know the Bible, or whose acquaint-
ance with it has begun in an unimpressionable age, will
probably never know that he is missing anything." —
J. B. PRATT.[23]

"The only precious thing in danger is the Church's rep-
utation for honesty and candor. The case of truth can
never be advanced by men who dare not face the facts.
It is disheartening that even in our day there are men of
intelligence and noble purposes who refuse to admit that
Paul was mistaken. . . .

"The traditional conception of inspiration must be reconstructed. . . . The image of the inspired and inerrant
Apostle, which still hangs in many a mind, is a creation
of the pious and uninstructed imagination. . . .

"He [Paul] wrote a letter to the Thessalonians which
stirred up so much commotion, that he had to write a
second letter to explain what he meant. He wrote a letter
to the Corinthians which contained statements so extreme, that it was necessary to write another letter to
tone these statements down." — C. E. JEFFERSON.[24]

"So we used to think of inspiration as a procedure
which produced a book guaranteed in all its parts against

22. *Ibid.*, pp. 11, 12, 1925.
23. James B. Pratt, "Religion and the Young Generation," *Yale
Review*, April, 1923.
24. *The Character of Paul*, pp. 37, 154, 155.

error, and containing from beginning to end a unanimous system of truth. No well-instructed mind, I think, can hold that now." — H. E. FOSDICK.[25]

"We know now that every idea in the Bible started from primitive and childlike origins, and, with however many setbacks and delays, grew in scope and height toward the culmination in Christ's gospel. We know now that the Bible is the record of an amazing spiritual development." —H. E. FOSDICK.[26]

"The Bible, therefore, is not only inspired as all other honest work is inspired, but in the same way. If it reveals a higher measure of inspiration than any other work, it is not because it was given it, but because it has reached it." — BASIL KING.[27]

"For the revelation with which the N. T. is charged is not a fixed dogma, supernaturally conveyed, but a Life generated by the Spirit of Jesus Christ. This Life implies no doubt certain truths or doctrines which have to be retained and from time to time restated. But they are only tenable in and through participation in the Life itself. What enforces them is not any dogma of Church tradition, not any arbitrary hypothesis of verbal inspiration, but the authority with which life speaks to life." — J. MOFFAT.[28]

"The Reformation insistance upon the authority of Scripture, as against the authority of the church, bears within it the perils of a new idolatry. Its Biblicism became, in time, as dangerous to the freedom of the human mind in searching out causes and effects as the old religious authority." — REINHOLD NIEBUHR.[29]

25. *The Christian Century*, Sept. 4, 1924.
26. *The Modern Use of the Bible*, p. 11.
27. "The Bible and Common Sense," in *Harper's Magazine*, July-Oct., 1934.
28. Cf., *Princeton Theological Review*, Oct. 1926, p. 608.
29. *The Nature and Destiny of Man*, Vol. II, p. 152.

Blood Atonement

MODERNISM:

"He [the primitive beast-like man] lived long before Harvey's discovery of the circulation, but when he slit a throat the blood spurted, and to him that spurting was a manifestation of life in the blood. He came to believe that blood was precious, sacred. It was his habit to divide with his gods whatever good things he gained; he thought the gods liked the flavor and smoke of cooking meat and that above all they liked blood. So bloody sacrifice entered into religions." — BRUCE BARTON.[30]

"Who can look on such a one as he hangs upon the cross and cries, 'It is finished,' and believe that it is indeed finished? Is this all of such a life as that? Are we living in a universe which produces such a man and then so wantonly destroys him? Our soul revolts at the conception. It is *not* finished. We must defend the world against such an indictment." — CHARLES C. MORRISON.[31]

"Christian theology was to find the explanation in the sacrificial system of Judaism; his death [Christ's] was to be the one grand sacrifice that would meet the Divine requirements forever. It is almost certain that Jesus himself did not think so." — W. A. GIFFORD.[32]

"A man's salvation at the cross does not depend upon accepting a certain view of what happened at the death of Jesus. Beware of the teacher who almost forgets savior and saved in his fascination with the operation, the transaction, the mechanics of the salvation. . . . Instead of getting down to the substantive question of who is saved from what for what, he ties us up in a consideration of how, by what arrangement, by what procedure salvation was effected. Instead of bidding us to the cross, which tells its own story and exhorts its own commitment, he demands subscription to a particular doctrine

---

30. *What Can a Man Believe?*, p. 21.
31. *The Christian Century*, April 14, 1927.
32. *The Story of the Faith*, p. 76.

about what actually happened a long time ago. It is as if we were told that the light switch under our fingers would not turn on the lights until we had initialed the blue prints of a certain special dynamo or turbine. . . .

"The how of the cross remains one of the deep mysteries of the faith, probed only superficially by the best of our metaphors. But the salvation we know there comes from whom we see there and what happens to us there. Some Christians see the Son of God hung there; others see the greatest and truest and best of men crucified. But all see alike who brought this Jesus to this cross . . . *we* brought him there . . . At the cross we see that God forgives us what we cannot forgive ourselves, that he wants us to be at home with him, not waiting for us to fix ourselves up enough to attract him, but desiring us so much just as we are, in all our confusion and wrongness, that he goes to this incomprehensible length and even — as some of us would say — suffers this ununderstandable agony to tell us that, to show us that, to give us a way back. . . ." — HAROLD E. FEY.[33]

The Christian

MODERNISM:

"The Christian shares with, or is like, other people in very many ways. He is like other people in his instincts, in having friendships, in being loyal to some purpose or some ideal. . . . He has his own distinctive temperament like other folks. He may be temperamentally jovial or melancholy, active or sluggish. . . . The Christian, however, whatever his original nature, is one who has made up his mind to live his life after the model or pattern of Jesus." — A. W. WISHART.[34]

"It might be subject to question how far one was entitled to call himself a Christian in any complete and ade-

33. Editorial, "What The Cross Certifies" in *The Christian Century*, Mar. 21, 1956.
34. *The Christian Life*, etc. Three sermons delivered in the Fountain Street Baptist Church, Grand Rapids, Mich.; 1925.

quate sense whose religion is chiefly concerned with his
personal salvation in another world, with doctrines, as-
sents to which he therefore calls fundamental." — PROF.
LYMAN of Union Theological Seminary.[35]

The Church

UNITARIANISM:

"The Church, according to the Unitarian understanding of things, is a purely human institution . . . The
Church is simply an organization of man's religious interests. The institution, no matter what its traditions and
claims and forms, can have no authority above that
which proceeds naturally from the intellectual and spiritual attainments of the persons composing it. Like
every other institution it has a right to require that those
seeking admission shall go through certain forms, but to
offer eternal rewards or pronounce eternal doom is wholly
beyond its right and power. To belong to a church cannot
secure anyone a privileged position after death.   The
Church is a saving and righteous force in a community
when and only to the extent that its members are living
examples of purest and noblest character." — CHARLES
GRAVES.[36]

MODERNISM:

"We Protestants should today be searching our hearts
with this question: Have we given to Jesus Christ the kind
of church that he deserves? He is the Head of the church
and as his disciples we are one in him. But we have failed
to honor him with a church through which he could manifest himself in the true dignity and power of his redemptive presence. In fact we have not given him a
church at all. Instead, we have given him a multiplicity of
'churches.' None of these 'churches' does he recognize as
his own. And few if any of us would for a moment tol-

35. *Union Theological Seminary Bulletin,* 1922.
36. *The Indianapolis Unitarian Bulletin,* II, p. 25, 1927.

erate the claim that our denominational church is the Church of Christ. He did not found any of them. They are every one man-made. At their origin his body was broken — 'by schisms rent asunder.' . . Those who look prayerfully forward to a great spiritual awakening in Protestantism — and who does not long for it? — may be sure that such a revival will not come to pass until we give back to Christ the church which he himself created and which his Lordship deserves. . . ." — CHARLES CLAYTON MORRISON.[37]

Creed

Dr. Charles Edwards Park, late pastor of the First Unitarian Church in Boston, answered the question of why Unitarians do not use the Apostles' Creed in its usual form. "We feel too much respect for it," writes the seventy-three-year-old minister in the July issue of the Unitarian monthly, *The Christian Register*. "Plenty of Christians can still repeat it with perfect honesty. We are not of that number. It does not express our belief." Dr. Park's version:

"I believe in (*a single, eternal, all-inclusive, all-pervading Life Principle whose source and perfect embodiment is God, who finds varying degrees of embodiment in all forms of life, who is the prototype of every grace, power, and nobility found in his creation, and whom I call*) God, the Father Almighty, Maker of heaven and earth; and in Jesus Christ (*not*) his only Son, (*for whose son am I? But*) our Lord (*because he is a more nearly perfect embodiment of the Life Principle than any one I know*) ; who was (*neither*) conceived by the Holy Ghost, (*nor*) born of the Virgin Mary, (*but was conceived and born exactly as we are all conceived and born; and who*) suffered under Pontius Pilate, was crucified, dead, and buried. He descended into (*no*) hell, (*for as hell is not a spiritual condition, he never saw the outer doormat of hell*). The third day (*the eager women found his tomb empty, and jumped*

---

37. Editorial in *The Pulpit*, Feb., 1951.

to the conclusion that in the night) he rose again from the dead; he ascended into (*no*) heaven, (*as heaven is not a place but a spiritual condition, he never left heaven,*) and sitteth on the right hand of God the Father Almighty (*if it is any comfort to you*). From thence he shall come (*if he is not already here*) to judge the quick and the dead. I believe in the Holy Ghost (*whom I call the Holy Spirit: the spirit in which God works;*) the holy catholic Church (*so long as it tries to be holy and catholic;*) the communion of (*what*) saints (*there are;*) the forgiveness of sins; the resurrection of the body (*if body means personality: not, if body means this mortal frame, for I am sick to death of my mortal frame and hope to be rid of it soon*) ; and the life everlasting (*meaning a chance to finish out the interrupted opportunities of this life*) Amen.[38]

Deity of Christ

UNITARIANISM :

"May I say, as clearly as I can, that I, as a Unitarian, believe in the divinity of Jesus? Then with the next breath say, I believe in the divinity of mankind. I believe, as well, in the divinity of every form of life. The dogma I deny is the exclusive divinity of Jesus. I do not believe the Eternal exhausted himself in one historic manifestation. I do not believe the Infinite can be compressed within the form of one being, even so exalted a personality as the Man of Nazareth. My difference with the Orthodox Church is not that it made Jesus God, but that it stopped there. I see the divine life sweeping on, filling every nook and cranny of the universe. It enters into every man; appears in every living thing. . . . The difference between the simplest form of life and the highest is not one of kind, but of degree. Jesus differs from other men only in His greater capacity for the one life."—F. S. C. WICKS.[39]

---

38. *Newsweek*, July 22, 1946.
39. *Indianapolis Unitarian Bulletin*, 4, 1, 1927.

MODERNISM:

"So I repeat, we are not left in the dark about the universal purpose which we have seen at work in the world producing ever finer and higher types of life. It is God, and Jesus is to us the symbol of that life, the noblest embodiment of it, the loftiest expression of it. He is the eloquent witness of the fact that we do not live in a material universe, where we are the slaves of physical forces, but we live in a world where man can conquer, where man can subject the world unto himself and live, not according to the will of physical forces, not bound hand and foot by heredity and environment, — but according to the creations of his spirit, his lofty conceptions of the good and the true, holding himself to these great tasks and refusing to be the slave of the forces around him or of his own body." — A. W. WISHART.[40]

"Perhaps it is sufficient to say that the Jesus of history actually created the Christ of faith in the life of the early church, and that his historic life is related to the transcendent Christ as a final and ultimate symbol of a relation which prophetic religion sees between all life and history and the transcendent." — REINHOLD NIEBUHR.[41]

"Christ is the symbol both of what man ought to be and of what God is beyond man."—REINHOLD NIEBUHR.[42]

Depravity

UNITARIANISM:

"Q. What gospel may we tell to 'the bad'?

"A. It is a gospel that the bad life is not man's true nature. It is a gospel that he can forsake and ought to forsake the evil way and that he will then become like a new creature as soon as he lets the electric touch of good-will move his soul." — DR. DOYLE.[43]

---

40. *God in Jesus*, a sermon.
41. *An Interpretation of Christian Ethics*, p. 120, as cited by Carnell, *op. cit.*, p. 162. "Christ is the true mythical symbol of both the possibilities and the limits of the human." *Ibid.*, p. 15.
42. *Beyond Tragedy*, p. 23, as quoted by Carnell, *op. cit.*, p. 144.
43. *Catechism of Liberal Faith*, p. 110.

"Unitarianism is an attitude of the soul towards men.
God being our Father, then we are all his children. This
is a rather obvious platitude. But its significance is far-
reaching. It undermines at once the doctrine of the total
depravity of man. . . . That God is our Father means that
man is in essence divine. . . . This fundamental thought
of Unitarianism has vast practical applications. It modi-
fies all our ideas of education and reform. The modern
education is trusting more and more to the natural instincts of the child. Its watchword is not repression, but
expression. . . . Character is the final goal of all our efforts." — JOHN H. APPLEBEE.[44]

"Christianity has at its heart the promise that no matter how much we may become involved in disobedience,
no matter how long our record of deliberate wrongdoing,
it is always possible, if we are honest with ourselves and
with God, to turn and be changed. We can begin again
without thinking of ourselves as under condemnation."
— JOHN C. BENNETT.[45]

The Devil

MODERNISM :

"He [Satan] never appeared again in the Old Testament until after Persian influence had begun its work. . . .
Having frankly recognized, therefore, the outgrown nature of the category [demons] we need not be troubled
by it when we read the Bible." — H. E. FOSDICK.[46]

The Fall

UNITARIANISM :

"The stories of the creation of Adam and Eve, of their
primal innocence, and of their fall, have become for us
folklore. In it the Fall explained the origin of sin; and
a horrible theory of the propagation of sin, reared by
Augustine on the basis of the Fall, was accepted by offi-

44. *Unitarianism: What It Is Not, and What It Is.*
45. *Christian Realism,* p. 40.
46. *The Modern Use of the Bible,* pp. 119, 121.

cial Catholic theologians. Darwin's triumph has destroyed the whole theological scheme." — BISHOP BARNES in St. Paul's Cathedral, London.[47]

"*The Real Difference Between Unitarian Christianity and Traditional Orthodoxy.* This difference is not about the Trinity. It goes deeper. What Unitarians and many liberals in other churches reject is the Calvinistic doctrine of the Fall of Man and the Depravity of Human Nature. We believe in the age-long Rise of Man, the dignity and divinity of human nature. We seriously, passionately, believe that we are the children of the Highest; that our nature is not ruined but incomplete; that within us a divinely beautiful nature is latent, waiting development. For Calvinistic pessimism we substitute an inspiring faith in human nature, not merely in what it is, but in what it is to be . . ."[48]

MODERNISM :

"That experience in the old theology has been labeled the 'fall of man,' but if it was a fall it was a fall forward. The man had become like God, knowing good and evil. It was the great upward step." — BRUCE BARTON.[49]

"The metaphysical connotations of the myth of the Fall are, however, less important for our purpose than the psychological and moral ones. It is in its interpretations of the facts of human nature, rather than in its oblique insights into the relation of order and chaos as such, that the myth of the Fall makes its profoundest contribution to moral and religious theory. The most basic and fruitful conception flowing from this ancient myth is the idea that evil lies at the juncture of nature and spirit. Evil is conceived as not simply the consequence of temporality or the fruit of nature's necessities. Sin can be understood neither in terms of the freedom of human reason alone, nor yet in terms of the circumscribed

47. *Indianapolis Unitarian Bulletin*, 11,18, 1927.
48. *Ibid.*, 11, 16, 1928.
49. *What Can a Man Believe?*" p. 22.

harmonies in which the human body is bound. Sin lies at the juncture of spirit and nature, in the sense that the peculiar and unique characteristics of human spirituality, in both its good and evil tendencies, can be understood only by analyzing the paradoxical relation of freedom and necessity, of finiteness and the yearning for the eternal in human life." — REINHOLD NIEBUHR.[50]

God

UNITARIANISM:

"Some day we shall be able to treat the myths and legends of the Bible as we do those of other peoples. Then Abraham and Prometheus, Samson and Hercules will appear alike as legendary heroes, while Zeus and Jehovah will be relegated to the dead man-made gods." — F. S. C. WICKS.[51]

MODERNISM:

"As preached in our Protestant churches the Trinity has often been little more than a mathematical formula about three being one and one three. Let it be said to the credit of the early fathers who introduced the church to the philosophical treatment of the Trinity, that they did not deal in such arithmetical absurdity as has characterized our modern pulpits in their identification of one person with three persons. If then, any one is troubled about this formula of the Trinity, the liberal prescription is familiar; translate the formula back into the experience from which it came. The Trinity that matters is the Trinity of experience." — H. M. FOSDICK[52]

"When, however, the metaphysical presuppositions of Hellenistic thinking are abandoned, the doctrine is regarded as a symbol of Christian faith rather than as a

---

50. *An Interpretation of Christian Ethics*, p. 76.
51. *Op. cit.*, 9, 29, 1926.
52. *Op. cit.*, p. 188.

literally exact description. Liberal Protestantism generally takes this position." — GERALD BIRNEY SMITH.[53]

"God is the work of human nature, imagination and will." — JOHN DEWEY.[54]

"I do not believe in any God that has ever been devised in any doctrine, that has ever claimed to be revealed, in any scheme of immortality that has ever been expounded. . . . there is no trustworthy evidence as to a God's absolute existence." — CARL VAN DOREN.[55]

"God is neither a Being nor existence of any sort, but rather an order of nature which includes men and all the processes of aspiring social life." — EDWARD SCRIBNER AMES.[56]

"Moses had had an extraordinary religious experience, that led him to enter into an exclusive covenant with Jehovah, or Yahweh, a storm god of Midian.

"It is unlikely that Moses was a monotheist, or even consciously looking towards monotheism." — GIFFORD.[57]

Holy Spirit

"There is simply no gainsaying the fact that the Good News was formulated in terms of a cosmology, a philosophy of history and a psychology, or of several of each of these, which if taken at face value are inadmissible to thinking men today. For example, the Christian is so familiar with the idea of the Holy Spirit as acting upon the believer or upon the sacramental elements that he hardly stops to consider what is implied, namely, a survival of a highly animistic point of view. Invasion of our bodies or selves by a 'spirit' either of God or of Satan is incredible with many today except as a figure of

---

53. G. B. Smith and S. Matthews, *A Dictionary of Religion and Ethics*, article on "Trinity."
54. *A Common Faith*, New Haven, 1934, p. 71.
55. "Why I Am an Unbeliever," in the *Forum*, Dec. 1926.
56. *Religion*, New York, 1929, p. 177.
57. *The Story of the Faith*, pp. 2, 15.

speech, and a Christian apologetics in these terms is under great handicaps."—AMOS N. WILDER.[58]

Judgment
MODERNISM:

"Personally, I do not pretend to know the details of the future life. . . . But I am likewise sure that the old Scriptural framework with its background of a Hebrew Sheol and a Zoroastrian judgment day is not in my mind." — H. E. FOSDICK.[59]

"It is unwise for Christians to claim any knowledge of either the furniture of heaven or the temperature of hell; or to be too certain about any details of the Kingdom of God in which history is consummated. But it is prudent to accept the testimony of the heart, which affirms the fear of judgment." — REINHOLD NIEBUHR.[60]

"The symbol of the last judgment in New Testament eschatology contains three important facets of the Christian conception of life and history. The first is expressed in the idea that it is Christ who will be the judge of history. Christ as judge means that when the historical confronts the eternal it is judged by its own ideal possibility, and not by the contrast between the finite and the eternal character of God." — REINHOLD NIEBUHR.[61]

"This fluidity of conception in the Jewish-Christian mythology is a commonplace of historical study. It should warn us against too literal a reading of the portrayals we find. If we take these pictures literally we do more than the Jews and early Christians did. What was important to them will, however, still be important to us: days of reckoning if not a day of reckoning, and God's governance of men and nations to the end of history."—AMOS N. WILDER.[62]

58. *New Testament Faith for Today*, p. 44.
59. *Op. cit.*, p. 102.
60. *The Nature and Destiny of Man*, Vol. II, p. 294.
61. *Ibid.*, p. 291.
62. *Op. cit.*, p. 102.

Man's Nature
UNITARIANISM:

"The difference between the Man of Galilee of the first century and the man of England and America in the nineteenth century, if I understand my gospels aright, is not in inherent capacity to draw near God, but in the relative degree of realization of a latent power common to humanity. It is this that has created the uniqueness of Jesus."—REV. ANSON PHELPS STOKES.[63]

MODERNISM:

"The incarnation was in man that it might be in men. O child of God, as God lived in his Son, so would he live in his sons and children."—C. S. MACFARLAND, former Secretary of the Council of the Churches of Christ in America.[64]

"Christ is essentially no more divine than we are or than nature is."—A. C. MCGIFFERT.[65]

"Doctrines of human depravity are alleged to enervation and resignation. Not a few Protestant writers have conceived the disctinctiveness and finality of Christianity in terms of this doctrine of the sacredness of human personality. This concept which has dominated so much of the Council's Federal Council of Churches of Christ in America social thought is clearly and ably expounded in the writings of Dr. F. Ernest Johnson. While his books are in no sense official pronouncements of the Council's position, no one has been in a better position to see and appreciate the real genius of its thought . . . Let us see what Dr. Johnson has to say about the doctrine of man. Candidly he states, 'If the Christian message is Jesus, its social and ethical character is inescapable, it is the embodiment of deity within the apprehension of the human.' Again, 'The essential truth . . . is that man is under absolute mandate to express di-

---

63. *Indianapolis Unitarian Bulletin*, 3, 25, 1927.
64. *The Spirit Christlike*, p. 68.
65. *The Rise of Modern Religious Ideas*, p. 208.

vinity in his own life and his whole nature.' Or, 'Little
by little though sometimes with a startling suddenness
mankind is learning that the essential divinity of man is
a first principle, not a derivative.' "—J. A. HUTCHIN-
SON.[66]

"We all, Christians, Buddhists, Shintoists, or whatever other faith, have much to learn from each other
and much to contribute to each other. Also we feel that
if we spiritual leaders are to accomplish anything constructive for the good of society as a whole we ought first
to get together as religionists and come to know each
other sympathetically."[67]

Man's Original Righteousness

"Christian theology has found it difficult to refute the
rationalistic rejection of the myth of the Fall without
falling into the literalistic error of insisting upon the
Fall as an historical event. One of the consequences of
this literalism which has seriously affected the thought
of the church upon the problem of man's essential nature, is the assumption that the perfection from which
man fell is to be assigned to a particular historical period,
i. e. the paradisaical period before the Fall. This chro-
nological interpretation of a relation which cannot be
expressed in terms of time without being falsified must
not be attributed to the authority of the Biblical myth
alone."—REINHOLD NIEBUHR.[68]

Miracles

MODERNISM:

"Biblical miracles will more and more become unreal
ghosts lost in antiquity and, gradually becoming dimmer,
will disappear in utter incredulity. . . .

"For this is the principle on which alone can Biblical
miracles have a vital part in our faith: Wherever a nar-

---

66. *We Are Not Divided*, p. 303.
67. *Rethinking Missions*, p. 34.
68. *The Nature and Destiny of Man*, Vol. I, p. 267.

rative in Scripture describes an experience in terms of miracle so that we recognize that the same kind of experience is open to us or would be open if we were receptive of God's incoming power, that narrative is fundamentally credible and useful."—H. E. FOSDICK.[69]

"One of the earliest of the prophet-teachers himself used magic to discredit the inferior magic of his opponents, the priests of the Baal. Elijah brought down fire from heaven to consume a water-sodden sacrifice, after making sport of the futile attempts of the Baal-worshipers. A third example of belief in magic can be taken from the regulations given in the book of Leviticus for cleansing a house after a visitation of plague or leprosy. These regulations read like the descriptions of magic one can find in many modern discussions of primitive practices among living peoples, in Africa, Australasia, and the South seas."—HAROLD E. B. SPEIGHT.[70]

Prayer

UNITARIANISM :

"Why pray since we live in a world governed by natural law? Can puny man importuning the Almighty, cause him to change his mind or break his laws to grant our petition? No — men did that in an ignorant, superstitious age, but we have enlarged our idea of God, and now we must revise our idea concerning prayer. We must accustom ourselves to think of prayer, not as supplication, but as co-operation; not as asking God to work for us, but as pledging ourselves to work with God."—AUGUSTUS P. RECCORD.[71]

"We seek to know the way of life that we may walk therein. We seek a revelation which will make known to us the way in which we should go. In vain we lift our eyes to the distant Heavens; in vain we turn to the

69. *Op. cit.*, pp. 157, 165.
70. "From Magic, Through Science, to Faith," in *The Christian Century*, Feb. 4, 1926.
71. *The Indianapolis Unitarian Bulletin*, Feb. 8, 1929.

printed page: for us no revelation from above, no revelation from beyond. And then, turning back in our unavailing search, we turn within and and there we find the light that lighteth every man that cometh onto the earth, the light that illuminates our understanding, the light of conscience and of reason. Finding truth in our minds and justice in our hearts, we have found our lights; and following their leadings, we are in the way of Eternal Life. Amen."—F. S. C. WICKS.[72]

MODERNISM:

"The only prayer which we have a moral right to pray is precisely the prayer which after all we ourselves must answer."—GEORGE BURMAN FOSTER.[73]

Prophecy

MODERNISM:

"That was the message of Jesus — that God is supremely better than anybody had ever dared to believe. Not a petulant Creator, who had lost control of his creation and, in wrath, was determined to destroy it all. Not a stern Judge dispensing impersonal justice. Not a vain King who must be flattered and bribed into concession of mercy. Not a rigid accountant, checking up the sins against the penances and striking a cold hard balance. Not any of these . . . nothing like these . . . but a great Companion, a wonderful Friend, a kindly, indulgent, joy-loving Father . . ."—BRUCE BARTON.[74]

"It cannot be too strongly insisted upon that predictive prophecy has always been immediately connected with a non-moral theory of inspiration."—KEMPER FULLERTON.[75]

---

72. "Words of Aspiration," in "The *Indianapolis Unitarian Bulletin*, July 15, 1927.
73. *The Function of Religion in Man's Struggle for Existence*, p. 184.
74. *The Man Nobody Knows*, p. 86.
75. *Prophecy and Authority*, p. 189.

Regeneration

MODERNISM:

"Yet another thing the historic Jesus has done: he has made men believe in the possibility of moral reclamation and renewal. He was the great specialist in the conservation of the waste products of humanity — its prodigals and outcasts . . ."—H. E. FOSDICK.[76]

"Modern interpretation inclines to return to the symbolical use of the conception of Regeneration. Our ethical realities deal with transformed characters. Regeneration expresses thus a radical, vital, ethical change, rather than an absolutely new metaphysical beginning. Regeneration is a vital step in the natural development of the spiritual life, a radical adjustment to the moral processes of life. More commonly a series of ethical renewals is taught. Psychologically, this does not express a miraculous 'new birth,' but new stages of contact with spiritual power."—HERBERT A. YOUTZ.[77]

Resurrection

MODERNISM:

"In the Bible immortality is associated with the resurrection of the body; among us immortality is conceived as escape from the body.

"I believe in the persistence of personality through death, but I do not believe in the resurrection of the flesh."—H. E. FOSDICK.[78]

"The idea of the resurrection of the body is a Biblical symbol in which modern minds take the greatest offense and which has long since been displaced in most modern versions of the Christian faith by the idea of the immortality of the soul. The latter idea is regarded as a more plausible expression of the hope of everlasting life."—REINHOLD NIEBUHR.[79]

---

76. *Op. cit.*, p. 225.
77. G. B. Smith and S. Matthews, *op. cit.*, article on "Regeneration."
78. *Op. cit,*, pp. 45, 98.
79. *The Nature and Destiny of Man*, p. 294.

"Though men crucified Jesus, the amazing thing," to quote R. L. Smith in his booklet, *The Greatest Question*, was that when he died he did not lose touch with his followers, but that he entered into a new life which made it possible for him to be always at the Christian's side. He became a living, reachable, spiritual presence, and any man who desired to do so might thereafter live a life which had an entirely new quality. This, John spoke of as 'eternal life,' because it was capable of surviving all experiences, even that of death."—J. W. MCKELVEY.[80]

Return of Christ
MODERNISM:

"I do not believe in the physical return of Jesus." — H. E. FOSDICK.[81]

" 'I go to prepare a place for you. And if I go and prepare a place for you, I will come again, and receive you unto myself; that where I am, there ye may be also.' 'I will come again.' When? Where? Now there are many who interpret this to mean the coming, the so-called Second Coming, when Christ shall come in glory, when the judgment, the division, and the final rounding up of things will take place. To very many that is a very dear doctrine. There are others, however, equally devout and faithful, who think that this refers to the coming of the Spirit of our Lord into the hearts of all who give him room, into our lives, where he comes again and again and again, and tarries with us when we give room to his Spirit. There are still others who think that it refers to his coming to meet us when death has 'kissed down our eyelids still.' Now it seems to me there is room here for a difference of opinion and that the main thing is the promise of companionship, the comradeship of our Lord's Spirit." — EDGAR DE WITT JONES.[82]

---

80. *The Pulpit*, Mar., 1946.
81. *Op. cit.*, p. 104.
82. *The coming of the Perfect*, p. 186.

"The time is past when such features of the New Testament could be skirted out of deference to cherished pieties. There are too many today for whom such doctrines are occasions of stumbling if not scandal. We must frankly concede that no such dramatic return of Christ with the clouds is to be expected in the course of history. He has his own way of coming but not this way. . . .

"Clarification of this matter should begin with a double recognition: (1) that the New Testament doctrine of the return of Christ (or Jesus' announcement of the coming of the Son of Man) belongs to the order of symbolic and mytho-poetic statement and was not understood literally in the late Jewish and early Christian religion: and (2) that (as Professor Minear has so well shown in his volume, *The Christian Hope and the Second Coming*) a just understanding of the teaching is only possible in the light of the whole complex of biblical experience." — AMOS N. WILDER.[83]

Sinlessness of Jesus

"Schleiermacher is quite right of course in suggesting that to be tempted means in a sense to have sinned; for temptation is a state of anxiety from which sin flows inevitably." — REINHOLD NIEBUHR.[84]

Substitution

MODERNISM:

"Guilt and merit are personal. They cannot be transferred from one person to another. We tamper with moral truths when we shuffle them about."
— W. RAUSCHENBUSCH.[85]

"Paul's idea of law, of penalty, of expiation, offends the modern sense of justice and contradicts our ethical values at every point of contact. Without caricature it may be compared to ideas that prevail in certain police

83. *Op. cit.*, pp. 103, 104.
84. *The Nature and Destiny of Man*, Vol. II, p. 73.
85. *A Theology for the Social Gospel*, p. 219.

circles today. A sensational crime is committed; the
public is greatly aroused and demands detection and
punishment of the criminal. This the police are unable
to accomplish, but obviously something must be done to
silence public clamor; so they 'frame up' a case against
someone who can plausibly be made the scapegoat. He is
convicted by perjury, the public is silenced, the majesty
of the law has been vindicated, justice is satisfied. But
we are no longer content with that brand of 'justice.' We
insist that the guilt of the guilty cannot be expiated,
justice cannot be satisfied by the punishment of the innocent. Yet our theology continues to teach that the Almighty could find no better expedient to save men than
'to frame up' a case against His own Son and put to
death the innocent for the guilty. And that which fills us
with horror when done by man to man, we praise and
glorify when done by God to God." — VEDDER.[86]

"In bearing sin for us there is a sense in which we
speak of Christ as our substitute. He in His life and on
the cross does something for us which we, thanks to Him,
are relieved from doing. Those of us who spend our holi-
days in the mountains know our indebtedness to trail-
makers, who blazed paths through the forest and set up
cairns on the slopes of the summits above the timber line
. . . In taking on His conscience the sin of the world and
in letting men slay Him, our Lord suffered the Righteous
for the unrighteous. He offered this sacrifice of Himself
once for all. He discovered the path to oneness with God
— the path of trust and devotion, the path of love which
beareth, believeth, hopeth, endureth all and never faileth.
He blazed that trail with His blood. Or (to employ a
New Testament metaphor) He opened a new and living
way. The trail once found and marked, the way once
opened, remains for all time. None can repeat the vicarious sacrifice of Him who gave Himself to discover the
route, to be the way. Forever all who attain like oneness

---

86. *Fundamentals of Christianity*, p. 191.

with God must come unto the Father through Him. And all will be grateful to Him 'the Pioneer and Perfection of faith,' 'the Author of eternal salvation.' But He is Saviour only to those who obey Him. The path of trust and devotion must be trod by those who wish to share His life with God. The trail of vicarious love is to be taken and pursued until we, too, bear the sins of men and offer ourselves in service for their redemption." — H. S. COFFIN.[87]

"Thomas Paine remarked truly that no religion can be really divine which has in it any doctrine that offends the sensibilities of a little child. Is there any reader of this page whose childish sensibilities were not shocked when the traditional explanation of the death of Jesus was first poured into his ears? Would any human father, loving his children, have sentenced all to death, and then persuaded to commute the sentence only by the suffering of his best beloved?" — BRUCE BARTON.[88]

The Virgin Birth

UNITARIANISM:

"Among the dogmas held by the Church has been that of the Virgin Birth of Jesus. This has come to be regarded as sacred. Now everyone who has studied and thought knows that there is not the faintest evidence of a fact on which this dogma was built. We know now how it began. It is due to the mistranslation of the Hebrew word, 'Alma,' which means only, a young woman. This word appeared in the Greek translation as 'Parthenos,' virgin. The writer of Matthew, having only the Greek version before him, repeated the mistranslation. Every scholar knows this, but most have been discreet in proclaiming it. . . . I dislike the dogma because it casts a slur on pure womanhood, on your mother and mine. Our birth was as

87. *The Meaning of the Cross*, Scribner, p. 101.
88. *The Man Nobody Knows*, p. 59.

divine as that of Jesus, and the love of our Fathers and Mothers as pure as the love of Mary."—F. S. C. WICKS.[89]

MODERNISM:

"The virgin birth is not to be accepted as an historical fact. To believe in virgin birth as an explanation of great personality is one of the familiar ways in which the ancient world was accustomed to account for unusual superiority. Especially is this true of the founders of great religions." — H. E. FOSDICK.[90]

"Salvation has come nigh us because we have found God, in Jesus, identified with us. We are to become saviours — which is the fulness of stature set before us in Christ — by becoming identified ourselves with the lives of others. This is the gospel of the incarnation." —PAUL HUTCHINSON.[91]

"Only when it is recognized that humanity is divinity in germ and that divinity is humanity raised to the *nth* power, does a solution become possible. We may disagree with the Creeds of Nicæa and Chalcedon in their methods of explaining the unity of divine and human, but we fully agree with what they were endeavoring to assert — the likeness of Christ to humanity and at one and the same time his difference from it.

"The Virgin Birth is, therefore, in no way connected with the divinity of Jesus unless we regard that divinity as material. We may accept it or may reject it for a more spiritual idea of divinity, and in either case hold fast to the essential underlying truth of the differences, the uniqueness, the majesty, the lordship of Christ, the eternal Son of God. We do not indeed venture to such a length as to say that Christ is God, for this would involve the inconceivable assertion that God Almighty was once born and died." — F. PALMER.[92]

89. *Indiana Unitarian Bulletin, Supplement* 3, 8, 1929.
90. *Shall the Fundamentalists Win?*
91. "Incarnation," a sermon in *The Christian Century*, Dec. 22, 1927.
92. *The Virgin Birth*, p. 28.

The Wrath of God

MODERNISM:

"Anger is a primitive emotion of resentment associated with the instinct of self preservation. In the history of religions, anger is frequently attributed to God. Primitive peoples think of their gods as subject to anger and revenge in naive anthropomorphic fashion. The Old Testament writers freely referred to the anger of Yahweh against those who opposed his will. The New Testament writers spoke of the wrath of God coming on those who reject Christ. Christian theology has regularly taught that God experiences anger against sin, but that His anger is not inconsistent with His love."[93]

"To a modern mind such acts of caprice are unthinkable in connection with God. . . . But the writers of J and E [documents] did not hesitate to endow Jahveh with their own passionate natures." — WILLIAM F. BADE.[94]

Goads to Thought

1. Mention some excellent features of modern religious liberalism.

2. In which ways are the evangelical churches to blame that so many upright souls have turned to Modernism?

3. What has Modernism in common with all false religious cults?

4. Was Dr. James Snowden right when he called Luther and similar progressives of their day Modernists?

5. Do Unitarianism and Modernism show a united front (a) as to methods of propagating their views, (b) as to contents of views?

6. Present evidence of the intellectual dishonesty of Modernists, dealing with the doctrinal tenets of historic Christianity (evidence lies spread through the chapter; an incisive indictment on this point may also be found in

---

93. G. Smith and S. Matthews, *op. cit.*, article on "Anger of God."
94. *The Old Testament in the Light of Today*, p. 68.

Machen's review of Fosdick's "Modern Use of the Bible," reprinted in *What Is Christianity?* by Machen).

7. Has Modernism changed essentially either after the first or the second World War?

8. Are Modernism and Fundamentalism the same religion? Are Fundamentalism and Orthodoxy, that is, historic Christianity, the same religion?

9. To which view of the Apocalypse does the author apparently adhere? What is your own view of the book of Revelation?

10. What is wrong with "the Lordship of Christ" as a basis for ecumenical unity? And what is wrong with Charles C. Morrison's basis for church unity? Could you possibly agree with Morrison's understanding of the character of the Church?

11. Prove from citations the wide divergence of Modernism from the Scriptural position on fundamental Christian doctrines.

14

SWEDENBORGIANISM

The cult of Swedenborgianism announces itself as "The New Church" or "The Church of the New Jerusalem." For all that, it is not nearly as new as the other cults described in this volume. Its founder lived in Sweden from 1688 and died in London in 1772. Consequently, one of our earliest great theologians, Dr. Charles Hodge of Princeton, took note of Swedenborg in his famed *Systematic Theology* in 1875.

As to the founder, he stands apart from, and intellectually miles above, founders of "new" religions as Joseph Smith, Mary Baker Eddy, Russell-Rutherford, the Fillmores, and others to whom the words of Henry Van Dyke apply: "There are many Americans who have too little respect for special training, and too much confidence in their power to solve the problems of philosophy and statesmanship extemporaneously."

Emanuel Swedenborg was a genius and a scholar of the first dimension who, as a confirmed bachelor, had more time than others to devote to his profound studies, and did so unstintedly. Recognized by his government, he was for thirty years the Royal Assessor of Mines, one of the body of men responsible to the government for the mineral wealth of Sweden. He wrote some thirty-three scientific works on metallurgy, mineralogy, physiology, geology, mathematics, cosmology, and the structure and functions of the human brain. He anticipated the airplane and the submarine. His name would have gone down in history as of one of mankind's greatest scientists, but at fifty-nine years of age he resigned from his government post, and began to spend another twenty-five years investigating the things of the spirit, and wrote another thirty works, no small pamphlets either, on "theology," being firmly convinced that the Lord had called him to revive a dying Church. This conviction he had in common with his contemporary, John Wesley (1703-1791), but the results of the two convictions and inspirations differed widely indeed.

Swedenborg's works are chiefly the *Arcana Coelestia, Heaven and Hell, The True Christian Religion, The Four Doctrines, The Divine Providence, Conjugial Love, Miscellaneous Theological Works.*

A great intellect, however, together, with a deep religious sense do not make a man right. In Swedenborg we encounter one more man who, interpolating Scripture in accordance with "revelations" that came on top of the inspired Scriptures, drifted into re-writing the Scriptures to make them tally with his pantheistic and spiritistic intuitions. And this, for all his intellectual superiority, vast scholarship and unquestionable integrity, he had in common with the untrained and unscrupulous founders of today's weird American religious cults.

It cannot be re-iterated strongly enough that divine revelation has terminated with the final book of the New Testament. The Mormon excuse that the curse pronounced in Revelation 22:18 upon those who add to "the words of the prophecy of this book" merely warns that no chapters are to be added to *this* particular book, whereas new revelations remain to be expected, is to be rejected as a mere subterfuge. Whatever man must know of God in His saving activity is to be found within the covers of the Bible; and it will be found that all those who have come with additional "revelations" have added and/or subtracted, thus robbing us of the cardinal doctrines of Scripture. This holds of Swedenborg, too.

When Swendenborg said that he had frequent communication with numerous spirits of the departed, who gave him all sorts of information that was supposed to be firsthand, but in addition to the Scriptures; and when he stated that all the history, symbols and parables of Scripture have a threefold sense, one for this life (the natural sense), one for the next life (the spiritual sense) and one for the life of angels (the celestial sense), he opened the floodgates to the most fanciful speculation.

Swedenborgianism, therefore, has become as much a type of gnosticism as, for example, Theosophy; and they who reject Swedenborgianism are written off as people who are unable "to struggle upward through the dogma of the past."[1]

To Swedenborg the Bible was fully inspired; but this inspiration is upon three levels: for the natural man (man seeking after God); for the spiritual man (men who, like Swedenborg, can live in two worlds at once, or alternatively) and for the celestial spirits (the angels in heaven).

By way of illustration, let us turn to one of the Ten Commandments. "Remember the sabbath day to keep it holy." What does it mean? According to the Swedish seer these words have a natural meaning. "With the children of Israel the Sabbath, because it represented the Lord, was the sanctity of sanctities, the six days representing His labors and conflicts with the hells, and the seventh His victory over them, and consequent rest; and as that day was a representative of the close of the whole of the Lord's work of redemption, it was holiness itself." But in the spiritual sense this command represents man's reformation and regeneration by the Lord. The six days of labor are his warfare against indwelling sin; the seventh day means victory in conjunction with the Lord. While in the highest, or celestial sense, the Sabbath means a state of peace that comes of perfect harmony with the Divine Will.

At times the natural sense is disregarded for the sake of the spiritual, as when Swedenborg said that the Mosaic account of creation, the story of the Flood, that of the

1. Bach, *Faith and My Friends*, p. 218.

Tower of Babel, are not literally true, but are the outer garments of imperishable truths.

Angels are in need of Scripture, not for the same reason sinners on earth are, but because they delight in the search of Truth, which is contained in the celestial sense of the words. And how did Swedenborg himself know of the spiritual and celestial meanings of Scripture? Because he lived in continuous report with spirits and angels who revealed to him many things. At times he would go without food for days when he was in trance condition. This man, who in truth was a psychic, would not read theology for fear of being misled; but he would let "spirits" guide his hand in writing.[2] He was also firmly convinced that God visited him as a man in order to divulge to him the spiritual sense of the Scriptures.[3]

Thus, although it is beyond doubt that our Swedish mystic was sincere and honest, he laid himself open to all sorts of suggestions from another world, in true spiritistic fashion; and the information he brought back from his journeys into the spiritual realm is often so contrary to the plain meaning of Scripture that it is impossible to receive it as a restoration of true Christian spirituality.

It may be true that Swedenborg wanted only Christ, and that he was afraid of being taken for a saint or seer, lest men might give to him the honor that is due only to Christ; but at the same time his *rationalism* which made him demand that Scripture should be in harmony with the human reason, led him astray. Rationalism, whether in its bold and unvarnished form like that of Russell-Rutherford-Knorr, or in its more refined cloak of mysticism, always ends in rejecting the cardinal doctrines of Scripture.

Thus Swedenborg, the son of a noted Lutheran bishop, rebelling against the cold intellectualism of his day, went so far as to identify the Reformation with the dragon of the Apocalypse. And he was quite convinced that he,

---

2. Cyriel O. Sigstedt, *The Swedenborg Epic*, pp. 207, 211.
3. *Ibid.*, p. 198.

Swedenborg himself, had succeeded after many efforts, to bring the spirit of Martin Luther to peace at last by causing that spirit to repent of Luther's nefarious doctrine of justification by faith!

For to Swedenborg sin is not something that needed expiation. God would not visit sin upon another than the sinner. Sin is something that has to be eradicated by repentance, which is the act of feeling sorry for sin and ceasing to sin. Here we deal with two errors: sin to Swedenborg was exclusively something that has to be wiped out ethically; and man, although a sinner, can repent at any time he feels like doing so. Regeneration is a process following upon man's initial repentance and faith. This, of course, implies a totally free will, unhampered by any sort of determinism. Sin is caused only by man's refusal to use his totally free will.

As to God, Swendenborg rejected the Trinity in the accepted sense. To him God is one Person, the Father. In order to reach and save man, this Father became incarnate, that He might thus unite Man with God by overcoming evil as a Man. The Holy Spirit is the energy that proceeds from God to man, as the human energy proceeds from man's body and soul.

Any man can attain to faith. This is done by living in accordance with the truth as one knows it. Unbelievers are impenitent sinners, who will go to hell, but not because God punishes them; for God knows no anger and is all compassion; but because they will choose to go to their own place. Heathen people who have not heard of Christ will receive an opportunity to learn of Him in the spirit world.

Swedenborg clung to the doctrines he had learned in his youth to such an extent as not to abandon, for example, such practices as baptism and the Lord's Supper. But he changed their meaning beyond recognition. The water in baptism to him meant the cleansing power of Truth; the bread in the Supper the Divine Goodness ("O, taste and see that the Lord is good"). What natural bread is to the body, that the goodness of the Divine Substance is to the soul. The wine represents the Lord's blood, the spiritual meaning of which is His Divine Truth.

The resurrection of Christ was, and that of believers will be, spiritual: the body decays and will not be resumed.

Such teachings naturally called only for a spiritual return of the Lord. This occurred about 1745, when Swedenborg had a revelation concerning the "New Church."

Numerically, this cult is not strong. Mead (Handbook of Denominations in the U. S.) listed in 1951, 52 congregations with 4,621 members for the General Convention of the New Jerusalem in the U.S.A., plus 10 churches with a total membership of 1,496 for the General Church of the New Jerusalem. Yet these small groups maintain theological schools in Cambridge, Massachusetts and Bryn Athyn, Pennsylvania. The Swedenborg Foundation in New York City distributes Swendenborg's writings. The names of such stars as Galli Curci, and Helen Keller (*My Religion*) have added lust to the movement.

We can perhaps best impress upon the reader the heterodox character of this cult by following the outline of previous chapters, giving a few authentic citations on the chief doctrines confessed through the ages by Christian churches of various names and antecedents.

A Few Samples from Thousands of Pages of Print

Revelation

"I went to my room, but that night the same man revealed himself to me again. I was not frightened then. He said that He was the Lord God, the Creator and Redeemer of the world, and that He had chosen me to declare to men the spiritual contents of Scripture; and that He Himself would declare to me what I should write on this subject.

"Then, on that same night, the world of spirits, hell and heaven were opened to me with full conviction. I recognized there many acquaintances of every condition in life. And from that day on I gave up all practice of worldly letters and devoted my labor to spiritual things."[4]

"I have written entire pages, and the spirits did not dictate the words, but absolutely guided my hand, so that it was they who were doing the writing . . . . it being allowed me only to tell such things as flowed from God Messiah mediately and immediately."[5]

"That men, therefore, may not continue to doubt whether the Word is Divine and most holy, the Lord has revealed to me its internal sense. . . . That sense is the spirit that gives life to the letter; consequently that sense can bear witness to the Divinity and holiness of the Word, and convince even the natural man, if he is willing to be convinced."[6]

"The essential reason why it is hurtful to confirm the appearances of truth that are in the Word, which thereby become falsities and thus the Divine truth concealed within the appearances is destroyed, is that each thing and all things of the sense of the letter of the Word communicate with heaven. For it has been shown above that within each thing and all things of the sense of the letter there is a spiritual sense, and this sense is opened in passing from man to heaven. All things of the spiritual senses are genuine truths; so when man is in falsities and applies the sense of the letter to those falsities, the falsities enter into that sense, and when they enter truths are dissipated, which is done on the way from man to heaven."[7]

"When understood spiritually this does not mean that the sun and moon would be darkened, that the stars would fall from heaven, and that the sign of the Lord was to appear in the heavens, and that they were to see Him in the clouds, and also angels with trumpets; but by each particular word here something spiritual pertaining to the church is meant

---

4. Quoted by Sigstedt, *op. cit.*, p. 198.
5. *Ibid.*, p. 211.
6. *Ibid.*, p. 192.
7. *Ibid.*, p. 258.

348 THE CHAOS OF CULTS

and its end here being treated of. For in the spiritual sense
the sun that shall be darkened means love to the Lord; the
stars that shall fall from heaven mean knowledge of what
is true and good; the sign of the Son of man in the clouds
of heaven with power and glory means the Lord's presence
in the Word and revelation; the clouds of heaven signify
the sense of the letter of the Word, and glory signifies its
spiritual sense; angels with the great sound of a trumpet
mean heaven from whence comes Divine truth. . . ."[8]

Trinity

"From the Nicene Trinity and the Athanasian Trinity
together a faith arose by which the whole Christian church
has been perverted. That both the Nicene and Athanasian
trinities are a trinity of Gods can be seen from the creeds
above quoted."[9]

Forgiveness

"And I have heard from heaven that the Lord forgives
to every man his sins, and never takes vengeance nor even
imputes sin, because He is love itself and good itself; nevertheless sins are not thereby washed away, for this can be
done only by repentance."[10]

Imputation

"That no faith imputative of Christ's merit is taught in
the Word, is very clear from the fact that this faith was
unknown in the church until after the Nicene Council had
introduced the doctrine of three Divine persons from
eternity. . . .

8. *Ibid.*, p. 198.
9. *Ibid.*, p. 177. Note: This is essentially the same misrepresen-
tation of the Christian creed of which Jehovah's Witnesses make
themselves guilty. Such misrepresentations would not have made
their sad inroad upon the churches had not the ministers in America
abandoned the teaching of doctrine to God's youth, listening to the
siren song of Modernism that "religion must be taught in the language of the man in the street." Neither Paul's Epistle to the
Romans, nor the adherents of modern cults teach religion in that
way!
10. *Ibid.*, p. 409.

"In order to know that an imputation of the merit and righteousness of Jesus Christ is impossible, what His merit and righteousness are must be known."[11]

Mixture of Doctrine

"The Divine Energy and Operation, which are meant by the Holy Spirit, are, in general, reformation and regeneration; and in accordance with these, renovation, vivification, sanctification and justification; and in accordance with these latter, purification from evils, forgiveness of sins, and finally salvation."[12]

Death

"When the body is no longer able to perform the bodily functions in the natural world that correspond to the spirit's thoughts and affections . . . man is said to die. This takes place when the respiration of the lungs and the beating of the heart cease. But the man does not die; he is merely separated from the bodily part that was of use to him in the world, while the man himself continues to live. . . . Evidently, then, the death of man is merely his passing from one world into another."[13]

Second Coming

"Since the Lord cannot manifest Himself in Person . . . it follows that He will do this by means of a man, who is able not only to receive these doctrines in his understanding but also to publish them by the press. That the Lord manifested Himself before me, His servant, and sent me to this office. . . . I affirm in truth. . . ."[14]

"By the New Jerusalem coming down from God out of heaven a new church is meant for the reason that Jerusalem was the metropolis in the land of Canaan, and the temple and altar were there. . . . This is why 'Jerusalem' signifies the church. . . .

---

11. *Ibid.*, pp. 639, 640. Cf. Romans 5.
12. *Ibid.*, p. 142
13. *Heaven and Hell*, p. 445.
14. *True Christian Religion*, p. 779.

"It is in accordance with Divine order that a new heaven should be formed before a new Church is established on earth, for the church is both internal and external, and the internal church makes one with the church in heaven, thus with heaven itself. . . .

"That his church is to follow those that have existed since the beginning of the world and that it is to endure for ages and ages, and is thus the crown of all the churches that have preceded, was foretold by Daniel. . . .

"What this church is to be is fully described in the *Apocalypse*, where the end of the former church and the beginning of the new are treated of . . .[15]

Little Children in Heaven

"I have talked with angels about children, whether they are free from evils, inasmuch as they have no actual evil as adults have; and I was told that they are equally in evil, and in fact are nothing but evil; but, like the angels, they are so withheld from evil and held in good by the Lord as to seem to themselves to be in good from themselves. For this reason when children have become adults in heaven, that they may not have the false idea about themselves that the good in them is from themselves and not from the Lord, they are now and then let down into their evils, and are left in them until they realize, acknowledge, and believe the truth of the matter. . . .

"In the other life one never suffers punishment on account of his inherited evil, that is, it is not his fault that he is such. . . . When, therefore, the children that have become adults are let down into the state of their inherited evil it is not that they may suffer punishment for it, but that they may learn that of themselves they are nothing but evil, and that it is by the mercy of the Lord that they are taken up into heaven from the hell in which they are, and

---

15. *Ibid.*, pp. 782-790, *passim*.

that it is from the Lord that they are in heaven and not from any merit of their own. . . .[16]

Autosoterism

". . . and they fail to understand that the Lord from mercy leads every one who accepts Him, and that He accepts him who lives in accordance with the Laws of Divine order, which are the precepts of love and of faith, and that the mercy that is meant is to be thus led by the Lord from infancy to the last period of life in the world, and afterwards to eternity."[17]

Questions

1. Is it sufficient in religious matters, to be "sincere," "deeply spiritual," and the like? Or is it perhaps more dangerous to be spiritual, sincere and zealous than to be apathetic?

2. Do the followers of Swedenborg have a right to deny that he was a Spiritist (or Spiritualist)?

3. Can you point out similarities between Swedenborgianism and other cults described in this textbook? If so, which are the cults, and on which points of teaching do they touch?

4. What is the root error in this system?

9. To which view of the Apocalypse does the author apparently adhere? What is your own view of the book of Revelation?

10. What is wrong with "the Lordship of Christ" as a basis for ecumenical unity? And what is wrong with Charles C. Morrison's basis for church unity? Could you possibly agree with Morrison's understanding of the character of the Church?

11. Prove from citations the wide divergence of Modernism from the Scriptural position on fundamental Christian doctrines.

16. *Heaven and Hell*, p. 342.
17. *Ibid.*, p. 420.

15

THE BOOK AND THE FAITH

The Main thought of the present volume has been cogently expressed by Professor Nathaniel Micklem of Mansfield College, Oxford, in these words: "The ultimate scandal of evangelical religion (which in this connection includes both historic Protestantism and the Church of Rome but excludes much of modern Protestantism) lies not in dogma or symbolism but in its intolerable offense to human pride. 'Nothing in my hand I bring; Simply to thy cross I cling' — it is *that* which the man of taste and culture cannot bring himself to say; he feels no need of so utter a salvation; to him therefore it is nonsense or mere mythology that the majesty of God should take a Servant's form . . . That is what the Master said: 'the publicans and the harlots go into the kingdom before you;' that is the reason for the aversion of men of taste to evangelical religion."[1]

This has been stressed throughout our discussion: "The great religions," together with the leading isms, object to the supernaturalism of the Christian religion. Yet Christianity, which is the fulfillment of Judaism in its pure form, is not the fruit of evolution, but the gift of revelation. It points man to the divine Source, outside himself, for salvation.

Paul did not deny to the men of Athens that their own poets had said certain good things; but he stated that Christianity is the fulfillment of truth. "The seed of religion" in the human heart needs the fertilization of the Holy Spirit to cause the plant of religion to blossom forth into a fracgrant flower, holy and acceptable to God. "Religion" is not enough; man stands in dire need of Christianity; and the

---

1. *Christendom.* A Quarterly Review, Autumn, 1936.

Christian religion, both as a faith and as a life, is the gift of God.

The fundamental error of the anti-Christian cults is their naturalism. They seek, to use Dr. E. Stanley Jones's terminology, syncretism rather than fulfillment. Only a virile, well-defined Christianity can bring fulfillment to the vague longings of the religious heart, not Charles Clayton Morrison's invitation to Judaism to become a universal religion by adding elements of Christianity. "If this position seems paradoxical," says Dr. Morrison, "the paradox will be revealed at once by considering the fact that when two religions meet on the cultured open field of democracy, for free conflict of opinions and comparison of values, the result is not likely to be annihilation or 'liquidation' of either, but the interpretation of both by the enduring values of each."[2]

The editorial from which we quote intimates that the "condemnable cruel injustice" which has been done to the Jews for centuries is, to a large part, due to "the historical fact that the most basic concept of Judaism through the centuries has been that of a covenant race, destined to be the instrument or medium through which God will perform, soon or late, 'some mighty act involving human destiny.' "

It is this that is resented. Judaism, or Christianity, may lay claim to being just another "great religion"! But if, with Dr. Samuel F. Zwemer, we call Christianity "the final religion," we may look for resentment, if not for ultimate persecution, at the hands of the many man-worshippers of one type or another.

We submit, however, that men who place Christianity on a level with the naturalistic, autosoteric religions of paganism have failed to grasp *the* essential of the Christian religion, no matter how greatly we honor them for their valiant fight for social and economic justice. They could never say with Toyohiko Kagawa, "I am grateful for Shinto, for Buddhism, and for Confucianism. I owe much to these

2. "Why Is Anti-Semitism?", in *The Christian Century*, July 7, 1937.

faiths. The fact that I was born with a spirit of reverence, that I have an insatiable craving for values which transcend this earthly life, and that I strive to walk the way of the golden mean, I owe entirely to the influence of these ethnic faiths.

"Yet these three faiths utterly failed to minister to my heart's deepest needs. I was a pilgrim journeying upon a long road that had no turning. I was weary. I was footsore. I wandered through a dark and dismal world where tragedies were thick . . .

"Buddhism teaches great compassion . . . But since the beginning of time, who has declared, 'this is my blood of the covenant, which is poured out for many unto remission of sins?' "[3]

Christianity differs from other religions. That some other religions come in the name of Christ, or borrow a few symbols, rites, and doctrines from Christianity, only makes them more dangerous.

The question therefore becomes, What is Christianity? To this query the reply of all the evangelical groups has ever been that the inspired Scriptures are the only source of saving knowledge and the determining factor of what is to be believed.

It is therefore an unhealthy sign when the modern man is so mortally afraid of the study of the contents of the Christian faith. Surely the isms are not afraid to parade *their* doctrines nor ashamed to demand that we shall study them. Some twenty years ago an American evangelist stated with remarkable clarity, "The common conception of theology is that it is dry, impractical, worthless, whereas it is the sweetest, liveliest, most inspiring of all studies. Christianity has always flourished under the teaching and preaching of a robust theology. And let it also be stated, with a tremendous emphasis, that when men are not sufficiently interested in Christianity to build a Christian theology, then Christianity must languish or perish."[4]

3. *Christ and Japan*, pp. 108, 113.
4. G. W. McPherson, *The Crisis in Church and College*, p. 64.

Today, we rejoice to note, some Modernists are again beginning to see this need of theology. Says Dr. H. Richard Niebuhr, "The revolters in the church are learning that without a Christian theory or theology the Christian movement must lose itself in emotions and sentiments or hasten to action which will be premature and futile because it is not based upon a clear analysis of the situation. They have learned from the Communists that years spent in libraries and in study are not necessarily wasted years but that years of activity without knowledge are lost years indeed. They have learned from history that every true work of liberation and reformation was at the same time a work of theology. They understand that the dependence of man upon God and the orientation of man's work by reference to God's work require that theology must take the place of the psychology and sociology which were the proper sciences of a Christianity which was dependent on the spirit in man."[5]

Nor is this conviction and practice limited to the more liberal type of church. The 100,000 ministers poll of "Great Churches of America" reveals that the same conviction, as might be expected, prevails among evangelical churches. Hollywood's First Presbyterian is a fair example. "Anyman who serves as an elder or a deacon in Hollywood gets a three-year course in church history and doctrine. And it is not just a lecture course; each member of session takes home after every meeting a four-page syllabus to encourage and guide him in further study." Moreover, this church has a "thriving College Department" which operates on the principle that "the greater the demands the greater the response." "They are accustomed to hard study in high school and college; give them study just as demanding in Sunday School."[6] Four rural churches made the grade of "great churches" in this poll, namely, the Evangelical and Reformed, New Knoxville, Ohio; Trinity Lutheran (Missouri), Freistatt, Missouri; Washington Prairie Evangel-

---

5. *The Church Against the World*, p. 153.
6. *The Christian Century*, Sept. 20, 1950.

ical Lutheran, Decorah, Iowa; and Olive Chapel Baptist, Apex, North Carolina. It stands to reason that doctrinal instruction would not, alone and by itself, make for a successful church but at the end of a brief study of what makes these churches great, Thomas Alfred Tripp, "a rural social scientist and national director of the town and country department of the Congregational Christian Churches," writes, "The final lesson of the *Christian Century* series is that rural ministers must teach and preach the Word of God. . . . No half-hearted Sunday school can relieve the rural pastor of his duty of teaching his youth the Christian gospel."[7]

Over against the cults and isms which vociferously advertise their own brands of "theology," we must again place a doctrine, a teaching concerning God and man and their interrelationship. We can have no "experience" that hangs in the air; no "life" except it be based upon, and emanates from, certain basal beliefs and convictions concerning God and Christ. "He that cometh to God must believe that he is and that he is a rewarder of them that seek after him." "And they continued stedfastly in the apostles' teaching and fellowship, in the breaking of bread and the prayers." "As a man thinketh in his heart, so is he."

Only one question remains, then, to be answered. It is this: Where is the true doctrine? For all quote Scripture.

This is a momentous question. If practice flows from theory, if life is based upon teaching, it follows that the wrong doctrine will issue in the wrong attitude toward God and Christ, and consequently in warped and twisted Christian life. Whither shall we go to be properly instructed?

To this our answer is of a twofold nature.

First of all and foremost one should go to the fountainhead. The sacred Scriptures of the Old and New Testament were given by inspiration of God, and they were given for our instruction, that they might make us wise unto salvation. God therefore intended that they should be read and

---

7. *Ibid.*, Jan. 24, 1951.

studied. It did not please the Almighty to present men with "a gospel engraved on a dime." He gave us a gold mine with sixty-six shafts that we might apply our hearts and minds, praying for the illuminating guidance of the Holy Spirit, the primary author of Scripture. Nor is it impossible to seek successfully one's own way through the Scriptures, to find in them the Saviour and the way of salvation. God the Spirit knows how to make His own work understood.

Nevertheless, there is a second consideration. Our blessed Lord who said, "Go and teach, and lo, I am with you always," did not begin to open the minds of men toward Scripture in this present day and age. It is base ingratitude, not to say detestable conceit, and ingratitude not only toward men but toward God, to ignore the results of the sincere and arduous labors of godly and Spirit-filled men of past generations.

We shall therefore consult the findings of the fathers. But where shall we look for the best doctrinal products of the ages? To this paramount question the answer is, *In the great historic creeds of the Church universal.*

True, the foes of the evangelical faith have not wearied to remind us that Protestantism lies prostrate and powerless by reason of its many divisions and subdivisions. There are undoubtedly far too many splits and divisions — groups and denominations innumerable. All of this is a great shame for the Christian world.

However, they who come with a method, not a creed, men who write books under such titles as "One Man's Religion," should not complain because there are those among us who follow Luther, and again those who admire Calvin's doctrine, or that of Arminius. It remains true, in the midst of a difference which is better than indifference, that the divergencies are there not to scare us away from the field. The God who gave us sheep, not woolen clothing, electricity, not refrigerators, air-waves, not radios, also gave us a Bible, not a system of truth.

Which system are we to teach our children and our fellowmen? For we must make disciples, teaching them to observe all thinggs whatsoever Christ commanded His disciples.

When we return to the great confessional writings of the fathers, to those shamefully neglected documents that have been composed as a result of days and years of prayerful study of the Church's most eminent and gifted leaders, we make a pleasant discovery. We find that these creeds are charming in their clarity of expression, in their passionate devotoin to the great supernatural teachings of the Christian religion, and sound a deeply and warmly spiritual note that pervades them as the breath of God.

What true Bible-lover could not subscribe to these opening words of the *Formula of Concord* of 1576, which happens to be Lutheran?

"We believe, confess and teach that the only rule and norm, according to which all dogmas and all doctors ought to be esteemed and judged, is no other whatever than the prophetic and apostolic writings both of the Old and New Testament, as it is written (Psalm 119:105) : 'Thy word is a lamp unto my feet, and a light unto my path.' And St. Paul saith (Gal. 1:8) : 'Though an angel from heaven preach any other gospel unto you, let him be accursed.'

"But other writings, whether of the fathers or of the moderns, with whatever name they come, are in nowise to be equalled to the Holy Scriptures, but are all to be esteemed inferior to them, so that they be not otherwise received than in the rank of witnesses, to show what doctrine was taught after the Apostles' times also, and in what parts of the world that more sound doctrine of the Prophets and Apostles has been preserved."

And among our persecuted Lutheran brethren in Germany, and even among our Russian brethren who tremble before the deadly hatred of Sovietism, who could not respond with a thrill in the heart to the concluding words of the *Belgic Confession of Faith,* which happens to be a Reformed document, written as a defense before the King of

Spain who had let loose the horrible Inquisition against the innocent citizens of the Lowlands? For these sentences tell of the bodily and visible return of our Lord Jesus Christ to judge the living and the dead, as follows.

"But on the contrary, the faithful and elect shall be crowned with glory and honor; and the Son of God will confess their names before God his Father, and his elect angels; all tears shall be wiped from their eyes; and their cause, which is now condemned by many judges and magistrates as heretical and impious, will then be known to be the cause of the Son of God. And, for a gracious reward, the Lord will cause them to possess such a glory as never entered into the heart of man to conceive. Therefore we expect that great day with a most ardent desire, to the end that we may fully enjoy the promises of God in Christ Jesus our Lord. Amen."

What have Mormonism or Russellism to say in the face of such confessions? What has Mother Mary Baker Eddy to lay alongside of them?

Why should Christains be ashamed of their inheritance?

I conclude this chapter, then, with the following practical observations:

1. We need much prayer for a world-wide revival of true, evangelical religion, increased church attendance, and godly living. But it should be a revival with a strong emphasis upon the intellectual aspects of the Christian religion.

2. We need clearcut, sound, fundamental preaching of the doctrinal, expository, and exegetical type.

3. We must develop a sense of the sinfulness of sin. Our study of a few popular isms have revealed that where the sense of sin is absent there can be no evangelical fervor.

We should do well to restore the pastor's catechetical class in the fundamentals of the Christian religion. This need not consume too much time. There is an age which is particularly approachable, and in that period of time much can be accomplished in one weekly session during school months. The numerous catechetical books by ministers in the Reformed and Christian Reformed Churches, *A Book of*

Instruction by John B. Gardner (Lutheran), *Coming to the Communion* by Charles R. Erdman, and *Preparing to Commune* by George Taylor (Presbyterian) prove that it is not beyond human power to present the main tenets of the Christian faith in a concise and accessible form.

Christian Scientists have their "reading room" with some one in perpetual charge. Baha'is, Rosicrucians, Unity School of Christianity maintain parlors equipped with libraries not alone, but, "We conduct classes twice a week to teach divine truth free of charge." The members of the denomination the writer serves may drift as do others; they may join "a church that is not so strict," but they do not fall for pantheism, because since the age of twelve they have been taught the difference between pantheism and the doctrine of the two natures of Christ. A minister who will sit down and study, and afterward stand up and teach, will do more for his people than one who runs from pillar to post and is present at a ceaseless round of "church activities."

5. I am indebted to Dr. Ralph J. White, pastor emeritus of Trinity Evangelical Lutheran Church of Grand Rapids, for the suggestion that it is incumbent upon the ministry in America to help their people in developing "a technique of the Christian life." The strength of today's isms lies partly in this. They have a technique whereby they foster a joyous conviction that their religion is the right thing. Thus, Unity bids its devotees repeat "Healing Thoughts" and "Prosperity Thoughts." So do New Thought and Christian Science, while "Father Divine" accomplished results in Harlem by making his followers exclaim, "Peace, it's wonderful!"

Martin Luther, says Dr. White, prescribed creeds and prayers to be recited by the father for his family. The simple rite for the morning was followed by these words, "And then thou shouldest go with joy to thy work, after perhaps a hymn has been sung, as the Ten Commandments, or what thy devotion may suggest." In a similar manner Luther suggested, "In the evening, when thou goest to bed, thou shalt make the sign of the holy cross, and say: In the name

of the Father, and of the Son, and of the Holy Ghost. **Amen.**
Then kneeling or standing, thou shalt say the Apostles'
Creed and the Lord's Prayer. Then, if thou wilt, thou
mayst add this prayer . . . Then thou shouldest go to sleep
immediately and joyfully."

Here is some sort of technique of Christian living. This
has been dropped by the Lutherans in the transition from
European to American soil. So have the Reformed people
dropped the beautiful prayers prescribed, or at least suggested, by their fathers for morning, mealtime, evening,
and public worship. The result is that our people have no
technique that may aid in fostering a joyful Christianity,
and so they fall a ready prey to New Thought and kindred
cults.

6. We owe our covenant God untold gratitude for the
great heritage He has bestowed upon us as heirs of the
British Pilgrims, the Dutch Knickerbockers, the French
Huguenots, the Scotch-Irish Presbyterians, the German
and Scandinavian Lutherans, the Michigan Dutch. Above
all, the fact that we may worship Him freely and unmolest-
ed, without interference from, and yet under the protection
of, our splendid democratic form of government, should fill
us with national pride and Christian humble thankfulness.
The times are out of joint. The Christian Church everywhere, for the first time in history, faces an organized
atheism, and that from some of the most powerful governments on earth. Moreover, recent German history has
taught us that vast and unexpected changes may occur on
the religious horizon almost overnight.

We do not know, then, what the morrow may bring. But
even if our religious liberties should be taken from us, and
even if freedom of worship should give way to religious
intolerance in the land of the free and the home of the
brave, may there yet be found tens of thousands in America who cannot be shaken in their firm convictions concerning the faith of our fathers which is living still. In the
darkest hour of the Church, may we yet be able to sing,

Like a mighty army
  Moves the church of God;
Brothers, we are treading
  Where the saints have trod.
We are not divided,
  All one body we;
One in hope and doctrine,
  One in charity.
Onward, Christian soldiers,
  Marching as to war,
With the cross of Jesus
  Going on before.

Can You Tell?

1. What is the main thought presented in this book (and some closely related thoughts)?

2. Why is a reference to the Bible insufficient for cultists who also claim to believe the Bible "from cover to cover"?

3. What is the relation between Scripture and creeds?

4. Do the great historic creeds reveal any sort of Christian unity? Have you ever read any of them?

16

APPROACHING ADHERENTS OF THE CULTS

Adherents of the cults — and we here use the word, as we have done throughout, in the sense of "any religion regarded as unorthodox or even spurious" (Webster) — are the most difficult people to evangelize. Let us face this fact lest we might grow discouraged after the first or second attempt. This is hard work because:

1. Cultists are not people who have to be aroused to an interest in religion. They are not folks who have drifted away from their moorings but, when duly approached, will grant that a return to "mother's religion" might be a good thing. The average devotee of a cult has left a traditional faith, in which he was more or less reared, and has adopted "something better." Was not Annie Besant the daughter of an English minister and later the wife of another? Did not Frank Buchman start out a Lutheran minister?

2. Not only has the cultist repudiated the orthodox religion you represent, he actually is hostile to it. Remember that every cult is, at bottom, autosoteric. The man who has surrendered God's supernatural plan of salvation for some system of self salvation cannot but resent the fundamental implications of the gospel that "all our righteousnesses are as a polluted garment" (Isa. 64:6).

3. Inseparable, though distinguishable from this hostility, is therefore a resentment against you as an intruder who ventures to come and lecture him who has found something so vastly superior. If your prospect is a woman, this feeling of ill will may be even more pronounced, as women are led more by intuition and sentiment. Who are you anyway that you deem yourself a teacher? Have you tasted the power of which your cultist boasts?

This resentment against you may assume various forms according to the character of your opponent and the nature of the ism which he represents. It may be haughtiness or even hatred in the case of a Jehovah's Witness, since you represent "Satan the devil's organization"; it may be a mild contempt for you as an "O. P.," (Ordinary Person) with a Theosophist; or it may be a kind indulgence on the part of a Modernist who recognizes you as a fellow Christian for all your mental ballast, and who trusts that some day you will arrive at the realization that his Christianity is just of a somewhat differing conception than your own.

4. Moreover, the well informed cultists is much alive to the shortcomings of your evangelical Protestant religion. There is first of all the hopeless division into endless varieties of Lutherans, types of Arminians, and shades of Calvinists. (Do not try to defend it: rather point out that your cultist adds just one more group). Take a Baha'i now, or a Spiritist, or a Theosophist: he has reached the heights from which he can scan the whole field of religion and, holding to the underlying foundation of them all, he can work for the unity of a world religion that will be the fulfillment of the Master's prayer that they may all be one. To him you are just behind the unifying spirit of the times with your denominationalism.

Or, take the Mormon. He has the positive revelation of God to Joseph Smith, Jr., the Prophet, or a later revelation; while a Buchmanite is in personal touch with a guiding God. What has your abstract and cold traditionalism to offer in comparison with that?

Make no mistake: the cults as well as the sects (the word "sect" is here taken in the sense of a somewhat odd denomination) owe their rise, in part at least, to the shortcomings of the churches. Should you doubt the truth of that statement, read the excellent article by Dr. Kuizenga.[1]

5. Again, many cultists have made sacrifices. They are a deeply religious type; that is why they went to so much

---

1. "The Cults: Phenomenon and Challenge," by John E. Kuizenga in *Theology Today*, Vol. 1, No. 1, April, 1944.

investigating. Now that they have finally found peace, and have braved the ridicule of kith and kin, do you think it easy for them to admit that they have erred after all?

6. This hatred, this self-sufficiency may assume such proportions that it proves altogether a waste of time to deal with many of the cultists. In his book *The Work of the Pastor* Dr. Charles R. Erdman has suggested that one should not waste his time on the paid propagandists of the cults. Dr. Kuizenga reminds us that "the cults believe that every member is to be trained as a salesman, and they do it efficiently." The Rev. I. Van Dellen, author of a good book on Mormonism, stated that he had never been able to convince a Mormon. "A man convinced against his will, Is of the same opinion still."

For such reasons as these it is of primary importance that you should assume the right attitude for this particular form of evangelization.

1. You may well postpone approaching adherents of cults until you have gained experience in dealing with human nature and presenting the gospel to others, say, to the large group of those who are just indifferent, of those who think they are "all right," of those who admit that "some day" they should give more attention to religion.

2. When finally you decide to go into the lion's den, if ever you were in need of "guidance," it is now. If ever you should pray for patience, it is here. The cultist you are about to visit is your *opponent.* He may lose his temper, or he may treat you with silken condescension, or again with icy disdain; you are to take it all with unruffled spirit. Bear in mind that in final analysis all his antagonism is not directed against your personality or your past life, but against the message you present.

3. You must be "clothed with humility." Your own church may boast that it has "the true and complete doctrine of salvation," yet your denomination has not gotten beyond Paul who admitted, "Now I know in part." Every race has its peculiarities, and even climate and latitude have left

their mark upon the religion of people. The cold Nordic will never be as emotional as the Negro, and the strict followers of Calvin cannot attain to the "holiness of beauty" of the Church of England, though they may know something of the "beauty of holiness."

Do not take an air of superiority. Your antagonist would soon puncture your self-inflation. Admit whatever he may advance against the peculiarities of the group you represent. You have come to represent Christ, not Christians.

4. Approach the cultist with a sympathetic heart. Hostility does not win. Only love can do that. No matter how much you may hate error, your first approach to an errorist should always be that of seeking love. You must love the sinner while hating the sin in him. There should always be something in you of Christ, who was moved with compassion when He found the multitude as sheep without a shepherd. And yet, how self-satisfied those same multitudes were as the result of faulty leadership!

5. Do not dispute what ever grain of truth or of good there may be in the particular cult you are dealing with. Paul praised the ultrapolytheistic people of Athens because in all things they were very religious, and from that point on he reasoned saying, "Now therefore, I would tell you of that God you try to worship in your ignorance." If, then, your own orthodox church has failed to emphasize Christ as healer of the body, admit that the Christian Science practitioner has something; and if New Thought, Unity and the "I Am" cult have "precipitated" wealth, grant that Jesus said He came that men might have life abundantly (John 10:10), and Paul stated that godliness also has the promise of the life which now is (I Timothy 4:8). You should, therefore, become all things to all men that you may gain some (I Cor. 8:20-22).

6. Above all, never show that you suspect the cultist of dishonesty or mercenary motives. Most all men's motives are highly complicated, and foreign elements may enter into the devoutness of all. There is also this further con-

sideration that there is a sufficient amount of common
grace working in most men for them to resent being suspected of evil. If, therefore, you show a man that you doubt
his sincerity, all further efforts to win him are useless. Besides, to do justice to your prospect, the circuitous ramblings
of the human mind are so baffling that it is needless to
ascribe wrong motives where we are unable to fathom all
that has led to a given conviction or course of life.

Though Joseph Smith's biographers do not fail to leave
the impression that he was unscrupulous and an impostor,
there can be no possible doubt that Brigham Young was
sincerely and completely sold on the conviction that Brother
Joseph was a prophet of the Lord. The Rev. D. M. Canright, ace exposer of the follies of S.D.A., after many years
of personal observation reached the conclusion that Mrs.
Ellen G. White came herself to believe in the divine character of her so-called revelations because others looked to
her as to a mouthpiece of God.

Or, to approach the matter from a different angle, had
your ancestors settled after untold hardships in a certain
region, and had grasshoppers threatened to eat the entire
first year's crop of grain, and if then in the nick of time
seagulls had come and destroyed those myriad grasshoppers, would you not be convinced that the Almighty had approved of this adventure of faith, and that He had at last
delivered from "persecution"? That happened to the Mormons in their first year in Utah — and yet, the Mormons
are not even monotheists! Would it not be wiser, therefore,
to admit that the Mormons have made excellent pioneers,
and as such have done much for the cultural development
of the West than to deny God's providence in the seagull
episode? And to point out that God may have spared their
forefathers that the goodness of God might lead them to
repentance (Romans 2:4)?

If 'Abdu'l-Baha said, "I am going to the United States to
establish the fundamental principles of our Cause and to
proclaim the oneness of the world of humanity and the
equality of all men," do not deny the high goal of the ideal

(certainly it is far superior to a "Christian" interpretation of Scripture which has misused Noah's curse in order to defend slavery and the colonization of "inferior" races;[2] but rather try to point out that this high ideal can only be realized "if ye abide in Me," while apart from Christ all such idealism ends in the deification of man, hence, in the spirit of antichrist.

You are now ready to begin.

1. In general you may remind your prospect that neither "sincerity," nor miracles, nor financial sacrifice are enough to convince of the rightness of a cause. Paul granted that the Jews had a zeal for God, but it was a zeal "not according to knowledge," hence worse than inadequate. Who was ever more zealous than Saul when he persecuted the Church? Yet his sincerity only made him the greatest of sinners. Propaganda and numerical growth are found among all sorts of cults; if they were a mark of the genuine, the Seventh-Day Adventist with his weekly output of a third of a million copies of *Signs of the Times* might as well sell out to Unity with its "batallions of typewriters . . . literature of every type to appeal to every taste in tons; telegraph, telephone, radio . . . pressed into service" (Ferguson).

What we need to know and to discuss is not the *chronique scandaleuse* of Blavatsky or Aimee MacPherson, is not the apparent statistical or tabulated result of a given cult. It is this: Is there a zeal according to knowledge?

2. Our problem therefore boils down to this question: Whence do we obtain religious knowledge with unerring certainty? As to that question, there are in the nominally Christian world three theories of the source of authority in religion:

a. that the principle of authority lies in the church (Rome);

---

2. See my *Our Christian Heritage* (Grand Rapids: Wm. B. Eerdmans Publishing Co., 1948).

b. that it is vested in man (either rationalism or mysticism). This ultimately casts man back upon his own resources and ends in autosoterism;

c. that God has spoken in His Son, the infallible record of which we have in the Bible (according to Heb. 1,2).

True, there are mediating views, such as that the Bible contains the word of God though it is not altogether that, or that the Bible contains a word of God that may mean one thing to one man and another to some one else; but such views finally cast man back upon his own judgment and end in a refined form of rationalism.

3. This should now be very clear: Combating cults is not a dunce's task. To the contrary, this is indeed a specialty of theology, and one that requires accurate knowledge of the fundamentals of other branches of the theological encyclopedia. Needed is a workable knowledge in two fields. First, one must be able to defend the principle of the "Protestant rule of faith" (Hodge) ; that is to say, one should be able to defend the inspiration, completeness, perspicuity and sufficiency of Scripture.[3]

4. Secondly: In an argument with an adherent of a different faith you should be able to attack and refute his stand. This can be done in two ways. One way is to refute his principle, the foundation of his system. You must therefore have a clear conception of the fundamental error of your opponent. Do not lose yourself in an argument with a Russellite on whether Luke 23:43 should be read, "Verily I say unto thee, Today shalt thou be with me in paradise," or, "Verily, I say unto thee today, Thou shalt be with me in paradise."[4] Do not argue with a Mormon the question whether the two stiks in Ezezkiel 37:15-20 represent the Old Testament and the Book of Mormon; nor if Luke 20:35 means that (plural) marriage must be

---

3. Material may be found in all standard works on Dogmatics (Systematic Theology) ; also in such a book as H. Rimmer's *Internal Evidence of Inspiration* (Grand Rapids: Wm. B. Eerdmans Publishing Co., 1938).

4. Max Heindel, Rosicrucian, reads it in the same way.

solemnized in this world in order to be effective in the next.
Do not debate with a Seventh-Day Adventist whether the
words in Mark 2:28 "that the Son of man is lord even of
the sabbath" mean that Jesus is Lord of Saturday, and
therefore Saturday is "the Lord's day" in the New Testament. For all such exegesis is *a priori* conditioned by an
entire theory which they claim to be Scriptural. Destroy
the foundation, and the excrescences will disappear; but
cut off the growths by dint of a stronger or of one more argument, and you will have gained nothing: the foundation still stands. Deal only with fundamental concepts.

5. There is a second way of dealing with this problem.
Your opponent, salesman by the grace of his theological
zeal, is by no means a lamb that before its shearers is
dumb; he is a mighty warrior, a hunter ready for the
kill. He may be in a belligerent mood, in which case he
will surely attack, say, your conception of the deity of
Christ. If he does not, you are to tackle his. This means
that besides debating the fundamental position of the man
you intend to convert, you may have to discuss his idea of
sundry doctrines of the Christian faith.

Only, let the debate be confined to major issues, such
as the Trinity, the two natures of Christ, His bodily resurrection, blood atonement, second coming, the supernaturalness of the work of salvation. Whether the latter is post-,
pre-, or nonmillennial should not enter into the discussion:
you are endeavoring to convert a man from a non-Christian
belief to the Christian faith, not far from a less correct to a
more correct understanding of the Christian tenets. So you
are not to lose yourself in a discussion of adult-only or also
infant baptism, nor of the "validity" of "sprinkling." And,
frankly, should you convert a Spiritist into a Christian you
would have won the main battle regardless of whether he
became a Christian like Luther, Spurgeon, or Moody.

6. It may be said in general that there are two distinct
types of cults. Some assert that they believe the Bible.
Among these are Jehovah's Witnesses (they write it with

a small "w"), Mormons, Christian Scientists, Unity adherents, British Israelites, Swedenborgians ("the Church of the New Jerusalem"). But there are also cults that reject the final authority of the Orient, and also Spiritism, Freemasonry, Rosicrucianism, and numerous smaller fry. Hence, not all the foregoing applies to all isms.

In dealing with the first named group it is sufficient to prove the completeness and sufficiency of the divine revelation in Scripture, plus the fact that the clear and historically accepted meaning of the Bible's main teachings is not what these cults distill from it. Difficult? As stated before, trying to convert those who are firmly rooted in and posted concerning an erroneous religious ism is no task for babes in the woods. It is more than time that some easygoing "personal workers" discover that not all classes of men can be gained for Christ with a superficial, "Come under the blood, brother!" Nor are people to be neglected because gaining them entails earnest mental labor.

7. If it be any comfort to you there is more to follow.

With the second group, who do not admit that the Bible is the end of contradiction, you will have to pursue a different tactic. Here you must be at home, in the fundamentals at any rate, of yet another theological study. This is the field of comparative religion, also called Christian Evidences. You should be able to speak of the reasonableness of monotheism over against both polytheism and dualism, of the superiority of theism to pantheism and deism. You should know that religion results from revelation, not from evolution.[5] You must know that in spite of the too numerous divergencies, there is such a thing as Christian belief and a Christian view of life, and that it is superior to all pagan views; that Christianity is the only religion that has a universal appeal; that it alone offers a divine salvation and thus delivers man from "broken cisterns that can hold no water." You will reason that Christianity, although it has never been tried upon a national scale, is

---

5. Cf. S. M. Zwemer, *The Origin of Religion.*

yet the only religion that has raised nations from savagery to a high cultural level; that it alone has given mankind freedom from want and fear, freedom of speech and of religion; and that it is the sole religion which for the life to come has offered something that is superior to the life we now have.

Yet this should not prove too arduous a task. When the Baha'i asks you to observe that "all these things we have today, wars and labor troubles, etc., have been predicted in the ancient writings," and hands you a copy of *The Wisdom of 'Abdu'l-Baha,* what a far cry that is from the eschatological address of Jesus, and from the apostles John and Paul! Only, bear in mind that when you set out to convince men like that, you cannot do it by leaving a tract: it will take hours and days of reasoning together. Converting the cultists will often prove a hopeless task because you cannot find a common ground upon which to stand, a mutual point of departure; in other cases it will demand much knowledge, skill, and endless patience.

If, however, "by their fruits ye shall know them," why should the Theosophist and the devotee of the swamis and yogis return to the wisdom of the East which has left women enslaved, children despised, nations illiterate and wallowing in filth?

You may point to the sinlessness of Jesus as an evidence of Christianity, or you may refer to His miracles and His resurrection as indisputable evidence of His deity.[6]

You may have heard the anecdote of the colored preacher who was asked by a committee from the church to resign his pastorate. "What's the matter, brethren?" inquired the astonished man. "Don't I splanify to suit yuh? Don't I argify to suit yuh?" "Yessuh, pastor Jones," was the reply, "yuh-all splanify to suit us and yuh argify to suit us; but yuh dohn tell us wherein." The colored brethren wanted a practical application!

---

6. Quite helpful is Dr. A. Pieters' *Facts and Mysteries of the Christian Faith* (Grand Rapids: Wm. B. Eerdmans Publishing Co., 1933).

Lest I be accused with the dusky minister, I shall endeavor to give an example or two of how I conceive of your
task. And this will be done the more gladly if it may appear that the work is not as forbidding as it seems when we
refer to the theory of it (no work ever is!).

1. No one can ever know too much, and the more thorough our knowledge, the more easily we can use it for
practical purposes. At the same time, a few facts that we
have truly mastered are of far greater use to us than many
facts of which we have a general idea but which we cannot defend against subtle attack. The school boy's retort,
"I know it but I can't say it," deceives only the school boy.
If you cannot answer the argument of a cultist, it is only
because you have not mastered the facts. It is your inadequate knowledge that makes you leave the field defeated
and that leaves your Lord dishonored.

2. Before entering upon this discussion, however, let us
make sure of our ground. We have fallen upon days in
which the "proof-text method" is repudiated as something
of the dark ages. Now it is true that everything can be
"proved" (or distilled) from the Bible by taking isolated
texts from their context, or by substituting a period for a
comma. Nonetheless, the proof-text method is legitimate
and even mandatory, provided it be used rightly. The
Bible authors were not men who expressed themselves in
indistinct and ambiguous speech. It is possible to quote
them so that others perceive what they meant.

In using the proof-text method you must be absolutely
fair and honest, and at the same time on your guard. Never
quote a text apart from its connection unless you are firmly
convinced that the context is not needed to make its implication clear or that you use it in a sense that is compatible
with the context. Never allow yourself to build upon a word
at the expense of another word that must be ignored in
order to press your preferred interpretation of the first text.
Always compare Scripture with Scripture.

But if you will bear these few simple rules in mind, here is a note of encouragement. You and I are not the first ones to tread this path. There are a number of charts, folders, and booklets dealing with these (and other) cults and sects, and some carry Scriptural and erroneous statements in parallel columns.[7]

3. Coming now to our concrete example, we may well begin with the doctrine of the two natures in Christ. Did not the apostle John state that a correct Christology is the earmark of orthodoxy (I John 4:1-3)? And did not the oldest and the most numerous errors in the early Church center around the person of Christ?

Yet, no one can speak scripturally concerning the Person of Christ who has not first a true conception of (a) the personality of God, and (b) the trinity in the unity of God. We may leave the discussion of polytheism versus monotheism, and that of deism out of the present phase of our argument; for it is evident that we must begin somewhere. We desire to direct attention now to the *deity* of Christ.

Christian Science says: "God is incorporeal, divine, supreme, infinite Mind, Spirit, Soul, Principle, Life, Truth, Love."

Unity states: "God is a mind Principle whose foundation is ideas . . . It does not matter what you call this fundamental Principle . . . God is, therefore, not a person, but omnipresent mind, principle, and law."

Theosophy asserts: "God is Universal Life, the Limitless Consciousness, the Eternal Love, the very source and heart of all that is."

Rosicrucianism maintains: "God is an expression of the positive pole of the Universal spirit (matter is the negative pole)."

---

7. Special mention should here be made of an organization called in existence in August, 1946, for the specific purpose of combating false religious cults and sects. This organization publishes and lists a voluminous literature, and also a bi-monthly paper, *The Discerner*. Address, *Religion Analysis Service, Inc.*, P. O. Box B, Traffic Station, Minneapolis.

Spiritism teaches: "We abrogate the idea of a personal God."

These are just a few samples, taken at random. Of all such pantheism Dr. Charles Hodge remarked (after discussing some nine theories of pantheism) that it is evidently a hypothesis, something which in the nature of the case cannot be proved. And also that it is impossible in any of its forms to reconcile it with what the Bible teaches concerning God. He further states that it does not only contradict the laws of belief which God has impressed upon our nature, but also subverts the very foundation of religion, and of morality, and that it involves even the deification of sin.[8]

You must, then, be able to show from Scripture that the Bible certainly does speak of God as personal, and as transcendent (for example, in Acts 17:24), and that this transcendence eliminates an immanence after the pantheism of the above named cults.

What interests us right now, however, is to show that when the Bible refers to our Lord Jesus Christ as divine, it speaks of a deity such as could not be attributed to any other man or to mankind as a whole. The Unitarian-Modernist theory that Jesus' deity ("divinity" they prefer to call it: why?) differs only in degree from that of our own deity must be disproved. If that can be done, you see, you will have defeated every pantheistic cult in such an important point that there can be little left.

Various cults would agree to Dr. Fosdick's statement, "In our theology no longer are the divine and human like oil and water that cannot mix," and with the saying of a prominent Ritschlian, "What He was in this world we hope to be in the next"; namely, sons of God whose "sonship is not disturbed by sin."

You may discover to your surprise that some adherents of the pantheistic cults are not even aware of their diver-

8. The last point has been demonstrated in our chapters on Spiritism, Theosophy and Christian Science.

gence from orthodox belief. Point out, therefore, that the Church universal has always held that the sonship of Christ differs in essence from that of other men. The Jews, who had been raised on the conviction that God is One and that He is far above the creature, realized full well that Jesus asserted His deity in a metaphysical sense, and they wanted to stone Him "because thou, being a man, makest thyself God" (John 10:33).

The entire Fourth Gospel was written for the purpose of proving first of all the deity of Christ (20:30), and it is made clear at the beginning that this deity put Him on an equality with God (1:1), and makes His Sonship to differ from that of others (1:12). What man would even today, after various pantheistic theories have been dinned into our ears, dare say with Jesus, "Before Abraham was born I am," John 8:58) ?[9]

Both Paul and James call Jesus "the Lord of glory" (I Cor. 2:8; Jas. 2:1) and both men were Jews, thoroughly sold on the idea that the Lord of Glory is Jehovah of the shekinah. Paul calls Christ a Jew, or Israelite, according to His human nature, but "God above all "according to His other side (Rom. 9:5). John states of Him, "This is the true God, and eternal life" (I John 5:20).

You will probably find, by probing the beliefs of your opponents, that their difficulty is more one of the heart than of the head (in speaking of Rom. 9:19, 20 Dr. Warfield remarked one day in class, "You see, gentlemen, that Paul lays down the rule that a bad theology comes from a bad heart"). What the sinner refuses to admit is the awful guilt of sin, so great indeed that we actually are *enslaved* by Satan, the originator of sin, and hence can only be redeemed, that is, bought back to freedom (or to God, which is the same) by the ransom of Christ's blood (Matt. 20:28;

9. Rosicrucian Max Heindel saw in these words proof for reincarnation: both Jesus and Abraham were reincarnations of an older Ego; hence the Jews were not Abraham's seed. But the evolutionistic theory of rebirth, and deliverance through it, runs contrary to all of Jesus' teachings. Certainly, His hearers did not understand Him in that way, v. 59.

I Peter 1:19). Hence this Jesus becomes Lord, that is, owner, master, proprietor. For "Lord" is *Kurios,* which is the Greek equivalent throughout the Septuagint of the Hebrew *Jahweh.* So while the Pharisees rejected Jesus because they wanted a Messiah who was David's Lord (Matt. 22: 41-46), Paul gladly called Him "Jesus Christ our Lord," and himself the bondservant, slave, *doulos,* of this divine master. And Thomas exclaimed, "My Lord and my God!"

4. However, even so you may not yet have reached the end of contradiction. You may encounter a Russellite (Jehovah's Witness). Ask him if he believes that Jesus is God. He cannot, of course, for he holds that Jesus was the archangel Michael changed into a man. Press him for his beliefs, and he will admit the deity of Jesus in a Socinian sense: the man Jesus did not arise from the tomb as a man, but a spirit, and this spirit was raised to the divine dignity because of his perfect righteousness and his sacrificial death while he was a man. Your Russellite will say, "He is not Jehovah-God." For there are few things these people hate worse than they do the doctrine of the Trinity. In dealing with such a man, then, you cannot suffice with quoting, say, Hebrews 1:3, 4. The Witness will interpret this as meaning that Jesus Christ, because of the perfect obedience rendered in the flesh, has been raised to the dignity of God. You cannot refer to John 1:1, for the Witness has grown smart: Where formerly he would refer you to your concordance, of late he has graduated from that and will ask you to "look into your polyglot Bible." If you inform him you thought only great libraries own such works, he will shake his head and inform you that if only you owned a polyglot Bible you might have known that John says, "the word was a God." And this he will explain in an Arian fashion, as something neither fully god nor fully a lower creature, as he will also do in the case of Romans 9:5b.

You will, then, have to show from Scripture that Jesus is indeed the Jehovah of the Old Testament. If you succeed in that, either the Witness will have to surrender, or he

must flatly contradict the Bible. Well then, Isaiah said that
he saw the glory of Jehovah (ch. 6:1-3), while John states
that Isaiah saw the glory of Jesus (John 12:4). Isaiah
says, "Jehovah of hosts, him shall ye sanctify (Isa. 8:13),
and Peter substitutes, "But sanctify Christ in your hearts
as Lord," (I Peter 3:15). When Malachi states that the
messenger shall prepare the way before the Lord (3:1),
Mark says that this prophecy is fulfilled in the coming of
John the Baptist before Jesus Christ (1:4), and so says
Luke (3:3-6, 15-17). What is more, Jeremiah calls the
name of the "branch of David" (i.e., a son of David, hence
a man, namely, Jesus) Jehovah: "And this is his name
whereby he shall be called: Jehovah our righteousness,"
(23:6). For that matter, John himself has cut off the translation, "The word was a god" when he stated in 17:3 that
there is but one true God.

At this point you might inquire of your Russellite friend
why it is that his organization leaves upon people's door-
steps folders that bear at the top a citation of Isaiah 9:6,
stopping short of the words, "Wonderful, Counselor." Do
they not know that the same verse calls the same *Child*
"Mighty God, Everlasting Father?"

You now have him cornered.[10] If he refuses to admit the
evidence (he most likely will), do not get angry, which
might be construed as a sign of weakness in argument, or
as a lack of saintliness (though there is a holy anger) ; but
let him go, and turn to another prospect. You cannot convince a man against his will. Tell him frankly that you and
he have come to the parting of the way. You might ask him
if he is willing to have a word of prayer with you before
you leave him, and inform him that prayer is going to be a

---

10. On January 18, 1952, two earnest and courteous Russellites
walked a considerable distance to my home in 20 degrees below zero.
We had a two-and-a-half-hour discussion of the doctrines of the Trinity and the Deity of Christ.   When I confronted them with this
question, one of them, who stated that he is "a barber, but also a
minister of the gospel," replied that Christ may be called "Mighty
God," but that does not identify Him with Jehovah, for the latter is
"Almighty God" (!)

petition that the Lord may speak to the mind of him who is in error. If he refuses, let him go; but impress clearly upon his mind this one cardinal point because of which you leave him. You two have argued a good deal; but you quit because he claims to believe the Bible, yet he cuts off words that do not appeal to him. That is the point. This he must remember. This should continue to ring in his ears.

If, however, he should grant your proposition, your next step might well be to show him that in yielding on this point he has wandered far away from Russellism which, like all rationalism, denies the Trinity. Make clear to him that the Church does not mean with the word "trinity" the horrible distortion that Russell - Rutherford have made of it ("that Jesus was his own father") ; or, that "the trinity is accepted and upheld by Christendom and heathendom" (Leaflet on public address by A. Nichol).

5. Christ's humanity is as vital as His deity. Christian Science denies the reality of the human nature. Its pantheism, its one-sided stress upon the spiritual and divine, led to this. But Scripture teaches that Jesus suffered in the *body*, which was nailed to the Cross, and that He was sorrowful in His *soul*. It is reprehensible from a psychological viewpoint to deny some of life's manifestations because of others (the muscles suffer though pain may be ultimately mental or spiritual). Logically, it is nonsense to say that the bodily pain was "an erroneous mental concept," while at the same time affirming that the mind is divine and cannot err. And it is morally indefensible to substitute meanings for words in the Bible that were never in a dictionary; for example, to read, "As in Adam (Error) all die, so in Christ (Truth) shall all be made alive."

6. And so it goes all along the line. Never lose yourself in a discussion of minor points. Always stay with the cardinal doctrines of the Christian religion. When you deal with a Mormon, you might perhaps grant with Dr. Kuizenga, "Mormonism has at least the merit of trying to bring sex life within the pale of religion"; but do not try to refute

them on this point by referring to the sexual exploits of Joseph Smith as reported by his enemies (even if you think their documents well authenticated). Rather show that polygamy is contrary to Genesis 2, to Matthew 19:6, to Ephesians 5:24-33 and to I Corinthians 7:2. For as to the first named passages, it is apparent that if *the two* (God created one wife for the one man) are to be one flesh, three, that is one man and two women cannot be one flesh, nor can the one man be one flesh with the one woman while his body does not belong to her in the same sense that hers belongs to him because it is partly some other woman's. As to Ephesians 5 it is evident that marriage is taken as an illustration of Christ's union with His Church. This can only be if the husband has one wife as Christ has one Church which is His entirely. The third passage, I Corinthians 7:2, teaches that every man should have his own wife in order to prevent fornication, and each woman her own husband. This prevents a sharing of one partner with two of the other sex. Hence Paul, in the midst of a polygamous world, directed that no one could occupy a position of leadership in the Church if he were the husband in a polygamous marriage (Titus 1:5, 6; I Tim. 3:2).

And here you are touching upon an error in Mormonism which is even more foundational than polygamy: the God with whom we are dealing was at one time the man Adam, a polygamous man, and Jesus was married to many women.

7. There remains but one more point. You may meet with people who adhere to a cult or sect that stresses several fundamentally Christian doctrines; such as S.D.A. or British Israelism. They will wonder why you debate with them. Tell them it is they who do the attacking. Inform them that a body is known by what it holds in common with all others but by what it defends in distinction from every other group. Seventh-Day Adventists decry every group of Christians as bearing the mark of the beast; British-Israelites lead Americans to the humanism of believing that they will save the world from war and distress merely by

being the chosen children of promise by the sole virtue of having been born in the United States.

If now the foregoing pages should have convinced the reader that approaching the adherents of cults is a work fraught with difficulty, there is neither the desire nor the attempt on the part of the writer to deny this.

And what of it? Evangelization has been altogether too much undertaken by well-meaning but ill-equipped witnesses. While the winning of one who has been part of a zealous, proselytizing group is worth more in its indirect results than the winning of one who may have been a lost sheep but never was one of a pack of detrimental wolves.

Above all: America's need of Christ is so great! In 1912 American women kissed the hands of 'Abdu'l-Baha, and one enthusiast said that she "had seen God." In Harlem a little man has been hailed as God for years by thousands of whites and blacks, and all because he supplied them with sixty-course, three-hour banquets. "Peace! It's wonderful."

Yes, it is. And it is sad beyond words.

Almost anything, perhaps positively everything, will sweep some people off their feet, and fill them with fake religious ecstasy.

Our country needs Jesus Christ, Him of the sacred Scriptures. And it needs to be told just what that means, and what it does not mean.

Recapitulation

1. How many reasons can you give why it is particularly difficult to convince a cultist of the error of his way? The text mentions six.

2. Can you state seven requisites in a personal worker who wants to attempt this hard task?

3. Mention from the text of this chapter instances of good principles emphasized by adherents of false religious systems. Do you remember additional ones from previous chapters?

4. Why is some knowledge of so-called Evidences of Christianity valuable in coping with the cults? What other names are given to this study?

5. Do all cults recognize the Bible as the final religious authority? Which do not?

6. Is it possible from the Christian standpoint to answer every argument of the cults?

7. Can sectarian opinions be silenced by quoting texts from Scripture? If so, what conditions must such citing measure up to?

8. How would you meet pantheistic assertions concerning Jesus' deity?

9. What is your answer to the Russellite assertion that the Logos was "a god" according to John 1:1?

10. Is Jesus' true manhood important? Who deny it?

11. How will you meet Mormon references to Scripture in favor of polygamy?

12. What does America and what does the war-stricken, sin-cursed world need most of all?

17

THE CHRISTIAN RELIGION

Surely there are too many denominations in the United States of America. In the thinly populated state of Washington I came upon a town of 2,400 in which twenty-eight churches are represented. People mockingly call it "the holy City."

Individualism, inability to co-operate, refusal to see eye-to-eye — these pronounced American weaknesses, rather than firm conviction, have, in all too many cases, given rise to disruption and schism.

Some day, perhaps, God will cleanse us by means of persecution from the filth of our disobedience to Christ's will that Christians should be one "that the world may believe that thou didst send me" (John 17:21). For if there are no atheists in foxholes, there can be little display of denominationalism in concentration camps.

A candid appraisal of facts, however, will lead to the frank admission that the Church's divided existence is not the sole reason why entire towns lie asleep when on Sunday mornings a few straggly worshipers answer the call to prayer. There are things that are worse than either radical or minor difference of opinion in matters religious. Among these is a total indifference to all religious conviction.

Moreover, if those who sneer at the Church would take the trouble to examine the credentials of the various Christian churches, they might discover a remarkable unity and agreement on fundamentals far beyond their expectation.

Our troubles lie far deeper. The great heritage of the Christian Church, so painstakingly arrived at, so profoundly thought through and so zealously guarded again and again at the cost of blood and tears, has been brushed aside by multitudes who have come to the loose belief that a varnish of outward morality will do as a substitute for Christianity. We have come to the point where a none too pessimistic religious weekly has stated editorially: "An honest appraisal requires the acknowledgment that American Protestantism is spiritually weaker today than at any time in its history."[1] And again: "It is no exaggeration to say that, since the time when the invention of printing gave the Bible to the common people . . . there has been no generation of Christians so religiously illiterate as our own."[2]

There are those among us who are convinced that the Christian religion has been God's greatest boon to mankind; that it has removed barbarism and illiteracy; that it has promoted the more abundant life of art and science, of high moral standards to be found nowhere outside the pale of Christendom.

They hold that when these by-products of Christianity are relished while their fountainhead is trodden under foot, God calls the Christianized nations back by turning their boasted civilization against them, lest a worse evil befall them.

Such a time is upon us even now.

Are we heeding the divine voice that calls us back to the Father? Or are we seeking oblivion in alcohol and fornication, in wholesale denunciation of other nations as evil and indiscriminate praise of our own American goodness?

It should not be an impossible task to determine what is the essence of the Christian religion.

This cannot be done by obliterating all differences of interpretation. No thing on earth can mean one thing and its opposite at the same time. That popular student and teacher of comparative religion of our day, Dr. Marcus Bach, recently wrote that "Mormonism and Christian Science have long since become denominations in every sense of the word, and their emergence from a modern cult or a

---

1. Chas. C. Morrison, "Protestant Reorientation," in *The Christian Century*, Oct. 27, 1943.
2. Morrison, in *Christian Century*, Dec. 1, 1943.

minority religious group is total and complete." But he could so recognize these un-Christian cults only by referring in almost the same breath to our historic Christian faith in these words, "The old symbolisms, the clichés, the ancient shibboleths out of which the meaning has gone, are irrelevant."[3]

Surely, there is a better way of determining what constitutes Christianity than this method of embracing everything half-Christian and non-Christian together with the tenets of the Christian faith.

If God is infinite and man finite, man can but know God because He has made Himself known.

It is equally certain that when God wants to be known, He can reveal Himself in such a manner that man may respond to His self-revelation. And His unveiling of Himself most needs be consistent throughout: there may have been progress but there can be no contradiction.

Ever since its beginning Christianity has believed that God has spoken to man in the Bible and, at the same time, that the Holy Spirit must guide the human mind that it may both understand the divine revelation in Scripture and love it.

For man is not only finite; he is also depraved. Sin has affected all men, at all times and in all places, so as to make them inclined to follow error instead of truth, to drift toward evil rather than to excel in goodness.

Above all, man is so sinful that he puts his own interests far ahead of God's honor and the promotion of His cause on earth: many men and women will dismiss the suggestion that they are sinful with the reply that they "have never done anything out of the way, and they fail to realize that their great sin is that "God is not in all their thoughts."

"All have sinned, and fall short of the glory of God," is the fundamental Biblical statement concerning man. This is written in Romans 3:23, but the same thought runs

3. In a review of C. S. Braden's *These Also Believe* in *The Christian Century*, July 6, 1949.

through all the Scriptures. "For we are all become as one that is unclean," said the greatest of the Old Testament prophets, "and all our righteousnesses are as a polluted garment: and we all do fade as a leaf; and our iniquities, like the wind, take us away" (Isa. 64:4). "You are," said Jesus, to those Jews who gloried in being Abraham's seed, "of your father the devil, and the lusts of your father it is your will to do" (John 8:44). Neither did Jesus distinguish between bad men and good men as though the latter were to be congratulated because there was so little of imperfection left in them; but, "Every one that committeth sin is the bondservant of sin" (John 8:34).

Isaiah's statement that our iniquities, like the wind, carry us away is but the poetic phrasing of the common scriptural teaching that "the wages of sin is death" (Rom. 6:23); "that God cannot be tempted with evil, and he himself tempteth no man: but each man is tempted when he is drawn away by his own lust and enticed. Then the lust, when it hath conceived, beareth sin; and the sin, when it is full grown, bringeth forth death" (Jas. 1:13-15).

According to Scripture neither sin nor death can possibly be the result of evolution; they are the fruits of a fall. Sin, therefore, is not a disaster, or a weakness to which man is heir as a result of his brute ancestry; quite to the contrary, it is the effect of willful, uncalled for rebellion against a good God who had created man able to know the will of his Creator and to recognize it as only good, wise and beneficial.

Thus the Christian religion, the only religion which offers a gospel worthy of the name, begins with condemning man and holding him solely responsible for the evil condition that has him in its iron grip. The Bible is not like a charlatan who puts some salve on a sore spot and calls it whole while underneath a deadly gangrene does its vicious work. It is rather like a surgeon who cuts deeply, but his cutting is an act of kindness because he removes the source of evil.

The very first requisite, therefore, in order to get rid of evil in its every form is the humble acknowledgment of one's lost condition. "Only acknowledge thine iniquity, that thou hast transgressed against Jehovah thy God" (Jer. 3: 13). Salvation begins with David's confession, "Against thee, only, have I sinned, and done that which is evil in thy sight; that thou mayest be justified when thou speakest, and be clear when thou judgest" (Psa. 51:4).

When man has arrived at the point where he blames neither God nor his fellow, ill luck nor circumstances, but only himself for his transgressions, he is ready to benefit by the gospel. "For the sacrifices of God are a broken spirit: a broken and contrite heart, O God, thou wilt not dispise" (Psa. 51:17).

For only the gospel, in contrast with every so-called "great religion" and every false cult, begins with casting man down in his pride and continues with holding before him the unfathomed, infinite love of God, who being offended, mended the breach in His own Person and at infinite cost.

It has become quite fashionable to refer to the devil, that archenemy of mankind, as to a mythical boomerang, and to speak of hell as a fictitious place to which we lightheartedly consign the enemy.

Back of this lies the hatred of the natural, that is, the sinful heart against divine truth. Ignoring the righteousness of God which cannot tolerate evil, this spirit steps lightly (Christian Science, Modernism) or roughly (Russellism) over Jesus' words, "There shall be the weeping and the gnashing of teeth" (Matt. 8:12). For it ignores or minimizes the Old Testament verdict, so clearly corroborated by the world in which we live today: "The heart is deceitful above all things, and it is exceedingly corrupt: who can know it? I, Jehovah search the mind, I try the heart, even to give every man according to the fruit of his doings" (Jer. 17:9). And the New Testament words, "It is appointed unto men once to die, and after this cometh judgment" (Heb. 9:27).

Since this cardinal truth has been tampered with and toned down, Christianity has been gradually diluted to a wishy-washy help-yourself-religiousness, in which Jesus Christ has become the pattern of clean living, just a few steps ahead of the rest of us in moral evolution.

The denial of the deadly character of sin is serious not only because it belittles God's holiness and righteousness; it also detracts from the love of God. Had sin been less enormous, God might have paid a smaller price for the redemption of mankind; but now it was only in the Cross of Christ that "righteousness and peace have kissed each other." The love of God, concerning which we thoughtlessly quote the most famous Bible verse (John 3:16), is so incomparably great: *First,* because it was for sinners that God gave His Son, though God is too pure to have a share in iniquity and can experience only revulsion against sin; *secondly,* because with His only begotten Son God gave His divine all to the point of entering into the sinful human race; and *thirdly,* because God "gave up" the Son "who is in the bosom of the Father" (John 1:18) to the point where He "was made sin on our behalf" (II Cor. 5:21) and "become a curse for us" (Gal. 3:13).

Refusal to accept this gift of infinite love therefore constitutes the greatest sin, whether it be done in blasphemous insolence or in politely passing by the supreme sacrifice. "Is it nothing to you, all ye that pass by? Behold, and see if there be any sorrow like unto my sorrow which is brought upon me, Wherewith Jehovah hath afflicted me in the day of his fierce anger," (Lament. 1:12), "All we like sheep have gone astray; we have turned every one to his own way; and Jehovah hath laid on him the iniquity of us all (Isa. 53:6). But our Bible is nothing if it is not consistent. God forsooth does not teach that "out of the heart come forth evil thoughts, murders, adulteries, fornications thefts, false witnesses, railings," (Matt. 15:19), only to state in the same breath that man may at any time change his Ethiopian's skin or his leopard's spots and "accept Jesus," as a good proposition which he considers worth his while to look into. Man must be "born anew, born of the Holy Spirit," says the Saviour (John 3:3,5).

Being born again, however, is as much a thing to undergo as is being born of a woman: the beginning of salvation is of God and of Him alone.

> *I sought the Lord, and afterward I knew*
> *He moved my soul to seek Him, seeking me;*
> *It was not I that found, O Saviour true;*
> *No, I was found of Thee.*

Thus the Bible deals with the sinner in true pedagogical style. Having laid the responsibility at man's door, it guards against indifference and false passivity; then, having reminded man that he cannot even begin to save himself, it casts him back upon the Lord as the sole author of his salvation.

This done, the Scriptures give the penitent sinner full encouragement in the words of Jesus: "No man can come to me, except the Father that sent me draw him"; consequently: "and him that cometh to me I will in no wise cast out" (John 6:37, 44). For the Father and the Son cannot but work together.

Let, therefore, him who has seen his sin and dreaded its result, rejoice: Jesus Christ is able to save to the uttermost "them that draw near unto God through him" (Heb. 7:25). God is more willing than man is, "not wishing that any should perish, but that all should come to repentance" (II Peter 3:9). The thirst for salvation at His once pierced hands is itself unmistakable evidence of the saving process of the Father, by means of the Son, and applied by the Holy Spirit: . . . he that is athirst, let him come: he that will, let him take the water of life freely," is the Bible's final word (Rev. 22:17).

There is another point at which full salvation halts in the case of many who call themselves Christian, yet fail to let their light shine before men.

The word of God does not teach that "the Son of man came to give his life a ransom for many" (Matt. 20:28), only to stop there.

God removes sin as well as its consequence. "If we confess our sins, he is faithful and righteous to forgive us our sins, and to cleanse us from all unrighteousness" (I John 1:9), and "the blood of Jesus his Son cleanseth us from all sin" (1:7).

Today the world is in a worse plight than it has ever been, not because Christianity has failed, but because it has never been seriously put to the test.

For where Christ holds undisputed sway He comes with His law of love, which is the only thing that can destroy hatred; and hate has bred all the world's woe.

Then the Golden Rule is put into practice as well as admired; to do unto men as we would have them do unto us because God requires it results in true altruism, an altruism of individual toward fellow man, of class toward class, of race toward race, of nation toward nation. Had there been a more universal and earnest endeavor to love God with all the heart and had we loved our neighbor as we should love ourselves — in other words, had there been more true Christianity — wars would have been abolished long ago, class hatred would have been a thing of the past, racial antagonism would have disappeared; the Christian nations, rather than exploit the backward races, would have raised them to our own level of abundance for all; the "four freedoms" would have been an accomplished fact after more than nineteen centuries of the Christian religion; religious intolerance among Christians would have been an unknown quantity.

The Scriptures, however, do not promise a gradual and total Christianization, of the world in this age. To the contrary, they warn us that unbelief, selfishness and greed will wax worse. *"But know this, that in the last days grievous times shall come. For men shall be lovers of self, lovers of money, boastful, haughty, railers, disobedient to parents, unthankful, unholy, without natural affection, implacable, slanderers, without self-control, fierce, no lovers of good, traitors, headstrong, puffed up, lovers of pleasure rather than lovers of God; holding a form of godliness, but having denied the power thereof: from these also turn away"* (II Tim. 3:1-5). (Here is the reason why this book has been written.)

But the Scriptures do promise the visible return of the Son of man in great power and majesty, to judge the living and the dead. Then shall all wrongs be righted. Then shall the righteous shine as the firmament. A new heaven and a new earth will appear out of the conflagration of this old, sin-stricken universe (II Peter 3:10). Then will the Son of man own His disciples, in spite of all the imperfection, and they shall enter with Him into the glory of eternal life (Matt. 10:32; 25:46; I John 3:2). Wars shall be no more (Isa. 2:4) nor tears (Rev. 21:4) " . . . And there shall be no curse any more" (Rev. 22:3). "For Christ, having been once offered to bear the sins of many, shall appear a second time, apart from sin, to them that wait for him, unto salvation" (Heb. 9:28).

Thus our Lord Jesus Christ, Son of God and born of a woman, once slain, now exalted above all, is the center of the Christian religion. It is He who leads us to the Father (John 1:12). It is He who is the Christian's object of loyal service and adoration. And He is Christ Jesus our hope, (I Tim. 1:1).

Like Paul, every Christian is a bondservant, that is, a slave, of Christ. But this bondage is true freedom: "If therefore the Son shall make you free, ye shall be free indeed" (John 8:36). For He delivers us from the bondage of Satan, and restores us "into the liberty of the glory of the children of God" (Rom. 8:21). This is the true freedom from want and freedom from fear. No evil can touch the Father's children, beloved in Christ. He may chasten, but He will never punish them. He cares for them to the point of having numbered their very hairs (Matt. 10:30), and whatever seems to be to their hurt, He makes to work together to their ultimate gain (Rom. 8:28).

Harassing times are upon us. The present unrest is beyond human ken, and its dire aftermath may well prove past all previous human experience. Today's problems are staggering, and they raise questions of such gigantic proportions that it will call for the accumulated wisdom of the best heads in all lands to bring order out of chaos.

Yet there is one question that is of paramount importance.

More weighty it is than questions of post-war reconstruction.

More pertinent is this question than all the world's quest after peace, goodwill and mundane happiness.

It is the question that must be answered by every soul in the privacy of the inner chamber.

This question was answered wrongly by him who first asked it; answered wrongly for political reasons; answered wrongly to his everlasting sorrow.

It is the question of the Roman procurator Pontius Pilate.

This question must now be faced by every one who has read through these pages:

"What shall I do then with Jesus which is called Christ?" (Matthew 27:22).

For the Classroom

1. Try to face sincerely the Roman Catholic accusation that Protestantism, by its many splits, has definitely shown that it is the rebellious daughter of the one holy Catholic Church.

2. Do you think the World Council of Churches is the right answer to the divided condition among the churches? If not, what are your objections to this movement?

3. Do you think it possible (a) over against the many cults, (b) in spite of the hopeless division and confusion of Christendom, to present the true Christian religion in its

main tenets, in such a maner that all born-again Christians will assent to the presentation?

4. Has the author, in your opinion, succeeded in doing so in this chapter?

5. Have you personally considered the implications of the final question?

Bibliography

SELECTED BIBLIOGRAPHY

The following bibliography is a rather complete list of works consulted by the author; it is not meant to be an exhaustive list of references for a study of the cults. The card index of the public libraries in large cities may give some of the titles which are not found here. An asterisk (*) indicates that the source is a pamphlet.

Chapter 1 — The Issue Defined

Atkins, G. G., *Modern Religious Cults and Movements* (New York, 1923).

Burrell, D. J.,*The Religions of the World* (Philadelphia, 1922).

Jones, J. P., *India, Its Life and Thought* (New York, 1911).

Lowman, I., *Non-Christian Religions. A Comparative Study* (Wheaton, Ill.)   ;

Radhakrishnan. *Comparative Studies in Philosophy.* Presented in Honor of His Sixtieth Birthday (New York, 1950).

Thomas, W., *Hinduism Invades America.*

Warfield, B. B., *The Plan of Salvation* (Philadelphia, 1915; Grand Rapids, 1946).

Chapter 2 — Spiritism

Colville, W. J., *Universal Spiritualism.* Spirit-Communion in All Ages Among All Nations. (New York, 1906).

Doyle, A. Conan, *The New Revelation* (New York, 1913).

———, *The History of Spiritualism*, 2 vols.

Fox, John, "Spiritist Theologians" in *Princeton Theological Review* (1920).

Hanson, T. F., *Demonology, Or Spiritualism, Ancient and Modern* (Belfast, Me., 1884).

Jones, R. B., *Spiritism in Bible Light* (London, 1921).

Lodge, Sir Oilver, *Raymond; or Life and Death with Examples of the Evidence for the Survival of Memory and Affection After Death* (New York, 1916).

Mind and Matter; The Banner of Light; and other spiritist periodicals.

Panton, D. M., the following pamphlets: *Gnosticism: the Coming Apostasy; The Medium and the Witch; Spiritualism: Its Origin and Character.*

Schofield, A. T., M. D., *Modern Spiritism, Its Science and Religion* (Philadelphia, 1920).

Stoddart, Jane T., *The Case Against Spiritualism* (New York, 1909).

Chapter 3 — Theosophy

Besant Annie, *The Changing World* (Chicago, 1910).
———, *Esoteric Christianity; or, The Lesser Mysteries* (Adyar, 1914).
———, *Man's Life in Three Worlds** (Adjar, 1919).
Blavatsky, Helena Petrovna, *The Secret Doctrine*, 3 vols.
Bouwman, H., *Boedhisme en Christendom* (Kampen, 1906).
Cooper, I. S., *Theosophy Simplified** (Krotona, 1919).
De Heer, J., *Anti-Christelijke Stroomingen* (Zeist, 1925).
De Korne, John C., *Chinese Altars to the Unknown God* (Grand Rapids, 1926).
Landau, Rom, *God Is My Adventure* (New York, 1936).
Rogers, L. W., *What Theosophy Is** (Chicago).
Sheldon, H. C., *Theosophy and New Thought* (New York, 1916).
Sinnett, A. P. *Nature's Mysteries and How Theosophy Illuminates Them* (Krotona, 1918).
Sloan, Mersene Elon, *Modern Theosophy; An Exposition and a Refutation with Corrective Bible Teaching* (Rome, Ga., 1922).
Williams, Gertrude Marvin, *The Passionate Pilgrim*: A Life of Annie Besant (1931).
———, *Priestess of the Occult*: Madame Blavatsky (New York, 1946).

A complete list of theosophical publications may be had by addressing the Chicago Theosophical Book Concern for their catalog.
Literature on the Liberal Catholic Church may be ordered from 2041 N. Argyle Ave., Los Angeles, Calif.

Chapter 4 — Rosicrucianism

The literature used in the chapter is from *The Rosicrucian Fellowship* as stated in the text. A rival group is A.M.O.R.C., i.e. *The Ancient and Mystic Order Rosae Crucis* with the "Supreme Temple for North and South America" at Rosicrucian Park, San Jose, Calif. Cecil A. Poole is "Supreme Secretary." They are "neither a religion, nor a creed, nor a church"; just a friendly organization, apparently, to help men gain control of their destiny, and to give every woman "an unseen guide." They number 35,000 members. For a statement of sincerity of purpose, a declaration that you believe in God, or a Divine Mind, or an Architect of the Universe, and that you are "of good moral repute," you may become an aspirant to the Grand Lodge, and receive the monthly *Rosicrucian Digest* and the bi-monthly *Rosicrucian Form*. There are numerous get-acquainted folders and pamphlets, in attractive form and well-illustrated; also such intriguing books (to those on the West Coast, at any rate) as *Lemuria, The Lost Continent of the Pacific*, telling about The First Races of Man in America. The Magic Dwellers of Mt. Shasta, etc.

Chapter 5 — Christian Science

Beasley, Norman, *The Cross and the Crown, The History of Christian Science* (1952).
"Christian Science," in *20th Century Encyclopedia of Religious Knowledge* (Grand Rapids, 1955).

Eddy, Mary Baker, *Science and Health with Key to the Scriptures.*
———, *Miscellaneous Writings.*
Orcutt, Wm. Dana, *Mary Baker Eddy and Her Books* (Christian
Science Publishing Society, 1951).
BIOGRAPHIES OF MRS. EDDY:
Bates, Ernest Sutherland, and Dittemore, John V., *Mary Baker
Eddy, The Truth and the Tradition* (New York, 1932).
Dakin, E. F., *Mrs. Eddy, The Biography of a Virgin Mind,* pub-
lished by Scribner's with a pamphlet telling of the attempt to
suppress its publication by intimidation on the part of the Chris-
tian Scientists.
Eddy, Mary Baker, *Retrospection and Introspection.* An auto-
biographical sketch by Mrs. Eddy.
Milmine, Georgine, *The Life of Mary Baker Eddy and the History
of Christian Science* (1909). This work was bought up and
suppressed. The plates were destroyed by arrangement with
the publisher.
Powell, Lyman, *Mary Baker Eddy* (1930). Supposed to be an an-
swer to Dakin.
Wilbur, Sibyl, *Life of Mary Baker Eddy.* This is the biography
officially approved by the Scientist Church.
REFUTATIONS OF EDDYISM: These are too numerous to mention;
among them are:
Bates, E. S., and Dittemore, John V., *Mary Baker Eddy* (New
York, 1932).
Haldeman, I. M., *Christian Science in the Light of Holy Scripture.*
Marsten, F. E., *The Mask of Christian Science* (New York, 1909).
Martin, W. R., and Klann, N. H., *The Christian Science Myth*
(1954).
Snowden, J. H., *The Truth About Christian Science.*
Swain, R. L., *The Real Key to Christian Science; A Surprising
Discovery* (New York, 1917).
Warfield, B. B., *Counterfeit Miracles* (New York, 1918).
Wyckoff, A. C., *The Non-Sense of Christian Science* (New York,
1922).
There is further an endless stream of pamphlets against Christian
Science by A. E. Bell, R. E. Neighbor, Wm. Evans, Wm. E.
Biederwolf, I. M. Haldeman, J. Ritchie, G. H. Cooper, and others.
These may be ordered for propaganda purposes from the Bible
Institutes, such as Moody, Los Angeles, Swengel, Pa. Excellent is
*The Religio-Medical Masquerade, A Complete Exposure of Chris-
tian Science* by F. W. Peabody, LL.B. of the Boston Bar (New
New York, 1910, 1915).

Chapter 6 — Unity

Atkins, Gaius Glenn, *Modern Religious Cults and Movements*
(1923).
Dresser, Horatio W., *The Quimby Manuscripts* (1921).
Ferguson, Charles W., *The Confusion of Tongues* (New York,
1929).
Fillmore, Charles, *Christian Healing*
———, *Talks on Truth*
Numerous other propaganda books are advertised in *Unity;*
propaganda literature is sent upon request from Unity School
of Christianity, Kansas City, Mo.

Marden, Orison S., *Peace, Power, and Plenty; Every Man a King;*
    and numerous other books.
Putnam, C. E., *The Unity School of Christianity and What Its
    Teachings Reveal** (Chicago, 1921).
Sheldon, Henry C., *Theosophy and New Thought* (1916).
Zweig, Stefan, *Mental Healers*: *Mesmer, Eddy, Freud* (1932).

Chapter 7 — Baha'ism

"Baha'ism" in *Encyclopedia of Religion and Ethics.*
"Baha'ism" in *20th Century Encyclopedia of Religious Knowledge*
    (Grand Rapids, 1955).
Baha'u'llah, *The Book of Assurance* (1924).
Esselmont, J. F., *Baha'u'llah and His Message**
Miller, Wm. *Baha'ism: Its Origin, History, and Teachings.* Intr.
    by R. E. Speer (New York, 1931).
Miller, Wm., "The Baha'i Cause Today," in *The Moslem World,*
    Oct. 1940.
"My Experience in the Baha'i Movement," in *The Sunday School
    Times,* Aug. 25 - Sept. 15, 1923.
Remey, Charles Mason, *The Baha'i Movement.* A Series of Nine-
    teen Papers Upon the Baha'i Movement (1912).
———, *Observations of a Baha'i Traveler* (1909).
The Baha'i World. A Biennial International Record. Vol. V.
    1932-1934 (New York).
The Wisdom of Abdu'l Baha. From Addresses Delivered in Paris
    (1910 - 1911).
White, Ruth, *Baha'i Leads out of the Labyrinth* (1944).
Wilson, S. G., *"Baha'ism and Its Claims* (New York, 1915).
———, "Is Baha'ism Anti-Christian?" in *Bible Magazine,* Aug.,
    1915.

Chapter 8 — Mormonism

Anderson, N. *Desert Saints.* The Mormon Frontier in Utah
    (Chicago). Written by a Mormon "by conversion, not by
    heredity."
Arbaugh, George, *Revelation in Mormonism* (Chicago, 1932).
    A good source book in the study of Mormonism, incorporating
    in its pages the findings of Shook, Lamb, Linn, and others.
Bales, James D., *Apostles or Apostates.* Have the Latter-Day
    Saints Perverted the New Testament Teaching Concerning
    Apostles of Christ? (Searcy, Ark., 1944).
Brodie, Fawn M., *No Man Knows My History.* The Life of Jo-
    seph Smith, the Mormon Prophet (New York, 1946). Said by
    reviewer in *The Christian Century,* June 5, 1946, to be "as un-
    predjudiced and honest a study of a baffling character as we
    are likely to get."
Davis, Inez Smith, *The Story of the Church,* 3rd ed. (Indepen-
    dence, Mo.), Mormon source, giving special attention to the rift
    which occurred after the murder of Joseph Smith.
Evans, John Henry, *Joseph Smith.* An American Prophet (New
    York, 1936).
Evans, Bishop R. C., *Forty years in the Mormon Church. Why I
    Left It!* (Toronto, Canada, 1920).

Gates, Susan Young, and Widtroe Leah, *The Life Story of Brig-
ham Young* (1930).
Hall, Thomas Cuming, *The Religious Background of American
Culture* (Boston, 1930).
Lamb, M. T., *The Mormons and Their Bible* (Philadelphia, 1903).
Larson, Gustave O., *Prelude to the Kingdom, Mormon Desert
Conquest.* A Chapter in American Cooperative Enterprise
(Francestown, N. H.). A history of the Mormon movement by
a Mormon, centering attention upon the economic and admin-
istrative aspects of the great migration to the Salt Lake re-
gion, the planting of prosperous communities, and the bring-
ing of 85,000 converts from Europe in the years 1840-'87.
Penrose, Charles, *"Mormon" Doctrine Plain and Simple;* or,
Leaves from the Tree of Life (1897).
Pratt, Parley, *Key to the Science of Theology,* 7th ed. (Salt
Lake City, 1925).
Pryor, Elinor, *And Never Yield* (New York). A novel dealing
with the Missouri and Nauvoo phases of the enterprise. Writ-
ten by a devotee of the cult.
Richards, F. D., *A Compendium of the Doctrines of the Gospel,*
1924 ed.
Shook, Charles A., *American Anthropology Disproving the Book
of Mormon* (1916). This is a resume of Shook's larger work,
Cumorah Revisited.
————, *The True Origin of the Book of Mormon* (Cincinnati,
1914).
Smith, Joseph, etc., *The Pearl of Great Price.* A selection from
their Revelations, Translations and Narratives (1913).
Snowden, James H., *The Truth About Mormonism* (New York,
1926).
Sorenson, Virginia, *A Little Lower than the Angels* (New York,
1942). A novel by a descendant of early Mormons, describing
life in Nauvoo under Joseph Smith, his death, growing friction
between Mormons and "Gentiles," and the departure of the
former from Illinois. With particular stress on the beginnings
of polygamy and its effect upon Mormon family life.
Talmadge, James E., *The Articles of Faith,* 5th ed. (Salt Lake
City, 1909).
Taylor, John, *The Mediation and Atonement of our Lord and
Saviour Jesus Christ.* (Salt Lake City, 1892).
The Book of Mormon, 7th ed. (Independence, Mo.).
The Doctrine and Covenants of the Church of Jesus Christ of
Latter Day Saints, Containing the Revelations Given to Joseph
Smith, Jr., the Prophet, for the Building up of the Kingdom of
God in the Last Days.
Werner, M. R., *Brigham Young* (1925).
Weston, Joseph H., *These Amazing Mormons,* large size, double-
column book, published and republished by the Deseret News
Co., Salt Lake City. Written by a recent convert to Mormon-
ism, it is very revealing of "how they do it."
Young, Ann Eliza, (Brigham Young's apostate wife), *Wife No.
19,* or, *A Life in Bondage,* being a Complete Expose of Mor-
monism (1876). This book is bought up by Mormon mission-

aries and shipped to Utah. It is difficult to obtain and is becoming valuable.

Young, Kimball, *Isn't One Wife Enough?* (New York, 1954). Written by a grandson of Brigham Young. ' "This scholarly book," writes *Newsweek* magazine, "is filled with astonishing little-known facts."

Numerous pamphlets against Mormonism may be ordered from the American Desert Mission, Inc., P.O. Box 1743, Phoenix, Arizona.

Chapter 9 — Destiny of America

There is a voluminous literature published in various places.

PRO: Chiefly publications from Destiny Publishers, Haverhill, Mass.; 313 Sherbourne St., Toronto, Ontario, Canada. Also Teggler Bldg., Edmonton, Alberta, Canada. Many pamphlets are issued by The British-Israel Association of Greater Vancouver, 163 W. Hastings St.

Dobbs, F. S., *Israel in the New Testament**

Goard, Wm. Pascoe, LL.D., F.R.G.S., *The Second Coming of our Lord**

Haberman, Frederick, *Tracing Our Ancestors* (St. Petersburg, Fla.).

————, *The Seven Times of Prophecy and the Seventy Weeks of Daniel.*

Harris, Reader, *The Lost Tribes of Israel**

Houghton, Henry D., *The Marks of Israel**

Rand, Howard B., *Who Shall Possess Palestine?**

Williams, R. Llewelyn, *God's Great Plan a Guide to the Bible.*

Destiny — The Magazine of National Life, Haverhill, Mass., and *The Interpreter,* a Journal for promulgating the Kingdom of God on Earth. Conrad Gaard, editor, Ruth Gaard, assoc. editor. P.O. Box 619, Tacoma, Wash.; and the radio broadcast *Destiny in America* from Tacoma; *British-Israelism* broadcasts on Sunday noons from Edmonton, Alberta.

CONTRA: A host of brochures and folders, many by the followers of the Scofield Reference Bible, but also by others.

Gispen, W. H., *Het Pyramide Geloof* (Kampen, 1953).

Moyer, Robert, *The British-Israel Delusion** (Minneapolis).

Pollock, A. J., *The British-Israel Theory Briefly Tested by Scripture* (London).

Roadhouse, Rev. W. F., *The Incredibility and Delusion of Anglo-Israelism* as shown by Scholarship and Scripture.

Smith, William Henry, M. A., Ph. D., D. D., *The Ten Tribes of Israel Never Lost.* An Answer to the British-Israel Theory. Here also a broad literature on certain phases of our problem may be found. Reference, among others, is made to Dr. Abraham Pieters' *The Ten Tribes in History and Prophecy.* This is perhaps the most scholarly and exhaustive work against the movement by a Vancouver, B. C., professor of theology.

Chapter 10 — Seventh-Day Adventism

Berry, David Anderson, *Seventh-Day Adventism* (Glasgow).

Canright, D. M., *Seventh-Day Adventism Renounced* After an Experience of Twenty-eight Years (Chicago, 1889).

Clark, Elmer T., *The Small Sects in America* (Nashville, 1937).

De Korne, J. C., *The Bible and Seventh-Day Adventism**. The best pamphlet for distribution against S.D.A., Faith, Prayer and Track League, Muskegon Heights, Mich.

Easton, W., *Seventh-Day Adventists and the Sabbath** (Swengel, Pa.).

Haynes, Carlyle B., *Our Lord's Return.*

———, *What Is Coming.*

and other booklets.

Health A Doctor's Magazine for Everybody (Mountain View, Calif.).

Hodge, Charles, *Systematic Theology*, Vol. III, pp. 321-348.

Kuyper, Abraham, *Tractaat van den Sabbath* (Amsterdam, 1890).

Leaves of Autumn, (Takoma Park).

Liberty, A Magazine of Religious Freedom.

Mauro, Philip, *Concerning the Sabbath**

The Ministry. Official Organ of the Ministerial Association of Seventh-Day Adventists. Review and Herald Publ. Assoc.

O'Hair, J. C., *The Sabbath or First Day of Week; Which for the Christian?**

The Present Truth, a Semi-Monthly by the Review and Herald Publ. Assoc. (Takoma Park).

Putnam, C. E., *Legalism and the Seventh-Day Question** (Chicago).

Signs of the Times, The World's Prophetic Weekly, Pacific Press Publ. Assoc., Mountain View, Calif.

Spicer, W. A., *Our Day in the Light of Prophecy.*

Tait, Asa Oscar, *Heralds of the Morning.*

Warfield, Benjamin B., *The Foundations of the Sabbath in the World of God** (Glasgow, 1918).

The Watchman Magazine (Nashville, Tenn.).

White, Elder, *The Life of William Miller.*

White, Ellen G., *The Ministry of Healing.*

———, *The Great Controversy Between Christ and Satan.*

———, *Patriarchs and Prophets,*

and other books.

Literature against several cults may be ordered from Religion Analysis Service, Inc., 902 Hennepin Avenue, Minneapolis, "a specialized False-Isms-Exposing, Soul-Saving Ministry, Evangelical, Denominationally Unrelated." They sell a reprint of Canright's standard work *S.D.A. Renounced.* Conradi's *The Founders of the S.D.A. Denomination*, and their own periodical *The Discerner.*

Mr. Henry Francis Brown, secretary of the Home Missions Department, Michigan Conference of Seventh-Day Adventists, writes: Mr. van Baalen should have read:

Andross, *Story of the Advent Movement* (Review and Herald, 1926).

Dick, Rev. and H., *Founders of the Message* (Review and Herald).

Froom, Le Roy Edwin, *The Prophetic Faith of Our Fathers*, 4 vols. (Review and Herald).

Howell, Emma E., *Great Advent Movement* (Review and Herald, 1935).
Loughborough, *Great Second Advent Movement* (Review and Herald, 1892).
Nichol, Francis, D., *The Midnight Cry*: A Defense of William Miller and the Millerites (Review and Herald, 1944).
Olsen, *Origin and Progress* (Review and Herald, 1925).
The Seventh-Day Adventist Bible Commentary, edited by Francis D. Nichol. Vol. I: Pentateuch, 1120 pp. (Review and Herald, 1955). First major effort of S.D.A., to deal with the whole Bible systematically. Six more vols. to follow.
White, Mrs. E. G., *Desire of Ages* (Pacific Press, 1898).
———, *Life Sketches* (Pacific Press, 1915).
White, J. E., *Life Incidents* (1868).
"The Voice of Prophecy" is the name of the "International Radio Broadcast" sponsored by S.D.A. In Canada S.D.A. publications are the work of Signs of the Times Publishing Association, Oshawa, Ontario.

Chapter 11 — Jehovah's Witnesses

Burridge, J. H., *Pastor Russell's Position and Credentials and His Methods of Interpretation** (New York).
———, *"Pastor" Russell's Date System and Teachings on the Person of Christ, the Atonement, etc.** (New York).
———, *"Pastor" Russell's Teaching on the Coming of Christ** (New York).
Cole, Marley, *Jehovah's Witnesses. The New World Society* (New York, 1955). A complete history of the movement from Russell, via Rutherford, through the present Nathan H. Knorr.
Cook, Charles C., *All About One Russell** (Philadelphia).
Cooper, C. H., *Millennial Dawnism, or Satan in Disguise** (Swengel).
Gray, James M., *The Errors of Millennial Dawnism** (1920).
Haldeman, I. M., *A Great Counterfeit, or, the False and Blasphemous Religion Called Russellism and Millennial Dawnism* (New York).
———, *Millennial Dawnism, or, the Blasphemous Religion Which Teaches the Annihilation of Jesus Christ*.
Martin W. R., and Klann, N. H., *Jehovah of the Watchtower*. A Thorough Expose of the Important Antibiblical Teachings of Jehovah's Witnesses (New York, 1953). The authors call attention to the fact that the endless stream of publications by the Witnesses contains "just rephrases of Russell's and Rutherford's works and contain no originality other than up-to-date information on world conditions and new approaches to old material" (p. 115). This judgment is correct. Such works as *Let God Be True, The Truth Shall Make You Free*, give a good sample of their theology.
Mayer, F. E., *Jehovah's Witnesses*. An Examination of the Religious Tenets, etc. Mayer is professor of Systematic Theology, Concordia Seminary. (St. Louis, 1943).
Metzger, Bruce M., "The Jehovah's Witnesses and Jesus Christ, a Biblical and Theological Appraisal" in *Theology Today*, April

1953. Positive as well as polemical, this essay is one of the best on this cult. It is available in pamphlet form from Theological Book Agency, Princeton, N. J., 8 copies for $1.00.

Pollock, A. J., *How "Pastor" Russell Died*

Reid, R. J., *How Russellism Subverts the Faith** (New York).

Ross, J. J., *Some Facts and More Facts About the Self-Styled "Pastor" Russell** (Philadelphia).

Russell, Charles Taze, *Studies in the Scriptures* 7 vols. (Brooklyn, New York).

Rutherford, J. F., *The Harp of God. Deliverance. Comfort for the Jews. Creation.* And numerous other books (Brooklyn, N. Y.).

Stroup, Herbert Hewitt, *The Jehovah's Witnesses* (New York, 1945). A competent review of this work may be found in *Westminister Theological Journal*, May 1946. Deals with social significance of Russellism.

The New World Translation of Hebrew Scriptures (Old Testament) Vol. I, 1953, Vol. II, 1955.

The New World Translation of the Christian Greek Scriptures by the New World Translation Committee (Watchtower Bible & Tract Society, 1950). A cursory look through this volume reveals it to be a version on which much labor has been bestowed. Its chief purpose seems to be the insertion of the name "JEHOVAH" in the New Testament wherever a text from the Old Testament is quoted having that name; and some few Appendixes on John 1: 1, Romans 9:5, and others, claiming that true exegesis repudiates the orthodox view of Jesus' deity, future punishment, etc. But their dislike of all that is Christian in the accepted sense appears from such facts as: for the word *church* they everywhere substitute *congregation;* impaled for *crucified;* and for the *cross* they write the *torture stake.* The latter is incorrect from a linguistic viewpoint, as it would mean that the stake went through Christ's body. Read the interesting debate between the Witnesses and a Greek scholar in *The Christian Century*, May 9, 1951, "How Bible Translators Work."

There is a vast amount of propaganda literature flowing continually from the Watch Tower Bible and Tract Society, Brooklyn, N. Y. This includes numerous pamphlets, such as *Where Are the Dead?; Hell What Is It?; Who Are There?; Can They Get Out?; The Kingdom, the Hope of the World; Universal War Near; World Distress — Why?; The Remedy;* etc.

Periodicals: *The Messenger. The Golden Age. The Bible Students Monthly. Consolation. Watchtower. The Dawn.*

The *Frank and Ernest* radio broadcast is sponsored by this cult.

Scholars interested in refutation of the mathematical calculations by "pyramid-believers" should consult J. P. Lauer, *Le Problème des Pyramides d'Égypte.*

Chapter 12 — Buchmanism

Begbie, Harold, *Life Changers.*

Brown, J. C., *The Oxford Group Movement. Is It of God or of Satan?** (Glasgow)

Brunner, Emil, *Meine Begegnung mit der Oxforder Gruppenbewegung* (Basel, 1933).

Clark, Walter Houston, *The Oxford Group, Its History and Significance* (New York, 1951).

Day, Sherwood Sunderland, *The Principles of the Group.*
Howard, Peter, *Ideas Have Legs.*
———, *Innocent Men.*
———, *Fighters Ever.*
———, *Men on Trial.*
Kraan, E. D., *De Buchman-Beweging* (Kampen, 1935).
Landau, Rom, "The Man Whose God Was a Millionaire" in *God Is My Adventure* (New York, 1936).
Layman with a Notebook, *What Is the Oxford Group?* (1933).
Russell, A. J., *For Sinners Only* (New York).
Shields, T. T., *The Oxford Group Movement Analyzed** (Toronto).
Shoemaker, Samuel M. Jr., "House-Parties Across the Continent," article in "Buchmansim Pro and Con," *The Christian Century,* Aug. 23, 1933.
———, *The Conversion of the Church* (New York, 1932).
———, *Children of the Second Birth* (New York, 1927).
Williamson, Geoffrey, *Inside Buchmanism.* An Independent Inquiry into the Oxford Group Movement, and Moral Re-Armament, (New York, 1955).
Additional literature and information on the Movement may be found in:
Christianity Today, Jan. 1934.
New World News. Issued monthly. Published by the Oxford Group — Moral Re-armament — MRA., Inc., Box 1516, Washington, D. C.
Rising Tide, a Bachmanite publication, 61 Gramercy Park, New York City, 1937.
The Banner, Feb. 10, 1934.
The Religious Digest, Oct. 1935, Mar. 1936.

Chapter 13 — Unitarianism-Modernism

Aubrey, Edwin E., *Present Theological Tendencies* (New York, 1936.)
Babson, Roger, and Zuver, Dudley, *Can These Bones Live?* (New York, 1945).
Baillie, J., *What Is Christian Civilization?* (New York, 1945).
Barton Bruce, *The Man Nobody Knows: A Discovery of the Real Jesus* (1925).
Bennett, John C., *Christian Realism* (New York, 1942).
Brown, Wm. Adams, *Pathways to Certainty* (New York, 1930).
Coffin, H. S., *The Meaning of the Cross* (New York, 1931).
Fosdick, Harry Emerson, *The Modern Use of the Bible* (1924). *On Being Fit to Live With* ("His final book of sermons") (New York, 1946).
Gifford, William Alva, *The Story of the Faith*: a survey of Christian history for the undogmatic (New York, 1946).
Hutchinson, John A., *We Are Not Divided.* A Critical and Historical Study of the Federal Council of Churches, etc. (New York, 1941).
Inge, W. R., *Christian Ethics and Modern Problems* (New York, 1930).
Jefferson, Charles E., *The Character of Paul* (New York, 1924).
Jones, Edgar DeWitt, *The Coming of the Perfect* and 16 other sermons (New York, 1946).

Knight, F. H., and Merriam, T. W., *The Economic Order and Religion* (New York, 1945).
Knox, John, *The Man Christ Jesus* (New York, 1942).
——, *Christ the Lord* (New York, 1945).
MacFarland, Chas. S., *The Spirit Christlike* (1904).
——, *Spiritual Culture and Social Service* (1912).
——, *Across the Years* (1936).
Mathews, Shailer, and Smith, Gerald B., *A Dictionary of Religion and Ethics* (1923).
Niebuhr, Pauck, and Miller, *The Church Against the World* (New York, 1935).
Niebuhr, Reinhold, *The Nature and Destiny of Man*, 2 vols. (New York, 1941, 1943).
Ogburn, Wm. Fielding, editor, *American Society in Wartime* (Chicago, 1943).
Palmer, Frederic, *The Virgin Birth* (New York, 1924).
Park, Wm. E., *Narrow Is the Way*. Addresses to Students by the President of Northfield Schools (New York, 1945).
Scott, Ernest T., *Man and Society in the N. T.* (New York, 1946).
Sweezey, Geo. S., *The Keeper of the Door*. Sermons (New York, 1946).
Van Dusen, Henry P., *God in These Times* (New York, 1935).
——, Editor *The Christian Answer* (New York, 1946).
Wishart, A. W., *Evolution and Religion: God in Jesus;* and other sermons (Grand Rapids).
The Christian Century, published weekly. *The Pulpit*, published monthly.
Further, an endless stream of books published without let-up and advertised from week to week. From the other side, either orthodox or at least critical of the liberal position, are:
Barth, Karl, *The Resurrection of the Dead* (New York, 1933).
Bergen, J. T., *Evidences of Christianity* (1916).
Berkhof, L., *Recent Trends in Theology* (Grand Rapids, 1946).
Gordon, Ernest, *The Leaven of the Sadducees* (Chicago, 1926).
Graebner, Theodore, *God and the Cosmos*, 3rd ed. (Grand Rapids, 1946).
Haas, John A. W., *The Unity of Faith and Knowledge* (New York 1926).
Henry, Carl F. H., *Remaking the Modern Mind* (Grand Rapids, 1946), *Fifty Years of Protestant Theology* (New York).
Horsch, John, *Modern Religious Liberalism* (Scottdale, Pa., 1921).
Hospers, G. H., *The Reformed Principle of Authority* (Grand Rapids, 1924).
Keyser, Leander S., *The Doctrine of Modernism* (Chicago, 1925).
Knox, John, *Chapters in a Life of Paul* (Nashville, Tenn., 1950). See the review by Dr. N. B. Stonehouse in *Westminster Theological Review*, Nov. 1950.
Kretzmann, P. E., "Modern News About Inspiration" in *The Princeton Theological Review*, April 1929.
Macartney, Clarence, *Twelve Great Questions About Christ* (New York, 1923).
McPherson, G. W., *The Crisis in Church and College* (Yonkers, N. Y., 1919)
——, *The Modern Conflict Over the Bible* (1919).
Mullins, E. Y., *Christianity at the Cross Roads* (New York, 1924).

Nash, Arnold, *The University and the Modern World* (New York, 1944).

Patton, Francis L., *Fundamental Christianity* (New York, 1926).

Rimmer, Harry, *The Harmony of Science and Scripture* (Grand Rapids, 1936).

————. *Modern Science and the Genesis Record* (Grand Rapids, 1937).

————, *Internal Evidence of Inspiration* (Grand Rapids, 1938).

————, *Dead Men Tell Tales* (Berne, Indiana, 1939).

————, *Crying Stones* (Grand Rapids, 1941).

————, *The Magnificence of Jesus* (Grand Rapids, 1943).

————, *That Lawsuit Against the Bible* (Grand Rapids, 1940).

Schaff, Philip, *The Creeds of Christendom* (New York, 1877).

Trueblood, Elton, *The Predicament of Modern Man* (New York, 1945).

————, *Foundations for Reconstruction* (New York, 1946).

Tulga, Chester E., *The Case Against Neo-Orthodoxy* (Chicago, 1951).

Warfield, B. B., *The Lord of Glory* (New York, 1907).

————, *Revelation and Inspiration* (New York, 1929).

Wilson, R. D., *A Scientific Investigation of the Old Testament* (Philadelphia, 1926).

Wood, H. G., *Christianity and Civilization* (New York, 1943).

Zwemer, Samuel M., *The Origin of Religion* (New York, 1935).

Chapter 14 — Swedenborgianism

The principal works of Swedenborg are these:
Arcana Coelestia
Conjugial Love
Heaven and Hell
Miscellaneous Theological Works
The Divine Love and Wisdom
The Divine Providence
The Four Chief Doctrines
The True Christian Religion
An exhaustive study which mentions many sources is:
Sigstedt, Cyriel Odhner, *The Swedenborg Epic. The Life and Works of Emmanuel Swendenborg* (New York, 1952).
A popular presentation is:
*The True Christian Religion. A digest of Swedenborg's larger work by the same name, prepared originally as a talking book for the blind by Rev. Arthur Wilde, now printed for general distribution by Swedenborg Foundation, Inc., 51 East 42nd St., New York 17, N. Y., 1952.

General

Anderson, J. N. D., *The World's Religions.* A new handbook presenting a factual survey of Animism, Judaism, Islam, Hinduism, Buddhism, Shintoism, and Confucianism. The author is a lecturer at the University of London, and one of the world's foremost authorities on Islam (Grand Rapids, 1950).

Bach, Marcus, *They Have Found a Faith* (New York, 1946). This book deals with Jehovah's Witnesses; The Four-square Gospel; Spiritualism; Oxford Group-MRA; The Kingdoms of Father Divine; The Baha'i Faith; Unity; Psychiana.

A sequel to this book is: *Faith and My Friends* (New York, 1951). It describes: The Trappist; The Vedantist; The Hutterite; the Penitente; The Swedenborgian. The first and last chapters are called, characteristically: I. "The Right to Believe"; VIII, "Something to Live By."

Braden, Charles Samuel, *These Also Believe* (New York, 1949). The author discusses: The Peace Mission Movement of Father Divine; Psychiana; New Thought; Unity School of Christianity; Christian Science; Theosophy; The I Am Movement; The Liberal Catholic Church; Spiritualism; Jehovah's Witnesses; Anglo-Israel; The Oxford Group Movement; Mormonism. Bach's book is brilliant and speaks of these movements from the standpoint of one who has spent time with them and reports his findings. Braden's is scholarly and reveals much knowledge of literary sources.

Henry, Carl F. H., *Re-making the Modern Mind* (Grand Rapids, 1946).

Kellogg, S. A., *A Handbook of Comparative Religion.* An authoritative guide to the chief concepts of the world's great religions. Contrasts in their positions on sin, salvation, moral conduct, immortality, etc., with the Christian view (Grand Rapids, 1951, reprint).

Machen, J. G., *Christianity and Liberalism* (Grand Rapids, 1956, reprint).

———, *What Is Faith?* (Grand Rapids, 1956, reprint).

———, *The Christian View of Man* (Grand Rapids, 1947, reprint).

———, *The Christian Faith in the Modern World* (Grand Rapids, 1947, reprint).

———, *The Origin of Paul's Religion* (Grand Rapids, 1947, reprint).

———, *God Transcendent* (Grand Rapids, 1949, reprint).

———, *What Is Christianity?* (Grand Rapids, 1951, reprint).

Dr. Machen's books are among the clearest and best against Modernism.

Martin, Walter R., *The Rise of the Cults* (Grand Rapids, 1955).

Mayer, F. E., *The Religious Bodies of America*, 2nd ed. (St. Louis, 1955).

Mead, Frank S., *Handbook of Denominations in the United States* (Nashville, 1951). The author is a Methodist and former editor of *The Christian Herald*.

Religion in the Twentieth Century, edited by Vergilius Ferm (New York, 1948). Contains 28 chapters on oriental and occidental religions. Each chapter is written by an outstanding representative of the cult described.

Smith, Wilbur M., *Therefore Stand.* A Plea for a Vigorous Apologetic in the Present Crisis of Evangelical Christianity (Grand Rapids, 1945).

20th Century Encyclopedia of Religious Knowledge (Grand Rapids, 1955), articles on "Social Gospel"; "World Council of Churches."